ILLUSTRATED COMPUTER DICTIONARY FOR DUMMIES™

by Dan Gookin,
Wally Wang, and Chris Van Buren

IDG Books Worldwide, Inc.
An International Data Group Company
San Mateo, California ✦ Indianapolis, Indiana ✦ Boston, Massachusetts

Illustrated Computer Dictionary For Dummies

Published by
IDG Books Worldwide, Inc.
An International Data Group Company
155 Bovet Road, Suite 310
San Mateo, CA 94402

Library of Congress Catalog Card No.: 93-78255

ISBN 1-56884-004-7

Printed in the United States of America

10 9 8 7 6 5 4 3 2 1

Distributed in the United States by IDG Books Worldwide, Inc.

Distributed in Canada by Macmillan of Canada, a Division of Canada Publishing Corporation; by Woodslane Pty. Ltd. in Australia and New Zealand; and by Computer Bookshops in the U.K. and Ireland.

For information on translations and availability in other countries, contact Marc Jeffrey Mikulich, Foreign Rights Manager, at IDG Books Worldwide; FAX NUMBER 415-358-1260.

For sales inquiries and special prices for bulk quantities, write to the address above or call IDG Books Worldwide at 415-312-0650.

Acknowledgments

I would like to thank the following folks who helped make this dictionary happen. First, kudos goes to my two coauthors, the ineffable Wally Wang and the earnest Chris Van Buren. Thanks also goes to the IDG staff: David Solomon, Mary "conniption fit" Bednarek, Laurie Smith, Drew Moore, Pam Mourouzis, Eric Dafforn, Kezia Endsley, Beth Baker, Cindy Phipps, and Tricia Reynolds. Final thanks go to Beth Slick, the technical editor. No one named "Webster" was involved with this project.

Dan Gookin
Coer d'Alene, Idaho

(The publisher would like to give special thanks to Patrick J. McGovern, without whom this book would not have been possible.)

About the authors

Dan Gookin, the author of *DOS For Dummies*, *DOS For Dummies,* 2nd Edition, *WordPerfect For Dummies*, *WordPerfect 6 For Dummies*, *Word for Windows For Dummies,* and coauthor of *PCs For Dummies,* is a writer and computer "guru" whose job is to remind everyone that computers are not to be taken too seriously. Presently, Mr. Gookin works for himself as a freelance writer. Gookin holds a degree in Communications from the University of California, San Diego, and is a regular contributor to *InfoWorld, PC/Computing, DOS Resource Guide*, and *PC Buying World* magazines. Dan recently moved to the wilds of Idaho with his wife and sons.

Wally Wang, a stand-up comic by night, also writes a software review column for a comedy newsletter, teaches computer classes for local companies, and has written other computer books. Both Dan and Wally once had a computer radio show on KVSD in San Diego.

Chris Van Buren, an author of several bestselling computer books, has over a dozen titles to his credit, including the *PC World You Can Do It With DOS* and *PC World You Can Do It With Windows* titles (IDG Books, 1992). He currently writes computer books full time and provides consulting services in the San Francisco Bay Area.

About IDG Books Worldwide

Welcome to the world of IDG Books Worldwide.

IDG Books Worldwide, Inc., is a division of International Data Group, the world's largest publisher of computer-related information and the leading global provider of information services on information technology. IDG publishes over 194 computer publications in 62 countries. Forty million people read one or more IDG publications each month.

If you use personal computers, IDG Books is committed to publishing quality books that meet your needs. We rely on our extensive network of publications, including such leading periodicals as *Macworld*, *InfoWorld*, *PC World*, *Computerworld*, *Publish*, *Network World*, and *SunWorld*, to help us make informed and timely decisions in creating useful computer books that meet your needs.

Every IDG book strives to bring extra value and skill-building instruction to the reader. Our books are written by experts, with the backing of IDG periodicals, and with careful thought devoted to issues such as audience, interior design, use of icons, and illustrations. Our editorial staff is a careful mix of high-tech journalists and experienced book people. Our close contact with the makers of computer products helps ensure accuracy and thorough coverage. Our heavy use of personal computers at every step in production means we can deliver books in the most timely manner.

We are delivering books of high quality at competitive prices on topics customers want. At IDG, we believe in quality, and we have been delivering quality for over 25 years. You'll find no better book on a subject than an IDG book.

John Kilcullen
President and C.E.O.
IDG Books Worldwide, Inc.

IDG Books Worldwide, Inc. is a division of International Data Group. The officers are Patrick J. McGovern, Founder and Board Chairman; Walter Boyd, President. International Data Group's publications include: **ARGENTINA's** Computerworld Argentina, InfoWorld Argentina; **ASIA's** Computerworld Hong Kong, PC World Hong Kong, Computerworld Southeast Asia, PC World Singapore, Computerworld Malaysia, PC World Malaysia; **AUSTRALIA's** Computerworld Australia, Australian PC World, Australian Macworld, Network World, Reseller, IDG Sources; **AUSTRIA's** Computerwelt Oesterreich, PC Test; **BRAZIL's** Computerworld, Mundo IBM, Mundo Unix, PC World, Publish; **BULGARIA's** Computerworld Bulgaria, Ediworld, PC & Mac World Bulgaria; **CANADA's** Direct Access, Graduate Computerworld, InfoCanada, Network World Canada; **CHILE's** Computerworld, Informatica; **COLUMBIA's** Computerworld Columbia; **CZECH REPUBLIC's** Computerworld, Elektronika, PC World; **DENMARK's** CAD/CAM WORLD, Communications World, Computerworld Danmark, LOTUS World, Macintosh Produktkatalog, Macworld Danmark, PC World Danmark, PC World Produktguide, Windows World; **EQUADOR's** PC World; **EGYPT's** Computerworld (CW) Middle East, PC World Middle East; **FINLAND's** MikroPC, Tietoviikko, Tietoverkko; **FRANCE's** Distributique, GOLDEN MAC, InfoPC, Languages & Systems, Le Guide du Monde Informatique, Le Monde Informatique, Telecoms & Reseaux; **GERMANY's** Computerwoche, Computerwoche Focus, Computerwoche Extra, Computerwoche Karriere, Information Management, Macwelt, Netzwelt, PC Welt, PC Woche, Publish, Unit; **HUNGARY's** Alaplap, Computerworld SZT, PC World, ; **INDIA's** Computers & Communications; **ISRAEL's** Computerworld Israel, PC World Israel; **ITALY's** Computerworld Italia, Lotus Magazine, Macworld Italia, Networking Italia, PC World Italia; **JAPAN's** Computerworld Japan, Macworld Japan, SunWorld Japan, Windows World; **KENYA's** East African Computer News; **KOREA's** Computerworld Korea, Macworld Korea, PC World Korea; **MEXICO's** Compu Edicion, Compu Manufactura, Computacion/Punto de Venta, Computerworld Mexico, MacWorld, Mundo Unix, PC World, Windows; **THE NETHERLAND'S** Computer! Totaal, LAN Magazine, MacWorld; **NEW ZEALAND's** Computer Listings, Computerworld New Zealand, New Zealand PC World; **NIGERIA's** PC World Africa; **NORWAY's** Computerworld Norge, C/World, Lotusworld Norge, Macworld Norge, Networld, PC World Ekspress, PC World Norge, PC World's Product Guide, Publish World, Student Data, Unix World, Windowsworld, IDG Direct Response; **PANAMA's** PC World; **PERU's** Computerworld Peru, PC World; **PEOPLES REPUBLIC OF CHINA's** China Computerworld, PC World China, Electronics International, China Network World; **IDG HIGH TECH BEIJING's** New Product World; **IDG SHENZHEN's** Computer News Digest; **PHILLIPPINES'** Computerworld, PC World; **POLAND's** Computerworld Poland, PC World/Komputer; **PORTUGAL's** Cerebro/PC World, Correio Informatico/Computerworld, MacIn; **ROMANIA's** PC World; **RUSSIA's** Computerworld-Moscow, Mir-PC, Sety; **SLOVENIA's** Monitor Magazine; **SOUTH AFRICA's** Computing S.A.; **SPAIN's** Amiga World, Computerworld Espana, Communicaciones World, Macworld Espana, NeXTWORLD, PC World Espana, Publish, Sunworld; **SWEDEN's** Attack, ComputerSweden, Corporate Computing, Lokala Natverk/LAN, Lotus World, MAC&PC, Macworld, Mikrodatorn, PC World, Publishing & Design (CAP), DataIngenjoren, Maxi Data, Windows World; **SWITZERLAND's** Computerworld Schweiz, Macworld Schweiz, PC & Workstation; **TAIWAN's** Computerworld Taiwan, Global Computer Express, PC World Taiwan; **THAILAND's** Thai Computerworld; **TURKEY's** Computerworld Monitor, Macworld Turkiye, PC World Turkiye; **UNITED KINGDOM's** Lotus Magazine, Macworld, Sunworld; **UNITED STATES'** AmigaWorld, Cable in the Classroom, CD Review, CIO, Computerworld, Desktop Video World, DOS Resource Guide, Electronic News, Federal Computer Week, Federal Integrator, GamePro, IDG Books, InfoWorld, InfoWorld Direct, Laser Event, Macworld, Multimedia World, Network World, NeXTWORLD, PC Games, PC Letter, PC World Publish, Sumeria, SunWorld, SWATPro, Video Event; **VENEZUELA's** Computerworld Venezuela, MicroComputerworld Venezuela; **VIETNAM's** PC World Vietnam

Credits

Publisher
David Solomon

Acquisitions Editor
Janna Custer

Managing Editor
Mary Bednarek

Project Editor
Laurie Ann Smith

Editors
Pam Mourouzis
Eric Dafforn
Kezia Endsley

Editorial Assistant
Patricia R. Reynolds

Illustrator
Drew R. Moore

Technical Reviewer
Beth Slick

Production Manager
Beth J. Baker

Production Coordinator
Cindy L. Phipps

Proofreader
Charles A. Hutchinson

Book Design and Production
Drew R. Moore

More Words!

We Want to Hear More Words!

Listen up, all you readers of IDG's *Illustrated Computer Dictionary For Dummies*! It's time for you to take advantage of a new, direct *pipeline* for readers of IDG's international bestsellers — the famous *. . . For Dummies* books.

Pipeline

Pronunciation: *pype lyne*

Meaning: The tunnel, gerbil tube, passageway, and conduit to the authors and editors of IDG Books Worldwide.

Sentence: "Keep those cards and letters comin' in, folks, and you'll soon be connected with the direct reader *pipeline* to the authors and editors of IDG Books Worldwide."

Seriously, we'd like your input for future printings and editions of this book. Tell us what you liked (and didn't like) about the *Illustrated Computer Dictionary For Dummies*. Feel free to suggest new terms if you want.

We'll add you to our *Dummies Database/Fan Club* and keep you up to date on the latest *. . . For Dummies* books, news, cartoons, calendars, and more!

Please send your name, address, and phone number, as well as your comments, questions, and suggestions, to:

. . . For Dummies Coordinator
IDG Books Worldwide
3250 N. Post Road, Ste. 140
Indianapolis, IN 46226

Thanks for your input!

Introduction

Here it is, the *Illustrated Computer Dictionary For Dummies,* your shield in the constant word battle that takes place between the nerds, geeks, and technoweenies and people like us who have to put up with the jargon. We've scoured the magazines, manuals, and books for these terms. Hunted them down in dark, programmers' dungeons, listened to taped conversations of bigwigs talking in acronym-speak, and we've even made up a few words ourselves. The end result is this light-hearted approach to understanding computer terms and — if you dare — learning how to incorporate such terms into your everyday conversation.

The Logical Approach

After long periods of careful thought, we decided to lay this book out in alphabetic format and, further, to alphabetize all the words for your referencing needs. Symbols ("@#$%^&*!") and numbers (0-9) are listed first in their own chapters. But after that, it's A to Z — with all the letters in between in proper order. (And we're assuming you know the alphabet here, sung to the tune of *Twinkle Twinkle* in case you forgot; ask any 4-year-old.)

The words are presented in the following format. First, we give you the word itself, then a pronunciation guide, followed by the word's meaning or a definition, and then comes sample usage:

dictionary

Pronunciation: *dik-shun-aery*

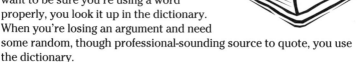

Meaning: A book that contains a list of words, their pronunciations, and meanings. When you don't know what a word means, you look it up in a dictionary. When you want to be sure you're using a word properly, you look it up in the dictionary. When you're losing an argument and need some random, though professional-sounding source to quote, you use the dictionary.

Sentence: "My kid keeps asking me what words mean, so I tell him to 'look it up in the *dictionary,*' since I'm too embarrassed to admit I don't know what the words mean myself."

Philosophical Stuff

Our purpose behind this dictionary is to both enlighten and inform. Oh, and we've tossed in some entertainment value as well. Computers are always thought of as these big, frowning, cold, and serious devices of torment — like nuns in a Catholic school. The truth is, they aren't. They aren't nuns, that is. (And the nuns aren't big and frowning either!) Instead, computers have a vast potential for humor and enjoyment (just like the nuns). This book presents technical information with that attitude in the hopes that you will understand it better. And if not that, then at least you'll be able to tolerate the terminology with a modicum of levity.

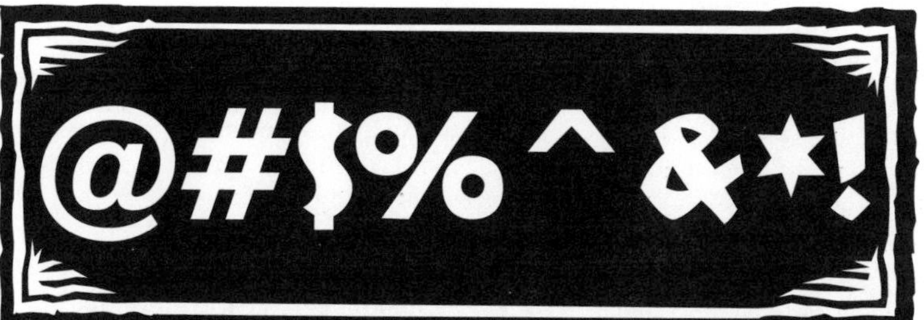

\

Symbol name: *backslash*

Uses: The symbol used in MS-DOS to separate directories and filenames such as C:\WINDOWS\SYSTEM or A:\PASCAL. Don't get the backslash key mixed up with the forward slash (/) that's found on the same key as the question mark (?). Otherwise, MS-DOS won't have the slightest idea what you're trying to do.

.

Symbol name: *star-dot-star*

Uses: The *.* designation uses the * wildcard which can take on any value. In MS-DOS, *.* refers to all files. To delete every file in a directory, you type **DEL *.*** and press the Enter key. (Don't try this at home unless you know what you're doing.)

&

Symbol name: *am-per-sand*

Uses: Sometimes this symbol is used to represent "and," as in "such & such" or "Baby want some c&dy?" Or more accurately, "Sterling, Worbletyme & Grockmeister." Most purists reject this form, prefering to spell out the letters A-N-D.

In computer programming, & sometimes represents a "logical and." For example:

```
IF(NUMBER=1 & LETTER=A) THEN "We're at the beginning."
```

In the C programming language, two ampersands are used — &&.

The character is correctly called an ampersand. *Ampers* comes from the ancient Vulcan for "this squiggly symbol means" and *and* meaning "and."

+

Symbol name: *plus*

Uses: This symbol is used in addition because (thankfully) it's on the keyboard and makes a poor imposter for the letter T.

```
2 + 2 = 5
```

(This used to happen a lot with older spreadsheets.)

The plus sign may also be used to connect two items. For example:

```
COPY A.DOC+B.DOC AB.DOC
```

In DOS, the preceding command glues the file B.DOC to the end of the file A.DOC, creating a new file AB.DOC. This is known as *concatenation,* which is literally translated as "sticking two cats together," though the more common "sticking two things together" is generally accepted.

#

Symbol name: *pound, num-ber, or tic-tac-toe*

Uses: The pound symbol, located above the 3 on American keyboards. This symbol is used in written language to represent numbers or items: "All right, Becky, you chose #3, 'Medical Instruments I've Found on the Beach.'"

In some versions of UNIX, the # is the system prompt.

The # symbol also has appeal as a nice solid character. Some people use it decoratively or to produce crude graphics:

```
  ######
#        #
#  # #   #
#        #
# ####   #
#   ##   #
#        #
  ######
```

On British keyboards, the # symbol is replaced by £, which really means pound. (# is the "hash" character.)

>>

Symbol name: *ap-end (as in append)*

Uses: There is really no way to pronounce any of these symbols, though "ugh-ugh" is often used. Some say "Double greater-than." Others may just say "append," which is what these characters do in DOS.

```
TYPE SIGNATUR.TXT >> LETTER.DOC
```

The preceding DOS command takes the information in the file SIGNATUR.TXT and sticks it to the end of the file LETTER.DOC. Note that this trick only works with text files, not documents created with a word processor or other formatted documents.

>=

Symbol name: *greater-than or equal to*

Uses: These symbols are used to compare two values in a test (as in a database query, for example). The test passes if the first value is greater than or equal to the second value. For example:

10 >= 9 is true

10 >= 10 is true

10 >= 11 is false

good >= evil — we hope is true

<=

Symbol name: *less-than or equal to*

Uses: These symbols are used to compare two values in a test. The test passes if the first value is less than or equal to the second. For example:

9 <= 10 is true

10 <= 10 is true

10 <= 9 is false

Hollywood <= "real life" is always true

!

Symbol name: *exclamation point; bang*

Uses: The exclamation point is used at the end of a sentence to denote excitement: "Your wife is here!" Or maybe surprise, "My heart!" In

Spanish, a preceeding upside-down explanation point pre-alerts the reader to the excitement level of the sentence: "¡Su esposa esta aqui!" Y "¡Mi corazon!"

In the C programming language, the ! is used to mean *not.* For example,

```
!TRUE = FALSE
```

The above means "not true is the same thing as false," almost a universal truth anywhere but in Washington D.C.

```
!=
```

This symbol means *not equal.* "Watching baseball on TV is just != to being at the ballpark."

In the USENET electronic mail system, ! is called a *bang,* and it's used in someone's electronic address — like a highly effective ZIP code. For example:

```
crash!dang
```

This is the electronic address of *dang* on the *crash* system. The address is "crash, bang, dang." (An actual address, by the way.)

Did you ever notice that all the sentences in *Mad Magazine* end in either an exclamation point or question mark?

"

Symbol name: *double quotes*

Uses: This symbol is often used to *hug* text, what's called a *string* of text. For example:

"The pastry was bad and the coffee tasted like it had been strained through a dirty gym sock."

The text between the quotes is the "string," but the quotes themselves are not.

$

Symbol name: *dollar sign; string; hex*

Uses: The dollar sign is used in a number of ways, most of which really have to do with money. Obviously, when followed by a number, as in $1,000,000, the dollar sign means dollars, big bucks, moola.

In the BASIC programming language, a dollar sign is used to identify a *string* or text variable. FIRST$ would be a variable named "FIRST" that holds a string value. It's pronouned first-string, by the way; not first-SS or first-dollar sign.

Some programming languages will use the dollar sign to denote a *hexadecimal* (base 16) number. For example $14 is the hexadecimal value 14 (20 decimal). $A1 would be the hexadecimal value A1 (161 decimal). In this usage, the $ is pronounced "hex." $A1 is hex-A-one.

In MS-DOS, one place the dollar sign is used is in the AUTOEXEC.BAT file to change the look of the C prompt, as in

```
Prompt $p$g
```

%

Symbol name: *percent sign*

Uses: The percent sign is used all over the place, sometimes actually to represent a percentage value: 15% means fifteen percent, or 15 times out of 100 or .15 or a value that's considered fairly good for weather forecasters and economists.

The percent sign plays numerous roles in various programming languages.

In BASIC, the percent sign denotes an integer variable: ITEM% would be an integer variable named ITEM. You don't pronounce the %.

In the C programming language the % is used as the "modulus" operator (which figures out the remainder when one number is divided by another). It's also used to format output.

'

Symbol name: *apostrophe; tick; single quote*

Uses: The apostrophe is used in text to mark the possesive "Bill's deficit" and sometimes in conjunction with the accent grave (backward apostrophe, `) in double quoting:

```
``This is more serious than we thought.''
```

In the BASIC programming language, the apostrophe at the start of a line marks a comment.

Symbol name: *parentheses, parens*

Uses: Parentheses are used in programming to group things together. Usually this happens in long mathematical operations; what appears between the paretheses is figured out first. Most programming languages also use parentheses to group together options and "arguments" for certain commands and keywords.

A single parenthesis is called a *paren*. When someone says "left paren," he's referring to the (character. The right paren is the). This comes in handy when reading computer typing instructions over the phone.

Symbol name: *copyright sign*

Uses: Many software packages will use a big C in parentheses to represent the © (copyright) symbol because the © isn't on most keyboards. Likewise, you may see (TM) for Trademark.

Symbol name: *asterisk; star; splat*

Uses: The asterisk is typically used in a decorative fashion. Occasionally it may appear to add emphasis when italics or underlines aren't available:

```
I was so *embarrassed*.
```

Or the asterisk may be used as a form of self-censorship while sending an e-mail message:

```
Eat **** and die!
```

Sometimes the asterisk appears to mark a footnote.

In DOS, the asterisk is used as a wildcard character, pronounced "star." The star can represent from 1 to several characters, matching other filenames for use with several DOS commands.

Nathan Hale did not say "I regret that I have but one asterisk for my country."

Other names for * include the "dingbat" and "splat." Splat is from the final result of dropping something mushy from a high altitude. The resulting spot would look like this:

Splat!

-

Symbol name: *minus sign; hyphen*

Uses: The minus sign is used in various corners of computer mathdom. First, it appears as the typical minus sign: 4-5, and so on. It's also used to identify a negative number: -5.

The minus sign's evil twin is the hyphen, which is the same character but used with words, such as Mary-Francis. Two hyphens can be used together in text to denote a clause or parenthetical element — like this!

In typographical terms, there are hyphens, en dashes, and em dashes, which are each used in different circumstances. The hyphen is the smallest one of the three. An *en dash* is a dash character with the same width as the letter *n*. The *em dash* is a longer dash, the same width as the letter *m*.

.

Symbol name: *period, dot*

Uses: The period is used in text to mark the end of a sentence.

In math, the period is used to mark the decimal portion of a number: 3.141. In that case, it's pronounced "point" as in "three point one four one."

In some countries, the period is used to separate the hundreds from thousands or thousands from ten-thousands: 1.000 is one thousand. (In these weird places, the comma is used as the decimal point. Strange.)

In DOS, the period is used to separate a filename from its extension. Other operating systems use the period as a separator as well.

In a hockey game, there are three periods: ...

/

Symbol name: *forward slash; division symbol*

Uses: The forward slash character is used in text to separate items: on/off, up/down, and so on.

In computer math, the / symbol is used for division. This is because the ÷ character isn't available on most keyboards. So 15/3 means "15 divided by 3."

Names for this character: slash, forward slash, solidus, stroke, virgule, the forward-pointing thing under the question mark key, and so on.

:

Symbol name: *colon*

Uses: In DOS, you use colons after drive names, such as in the C: drive to refer to your hard drive, and after device names, such as in PRN: to refer to the printer. In C programming, the colon is sometimes used, such as when you're declaring structure templates for bit fields.

;

Symbol name: *semicolon*

Uses: In Windows INI files, as well as DOS's CONFIG.SYS file, a line starting with a semicolon is taken to be a comment:

```
;This line will be ignored: The computer is afraid of it!
```

<>

Symbol name: *less than, greater than; not equal; angle brackets*

Uses: These are the angle brackets, sometimes used when straight-edged people tire of parentheses.

In some European languages, these characters are used as quotes, though they're doubled up: « is the start quote and » is the end quote. «Françios! Behold this lovely yellow pencil box!»

=

Symbol name: *equal sign*

Uses: Used to denote equality or that something is equal to something else. For example, CALORIES = TASTES GOOD.

==

Symbol name: *double equal sign; "is equal to"*

Uses: Used in some instances to denote that two things are equal. In the C programming language, the double equal sign is used when comparing two values.

Symbol name: *question mark*

Uses: Sometimes the question mark sits at the end of a sentence when the sentence is a question. For example: Is that so?

Used occasionally as a "wildcard" character, a placeholder for other characters to be matched in a search.

Symbol name: *at sign; about; strudel; rose; cabbage*

Uses: Could mean "at," though this little cryptic guy is a favorite for multiple uses.

[]

Symbol name: *square brackets; brackets*

Uses: Parentheses who just never really caught on. Mostly you'll find square brackets used to describe options for a command. For example:

```
spin [/fast] [/backward]
```

The brackets mean the items enclosed within them are optional. (In this dictionary, the brackets are used to guide pronunciation.)

^

Symbol name: *caret; hat; control*

Uses: Used as an abbreviation for "control," for example when typing out a key combination or the character produced by that combination. So Ctrl-S produces the ^S (control-S) character.

Used as a mathematical operator for "raising to the power of" in some languages. 2^4 means 2 to the 4th power. Other programming languages may have other interesting uses for the hat.

_

Symbol name: *underline; underscore*

Uses: Not normally used for anything, though some programmers and computerphiles like to use the underscore instead of a space between words. For example, FILE_NAME would be the way they write FILE NAME when it's forbidden to put a space between two words.

`

Symbol name: *accent grave*

Uses: The hardest part about dealing with this doodad is how to pronounce it. Is it "grave" as in serious or a place where dead bodies go to relax? Or could it be gravè, as in the way a French person would say gravey?

Some people use the accent grave to simulate double quotes. For example, "Oui, oui. It is a sauce we make from grease and flour." The double apostrophe is used to end the quote.

{}

Symbol name: *curly brackets; braces*

Uses: An alternative form of parentheses, most often found in C language programs. The curly brackets are used to "hold" various items in the program, items that belong to certain parts of the program or which carry out specific functions.

|

Symbol name: *vertical bar; pipe*

Uses: The pipe symbol is used as the logical OR mathematical operator in many programming languages. So SIX-OF-ONE | HALF-A-DOZEN-OF-THE-OTHER.

In DOS and UNIX, the pipe is used to control the output of a command. The pipe follows the DOS command and sends its output — what would normally go to the screen — to a special program called a *filter*. The filter modifies the output.

~

Symbol name: *tilde*

Uses: In some languages, the tilde appears over characters to give them special twangs. For example *año* means "year" in Spanish.

Some programming languages may use ~ to mean "not." See **!** (exclamation point).

101-key keyboard

Pronunciation: *one-oh-one-kee kee-bored.*

Meaning: A keyboard that has four distinct parts: a typewriter keyboard, a cursor keypad, a numeric keypad, and a row of function keys.

Sentence: "My new computer had a tiny little keyboard that didn't have a separate numeric or cursor keypad. That's why I bought a *101-key keyboard* to replace it."

16-bit

Pronunciation: *six-teen-bit.*

Meaning: An adjective describing that something can transfer or process 16 bits of information at any given time.

Sentence: "My first computer was an old 8-bit Apple IIe. My next computer was a *16-bit* IBM AT. Now my kid is talking about 16-bit Nintendo games. Boy, do I feel old."

2-bit

Pronunciation: *too-bit.*

Meaning: Something cheap, insignificant, or not worthy of attention, such as some people you may know.

Sentence: "Ignore him. He's just a *2-bit* player. We don't have to worry about him."

286

Pronunciation: *too-ay-dee-six.*

Meaning: Abbreviation for the 80286 microprocessor, used in the IBM AT class of computers.

Sentence: "Nobody sells a *286* any more. I use my old 286 as a doorstop."

3-D

Pronunciation: *Three-Dee.*

Meaning: Abbreviation for Three-Dimensional.

Sentence: "The latest spreadsheets offer the ability to analyze data in *3-D.* I have enough trouble just moving the cursor around the worksheet."

32-bit

Pronunciation: *thir-dee-too-bit.*

Meaning: An adjective, describing that something can transfer or process 32 bits of data at any given time.

Sentence: "My old computer has a *32-bit* processor, so it's faster than a 16-bit processor. I can't wait until they come out with a 128-bit processor. That way my computer can confuse me faster than before."

386

Pronunciation: *three-ay-dee-six.*

Meaning: Abbreviation for the 80386DX processor.

Sentence: "When I was the first on the block to own a 286 computer, everyone around me got green with envy. When I was the first to own a *386* computer, everyone got even more jealous. Now that I have no money to buy food or pay for rent because I bought so many computers, nobody cares about me at all."

486

Pronunciation: *for-ay-dee-six.*

Meaning: Abbreviation for the 80486DX processor.

Sentence: "Just when I thought a *486* processor would be sufficient, they had to come out with the more advanced Pentium processor and make my computer obsolete. How come I feel like I'm wasting my time trying to keep up?"

640K limit

Pronunciation: *six-for-dee-kay lim-it.*

Meaning: The restriction on IBM-compatible computers that restricts them to using a maximum of 640K of conventional memory.

Sentence: "I stuffed my computer with 8 megabytes of memory, but my programs still couldn't access all of it because of the *640K limit.* Who was the goofball who thought 640K of RAM would always be enough?"

6502, 65C02, 65C16

Pronunciation: *six-dee-five-oh-too, six-dee-five-see-oh-too, six-dee-five-see-one-six.*

Meaning: The family of processors used in the Apple IIe, IIc, and IIgs.

Sentence: "My old Apple IIe only had a tiny *6502* processor in it. Now I have a Macintosh with a 68030 processor. That's like going from a tricycle to a sports car."

68000

Pronunciation: *six-dee-ayt-thow-zand.*

Meaning: The numeric designation for the Motorola processor used in the original Macintosh computers.

Sentence: "When I bought a Macintosh Plus back in 1985, its *68000* processor seemed like the most powerful thing on earth. Now it looks like a pop gun compared to my Macintosh IIfx."

680x0

Pronunciation: *six-dee-ayt-oh-ex-oh.*

Meaning: Abbreviation to indicate the Motorola 68000 family of processors, including the 68000, 68020, 68030, and the 68040.

Sentence: "All Macintosh computers use the *680x0* processor. Who cares, just as long as the thing works okay?"

68881

Pronunciation: *six-dee-ayt-ayt-ayt-dee-one.*

Meaning: The math coprocessor used with the 68000 processor.

Sentence: "If you want real number-crunching capabilities, plug a *68881* math coprocessor in your computer. This will make your computer run faster, unless you're just playing video games or something."

8-bit

Pronunciation: *ayt-bit.*

Meaning: An adjective, describing that something can transfer or process 8 bits of data at any given time.

Sentence: "My old Apple IIe was an *8-bit* computer. And to think that when I bought it in 1979, I thought it was the most advanced computer in the world."

80286

Pronunciation: *ay-dee-too-ay-dee-six.*

Meaning: Numeric designation for the processor used in the IBM AT family of computers.

Sentence: "I found a computer with an *80286* at a garage sale. The guy only wanted $100 for it, so I bought it for my kids. Too bad their Nintendo games are now more powerful than that."

80386, 80386DX

Pronunciation: *ay-dee-three-ay-dee-six, ay-dee-three-ay-dee-six dee-ex.*

Meaning: Numeric designation for the processor used in some IBM-compatible computers. The 80386 is an abbreviation for the official designation of the 80386DX processor.

Sentence: "The minimum requirement to run Windows is an *80386* processor. Then again, you'd be better off with an 80486 or a Pentium, unless you like staring at the hourglass icon forever."

80386SL

Pronunciation: *ay-dee-three-ay-dee-six ess-ell.*

Meaning: A specially designed version of the 80386 processor for conserving energy, often found in laptop computers.

Sentence: "I told the salesman I wanted an 80386 in a laptop, but he told me that all the laptops used an *80386SL*. So now I carry a wagon behind me to drag my desktop 80386 with me wherever I go."

80386SX

Pronunciation: *ay-dee-three-ay-dee-six ess-ex.*

Meaning: A low-cost and slower version of the 80386DX processor. Like the 80386DX, this processor can process 32 bits of data at any given time, but it can only transfer 16 bits of data at once.

Sentence: "In the old days, you could save money by buying an 80386SX instead of a real 80386. Nowadays, an *80386SX* is way too slow to run anything more demanding than PacMan."

80387

Pronunciation: *ay-dee-three-ay-dee-sev-en.*

Meaning: The math coprocessor designed to work with the 80386DX, 80386SX, and 80386SL processors.

Sentence: "I plugged an *80387* math coprocessor into my computer to make it run faster. But it's still not as good as an 80486 processor, so I tossed the whole thing and bought a new computer instead."

80486, 80486DX

Pronunciation: *ay-dee-for-ay-dee-six, ay-dee-for-ay-dee-six dee-ex.*

Meaning: Numeric designation for the processors used in many IBM-compatible computers.

Sentence: "I sold my old 80386 computer so I could buy an *80486.* Now I have no money for rent, so I sold my car so that I could buy a super VGA color monitor."

80486SX

Pronunciation: *ay-dee-for-ay-dee-six ess-ex.*

Meaning: Low-cost and slower version of the 80486DX processor. The main difference is that this processor lacks the math coprocessor capabilities of the 80486DX.

Sentence: "If you're too cheap to spend an extra $100 and you don't do much number-crunching, you could probably get by with an *80486SX.*"

80487

Pronunciation: *ay-dee-for-ay-dee-sev-en.*

Meaning: The math coprocessor designed to work with the 80486SX. Together the two of them give almost equivalent speed and power of an 80486DX.

Sentence: "If you really want to waste your money, buy an 80486SX and an *80487* math coprocessor. Not only will this cost more than buying an 80486DX right from the start, but it won't run as fast either."

80586

Pronunciation: *ay-dee-five-ay-dee-six.*

Meaning: The unofficial designation for the Pentium processor. The main reason Intel chose not to name their latest processor the 80586 is because they couldn't trademark the name and threatened to sue anyone who used it without their permission.

Sentence: "I asked for an *80586* computer, and the junk salesman thought I meant an 80486 instead of a Pentium processor. What a dope. I bet last week this same salesman was selling door to door."

8086

Pronunciation: *ay-dee-ay-dee-six.*

Meaning: A 16-bit processor used in the later versions of IBM PC-compatible computers.

Sentence: "Although the first IBM PC used the 8088 processor, the later compatible computers used an *8086* processor because it was slightly faster. (The "6" is for "16-bit" and the "8" is for "8-bit," so the 808*8* is actually slower than the 808*6*.) Then again, it's still slower than an 80486."

8087

Pronunciation: *ay-dee-ay-dee-sev-en.*

Meaning: The math coprocessor designed to work with the 8088 and the 8086 processors.

Sentence: "Lots of IBM PC users bought an *8087* processor so their Lotus 1-2-3 spreadsheets would run faster. Now these same computers are collecting dust in somebody's closet or garage."

8088

Pronunciation: *ay-dee-ay-dee-ayt.*

Meaning: The first processor used in the IBM PC. Although this is a 16-bit processor, it can only transfer 8-bits of data at any given time.

Sentence: "IBM chose the *8088* over the 8086 because they wanted compatibility with 8-bit peripherals. Then when the market shifted towards 16-bit computing power, IBM-compatible computers started using the 8086 instead."

80x86

Pronunciation: *ayt-oh-ex-ayt-dee-six.*

Meaning: Designation that covers all the Intel family of microprocessors including the 8088, 8086, 80286, 80386, and 80486.

Sentence: "Lots of programs only work on *80x86* processors, which usually means IBM compatibles. Scientists like using the '80x86 designation' instead of 'IBM-compatibility' because it looks more scientific and important."

aardvark

Pronunciation: *ard-vark.*

Meaning: One of the first words listed in good dictionaries. Comes from the old Afrikanns phrase meaning "earth pig," which refers to a nocturnal mammal known to burrow its way through African terrain eating termites and dragging its big floppy ears and heavy tail.

Sentence: I have no idea what an *aardvark* has to do with computers, but I thought we'd probably get in trouble if we left it out of the dictionary."

ABC

Pronunciation: *Ay Bee See*

Meaning: Abbreviation for Atanasoff-Berry Computer; a device which was a precursor to the ENIAC and therefore, is sometimes considered to be the first electronic digital computer. The ABC was created by Professor John Atanasoff and student Clifford Berry at Iowa State University in the early 1940s.

Sentence: "The *ABC* had enough vacuum tubes in it to fill a room full of old televisions. I'd like to see the air conditioner those guys must have had to keep it cooled off."

abort

Pronunciation: *ah-bort.*

Meaning: To stop something before it's too late, such as a program running out of control. Popular methods include frantically hitting Esc, Ctrl-C, or the Break key. Rent the movie *WarGames,* and you'll see what we mean.

Sentence: "I broke into the Pentagon's computers and launched a nuclear missile at Cleveland, but then I had to *abort* when my mom found out."

Abort, Retry, Fail, Ignore?

Pronunciation: *Ah-bort, Ree-tri, Fay-el, Ig-nor.*

Meaning: The cryptic message that MS-DOS displays when it can't figure out what to do next. Typing **A** stops whatever program was running at the time. Typing **R** forces the computer to try again. Typing **F** stops the current command that caused the problem but keeps the program still running . Typing **I** tells the computer to pretend the problem never existed and keep running anyway. This Ignore command sometimes can cause the computer to lose or scramble data. (See also *MS-DOS.*)

Sentence: "I tried to display the directory of my floppy drive, but I forgot to put a disk in it. Then the computer asked, `Abort, Retry, Fail, or Ignore?` Because I hate making decisions, I turned the computer off instead."

About box

Pronunciation: *Ah-bowt box.*

Meaning: A tiny little window that appears in the middle of the screen, displaying the program's name, version number, and anything else the programmers thought the general public might want to know. (For an example, see the "About Program Manager" option under the Help menu in Windows.)

Sentence: "Whenever I'm bored at work and can't figure out anything to do, I display the *About box* on my screen so it looks like I know what I'm doing."

ABS

Pronunciation: *Ay Bee Ess.*

Meaning: An abbreviation for ABSolute value. ABS is a command used in many programming languages and spreadsheet programs for calculating the absolute value of a number.

Sentence: "According to my spreadsheet, my tax balance comes out to –$12,500, meaning I owe back taxes to the IRS. But when I calculate the *ABS* value of my debt, it looks like the IRS owes me $12,500."

absolute reference

Pronunciation: *ab-so-loot ref-er-rentz.*

Meaning: A term used in spreadsheets that tells a formula to use a specific cell or group of cells. If you move the formula from one cell to another at a later date, the formula will still use the specific cell defined earlier.

Sentence: "Most of the time, spreadsheets use relative references for calculating formulas. *Absolute reference* is something you have to specifically declare if you want to make sure your formulas don't get all screwed up."

AC

Pronunciation: *Ay See.*

Meaning: Abbreviation for Alternating Current.

Sentence: "Every home in America uses *AC* electricity instead of DC. That's good information to know in case you ever get asked this question on the game show *Jeopardy*."

accelerator board

Pronunciation: *ex-sel-ler-rate-ter bord.*

Meaning: A special circuit board that plugs into a computer and makes it run faster. Accelerator boards usually contain a faster processor that replaces or supplements the computer's existing processor. (See also *processor.*)

Sentence: "Instead of buying a new computer, I plugged an *accelerator board* into my old computer. Now my computer runs faster, but it still looks like a piece of trash."

access time

Pronunciation: *ax-sess time.*

Meaning: The amount of time needed for a storage device to retrieve information.

Sentence: "My hard disk has an *access time* of 28 milliseconds. Not only do I think that's fast, but I think that whoever takes the time to measure these things needs to set higher goals in life."

ACK

Pronunciation: *Ack.*

Meaning: Abbreviation for ACKnowledge, often used when a computer dials another one through a modem. Before two computers can transfer information, they must first ACKnowledge that the other one exists and is ready. (See also *modem.*)

Sentence: "For the longest time, my computer refused to get an *ACK* signal from the other computer. Then I realized I had to plug the modem in the phone jack."

acoustic coupler

Pronunciation: *ah-koo-stik cup-ler.*

Meaning: An old style modem device that works by shoving the handset of a telephone into two rubber cups that look like a high-tech bra from the future.

Sentence: "You kids these days have it easy. Not only did I have to walk five miles to get to school everyday, but I had to use an *acoustic coupler* if I wanted to connect my computer to the phone line."

acronym

Pronunciation: *ak-ro-nim.*

Meaning: A word created by taking letters from two or more words to create a new word. Examples are BASIC, FORTRAN, and DOS.

Sentence: "This computer manual is so full of *acronyms* that I can't understand a thing. Fortunately, I don't have to because I'm the boss."

active window

Pronunciation: *ak-tiv win-do.*

Meaning: The window on the screen that's currently in use. If two or more windows appear on the screen, the active window usually appears brighter around the edges. (See also *window.*)

Sentence: "When I have my word processor, spreadsheet, and database running in different windows, I have to make sure my word processor is the *active window* before I start typing threatening letters to my cat."

Ada

Pronunciation: *Ay-da.*

Meaning: A structured programming language that was supposed to be the standard language for all defense-related programming work. Naturally, hardly anyone uses it although we all paid for its development with our tax dollars. Ada was named after Ada, the Countess of Lovelace, who is generally credited with writing the first computer program for a machine that Charles Babbage designed.

Sentence: "Back in the '70s, the Department of Defense decided to create their own language called *Ada* that they wanted everyone to use. Now almost everyone uses C, which means Ada is pretty much a waste of everyone's time and money."

Adam West

Pronunciation: *Ad-um West.*

Meaning: The star of the *Batman* TV series that appeared during the '60s.

Sentence: "I got bored with computers, so I went to an RV show where I saw *Adam West* and the Batmobile on display."

adapter

Pronunciation: *ah-dapt-er.*

Meaning: A piece of equipment that plugs into a computer and into another piece of equipment such as a monitor or printer. Allows mismatched cables, plugs, or systems to work together. (See also *EGA* and *network adapter.*)

Sentence: "I couldn't plug my modem into my printer because the plugs were different sizes. After I bought an *adapter,* everything plugs together just fine."

add-on program

Pronunciation: *add-on pro-gram.*

Meaning: A program that works with and enhances the features of another program.

Sentence: "The problem with Lotus 1-2-3 is you can't use it for simple word processing. That's why I bought a special *add-on* program that gives me word processing while using Lotus 1-2-3. Too bad I still don't know how to use Lotus 1-2-3."

address

Pronunciation: *ad-dress.*

Meaning: The location of an item in memory or in a spreadsheet. Items stored in memory have a memory address. Items stored in a spreadsheet have a row and column address.

Sentence: "The *address* of the first cell in a spreadsheet is A1. That's also the name of my favorite steak sauce, which I can buy at the supermarket address of 123 Main Street."

AI

Pronunciation: *Ay Eye.*

Meaning: Abbreviation for Artificial Intelligence, which is the fascinating science of making computers as smart as human beings (which may be a step backward in some cases).

Sentence: "The military uses computers that have *AI.* That's why their projects usually cost more than they should and don't work the way they're supposed to. Their computers really do think like people."

ALGOL

Pronunciation: *Al-gall.*

Meaning: An early programming language that's an acronym for ALGOrithmic Language. ALGOL was one of the first programming languages to encourage structured programming. Pascal is a direct descendent of ALGOL.

Sentence: "I tried programming in *ALGOL* once, but nobody uses the language any more. That's why I switched to Ada. Nobody uses that language either, but at least the government pays me big bucks not to do anything with it."

algorithm

Pronunciation: *Al-Gore-rhythm.*

Meaning: A step-by-step set of instructions that actually does something worthwhile. Often used to describe the instructions written in a programming language like C, BASIC, or Pascal. (See also *billclintonrithm.*)

Sentence: "My program works perfectly because my *algorithms* are flawless. As long as nobody uses my program, it will keep on working perfectly too."

alias

Pronunciation: *ay-lee-ess.*

Meaning: Used with System 7.x on the Macintosh, an alias lets you make one or more copies of a program icon to display in other windows. An alias file works by running the original file it was created from. By

creating one or more alias files, you can have access to your programs no matter which window may be displayed. Think of alias files as Elvis impersonators that can appear everywhere you look.

Sentence: "I created two *alias* files from my word processor and stored one in my Home Business Folder and the other in my Job Folder. That way I can quickly run my word processor by clicking on the alias file, instead of trying to find where I stored the word processor file."

aliasing

Pronunciation: *ay-lee-ess-sing.*

Meaning: The ugly-looking jagged or stair-stepped appearance of diagonal lines in computer graphic images. Sometimes referred to as "the jaggies."

Sentence: "Trying to draw diagonal lines on a computer is about as easy as drawing circles on an Etch-A-Sketch. Because whenever you draw a diagonal line, you get *aliasing,* which makes your straight line look more like a poorly drawn staircase."

alignment

Pronunciation: *uh-line-mint.*

Meaning: When used to describe hard disks, the alignment refers to the drive head's ability to read and write information without error. When used to describe text, the alignment refers to the text's relationship to the left and right margins, as in "centered," "left-justified," and so forth.

Sentence: "While trying to adjust the *alignment* of text in my word processor, I bumped my computer and knocked the hard disk out of *alignment.*"

allocate

Pronunciation: *al-o-kate.*

Meaning: The process of dividing a computer's resources between two or more items.

Sentence: "When my program runs, the computer *allocates* a certain amount of memory for it to work. When my program doesn't work, I allocate a certain amount of emotional anger and frustration towards the computer."

alpha test

Pronunciation: *al-fa test.*

Meaning: The initial testing of a new program, usually conducted by the programmers and their trusted friends. Alpha test programs usually don't work correctly.

Sentence: "Before Microsoft released MS-DOS 6.0, they ran it through an *alpha test* of their own employees. Once they found the first few bugs, they released the program into beta test so that everyone else could find those same mistakes."

alphanumeric characters

Pronunciation: *al-fa-noo-mar-rik kar-rak-ters.*

Meaning: Characters that consist of letters and numbers.

Sentence: "Whenever you type a command, the computer usually expects an *alphanumeric* command. If you type something nonsensical like '| __|+_,' your computer won't understand it."

Alt

Pronunciation: *Alt.* (Can't get much simpler than that!)

Meaning: The key on IBM computers that is used with other keys to give commands to the computer. Common commands are Alt-X to quit and Alt-P to print a file.

Sentence: "In some programs, you press *Alt-X* to exit the program. In other programs, you press Alt-X to cut data from a document. Because computers never seem to work the way you expect, now you can understand why so many computer programmers go crazy."

Altair

Pronunciation: *Al-tar.*

Meaning: The name of one of the first personal computers available.

Sentence: "Before Apple, IBM, or even Radio Shack sold a microcomputer, the only one you could buy was an *Altair.*"

alternating current

Pronunciation: *al-ter-nat-ting ker-rent.*

Meaning: The type of electricity used in America. Often abbreviated as AC.

Sentence: "Today, everyone uses *alternating current.* Back when electricity was still new, Thomas Edison tried to get everyone to use DC instead because he had a financial stake in the matter."

Amiga

Pronunciation: *Ah-mee-ga.*

Meaning: The name of the most technological advanced, inexpensive personal computer on the market today that hardly anyone cares about.

Sentence: "I wanted to buy an *Amiga* for its low price and great color graphics, but everyone else seems to be using IBM or Macintoshes. So to remain compatible with the rest of the world, I spent three times as much on a Macintosh and got only half the graphics capability of an Amiga."

amp

Pronunciation: *am-pa.*

Meaning: Abbreviation for AMPere, which is a unit for measuring electric current.

Sentence: "Your computer uses too many *amps.* No wonder our lights keep dimming every time you turn it on."

analog

Pronunciation: *an-a-log.*

Meaning: A way of storing information as multiple values. Analog is the opposite of; storing information as discrete values (digital). Sound waves, for example, may be analog because they have a signal that varies continuously. When sound is digitized, it is sampled as discrete values that can be stored as ones and zeros in a computer or other device. That's why your CD player sounds so good. (See also *digital.*)

Sentence: "Computers are digital, which means they understand On and Off, Yes and No. People are *analog* because they understand Yes, No, I dunno, who cares?, why are you asking me this?, and maybe."

animation

Pronunciation: *an-i-may-shin.*

Meaning: To use your $3,000 computer to create Saturday-morning-style cartoons. Creating the appearance of movement of drawn objects. (See also *Mickey Mouse.*)

Sentence: "I bought a graphics program that lets me create *animation.* That way my business reports look more like cartoons. All I need now is a laugh track to go with them."

ANSI

Pronunciation: *An-zee.*

Meaning: Abbreviation for American National Standards Institute, an organization that defines standards for different industries that most people ignore anyway. In the computer industry, ANSI standards refer to the way programming languages are supposed to work, to the way computer screens display characters, and to the way computers on networks communicate. This standard is often called ANSI graphics. (Also, the technical term for how kids get when they've been riding in the car too long.)

Sentence: "If you buy a FORTRAN compiler, make sure it follows the *ANSI* standard for FORTRAN. That way you can run your program on different computers without modifying it."

ANSI C

Pronunciation: *An-zee See.*

Meaning: A standard definition for the C programming language as defined by the American National Standards Institute. Nearly every C compiler tries to follow the ANSI C standard as closely as possible, and then they add enhancements that pretty much destroy the whole purpose of a standard in the first place.

Sentence: "Lots of C compilers claim 100 percent compatibility with the *ANSI C* standard. Then again, lots of people claim that Elvis is still alive."

ANSI character set

Pronunciation: *An-zee kar-rak-ter set.*

Meaning: A list of predefined characters that computers use. The ANSI character set includes ordinary letters and numbers plus strange little symbols such as foreign language symbols, smiley faces, and lines and boxes.

Sentence: "Every computer uses the *ANSI character set* these days. So tell the salesman that he doesn't know what he's talking about."

ANSI graphics

Pronunciation: *An-zee gra-fiks.*

Meaning: Special characters that create simple graphics such as lines, boxes, and colors. Often found on BBSs for displaying information on the screen.

Sentence: "The first time I dialed in to a BBS, it asked if I wanted to use *ANSI graphics.* If I would have said no, the BBS screen would have looked plain. Since I said yes, the BBS screen looks nice and colorful. I'm still confused, but at least the pretty colors keep me amused."

ANSI screen control codes (ANSI.SYS)

Pronunciation: *An-zee skreen kon-troll kodz.*

Meaning: Yet another standard that specifies a series of characters that clear computer screens. IBM computers only use *ANSI screen control codes* if the CONFIG.SYS file contains the line:

```
DEVICE = ANSI.SYS
```

ANSI screen control codes begin with Esc and are often called escape codes.

Sentence: "If a computer doesn't have the DEVICE=*ANSI.SYS* line in its CONFIG.SYS file, you'll see all sorts of strange symbols like square brackets ([), numbers, letters, and characters (@) instead of boxes and lines."

answer mode

Pronunciation: *an-ser mowd.*

Meaning: The state of a modem when it's ready to receive calls from other computers.

Sentence: "I had to set up my modem in *answer mode* before it would accept calls from other computers. Then I had to set my teenage daughter off answer mode so boys would stop calling her."

API

Pronunciation: *Ay Pee Eye.*

Meaning: Acronym for Application Program Interface, which is yet another way that's supposed to make computers easier than they really are. API defines a standard way that programs work with pull-down menus, dialog boxes, and windows. Microsoft Windows, OS/2, and the Macintosh are examples of API in action.

Sentence: "Macintosh programs tend to look the same because they follow the same *API.* DOS programs tend to look like a mixture of everything because few of them follow the same API."

APPEND

Pronunciation: *Ah-pend.*

Meaning: An MS-DOS command that tells your computer which directories to look in for data files. This is similar to the PATH command that tells MS-DOS which directories to look in for program files.

Sentence: "Whenever I ran my database program, I kept getting a `File Not Found` error message. Then I used the *APPEND* command to tell DOS to look in my C:\DATA directory, and everything works fine. I thought computers would be smarter than this."

Apple Computer Inc.

Pronunciation: *Ap-pull Kom-pewt-er Ink.*

Meaning: The makers of the Apple II series, the Macintosh series, and several other new, very successful products. Based in Cupertino, California. Steve Jobs and Steve Wozniak, who had been teen-age friends, founded the company in a family garage in Silicon Valley. The Apple Macintosh introduced the now famous user interface that enhanced the use of icons, a mouse, pull-down menus, dialog boxes, and so on. Many of these ideas were born out of research done at Xerox's Palo Alto Research Center. Although the Apple computers have been the main counterpart to IBM-compatible technology for several years, the lines of distinction have become blurred as Microsoft Windows now provides a similar interface on the DOS platform. Nonetheless, DOS users and Mac users still tend to view each other as coming from different planets.

Sentence: "If I had as much money as *Apple Computer Inc.*, I wouldn't need a computer. I could be like our CEO at work — he's the only one I know who doesn't have a computer on his desk. That's because his secretary does all of his work."

Apple Desktop Bus (ADB)

Pronunciation: *Ap-pull Desk-top Bus.*

Meaning: Sometimes abbreviated as ADB, this defines an interface standard for connecting keyboards, mice, trackballs, and other input devices to Apple Macintosh computers.

Sentence: "Since every Macintosh computer has the *Apple Desktop Bus,* you can be sure that any printer that Apple sells will work with your computer. Too bad every printer that Apple sells costs twice as much as I can afford to pay."

No ma'am, the Apple Desktop Bus doesn't stop here.

Apple II

Pronunciation: *Ap-pull Too.*

Meaning: One of the first personal computers that actually did something useful. After introducing the Apple II, Apple released enhanced models called the Apple IIe, Apple IIc, and finally the Apple IIgs. Finally, Apple decided to drop the whole Apple II family altogether and focus on selling Macintoshes.

Sentence: "My first computer was an *Apple IIe* with 48K of RAM and one floppy disk drive. I paid $2,500 for it, and now it's worth about $10."

Apple III

Pronunciation: *Ap-pull Three.*

Meaning: A computer that was supposed to replace the Apple II but wound up being ignored by the general public. After turning into a public embarrassment to Apple, the Apple III quietly disappeared and can now be found in landfills all across America.

Sentence: "After spending $2,500 for an Apple II, I spent $3,000 for an *Apple III,* thinking I was making a good investment. Boy, do I feel stupid."

Apple menu

Pronunciation: *Ap-pull men-yoo.*

Meaning: The tiny little apple (with a bite taken out of it) that appears in the far left corner of the menu bar in Macintosh computers. Clicking on the Apple Menu pulls down desk accessories and simple programs to use while another program is already running.

Sentence: "To tell your Macintosh which printer to use, you have to choose the Chooser from the *Apple menu.* If you have no idea what I just said, then your computer is probably collecting dust right about now."

AppleShare

Pronunciation: *Ap-pull-share.*

Meaning: A network operating system developed by Apple to work with Macintosh computers.

Sentence: "After connecting all our Macintoshes in a network, we had to use *AppleShare* to get them all to work together. Now, if it could only be this easy to get our people to work together, we'd be all set."

AppleTalk

Pronunciation: *Ap-pull-talk.*

Meaning: A local area network standard developed by Apple to hook Macintosh and IBM PC computers together. Every Macintosh computer has an AppleTalk port built-in (the same can't be said for IBM computers). AppleTalk is an inexpensive way to create a network but it tends to be slower than other types of networks. (See also *network.*)

I heard he has worms!

Sentence: "We needed to hook up our Macintoshes to a single laser printer and one IBM. We didn't have much money or technical expertise, so we used *AppleTalk.*"

application

Pronunciation: *ap-lik-ka-shin.*

Meaning: Another name for a program such as a word processor, spreadsheet, or database.

Sentence: "Try running the *application* on *my* computer. Then we can tell if the program really is screwed up or your computer is."

ARC

Pronunciation: *Ark.*

Meaning: The name of a popular data-compression program that takes multiple files and smashes them into a single, smaller one. Once used heavily on IBM computers, the ARC file standard has been replaced by the ZIP standard.

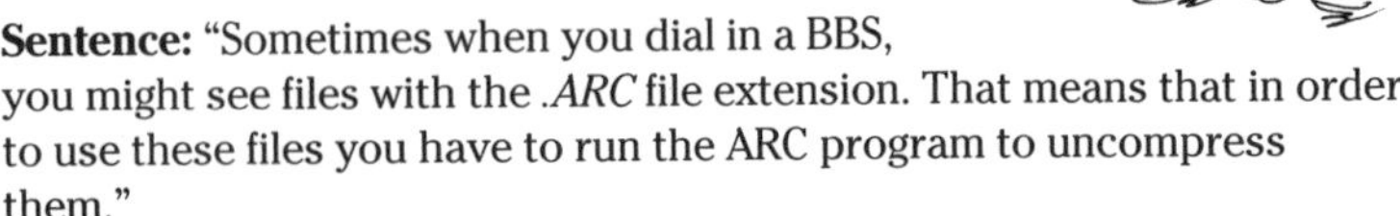

Sentence: "Sometimes when you dial in a BBS, you might see files with the *.ARC* file extension. That means that in order to use these files you have to run the ARC program to uncompress them."

architecture

Pronunciation: *ark-i-tex-sure.*

Meaning: The particular (and arbitrary) way computer equipment is designed. Also may refer to the design of a communication system as in "network architecture." (See also *open architecture.*)

Sentence: "The IBM *architecture* is very easy to understand, which explains why some people can build their own IBM-compatible computer. In comparison, the Macintosh architecture is more complicated. That's why hardly anyone has built his or her own Macintosh computer."

archive

Pronunciation: *ark-ive.*

Meaning: To store important files in a place where you can never find them again.

Sentence: "I made an *archive* copy of my tax returns so that I would always have it if I needed it. I still have it, but I don't know where it is."

argument

Pronunciation: *arg-yoo-mint.*

Meaning: A value given to a subprogram. A term used most often when you write your own programs.

Sentence: "The main program needs to give two *arguments* to the subprogram so that it can work properly. Once the subprogram gets these two arguments, it can plot the next most likely sighting of Elvis, Bigfoot, and the Loch Ness Monster."

ARPANET

Pronunciation: *Arp-pa-net.*

Meaning: A nationwide computer network created by the Department of Defense to link research institutions and universities together. ARPANET has now merged with several other networks to create the INTERNET.

Sentence: "I used the *ARPANET* to dial into a computer back in Boston. Now I have to use the INTERNET. Tomorrow I'll have to remember a new acronym to use to do the same thing."

array

Pronunciation: *ah-ray.*

Meaning: A collection of similar data (such as numbers, letters, or strings) stored under the same name. Data is assigned a different number in the array. An array to store five numbers might look like NumberArray[1..5] of Integer, depending on the language you use.

Sentence: "If you ever write programs for your computer, you'll probably use *arrays* to group related information together. Then again, you might just hire a programmer to do your work for you so you can go off surfing or something."

arrow key

Pronunciation: *air-row kee.*

Meaning: Special keys on the keyboard that move the cursor up, down, left, or right. Not surprisingly, the arrow keys have little arrows on them.

Sentence: "To move the cursor up one line, just press the up *arrow key.* To move the cursor down one line, press the down arrow key. To absolutely confuse the computer, press all the arrow keys simultaneously."

artificial intelligence

Pronunciation: *art-i-fish-al in-tell-i-jentz.*

Meaning: Sometimes abbreviated as AI. (See also *AI.*)

Sentence: "My favorite button is the one that says '*Artificial Intelligence* is better than none!'"

ascender

Pronunciation: *ass-sen-der.*

Meaning: The part of a letter that extends upwards. The letters *t* and *h* have ascenders. The letters *l, u,* and *n* do not.

Sentence: "Letters with *ascenders* can get in the way of the line on top unless you make the line spacing big enough."

ascending order

Pronunciation: *ass-sen-ding or-der.*

Meaning: To arrange information from lowest to highest.

Sentence: "My inventory database lets me arrange data in *ascending order.* That way I can see which item is selling the slowest and which item is selling the fastest."

ASCII

Pronunciation: *Ass-kee.*

Meaning: An acronym that stands for American Standard Code for Information Interchange. ASCII defines a standard way for representing characters on computers.

Sentence: "As long as you use *ASCII* characters in your report, we can copy and use it on different computers. If you don't use ASCII characters, then we won't have even the slightest idea what you wrote."

ASCII file

Pronunciation: *Ass-kee fi-ell.*

Meaning: A file that only contains ASCII characters. Sometimes called a Text File.

Sentence: "The only sure way to transfer files between different word processors is to store everything in *ASCII files.* You won't be able to use underlining, fonts, or typesizes, but at least the information will be the same."

aspect ratio

Pronunciation: *ass-pekt ray-she-o.*

Meaning: The ratio of the horizontal dimension of an object to its vertical dimension. A term used in graphics.

Sentence: "I tried drawing a circle on my computer, but the *aspect ratio* was all wrong so it looked like a sausage instead. After I changed the aspect ratio, my circles still looked funny, but that's because I can't draw anything to save my life."

assembler

Pronunciation: *ass-sem-bler.*

Meaning: A special program used to convert programs written in assembly language into machine code that the computer can understand.

Sentence: "After I wrote a program using assembly language, the computer still couldn't use it. Then someone told me I needed an *assembler* to make my program work. Wow, all these computer terms make my head want to explode."

assembly language

Pronunciation: *ass-em-blee lan-gu-uj.*

Meaning: A type of programming language that directly manipulates the microprocessor of a computer. Assembly language programs are usually longer and harder to read than programs written in C or BASIC. On the other hand, assembly language programs run faster and take up less space than similar programs written in other languages. Assembly language is used when speed and efficiency are more important than clarity and portability (the capability to run on different computers without modification).

Sentence: "After most companies write a program using C or Pascal, they optimize it by replacing large chunks with *assembly language.* Of course the programs run faster, but they are harder to modify at a later date. To remedy this problem, most companies just charge more."

asterisk

Pronunciation: *ass-ter-risk.*

Meaning: The * symbol on the keyboard. Many operating systems, such as MS-DOS, treat the asterisk as a wildcard when used with ordinary operating system commands.

Sentence: "If you wanted to delete every file in a directory using MS-DOS, type **DEL *.*** and press the Enter key. If you wanted to delete every file with the .EXE file extension, type **DEL *.EXE** and press the Enter key. If you wanted to delete every file permanently from the face of the earth, pour kerosene on your computer and light a match."

asynchronous

Pronunciation: *a-sink-ron-us.*

Meaning: Any process that isn't synchronized. Often used when sending or receiving data through a phone line. Most likely a term you'll never use in your life, but it can make you sound knowledgeable around other computer geeks.

Sentence: "Most computers use *asynchronous* transmission, which sends characters one at a time. Some computers use synchronous transmission, which sends more than one character at a time."

AT

Pronunciation: *Ay-tee.*

Meaning: An acronym (isn't the computer industry full of them?) that IBM invented that stands for Advanced Technology. When IBM introduced a new computer using the 80286 processor, they called the computer the IBM AT.

Sentence: "Back in 1985, I bought an IBM *AT* for $4,000. Now it's worth about $200. This is known as advanced technology."

AT&T

Pronunciation: *Ay Tee and Tee.*

Meaning: An acronym that stands for American Telephone and Telegraph. Familiar with telephones, AT&T tried to break into the computer market and threaten IBM. This was like McDonald's trying to break into the software business and put Microsoft out of work.

Sentence: "*AT&T* acquired NCR as a further attempt to bust into the computer market."

audio

Pronunciation: *aw-dee-o.*

Meaning: The reproduction or creation of sound.

Sentence: "My computer has *audio* capability. Every time I turn it on, I hear a voice that tells me that I screwed up again."

AUTOEXEC.BAT

Pronunciation: *Aw-toe Ex-ek Bat.*

Meaning: Short for AUTO EXECutable BATch file. Commonly found on IBM computers, this file contains instructions that the computer follows before waiting for any commands from you. If you ever feel like your computer is ignoring you when it first starts up, the AUTOEXEC.BAT is responsible.

Sentence: "My *AUTOEXEC.BAT* file got erased, so I had to type all the commands in myself before it was ready to work."

AUX

Pronunciation: *Ay Yoo Ex* or *Ox.*

Meaning: In MS-DOS, an abbreviation for the AUXiliary port, which is the communications (COM) port that MS-DOS uses by default.

Sentence: "Plug your modem in the *AUX* port. If it doesn't work, then you plugged it in the wrong port."

Avogadro's Number

Pronunciation: *Av-o-god-rowz Num-ber.*

Meaning: A constant value used by scientists that represents something so important they decided to name it after the guy who discovered it. Rumor has it that if you dial Avogadro's Number backward, you can hear demonic messages.

Sentence: "I'm tired of calling up girls for dates who turn me down. Give me *Avogadro's Number* and maybe I can talk physics to him or something."

axis

Pronunciation: *ax-iss.*

Meaning: Imaginary guidelines used for plotting graphics on a computer screen. To measure a point horizontally, you use the X-axis. To measure a point vertically, you use the Y-axis.

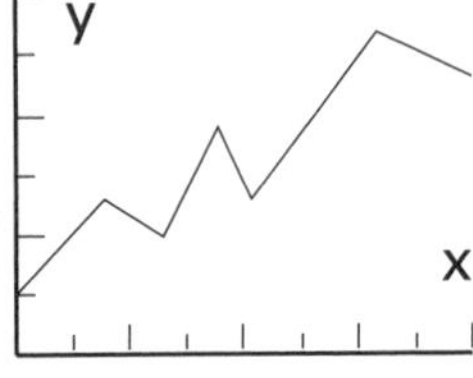

Sentence: "The upper left corner of the computer screen is often considered to be point (0,0) along the X and Y-*axis.* Don't you remember this from geometry class?"

back door

Pronunciation: *bak door.*

Meaning: A secret way of getting into a program that usually only the original programmer knows about (such as a secret password).

Sentence: "A lot of disgruntled programmers put *back doors* into their programs. That way if they ever get fired, they can still get in and use the program without anyone knowing."

background

Pronunciation: *bak-grow-nda.*

Meaning: To hide a window or another program out of sight without removing it from the computer altogether. Opposite of *active*. (See also *active window.*)

Sentence: "Whenever you run two or more programs simultaneously, you can use only one program at a time. Any other programs you load run in the *background* until you need them or until your computer crashes altogether."

backlit

Pronunciation: *bak-lit.*

Meaning: To illuminate a screen with additional lighting from behind. Often used to highlight LCD screens found on laptop computers.

Sentence: "My laptop is hard to use because it doesn't have a *backlit* screen. I get eye strain every time I use it and feel like I'm going blind."

backslash key

Pronunciation: *bak-slash kee.*

Meaning: The \ key that everyone always confuses with the forward slash key /. The backslash key is used to separate directory names such as in the command

```
DIR C:\WINDOWS\SYSTEM
```

Sentence: "Over the phone, you might say: 'Type CD *backslash* DOS and press the Enter key.' This moves you to the DOS directory if everything works the way it's supposed to."

BackSpace

Pronunciation: *Bak-Spay-sa.*

Meaning: The key on the keyboard that has the word BackSpace printed on it. In most programs, the BackSpace key erases the character to the left of the cursor (like a little PacMan).

Sentence: "I kept pressing the *BackSpace* key to erase everything I wrote. Then I discovered I could just turn off my computer without saving my file instead."

backup

Pronunciation: *bak-up.*

Meaning: A copy you make of a file in case the original file gets destroyed. Can also refer to the actual copy of the file. In MS-DOS, you use the BACKUP command to make backups of your files.

Sentence: "We made *backups* of all our important data. Now we have twice as many disks storing the same amount of useless information."

BAK

Pronunciation: *Back* (as in "Ahl be bahk!").

Meaning: A three-letter file extension given to backup files, especially the ones created automatically by some applications (such as some word processors).

Sentence: "If you want to save space on your hard disk, erase all the *.BAK* files. Just make sure you don't need these backups in case your original files get screwed up."

balloon help

Pronunciation: *ball-oon help.*

Meaning: Starting with System 7 on the Macintosh, Apple introduced balloon help, which provides little windows of helpful information on the screen. Balloon help gets its name because the windows it displays look like the speaking balloons seen in comic strips.

Sentence: "*Balloon help* just displays a little bit of help, unlike the normal help menu that displays gobs of helpful information that you can't use or understand."

bank switching

Pronunciation: *ba-nk switch-ing.*

Meaning: A way of quickly switching between two different groups of memory chips, giving the illusion that it's part of the same amount of memory. Bank switching is used to overcome any built-in limitations. IBM computers have a built-in 640K limitation of RAM. Expanded memory lets you add up to 16MB of RAM, but the computer still uses only 640K of RAM at any given time. Unless you're a technician, you'll never have to worry about bank switching for the rest of your life. (See also *expanded memory.*)

Sentence: "My computer has 16MB of RAM, but it still thinks it only has 640K of RAM. Fortunately, *bank switching* lets my computer use the extra memory in chunks of 640K so that it can use all of this memory."

bar code

Pronunciation: *bar kode.*

Meaning: A striped pattern of narrow and wide black and white strips. Found on almost everything you buy, bar codes provide information that scanning devices understand.

Sentence: "Many businesses use computers to scan in *bar codes* so that they can keep track of inventory. Our prison uses bar codes to keep track of prisoners."

base

Pronunciation: *bayss.*

Meaning: The number of digits used in a counting system. Base ten uses ten digits, base two (binary) uses two, and base sixteen (hexadecimal) uses sixteen.

Sentence: "Most people use *base* ten because we have five fingers on each hand. My cat only has four toes on each paw, so he counts using base eight."

BASIC

Pronunciation: *Bay-sik.*

Meaning: A programming language specifically designed to make programming easier. An acronym for "Beginners All-purpose Symbolic Instruction Code." Although BASIC is easy to use, many programmers look down on it as a "toy" language because early versions of BASIC prevented you from creating really cool programs that would wipe out your hard disk or blow up your modem. Newer versions of BASIC offer as much flexibility and power as C and Pascal, but it's still fashionable to snub BASIC, just to make BASIC programmers feel inadequate and insecure.

Sentence: "Most computers come with *BASIC* so you can experiment with writing your own programs. That sounds great, but I can't even program my VCR."

BAT

Pronunciation: *Bat* (like the animal that gets in your hair and eats bugs during the night).

Meaning: A three-letter file extension used to identify batch files.

Sentence: "I erased all my *BAT* files by mistake. Now I have to create a new AUTOEXEC.BAT file so my computer will work the same as before."

batch file

Pronunciation: *bat-ch fi-ell.*

Meaning: A special file that contains lists of operating system commands. Typing the name of a batch file tells the computer to follow all the instructions stored in the batch file.

Sentence: "I created a *batch file* to load WordPerfect and copy my files to a backup directory automatically. Instead of typing these commands myself, I just type the name of the batch file and let the computer do all the dirty work."

Batman

Pronunciation: *Bat-man.*

Meaning: A popular comic book character who dresses like a bat and goes around doing good deeds in crime-ridden Gotham City.

Sentence: "I like *Batman* because he's the only super-hero who isn't radiated or mutated in some way to get his superhuman powers."

battery backup

Pronunciation: *bat-er-ree bak-up.*

Meaning: A battery that's ready to supply electricity the moment a power outage occurs. (See also *UPS.*)

Sentence: "If the power goes out, I can still use my computer because I have a *battery backup.* Then again, I don't know what I'll do if my batteries go out at the same time."

baud

Pronunciation: *bawd.*

Meaning: A unit that measures the speed of transmission, such as for data through a modem. Modems are rated by baud rate, which varies from 300, 1200, 2400, 9600, to 14,400. Eventually, the baud rate will go as high as our national deficit.

Sentence: "I couldn't dial into the computer because my modem only has a *baud* rate of 300, but the other computer needed at least 1200 baud."

BBS

Pronunciation: *Bee Bee Ess.*

Meaning: Acronym that stands for Bulletin Board System, a program that lets other people dial into a computer and copy files, leave messages, and run up their phone bill.

Sentence: "Most cities have a list of *BBS* numbers that you can call with your modem."

BCD

Pronunciation: *Bee See Dee.*

Meaning: Another acronym that stands for Binary Coded Decimal, which is a technique that programs use to ensure accuracy for financial calculations.

Sentence: "Most spreadsheets use *BCD* so that rounding errors won't mess up your calculations. I just pay an accountant not to mess up my calculations."

beachball pointer

Pronunciation: *beech-ball poin-ter.*

Meaning: A symbol that appears on the screen to let you know that the computer is actually doing something although nothing seems to be happening. The symbol looks like a beachball, spinning around, hence its name. The beachball pointer is the Mac counterpart to the Windows hourglass.

Sentence: "My computer is so slow that I stare at the *beachball pointer* more often than I do the rest of my work."

bells and whistles

Pronunciation: *bells and wis-els.*

Meaning: A slang term to describe the multitude of extra features a program offers.

Sentence: "Each time they upgrade WordPerfect, they add more *bells and whistles*. Why can't they just make the thing easier to use in the first place?"

benchmark

Pronunciation: *ben-cha-mark.*

Meaning: A special test that measures the performance of a program or equipment against a basic standard. A benchmark is supposed to be a fair measurement of performance, but nobody thinks so except for the company whose product comes out on top.

Sentence: "Programs often tout how fast they run certain *benchmarks.* I just want to know which programs will work without requiring me to waste the rest of my life trying to use them."

Bernoulli box

Pronunciation: *Ber-new-lee box.*

Meaning: A mass storage system that uses removable cartridges. Named after a Swiss scientist who predicted the dynamics of a rapidly spinning, flexible disk around a fixed object and decided that his college education hadn't been a waste of time after all.

Sentence: "To store all our files, we bought a *Bernoulli box.* It was more expensive than another hard disk, but we just received a nice inheritance from great-uncle Louie. (May he rest in peace.)"

berserk

Pronunciation: *ber-zerk.*

Meaning: A fit of rage that Vikings often went into during the heat of battle. Today, it refers to the fit of rage computer users go into when their computer fails to work the way they thought it would.

Sentence: "Watch out for Fred. I think he's about to go *berserk* on us again."

beta test

Pronunciation: *bay-ta test.*

Meaning: The second stage of testing (alpha test is the first) of a program before releasing it to the general public. People who use a beta test program are called beta testers. Beta test programs are sometimes called "Version 1.0" by companies who want to rush their program on to the market before it's ready.

Sentence: "Before Microsoft released MS-DOS, they gave it to 50,000 people around the country to *beta test* it for them. After the program survived the beta test, they finally sold it to the rest of us."

Bézier curve

Pronunciation: *Bez-ee-ay kurv.*

Meaning: A mathematically generated line for displaying irregularly shaped curves. To create Bézier curves in most computer graphics programs, you plot a straight line and then manipulate two points somewhere in the middle, called control handles. Moving these control handles in different directions twists the line into a Bézier curve.

Sentence: "*Bézier curves* look like the twisted nightmare of some highways I've driven on."

big iron

Pronunciation: *big i-ron.*

Meaning: Slang term for a mainframe computer that costs millions of dollars, takes up half a room, and performs as much work as a $10,000 personal computer of today.

Sentence: "When our company finally switches over to personal computers, we'll give our *big iron* to a computer museum."

billclintonrhythm

Pronunciation: *Bill-Clinton-rhythm.*

Meaning: A step-by-step set of instructions that attempts to do something worthwhile. (See also *algorithm.*)

Sentence: "My new tax program works perfectly because my *billclintonrhythms* are flawless. As long as nobody sees me on the Arsenio program, my new sax program will keep on working perfectly, too."

billisecond

Pronunciation: *bill-a-sek-ond.*

Meaning: A billionth of a second, abbreviated as BS.

Sentence: "Some computer consultants cost so much it seems like they charge you a bill a second. Sometimes the programs they give you run in terms of *billiseconds,* which is slow by computer standards."

BIN

Pronunciation: *Been* (as in "I've been there").

Meaning: A three-letter file extension to identify files containing binary data.

Sentence: "Don't erase your *BIN* files because your program won't work without them."

binary

Pronunciation: *bi-nar-ree.*

Meaning: A counting system that uses two digits, 0 and 1. Sometimes used to describe other systems that offer only two choices, such as the Republican and Democratic parties.

Sentence: "Computers only count by twos, using *binary* arithmetic. People count by tens, using decimal arithmetic."

binary file

Pronunciation: *bi-nar-ree fi-ell.*

Meaning: A file containing bits and bytes of information that only a computer (or a computer geek) would understand. Often identified with the three-letter BIN file extension.

Sentence: "Most programs store additional information in *binary files* in case they need them later."

BIOS

Pronunciation: *Bi-os.*

Meaning: Acronym that stands for Basic Input/Output System. The BIOS is a set of instructions that tells the computer how to act. Most computers have the BIOS built in as a chip plugged into the computer.

Sentence: "Many IBM computers use the Phoenix *BIOS,* which mimics the IBM *BIOS* and makes the computer think it's really an IBM computer."

bit

Pronunciation: *bit* (as in "I bit my lip").

Meaning: Abbreviation for BInary digiT, which can be either a 0 or a 1. Bits are often used to measure the capability of a microprocessor to process data, such as 16-bit or 32-bit. Four bits make up a nibble, and eight bits make up a byte.

Sentence: "Old computers used an *8-bit* processor. The more powerful ones use a 32-bit processor, and they can handle roughly four times as much information. Too bad a computer with a 32-bit processor is still just as hard to use as one with an 8-bit processor."

bitmap

Pronunciation: *bit-map.*

Meaning: A graphic image represented by tiny little points of light called pixels. The more pixels used, the sharper the image looks.

Sentence: "If you want to display 'wallpaper' in Microsoft Windows, you have to use a *bitmap* graphic."

bitmapped font

Pronunciation: *bit-mapd fawnt.*

Meaning: A typeface style stored as a matrix of tiny dots. When you enlarge the size of a bitmapped font, the font tends to look jagged. Bitmapped fonts gobble up lots of memory.

Sentence: "You can always tell a *bitmapped font* because when you change its size, the letters start looking rough and jagged like they were printed on a cheap dot-matrix printer instead of an expensive laser printer."

bitmapped image

Pronunciation: *bit-mapd im-age.*

Meaning: A picture formed by patterns of tiny dots (pixels). Most paint programs, such as MacPaint or PC Paintbrush, create bitmapped images. Bitmapped images can be difficult to modify because you have to change pixels one at a time.

Sentence: "Creating a decent-looking *bitmapped image* is about as easy as trying to create a picture of a dog using colored bits of sand."

black box

Pronunciation: *blak box.*

Meaning: A collection of circuit boards that perform a specific function without the user knowing how the circuitry works.

Sentence: "Since equipment is so complicated these days, companies make them out of *black boxes.* Instead of trying to troubleshoot and repair something, they just yank out the black box causing the problem and replace it with one that works."

block

Pronunciation: *blok.*

Meaning: A collection of information lumped together for convenience. (1) When transferring files using a communications protocol such as XModem or ZModem, data gets transferred in blocks. With XModem, the size of the block is 128 bytes. With ZModem, the size of the block is 1024 bytes. (2) In a word processor, a block is a highlighted chunk of text.

Sentence: "Every time I send a file through my modem, it tells me how many *blocks* it has sent and how many more blocks remain until the whole file is transferred. This can be fun to watch for about ten seconds before you get bored and decide to do something else."

BMP

Pronunciation: *Bee Em Pee.*

Meaning: A three-letter file extension used to identify bitmap graphic files.

Sentence: "If you don't want to display wallpaper using Microsoft Windows, you can erase all your *BMP* files without a problem."

BNC connector

Pronunciation: *Bee En See kon-neck-tor.*

Meaning: A metal jobbie at the end of a cable that twists to connect the cable to the back of your computer or to another cable. BNC must mean Big Nobby Connector.

Sentence: "I need a cable with a *BNC* connector because I paid way too much for my network hardware."

boat anchor

Pronunciation: *bowt an-kor.*

Meaning: Slang term for something so useless it might as well be tied to a chain and used for dead weight to keep boats from drifting away.

Sentence: "Hardly any programs these days run on my old IBM PC with 128K RAM and one floppy disk drive. This thing's a *boat anchor.* I might as well throw it away."

bogus

Pronunciation: *bow-gus.*

Meaning: Something that's phony.

Sentence: "What a *bogus* program. And I thought it really would give my computer artificial intelligence."

boilerplate

Pronunciation: *boil-er-playte.*

Meaning: A predefined document you can use over and over again when you don't feel like thinking. Common uses for boilerplate documents are for form letters, legal documents, or love letters to multiple partners.

Sentence: "I had to write a business report, and I had no idea how to start. Fortunately, I just used a *boilerplate* document and changed a few words. In business, this is called *productivity.* In school, this is called *plagiarism.*"

bold

Pronunciation: *bowld.*

Meaning: To display or print text more darkly.

Sentence: "For emphasis, many people like to display their words in *bold.* So I had this bold idea of changing them all to italics."

bomb

Pronunciation: *bom.*

Meaning: A program designed to do something sneaky at a specified time. Many disgruntled programmers write bombs in their programs so that if they get fired, the bomb will go off on its own and wreck the company's program. Also, when a Mac crashes, you get a dialog box with a bomb in it.

Sentence: "I wrote a *bomb* and put it in my company's accounting system. That way if they don't give me a raise, my bomb will erase all their information for good."

boogie man

Pronunciation: *boo-gee man.*

Meaning: An imaginary monster that parents use to scare their children into behaving, such as "If you don't stop crying, the boogie man will come get you."

Sentence: "I used to believe that the *boogie man* was just a story. Now I believe he works for the IRS."

boolean

Pronunciation: *boo-lee-on.*

Meaning: True or false values, often used in programming.

Sentence: "If I need the car for the weekend, I check Dad's *boolean* value. If it's true that he's in a good mood, then I ask him for the keys. If it's false, then I ride the bus."

boot

Pronunciation: *boot* (like the kind cowboys wear on their feet).

Meaning: To start up a computer. Derived from the idea that the computer has to "pull itself up by the bootstraps" or from the feeling that the only way to get a computer to work is to threaten to kick it with a boot.

Sentence: "*Boot* up the computer without a floppy disk in your disk drive. That way the computer has to use the hard disk instead."

bootstrap

Pronunciation: *boot-strap.*

Meaning: To create something out of nothing, such as "pulling yourself up by the bootstraps."

Sentence: "We started this company with absolutely nothing. We had to *bootstrap* our way to the top."

bozo

Pronunciation: *bo-zo.*

Meaning: Someone with no clue what he's doing but with enough authority to keep others from ignoring him completely.

Sentence: "My boss is such a *bozo.* He thought that backing up a computer meant pushing it back against the wall."

BPS

Pronunciation: *Bee Pee Ess.*

Meaning: Acronym for Bits Per Second, which measures the speed of transmission for data. Used interchangeably with baud.

Sentence: "I have a modem that runs at 2400 *bps,* but I want to get a faster one that runs at 9600 baud."

brain damaged

Pronunciation: *brane dam-aged.*

Meaning: Something that looks okay from the outside but internally is crippled or limited.

Sentence: "The 80486sx processor is *brain damaged* because it doesn't have the math coprocessor that the regular 80486 has."

branch

Pronunciation: *bran-cha.*

Meaning: When the computer follows a series of instructions and then suddenly starts following a completely different set of instructions. Often used by programmers to describe the logic of their programs.

Sentence: "First, the computer runs these instructions, and then it *branches* over to the instructions over here. Then a miracle occurs and the program works perfectly."

break

Pronunciation: *bray-ka.*

Meaning: To stop the computer from doing whatever it happens to be doing at the moment. (See also *abort* and *Esc.*)

Sentence: "I was sending a file through my modem when the police showed up, and I had to *break* the connection and pretend I was playing video games instead."

breakpoint

Pronunciation: *bray-ka-poin-ta.*

Meaning: A place in a program where the computer temporarily stops running. Breakpoints are used for debugging so programmers can see how the program is behaving up to a certain point.

Sentence: "If your program doesn't work, put a *breakpoint* halfway in between. If the program works up until the breakpoint, then you'll know that it's the last half of your program that is screwing up."

broken disk

Pronunciation: *brow-kin disk.*

Meaning: Slang term for a hard or floppy disk drive that refuses to work any more.

Sentence: "Don't use that computer because it has a *broken disk.* It shredded the last guy's floppy disk and erased all his files, too."

brute force

Pronunciation: *broot forsa.*

Meaning: To get something to work without regard to appearance, elegance, or finesse.

Sentence: "My program has a command that's supposed to move the paper in my printer up one sheet. Rather than use this command, I just use *brute force* and pull the paper out of the printer myself."

bubble memory

Pronunciation: *bub-bull mem-or-ree.*

Meaning: A type of memory that retains its contents even after the power has gone off. Bubble memory is often used in tiny laptop computers that don't have room for a hard disk.

Sentence: "One day you might even see *bubble memory* on desktop computers. That way you wouldn't have to remember to save your file every time you turn the computer off."

buffer

Pronunciation: *buf-er.*

Meaning: A storage area for temporarily holding data. A printer buffer, for example, copies data from the computer and holds it until the printer is ready to print it.

Sentence: "If you don't like waiting for your printer, get a printer *buffer* so that you can print and use your computer at the same time. If this gives you a headache, then use a Bufferin to make it go away."

bug

Pronunciation: *bug* (as in insect).

Meaning: A problem that prevents a program from working properly. Something every program has.

Sentence: "This program doesn't do a thing that it's supposed to do. It must be full of *bugs.*"

bulletproof

Pronunciation: *bull-it-proof.*

Meaning: Software that works no matter how many keys the user presses incorrectly. A myth that programmers tell their children along with fairy tales like Snow White and Bambi.

Sentence: "This program is *bulletproof.* No matter what you try to do, it still works perfectly. Then again, maybe it's just not working at all, and I can't tell the difference."

bundled software

Pronunciation: *bun-dulled soft-ware.*

Meaning: Software that comes free (supposedly) when you buy a computer. Usually bundled software is stuff you need anyway (like MS-DOS) or programs that aren't selling well, so the publisher's trying to give it away just to clean out their warehouse.

Sentence: "Most computers offer *bundled software* such as MS-DOS and Windows. For added enticement, some dealers will toss in a word processor or spreadsheet as part of the bundled software."

burn in

Pronunciation: *bern in.*

Meaning: The process of testing electronic equipment to make sure that it works. Whenever you get a new computer, you should leave it on for 48 hours straight. If anything will go wrong, it will likely go wrong during this burn-in period.

Sentence: "Before selling a computer, most dealers let it *burn in* for 48 hours. Even so, you should let it burn in for 48 hours too, just to make sure. Then again, most problems with computers occur with software and not with the hardware."

burn out

Pronunciation: *bern owt.*

Meaning: What happens when you stare at your computer screen for long periods of time, such as when you're typing a long list of computer terms for publication in a computer dictionary. A tired, sluggish feeling that makes you want to collapse on the nearest flat surface that can support your weight.

Sentence: "Working on my computer really makes me feel *burned out.* After eight hours of staring at a computer screen, I can't wait to go home and stare at my TV for the rest of the night to unwind."

bus

Pronunciation: *bus.*

Meaning: An electronic transportation system for sending electrons around. Unlike a normal city bus system, a computer bus actually runs efficiently and gets electrons to the correct destination on time.

Sentence: "Every computer has a *bus* for sending data. Too bad every computer doesn't have data worth remembering."

bus mouse

Pronunciation: *bus mow-sa.*

Meaning: A mouse that plugs into an expansion board, connected to a computer's bus, in contrast to a serial mouse that plugs into a computer's serial port.

Sentence: "A *bus mouse* is good if you don't have a spare serial port to plug a normal mouse in."

button

Pronunciation: *butt-on.*

Meaning: A small rectangle that appears on the screen to let the user communicate commands to the computer. Buttons typically appear on the screen as gray rectangles with the commands printed on them. (See also *mouse button.*)

Sentence: "When you exit from Microsoft Windows, the program displays two *buttons.* One button says OK and the other says Cancel. Just click on the button that you want to select."

byte

Pronunciation: *bite.*

Meaning: The amount of memory needed to store one character such as a letter or a number. Computer memory and disk space is measured in kilobytes, megabytes, and gigabytes. (See these latter terms later in the book.)

Sentence: "My floppy disk is full. It only has 5,630 *bytes* free. My brain is full from reading these computer terms. I think I must have only 1,030 bytes left in my head."

C

Pronunciation: just like it looks, *SEE?* (And for you Spanish-speaking folks, just say yes. Si?)

Meaning: A programming language developed at Bell Laboratories back in the '70s when disco was popular. C is a general-purpose language like BASIC and Pascal, but with the ability to manipulate the internal guts of a computer like assembly language. C has been used to write many popular programs, including the UNIX operating system, Lotus 1-2-3, and Microsoft FoxPro.

C has three advantages over other languages:

1. C programs are almost as easy to write and understand as BASIC or Pascal programs. (Note the emphasis on "almost.")
2. C programs run almost as fast as assembly language but are easier to understand.
3. C programs are *portable,* meaning that you can run the same C program on different computers such as an IBM, a Macintosh, and an Amiga without changing the program.

In contrast, BASIC and Pascal programs usually run slower than C programs and cannot run on different computers without extensive modifications that usually aren't worth the effort. Unfortunately, because C was designed for maximum efficiency, it can also be hard for beginners to learn.

Sentence: "Only wimps use BASIC or Pascal. Cool programmers use *C* so that they don't have to write the same program over again to run on different computers."

Sample C program:

```
#include <stdio.h>
main ()
{
  printf ("Only wimps use BASIC or Pascal.\n");
  printf ("Cool programmers always use C.");
}
```

C++

Pronunciation: *See plus plus.* Just like saying "C+" but with a stutter at the end.

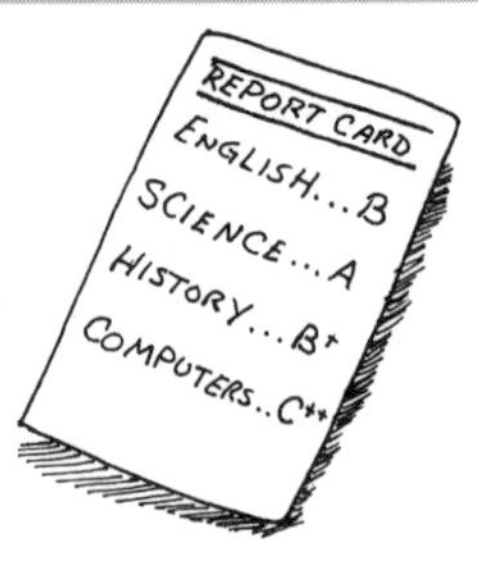

Meaning: An improved version of the C language that adds object-oriented extensions. C++ has become popular because it's easy for C programmers to learn, provides object-oriented features to make programming large projects easier, and sells a lot of computer books. Like C, C++ is fast, portable, and confusing to learn and understand.

Sentence: "Only wimps use C. Cool programmers use *C++* so that they can write bigger programs without losing their mind."

Sample program:

```
#include <iostream.h>
main
{
  cout << "Only wimps use C.\n";
  cout << "Cool programmers always use C++.";
}
```

cable

Pronunciation: *kay-bull.*

Meaning: Cables connect different parts together so that they actually do something useful. For example, a cable connects your monitor to your computer, your computer to your printer, and your modem to your computer. Cables always need to be plugged into a port, which is usually an oddly shaped hole in the back of your computer.

The cable that connects your monitor to your computer plugs into your computer's video card. The cable that connects your computer to your printer, called a *printer cable,* plugs into a parallel or serial port. The cable that connects your computer to your modem, called a *serial cable,* plugs into a serial port.

Sentence: "I couldn't get my printer to work because the salesman forgot to sell me a printer *cable.* Then he sold me a printer *cable* that wouldn't fit my computer's parallel port. Now I'm serving five to seven for aggravated assault."

cache

Pronunciation: sounds like *cash.*

Meaning: A place in memory where the computer can temporarily store data to avoid accessing the slow hard or floppy disk drive over and over again. Often called a RAM cache. Some computers have a built-in cache which they advertise as "Includes a 256K cache!" You can also carve a cache out of your computer's memory using a special utility program such as PC Tools Deluxe.

Sentence: "Bob's computer runs faster because his has a built-in cache. I would use a utility program to create a *cache* on my computer, but the cache would gobble up some of my computer's memory. So I'll just use Bob's computer instead."

cache memory

Pronunciation: sounds like *cash memory.*

Meaning: The specific memory chips or portion of memory used as a cache to make a computer run faster.

Sentence: "My computer has a built-in 256K *cache memory*, and I have a utility program that creates an additional 1MB of cache memory. My computer would be the fastest one around if only I could figure out how to plug it in."

CAD

Pronunciation: sounds like *kad* and rhymes with *sad, bad,* and *rad.*

Meaning: An acronym that stands for Computer-Aided Design, which substitutes a computer's graphics capabilities for drawing with paper and pencil. Computers running CAD programs often require huge amounts of hard disk space, high-resolution video displays, and a fast microprocessor. CAD has been responsible for designing the most recent engineering achievements including the gas tank for the 1972 Ford Pinto, the nuclear reactors for Three Mile Island, and the focal lens for the Hubble Space Telescope.

Sentence: "I can't even draw a straight line with a pencil, but I designed my own car using *CAD.* Of course, it blew up when I turned the ignition key."

CAD/CAM

Pronunciation: sounds like *kad/kam* and rhymes with *sad Sam.*

Meaning: A combination acronym that stands for Computer-Aided Design and Computer-Aided Manufacturing. CAM means letting computers actually make the stuff that somebody designed using CAD or pencil and paper.

Sentence: "A lot of companies use *CAM* to make products more efficiently and less expensively. Our company can't afford to buy computers, so we use child labor instead."

call

Pronunciation: combine the choking sound of a cat coughing up a hairball and make it rhyme with *ball.*

Meaning: A programming term that describes the temporary transfer of control from the main program to a subprogram. May be used in batch files, for example, to start another batch file.

Sentence: "I wrote a program that *calls* three subprograms. To add more features, I'll just need to call more subprograms. If that doesn't work, I'll just call another programmer and ask for help."

call waiting

Pronunciation: *kall ooayt-ing*

Meaning: A telephone option that beeps if someone is trying to call you while you're already using the phone. You then can put your current caller on hold and talk to the second caller without hanging up the phone first. If you're talking on the phone, call waiting can be handy. If you're communicating through a modem, then call waiting can break your connection. To temporarily disable call waiting when you use your modem, dial * 7 0, wait for the dial tone, and then dial the number normally. If you're using a Hayes-compatible modem and want to dial 555-1234, you would have to dial *70W555-1234 or *70,,555-1234.

Sentence: "I was just about to electronically transfer a million dollars out of my bank and into my personal account when my mother-in-law called and *call waiting* broke my connection. Even worse, then I had to talk to my mother-in-law."

camera-ready

Pronunciation: *kam-er-ra red-dee.*

Meaning: A photograph, drawing, or printed text that looks so squeaky clean you can make a zillion photocopies of it and the zillionth copy still looks good. This term is often used by publishers using desktop publishing software.

Sentence: "When professional photographers take pictures of bikini-clad models frolicking on exotic beaches, they produce *camera-ready* pictures for the *Sports Illustrated* annual swimsuit issue. When I take pictures of Uncle Fred in his bathrobe with my Kodak Instamatic, I can't produce camera-ready pictures of anything at all."

cancel

Pronunciation: *kan-sell.* Say it fast enough and it sounds like *can't sell.*

Meaning: To take back or reverse an action. When you give the Cancel command, you're essentially telling your computer, "Ooops, forget I did that and make everything like it was before." Windows dialog boxes often give the Cancel command as an option.

Sentence: "I typed **FORMAT C:** and almost erased my entire hard disk. Luckily when DOS asked me, `Proceed with format (Y/N)?` I typed **N** to *cancel* that command."

Caps Lock

Pronunciation: *kaps lock.*

Meaning: The key on every computer keyboard that lets you type capital (or uppercase) letters without having to press the Shift key each time. Most computers have a little light in the upper right corner of the keyboard that lights up when you have pressed the Caps Lock key once. If you press the Caps Lock key again, the light goes off. Unlike typewriters, pressing the Caps Lock key on a computer only produces uppercase letters. If you want to print ! or @ or any other symbol, you still have to hold down the Shift key first.

Sentence: "Sometimes my fingers slip and I press the *Caps Lock* key BY MISTAKE, AND THEN ALL MY TYPING LOOKS AS SCREWED UP AS THIS."

capture

Pronunciation: *kap-sure.*

Meaning: To store a screen image to a file on a floppy or hard disk. Often used with desktop publishing and telecommunications.

Sentence: "To illustrate computer books, many publishers must *capture* the image on the screen so that people can see what they should do next. When people call a BBS, the instructions sometimes scroll by too fast to read. Rather than take a speed reading class, many people capture the instructions on disk so that they can read it later at their leisure."

caret

Pronunciation: sounds like *carrot.*

Meaning: The symbol that appears when you press Shift-6, ^. Used in programming languages and certain programs as a specific command. In Pascal, the ^ symbol identifies a pointer. In C, the ^ symbol represents the exclusive OR (XOR) operator. In BASIC, the ^ symbol is used for exponential expressions. In spreadsheets such as Lotus 1-2-3, the ^ symbol centers labels or numbers. In word processors, the ^ symbol usually represents a typo.

Sentence: "In a C program, the command 'tax ^ salary' actually makes sense. This explains why programmers tend to be nerds."

carriage return

Pronunciation: *kar-edge ree-turn.*

Meaning: An invisible character used to end a line of text and move the cursor to the next line below. Created by pressing the Enter or Return key.

Sentence: "People who have never used a word processor before tend to put *carriage returns* after each line as if they're using a typewriter. When you edit their text, the carriage returns screw up all the formatting."

carrier (detect)

Pronunciation: *kar-ree-er (whispered) dee-tect.*

Meaning: A signal used by modems to detect the presence of another modem. When modems talk through the telephone lines, they emit a signal called a *carrier.* When one modem calls another modem, the two modems send carriers to each other. The moment each modem detects the carrier of another modem, it sends a carrier detect, letting the computer know that it is now connected to another computer.

Sentence: "I didn't think I actually dialed into NASA's computer until my modem got a *carrier detect.*"

carrot

Pronunciation: *kar-et.*

Meaning: The vegetable that parents claim will improve your vision. The favorite snack of Bugs Bunny.

Sentence: "While flying on American Airlines, the flight attendant told me to eat all my *carrots* because there were passengers starving on Air India."

cartridge

Pronunciation: *kar-tridge,* rhymes with *partridge.*

Meaning: A self-contained, removable part of a computer or printer that is usually plastic, expensive, and hard to find when you need it. Laser printers use toner cartridges and font cartridges. Nintendo units are worthless unless you plug in a game cartridge.

Sentence: "My laser printer couldn't print any fonts until I plugged in a font *cartridge.* Unfortunately, the font cartridge cost so much that I had to sell my computer to pay for it."

cascade

Pronunciation: *kass-kade.*

Meaning: To arrange several windows neatly on a computer screen so that you can still see the title bar and upper left corner of each one.

Sentence: "Until I had my computer *cascade* all my windows, some of my windows had been completely hidden from view. I still can't find anything I need, but at least the cascaded windows make me look nice and organized."

CASE

Pronunciation: sounds like *Kase* and rhymes with *base.*

Meaning: (1) In text formatting terms, case means the style of letters, either UPPERCASE or lowercase. (2) In programming terms, CASE is a special command that lets the computer choose two or more possible options. (3) In techno-dweeb talk, CASE is an acronym that means Computer-Aided Software Engineering.

Sentence: "As a computer science major, my *CASE* courses in school taught me that I could use the CASE command in Pascal to replace multiple IF-THEN statements. To make programs easier to read, my teachers told me that the *case* of my typing would matter too. That's why I dropped out and became a taxi cab driver instead."

case sensitive

Pronunciation: *kase sen-si-tive.*

Meaning: The distinction made between UPPER- and lowercase letters. Some programs or systems require that certain commands be in either uppercase or lowercase. UNIX is a good example. Also, modems can be fussy in that way, too.

Sentence: "Bob is so *case sensitive.* He thinks 'Hello' and 'HELLO' are two completely different words."

cassette tape

Pronunciation: *kass-et tape.*

Meaning: A reel of magnetic strip that can store information. Ancient computers used to use cassette tapes to store programs. Today, everyone uses floppy disks or hard disks. (See also *tape* and *tape drive.*)

Sentence: "I bought an old Timex/Sinclair computer that uses programs stored on *cassette tape.* I really screwed up my computer when I gave it a Led Zeppelin cassette tape by mistake."

catatonic

Pronunciation: *cat-a-ton-ic.*

Meaning: A state of near total paralysis, usually brought on by staring at a computer screen too long.

Sentence: "At first I thought Bob was *catatonic* from trying to figure out how to configure Windows to run on his computer."

CD

Pronunciation: *See Dee.*

Meaning: Sometimes referred to as the Change Directory command because that's what it stands for. Shortcut command to change directories using MS-DOS. Easier to type than CHDIR. Typing **CD ** changes to the root directory. Typing **CD..** changes to the parent directory of the current directory. Typing **CD** displays the name of the current directory.

(Also stands for Compact Disc, as in the favorite digital audio storage devices. See also *CD-ROM.*)

Sentence: "I used the *CD* command to change directories. Now my head feels like it's about to explode."

CD-ROM

Pronunciation: *See Dee Rahm (don't pronounce ROM as "Rome").*

Meaning: Acronym that stands for Compact Disc-Read Only Memory. Often used to describe a CD-ROM drive, which is a special disk drive that only reads compact discs. As a bonus, many computer CD-ROM disk drives can also play audio compact discs. This lets you turn your $2000 computer into a $49 Walkman. CD-ROM discs usually contain massive amounts of information (600MB or more of data, text, graphics, video, or sound). A compact disc is round, silver, flat, and looks like a UFO if you toss it in the air and use an out-of-focus camera to take its picture.

Sentence: "My new *CD-ROM* drive lets me display entire encyclopedias, classical novels, and maps from every country in the world. Now all I have to figure out is why I would want all of this information on my computer in the first place."

cell

Pronunciation: sounds like *sell.*

Meaning: The intersection of rows and columns in a spreadsheet used to store text, numbers, and formulas.

Sentence: "My inventory spreadsheet uses 300 *cells* to store all my vital business information such as salaries, sales regions, and taxes. Too bad I erased it all by mistake."

central processing unit

Pronunciation: *sometimes called the CPU or the processor.*

Meaning: The little chip in personal computers that controls everything. Sometimes referred to as the "brains" of the computer because it is where the basic calculating is done that translates into your favorite GIF file or spreadsheet. A central processing unit looks like a thin wafer or a headless cockroach. (See also *microprocessor.*)

Sentence: "I'm going to replace the 80386 *central processing unit* with an 80486 central processing unit so that my computer will run faster. Then I'll turn my old 80386 central processing unit into an earring for my girlfriend."

Centronics port

Pronunciation: *Sen-tron-iks port.*

Meaning: The parallel port on a computer. Originally used to connect computers to Centronics printers.

Sentence: "I tried to plug my printer into my serial port by mistake. Once I plugged my printer into the *Centronics port,* everything worked fine."

CGA

Pronunciation: *See Gee Ay.*

Meaning: An acronym that stands for Color Graphics Adapter, the original color graphics standard for IBM and compatible personal computers. CGA graphics produces fuzzy images that are perfectly calculated to strain your eyes and give you splitting headaches. Newer computers use VGA or SVGA graphics instead. (See also *EGA, VGA,* and *SVGA.)*

Sentence: "Because my computer only has *CGA* graphics, I can't play any of the cool games that look super-realistic. Instead, I can see only grainy images that don't look like anything natural."

character

Pronunciation: *kar-act-ter.*

Meaning: Any symbol that you can type from the keyboard. Letters are characters, numbers are characters, and even $, @, _, ^ and ~ are considered characters.

Sentence: "When I ran a word count in my word processor, it told me I have 4,128 *characters* in my document. Who's the goffy programmer who actually thought people would need this kind of information?"

character code

Pronunciation: *kar-ak-ter kode.*

Meaning: An agreed-upon collection of symbols that represent something else. The ASCII table is one collection of character codes; the seldom-used EBCDIC standard is another. Many programs, such as WordPerfect, use character codes mixed in with normal letters to represent underlining, superscripts, or bold.

Sentence: "I thought the letter was full of weird symbols until I realized that they were *character codes* to format the document for WordPerfect."

character graphics

Pronunciation: *kar-act-ter graf-iks.*

Meaning: Funny little symbols that you can create by pressing certain keys on your keyboard. To create character graphics on an IBM computer, press the Alt key and type a number on the numerical keypad. To type ⊤, hold down the Alt key and type 176.

Sentence: "My computer doesn't display graphics, but with *character graphics* I can still draw little boxes on my screen. Then again, I could do the same thing with an Etch-A-Sketch."

character set

Pronunciation: *kar-act-ter set.*

Meaning: An organized list of symbols such as an ASCII table.

Sentence: "The normal ASCII *character set* displays only letters and numbers, but the extended ASCII character set includes character graphics for displaying characters not found on a keyboard."

CHDIR

(See *CD.*)

cheap

Pronunciation: *cheep.*

Meaning: An adjective that denotes poor quality no matter what the actual cost may be.

Sentence: "If our company wasn't so *cheap,* they'd buy us new computers instead of forcing us to use these cheap dedicated word processors."

check boxes

Pronunciation: just like it looks.

Meaning: A blank box that appears next to two or more options that the user can choose from. When a check box is empty, the option has not been chosen. When the check box is marked, the option has been chosen. Two or more check boxes can be checked at the same time.

Sentence: "Rather than choose multiple options through different menus, I can choose them all at once using *check boxes.*"

Sample check boxes: Why do you hate computers?

[ ] Don't work the way you want

[X] Too expensive for what they offer

[ ] Too complicated

[X] Not easy to use

checksum

Pronunciation: just like it looks, such as, "Would you like to 'check some' of our lovely vegetables, or would you prefer to eat a big juicy steak instead?"

Meaning: A number calculated to verify the accuracy of data transmitted through a modem. During transmission, the sending computer breaks the data into several smaller chunks or *packets* of information. Then it calculates a checksum for each packet.

When transmitting, the sending computer sends each packet, followed by its corresponding checksum. The receiving computer recalculates the checksum of the incoming data and compares it with the checksum received from the sending computer. If the checksums are equal, the data has been received correctly. If they differ, the data is assumed to have been garbled somewhere along the line and the sending computer must send the information packet again. Checksum is most commonly used with the XModem transmission protocol.

Sentence: "I received your file, but my computer calculated a different *checksum* than yours. Either that means I received a different file than the one you sent or my computer is screwing up again."

chicklet keyboard

Pronunciation: *chick-let key-bored.*

Meaning: A keyboard that consists of tiny keys that resemble candy Chicklets. Chicklet keys are usually too tiny to type on comfortably. IBM developed the most popular chicklet keyboard for the IBM PCjr. The idea was to make the IBM PCjr unattractive for business use. They succeeded to the extent that nobody bought the IBM PCjr.

Sentence: "I could type better on a normal keyboard, but this *chicklet keyboard* is nearly impossible to use."

child process

Pronunciation: *chi-eld pro-sess.*

Meaning: One program on your computer has started another program. They can do that, you know. When WordPerfect spell-checks a document, it runs another program, the Spell Checker. WordPerfect is the "parent" program; the Spell Checker is the "child." Sadly, child processes are eventually killed by their parents processes because computer programs are greedy and must maintain control.

Sentence: "It's understandable why so many *child processes* run away from home."

Chooser

Pronunciation: sounds like *Choose her.*

Meaning: A Macintosh desktop accessory (DA) that lets you select which printer to use, whether to turn AppleTalk on or off, and whether to use the serial or parallel port. The Chooser always appears in the Apple menu, located at the far left side of the menu bar.

Sentence: "I couldn't get my Macintosh to print anything until I first selected my printer through the *Chooser.* I just did that once, and now I'll never have to do it again unless I get a new printer or totally screw up my Macintosh."

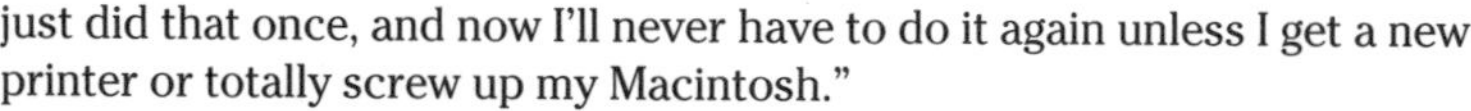

CI$

Pronunciation: *sis*

Meaning: Acronym for CompuServe Information Services. The dollar sign ($) replaces the S to let people know that this is going to cost them a lot of money. (See also *CompuServe.*)

Sentence: "By subscribing to *CI$* I can get the latest stock market prices from Wall Street. Of course, now I don't have any money to invest any more."

circuit breaker

Pronunciation: *sir-cut braker.*

Meaning: A device that monitors the flow of electricity and cuts it off if it exceeds a certain level that may cause overloading, short-circuiting, and death or destruction to massive amounts of personal property.

Sentence: "I almost burned my house down when I plugged my computer, monitor, printer, microwave, electric car, and high-powered, anti-satellite laser into one electric outlet. Good thing my *circuit breaker* worked or else I might be living in the street."

Class A / Class B

Pronunciation: *Klass A / Klass Bee.*

Meaning: Two similar and confusing labels that the Federal Communications Commission (FCC) uses to distinguish between computers that emit different levels of high-frequency electrical energy. The Class A label means that the computer has been approved for use in an office. The Class B label means that the computer has been approved for both the home and office. Ideally, you want a computer with a Class B label. If you put a computer with a Class A label in your home, it could screw up your radio and TV reception.

Sentence: "The lame salesman tried to sell me a home computer with a *Class A* label, but I told him I needed one with a *Class B* label instead. To prove my point, I had him stand next to a Class A-rated computer so he could see what it did to his pacemaker."

Clear key

Pronunciation: *Kleer kee.*

Meaning: The key that erases highlighted text or drawings.

Sentence: "I wanted to erase a sentence in my word processor, but I couldn't find the *Clear key*. So I painted White-Out across my screen instead."

click

Pronunciation: sounds like *clique.*

Meaning: To press and release once on the mouse button, usually to select or activate an option or command.

Sentence: "When I moved the mouse cursor on the menu and *clicked,* I erased the most important file of my career. Boy, am I glad a mouse makes a computer easier to use."

client

Pronunciation: *kli-ent.*

Meaning: (1) A local area network term that describes a computer that can request information, such as an application, from a file server, and can also perform independently from the network server by using a client application. (2) A Windows program that receives data through DDE. (See also *DDE.*)

Sentence: "Every computer on this network is a *client.* That way if the network breaks down, everyone can still keep working."

client application

Pronunciation: *kli-ent app-lick-kay-shin.*

Meaning: (1) A term used by local area network geeks and administrators to describe a program that only works on the computer that actually has the program on its hard disk. On most networks, one big computer usually contains all the programs that everyone else uses. If that one computer fails, then none of the computers can do anything. Because client applications only run on one computer and cannot be accessed by other computers in the network, a failure in one part of the network doesn't affect a client application (unless, of course, the part of the network that fails is the one computer holding the client application). Client applications cannot be used by anyone else in a network. (2) A Windows program with documents that can accept linked or embedded objects. (See also *OLE.*)

Sentence: "When the network crashed, everyone had to stop working but me because I had the word processor stored on my computer as a *client application.* Now everyone but me is getting paid to loaf around."

client/server network

Pronunciation: *kli-ent serve-her net-work.*

Meaning: A network where some programs and files are shared in one big computer, but each computer connected to the network can also run on its own.

Sentence: "We have a *client/server network* that lets everyone share the same database program and files with each other but gives each user the freedom to use whatever word processor she want on her own computer."

clip art

Pronunciation: *klip art.*

Meaning: Pre-drawn art that you can freely copy and use. Often used for desktop publishing.

Sentence: "I can't draw a line, and I'm too lazy to use a computer drawing program either. So I bought some *clip art* to add good-looking pictures to my letters so that nobody will notice that I have nothing important to say."

clipboard

Pronunciation: *klip-bored.*

Meaning: A temporary storage area used by the Macintosh, Windows, and certain DOS programs for holding text or graphics. Items are automatically placed in the clipboard whenever the user chooses the Cut or Copy command. Items remain on the clipboard until the user chooses a new item with the Cut or Copy command. Items stored on the clipboard may be transferred to other programs.

Sentence: "To hide my résume from the boss, I Cut it and put it in the *clipboard* where he wouldn't see it. Then I Copied it back to my word processor and printed it out on the company laser printer."

clock

Pronunciation: *klok.*

Meaning: The circuit in the computer that keeps track of the date and the time, even when the power is shut off.

Sentence: "My old computer didn't have a *clock*, so every time I turned it on, it thought the date was 1/1/80. Now everyone thinks I only worked on my computer once on January 1, 1980."

clock ticks

Pronunciation: *klok tix.*

Meaning: Evenly spaced pulses that determine the speed of a computer. During each clock tick, the computer actually does something. In between clock ticks, the computer does nothing, just like a typical office worker. The more clock ticks a computer has, the faster it will run. Clock speed is measured in megahertz (MHz) where 1 MHz = 1,000,000 clock ticks per second. Most modern personal computers have CPU clocks that run between 33 MHz and 66 MHz.

Sentence: "The salesman told me that the computer ran at 6 million *clock ticks* per second. I thought that was great until I realized that was just 6 MHz."

clone

Pronunciation: *klone,* rhymes with *alone.*

Meaning: A term that refers to any computer that imitates a better-known computer or program. In the hierarchy of computer brands, name-brands such as IBM, Apple, and Compaq are considered *top-of-the-line*. The next level down are computers called *compatibles,* which sport lesser-known names such as Dell, AST Research, and Epson. The bottom level are *clone* computers, usually generic, no-name computers that somebody slaps together in his garage late at night. Clones are attractive because they are inexpensive.

Sentence: "I wanted to buy a Macintosh *clone,* but none exist. So I had to buy a real Apple Macintosh instead and pay a lot more than someone who could buy an IBM compatible or an IBM clone."

close

Pronunciation: *kloze,* rhymes with *doze.*

Meaning: To remove a window from the screen. The two most common ways to close a window are to click in the window's close box with the mouse or to choose the Close Window command from a menu.

Sentence: "My word processor lets me open up to six different windows on the screen. The more windows I open, the less I see of any of them, so I have to *close* a few windows so that I can see what I'm doing. Instead of doing any productive work, I spend more time closing windows. Aren't computers wonderful?"

close box

Pronunciation: *Kloze bocks.*

Meaning: The tiny little box that appears in the upper left corner of a window. Clicking the mouse cursor inside the close box removes the window from view. In most programs, the close box can be used only by a mouse.

Sentence: "Instead of hunting around for the Close Window command from the menus, I just click in the *close box.* That's about the extent of my computer literacy knowledge."

closed architecture

Pronunciation: *klozed arki-tex-sure.*

Meaning: Equipment specifically designed to work only with the accessories made by the same company, usually the most expensive and least reliable equipment around.

Sentence: "The original IBM PC had an open architecture, so accessories were cheap and plentiful. Then IBM introduced the PS/2 with a *closed architecture,* hoping that people would buy only expensive IBM accessories. Instead, people nearly stopped buying IBM computers altogether."

CMOS

Pronunciation: *Sea-Moss.*

Meaning: An acronym that stands for Complementary Metal-Oxide Semiconductor, which is a specially designed circuit that consumes very little power. CMOS circuits are often used in devices such as wristwatches, pocket calculators, and laptop computers. CMOS RAM keeps track of system setup information, date, time, and so on. Whatever you do, don't change your CMOS setup password and then forget it; you won't be able to get back into your computer.

Sentence: "If it wasn't for my *CMOS* processor and RAM chips, my laptop computer couldn't run on batteries for five minutes."

coaxial cable

Pronunciation: *ko-ax-eel kay-bull.*

Meaning: A cable consisting of an insulating shield wrapped around a conductor. Coaxial cables are used for local area networks because they carry more data than ordinary telephone wires. TVs use a type of coaxial cable.

Sentence: "We have *coaxial cables* connecting our network together. That doesn't mean anyone knows what he's doing, but at least we used the right cables for networks."

COBOL

Pronunciation: *Ko-Ball.*

Meaning: An acronym for COmmon Business Oriented Language, COBOL is a language used primarily for business applications for large mainframe computers. (Now you know which language is responsible for screwing up your bank accounts.) Developed in the '60s by several computer companies and the U.S. Department of Defense, the language shows the influence that the drug-crazed, free-love era had on technology. COBOL programs tend to resemble plain English sentences. Unfortunately, the plain English sentences usually resemble those uttered by politicians or lawyers.

Sentence: "I learned to program in *COBOL* so that I could update our bank's accounting and billing system. With this power, I programmed the bank to electronically transfer all its money to my Swiss bank account."

code (coding)

Pronunciation: *kod (ko-deen).*

Meaning: To actually write a program using a specific programming language such as C, BASIC, or Pascal.

Sentence: "I tried *coding* in COBOL until I switched to C. Now it takes me half as long to *code* with only twice as many mistakes."

cold boot

Pronunciation: *kold boot.*

Meaning: To restart equipment that has been turned off. (See also *warm boot.*)

Sentence: "Sometimes when the computer crashes, pushing its reset button doesn't even work. In these cases, you have to *cold boot*

your computer by turning it off, waiting for ten seconds, and then turning it on again."

color monitor

Pronunciation: *kull-er mon-i-ter.*

Meaning: A computer screen that can display several colors at once. Color monitors follow specific video graphics standards such as CGA, EGA, VGA, and SVGA.

Sentence: "My first computer had a boring black-and-white monitor, but my newest computer has a *color monitor* that lets me view Carmen Sandiego on-screen."

columns

Pronunciation: *kahl-ums.*

Meaning: A vertical strip of text that appears on a page. Newsletters commonly display two, three, or four columns side by side. Columns are also common in spreadsheets and other documents.

Sentence: "My report looked better when I displayed it in two *columns.* That way it looked easier to read than it really was."

COM

Pronunciation: *kom.*

Meaning: (1) Short for COMmunications port. When dialing through your modem, your communications program needs to know which COM port the modem is attached to. (2) A description for a special executable file that is small and simple. A COM file has the .COM file extension.

Sentence: "I tried to send my COMMAND.*COM* file through my modem, but I had my modem connected to COM 1 instead of COM 2. So it didn't work."

COMDEX

Pronunciation: *Kom-Dex.*

Meaning: Acronym that stands for COMputer Dealers EXposition. Usually held twice a year, once in Las Vegas in the Winter and another city near the East Coast in the Spring. COMDEX is one of the most widely attended computer conferences in America and one of the easiest to get tired of real fast. Many companies introduce new products at COMDEX.

Sentence: "I went to *COMDEX* to see the latest computer equipment and software displayed. Then I decided it didn't make a difference in my life after all, so I went out to Binions and played Craps with Dan, Wally, and Chris."

Command key

Pronunciation: *kom-mand kee.*

Meaning: The key on the Macintosh keyboard that has an apple and cloverleaf symbol on it. This key is used with other keys to perform commands. To Cut an item, you press Command-X. To Copy, press Command-C. To paste, press Command-V.

Sentence: "Instead of choosing the Copy command from the Edit menu, I just pressed *Command-*C."

command line

Pronunciation: *kom-mand line.*

Meaning: The place on the screen where you type in a series of commands (such as at the DOS prompt).

Sentence: "To load WordPerfect, just type **WP** at the *command line.* If you want to load WordPerfect and a document named LETTER.WP, all you have to type is **WP LETTER.WP** at the command line."

COMMAND.COM

Pronunciation: *kom-mand kom.*

Meaning: The MS-DOS file that contains the command processor for DOS to run. Never delete this file.

Sentence: "My computer wouldn't run off my hard disk until I formatted it with the system and put the *COMMAND.COM* file on it."

comment

Pronunciation: *kaw-mint.*

Meaning: A brief note of explanation inserted into programs to describe what the program is supposed to do. Programmers use comments in their programs so that other programmers (and themselves) can understand what the program does and how it works.

Sentence: "It's good programming practice to insert plenty of *comments* in your programs, explaining what the program does, how it works, and any assumptions you may have made."

communications

Pronunciation: *kaw-me-u-ni-ka-shins.*

Meaning: A shortened version of *telecommunications* or *data communications.* Often used to describe transferring data from one computer to another through a modem or a network.

Sentence: "My modem would be useless without a *communications* program. Now I can break into all the computers I want."

compatibility

Pronunciation: *kom-pat-i-bill-i-tee.*

Meaning: The ability to work with equipment or software designed by other manufacturers.

Sentence: "In the early days, not all home computers were compatible with the IBM standard. Nowadays, nearly every computer offers IBM *compatibility.*

compile

Pronunciation: *kom-pile.*

Meaning: To convert a program written in a programming language (BASIC, C, Pascal, etc.) into a language that the computer can understand (machine code). A term that only programmers care to know about.

Sentence: "After I wrote my C program, I had to *compile* it to see if it would work. Of course it didn't, so I sold it to the government instead."

compiler

Pronunciation: *kom-piler.*

Meaning: A special program that converts programs written in a programming language (C, BASIC, Pascal, and so on) into something the computer can understand (machine code).

Sentence: "To write your own programs, you need to learn a programming language and buy a language *compiler.* Then you too can write programs that don't work and charge people a lot of money to use them."

composite video

Pronunciation: *kom-pos-it vi-dee-o.*

Meaning: A video signal used by TV sets, usually transmitted by one wire. By contrast, an RGB signal uses separate wires for red, green, and blue.

Sentence: "If you really want to see a blurry screen, use *composite video* to display your information on your TV set."

compression

Pronunciation: *kom-press-shin.*

Meaning: To take a file and smash it (or squish it) so that it takes up less space.

Sentence: "To double my hard disk space, I used the *compression* program provided in MS-DOS version 6.0."

CompuServe

Pronunciation: *Kom-pew-Serve.*

Meaning: A subscription-based on-line service that charges you a lot for every second you're connected to it. In return, CompuServe provides files to copy, games to play, and services to use such as making your own airline reservations or searching for information in newspaper articles.

Sentence: "I needed to spend more money on my computer habit, so I bought a modem and a subscription to *CompuServe.* Now I can buy and sell my own stocks. Unfortunately, I don't have any money left to invest because I'm spending it all on CompuServe charges."

compute

Pronunciation: *kom-pewt.*

Meaning: To calculate an answer using a variety of problem-solving techniques including mathematics, heuristics, and looking over someone else's shoulder.

Sentence: "I tried to *compute* my own taxes with my personal computer. Now the IRS wants to audit me and compute their own results."

computer

Pronunciation: *kom-pewt-her.*

Meaning: Any calculating device that processes data according to a series of instructions, that costs a lot, that doesn't work the way you think it should, and that becomes obsolete three days after you buy it.

Sentence: "I bought a computer to balance my budget. Now I need a *computer* to help me figure out how to use it."

CON

Pronunciation: *Kon, as in "con game."*

Meaning: A device name that refers to the keyboard and monitor, short for CONsole.

Sentence: "To create a file called AUTOEXEC.BAT without using a text editor, you can just type **COPY CON AUTOEXEC.BAT.** This command tells your computer to create a file and store everything you type in it. To stop storing every keystroke in the file, press Ctrl-Z and then press Enter. This is a great trivia feature that only hard-core computer users know about. Amaze your friends! Stump your boss! (But don't fool around with the AUTOEXEC.BAT file unless you know what you're doing or you can really cause some trouble!)"

concatenate

Pronunciation: *kon-cat-en-nate.*

Meaning: To join two character strings into one character string such as "ABC" + "DEF" = "ABCDEF." You can also concatenate files.

Sentence: "In my last program, the user had to type the first and last name. Then my program would *concatenate* them into one and use that as the user's password. So John Smith's password would be JohnSmith."

concurrent processing

Pronunciation: *kon-kur-rent pros-ses-ing.*

Meaning: To appear to run two or more programs at the same time, but in reality run only one. In comparison, multitasking runs two or more programs at the same time.

Sentence: "The latest versions of MS-DOS offers *concurrent processing.* You can load several programs at once and switch between them. But the moment you switch out of one program, it stops running."

confidence factor

Pronunciation: *kon-fi-dense fak-ter.*

Meaning: A term used by expert systems to place an abstract numerical value on an answer. Often used as an educated way of saying, "I don't have the slightest idea, but here's my best guess."

Sentence: "The used car salesman had a *confidence factor* of 99 that the car he was selling would work perfectly. Because used car salesmen tend to lie as much as lawyers and politicians, I only had a confidence factor of 10 that he was telling me the truth."

CONFIG.SYS

Pronunciation: *Con-Fig Siss.*

Meaning: A configuration file used on MS-DOS computers that specifies the keyboard, device drivers, and amount of buffers for the computer to use. One of the most important files and also the least understood by beginners.

Sentence: "To configure my computer to run Microsoft Windows, I had to change the settings in my *CONFIG.SYS* file. Because I didn't know what I was doing, I totally screwed up my computer. Boy, I'm glad computers are making my life easier."

configure

Pronunciation: *kon-fig-yur.*

Meaning: To modify or customize a computer a certain way. Any time you add a new piece of equipment or program to your computer, you have to configure it so that it will work properly.

Sentence: "When I tried to add a mouse to my computer, it didn't work because I didn't *configure* my computer properly. Now it doesn't work because I put my foot through the computer screen out of frustration."

console

Pronunciation: *kon-sole.*

Meaning: Another term for the computer monitor and keyboard.

Sentence: "Keep that coffee cup away from the *console.* If it spills on the keyboard or in the monitor, you could short-circuit your computer."

constant

Pronunciation: *kons-tant.*

Meaning: A value in a program that never changes.

Sentence: "If a program needs to use geometry, the value of pi is often stored as a *constant.* If a program needs to use calculus, the programmer is often out of luck."

context-sensitive help

Pronunciation: *kon-text sen-si-tive help.* (How much more basic can you get than that?)

Meaning: Help provided by a program that changes according to what the user is doing at the time that the help is requested. If the user has chosen the Print command, context-sensitive help provides help only about printing. If the user has chosen the File Save command, context-sensitive help only provides help for saving a file. If the user doesn't have the slightest idea what to do next, context-sensitive help simply confuses him even more.

Sentence: "Before *context-sensitive help,* most programs just displayed a standard help menu, which was about as useful as looking at the manual every time you had a problem. Context-sensitive help is like turning to the exact page in the manual that gives you the answers you need."

contiguous

Pronunciation: *kon-tig-u-us.*

Meaning: When two objects are physically next to each other. Often used when describing files stored on a disk or data stored in a file.

Sentence: "My hard disk is fragmented because the files are no longer *contiguous.* After using a defragmentation program, my hard disk runs faster."

control code

Pronunciation: *kon-troll kode.*

Meaning: A special symbol that controls the computer or printer. Examples of control codes are line feeds, carriage returns, and form feeds. Formatting commands trigger control codes to be sent to the printer to create the desired appearance of text.

Sentence: "If you really want to mess up somebody's document, throw in a lot of *control codes.* That way when she tries to print the document, the control codes take control and make the printer act erratically."

Control key

Pronunciation: *Kon-troll kee.*

Meaning: A special key, often abbreviated as *Ctrl,* that works with other keys to give commands to a program.

Sentence: "To save a document in many Windows programs, you can press *Ctrl-S* simultaneously instead of choosing the same command from a menu."

Control Panel

Pronunciation: *Kon-troll Pan-ell.*

Meaning: A utility program that lists options for modifying hardware devices such as the mouse, keyboard, and monitor. Found in the Macintosh, Windows, and OS/2 Presentation Manager.

Sentence: "It's easy to change the colors that your monitor displays by using the *Control Panel.* Of course, it's also easy to really screw up your computer if you don't know what you're doing."

controller

Pronunciation: *kon-troll-er.*

Meaning: The circuitry that controls the data transfer from the floppy and hard disks connected to a computer and the monitor. Sometimes called a *disk drive controller.*

Sentence: "I added a new hard disk to my computer, but I had to buy a *controller* before it would work."

conventional memory

Pronunciation: *kon-ven-shin-null mem-or-ree.*

Meaning: On IBM PC and compatible computers, the first 640 kilobytes of memory (of RAM). This was the limit for a long time, and many programs still can access only conventional memory. (See also *upper memory, expanded memory,* and *extended memory.*)

Sentence: "Most memory-management programs work by shoving all possible programs in upper memory. That way there's more room in *conventional memory* to run your programs."

converter

Pronunciation: *kon-vert-her.*

Meaning: Hardware or software that changes one item into another, such as an AC to DC converter or a WordPerfect to Microsoft Word file converter.

Sentence: "Tim's too lame to buy WordPerfect. So I had to use a special file *converter* so that he could use my WordPerfect files in WordStar."

cookie

Pronunciation: *koo-kee.*

Meaning: A thin, baked piece of flavored dough that tastes great and contains nearly every chemical and substance known to man that causes heart disease, cancer, and tooth decay.

Sentence: "I've been working on my computer for five hours straight without eating. I need a *cookie* or I'll pass out on my keyboard."

coordinates

Pronunciation: *kor-din-ates.*

Meaning: A term used to divide any area into definable parts. On computer screens, coordinates measure the horizontal (X) and vertical (Y) axis for plotting points. Also used on *Star Trek* for giving locations for beaming people from or to a planet's surface.

Sentence: "I programmed my computer to draw a line from the (2,10) *coordinate* to the (45,20) *coordinate.* Now if only I could get someone to pay me to do this on a regular basis, I wouldn't have to finish college."

coprocessor

Pronunciation: *ko-pros-ses-her.*

Meaning: A separate processor designed to take some of the load off the main processor to make the computer run faster. A graphics coprocessor takes care of displaying images on the screen, resulting in faster, more colorful, and more detailed images. A math coprocessor takes care of numerical calculations, making spreadsheets and graphics programs run faster.

Sentence: "A lot of people buy a math *coprocessor* so that their spreadsheets will run faster. I think differently. I just hire someone to work for me at minimum wage. That way it doesn't matter how fast my computer runs at all."

copy

Pronunciation: *kop-ee.*

Meaning: To make an exact duplicate of an item, such as text, data, or files stored on a disk.

Sentence: "Rather than buy games, many people just *copy* them instead. Although this is cheaper, it's illegal. So unless you're a politician or a lawyer, you probably won't get away with this."

copy protection

Pronunciation: *kop-ee pro-tec-shin.*

Meaning: A way to prevent a computer from copying one or more files.

Sentence: "Because the cost of a single program overseas is almost as much as the yearly salary of most people, software publishers put *copy protection* on any software they sell outside of America. Although copy protection doesn't guarantee that someone can't copy the software, it does prevent most people from doing it."

CP/M

Pronunciation: *See Pee Em.*

Meaning: An acronym for Control Program for Microcomputers. An ancient operating system that was popular on personal computers back in the late '70s and early '80s, before the introduction of MS-DOS.

Sentence: "When personal computers first came out, I had to learn to use the *CP/M* operating system. Now everyone uses MS-DOS. Oh, well."

cps

Pronunciation: *see pee ess.*

Meaning: Acronym that stands for *characters per second.* Used to rate the printing speed of dot-matrix and inkjet printers.

Sentence: "This model can print at over 200 *cps*, but the paper jams every time I try to use it."

CPU

Pronunciation: *See Pee U.*

Meaning: Acronym for central processing unit. (See also *central processing unit.*)

Sentence: "That computer isn't worth buying because it has only an 8088 *CPU.* If you want a good computer, get one with an 80486 CPU instead and pay thousands of dollars more. Isn't this good advice?"

CR/LF

Pronunciation: *carriage return/line feed* or *seer/elf.*

Meaning: End of line characters. A term used with printers that use continuous form-feed paper. A CR/LF advances the paper in the printer by one line. Some systems use only one or the other; that is, either the CR or the LF.

Sentence: "Keep adding *CR/LFs* into the document so that the printer will print it out with the title centered in the page."

crash

Pronunciation: *krash.* Think of the sound of a Ford Pinto backing into the side of a GM pickup truck.

Meaning: When the computer or a network suddenly stops working. Often used to describe the smashing of the hard disk drive heads into the disk drive.

Sentence: "My computer *crashed,* so I had to stop working. It's amazing what a little paper clip jammed into the disk drive can do for employee morale around here."

CRC

Pronunciation: *cyclical redundancy check* or *see-r-see.*

Meaning: An error-detection technique used to verify the accuracy of data transmission. Often used with various transmission protocols such as XMODEM.

Sentence: "XMODEM with *CRC* is more reliable for transferring data than plain XMODEM by itself. Then again, why don't I just hand you a copy of the file on disk, and we can forget about hooking up all these cables and stuff?"

crosshairs

Pronunciation: *kross hares.*

Meaning: The shape of the cursor when using certain programs such as a drawing or painting program. The cursor often appears as a crosshair symbol when you are drawing squares, circles, or lines.

Sentence: "You can tell when you've chosen to draw a line when the cursor turns into *crosshairs.* Otherwise, the cursor just appears as a silly little arrow pointing to the left."

CRT

Pronunciation: *See Ar Tee.*

Meaning: An acronym that stands for *cathode ray tube*. CRTs appear in computer monitors and TV screens.

Sentence: "Don't sit too close to the *CRT* or your eyes might get radiated and explode out of your head."

Ctrl

(See *control key.*)

Ctrl-Alt-Del

Pronunciation: *Kon-troll Alt Del-eet.*

Meaning: Three keys that appear on IBM-compatible keyboards. Pressing them in sequence (and simultaneously holding them down) — Ctrl-Alt-Del — will restart your computer. It will also cause you to lose whatever you were doing that you haven't saved and also will risk damaging any open files. When your computer *locks up,* you have no choice but to press Ctrl-Alt-Del. (See also *lock.*)

Sentence: "Whenever my computer stops working for no apparent reason, I have to press *Ctrl-Alt-Del* to start all over again. Sometimes this works, and sometimes I have to sacrifice a cheeseburger instead."

CUA

Pronunciation: *See Yoo Ay.*

Meaning: Acronym for Common User Access. A set of guidelines developed by IBM to provide a standard user interface for computer programs.

Sentence: "Nearly all Macintosh and Windows programs follow the *CUA* guidelines."

current directory

Pronunciation: *kur-rent dir-ect-to-ree.*

Meaning: The directory that you are working in at any moment is the current directory and is the one from which DOS stores and retrieves files (unless told otherwise). Any directory on a hard or floppy disk can be the current directory, but only one directory can be the current directory at any given time.

Sentence: "The first time I turn on my computer, I see the C:> prompt, which means that the *current directory* is C:\. If I type **CD \DOS** and press Enter, then the current directory becomes C:\DOS."

cursor

Pronunciation: *kurs-er.*

Meaning: The annoying little blinking light that appears on the screen to let you know where your next typed character will appear.

Sentence: "Move the *cursor* to the top of the page by pressing Ctrl-Home. Or just press the PgUp key a million times until you get there or give up."

cursor keys

Pronunciation: *kurs-her kees.*

Meaning: The keys on the keyboard that let you move the cursor around. On IBM keyboards, the cursor keys double up as the numeric keypad. (What a stupid engineering design.) The eight cursor keys are the Up/Down arrows, Right/Left arrows, Home/End keys, and the PgUp/PgDn keys. Many new keyboards have separate arrow keys available as well. (See also *101-key keyboard.*)

Sentence: "You can use the *cursor keys* or the mouse to move the cursor around the screen."

cut

Pronunciation: *kut.*

Meaning: To remove text or graphics from the screen. You can use the Paste comand to retrieve the most recent text or graphics that you cut.

Sentence: "To erase a paragraph in WordPerfect, don't press the Backspace key until you're blue in the face. Just highlight the whole thing and choose the *Cut* command instead."

cut and paste

Pronunciation: *kut and paste.*

Meaning: To remove text or graphics from the screen and make it reappear it somewhere else.

Sentence: "To copy homework more easily, just *cut and paste* from someone else's document and put it in your own."

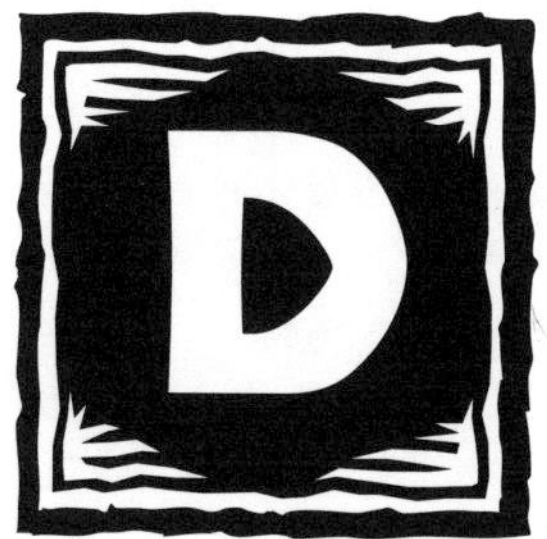

DA

Pronunciation: *Dee Ay.*

Meaning: Acronym for the *Desk Accessory* on the Macintosh. A desk accessory is a simple utility program, such as a calculator or notepad, that runs while another program is running.

Sentence: "Whenever I'm using Microsoft Word on my Macintosh and come up with a new idea to cheat the government out of taxes, I run my notepad *DA* and jot down my ideas before I forget."

daisy chain

Pronunciation: *day-zee chayn.*

Meaning: The linking of items one after another. In word processing, daisy chain printing means to print documents one after another.

Sentence: "My word processor lets me do *daisy chain* printing so that I don't have to waste time telling it to print each document individually. Too bad I have to waste time standing by the printer to make sure the paper doesn't jam."

daisy wheel

Pronunciation: *day-zee wee-ell.*

Meaning: A plastic wheel on which each spoke contains a character for printing. Daisy wheels appear in old-fashioned printers (unimaginatively enough called *daisy wheel printers* because the wheels look like petaled daisies). Whenever the printer needs to print a character, it spins the daisy wheel around until the correct character appears. Then it strikes the daisy wheel spoke so that it smacks against an inked ribbon, printing the

character on the page. (Sounds like a lot of trouble to go through, simply to print a single character, doesn't it?) (See also *dot matrix* and *laser printer.*)

Sentence: "Pages printed on a *daisy wheel* printer look like they came out of an ordinary typewriter. But nobody uses typewriters anymore."

darnthing

Pronunciation: *darn-thing.*

Meaning: A phrase commonly uttered by novices and experts alike when confronted by a problem that the computer refuses to solve. (Actually, there are lots of other more common phrases, but this is a family dictionary.) Otherwise known as *&^%$!!.

Sentence: "This *darnthing* won't let me delete this word. I hate computers. Somebody give me a sledgehammer."

Data

Pronunciation: *Day-tah.*

Meaning: Information people think is important and useful to save. Also the name of the android character on *Star Trek: The Next Generation.*

Sentence: "My hard disk contains megabytes of *data* on every aspect of my business. I wonder how many megabytes of data Commander Data retains on every aspect of the Enterprise."

data compression

Pronunciation: *day-tah kom-press-shin.*

Meaning: To take files on a disk and make them smaller. Often used for transmitting files through a modem (thereby reducing the time spent on the phone) and for storing files on a hard disk so that they take up less space. You have to uncompress them before you can use them.

Sentence: "The best program for *data compression* is PKZIP because it works faster and makes smaller files than similar data compression programs such as ARC or LHA. Now that my files are smaller, I can clutter up my hard disk with twice as much useless information."

Data Encryption Standard

Pronunciation: *Day-tah En-krip-shin Stan-dard.*

Meaning: Often abbreviated as DES. A government specification for encoding files using a password. A supposedly secure specification that no one can crack except maybe the government, which is why it wholeheartedly endorses this standard.

Sentence: "The *Data Encryption Standard* can scramble text so badly that no one can read it without the right password. This explains why government tax forms are so difficult to understand."

data fork

Pronunciation: *day-tah fork.*

Meaning: On the Macintosh, all files have two parts to them: a resource fork and a data fork. The data fork usually contains information (that is, the actual data) that the program needs to run. The resource fork usually contains the instructions for running a program or other resource information needed such as fonts, icons, menus, and so on.

Sentence: "Many MS-DOS programs consist of a separate .EXE file and one or more .DAT files that store the program data. On the Macintosh, you can smash this information into a single file by using a *data fork.*"

data structures

Pronunciation: *day-tah struk-sures.*

Meaning: A term programmers use to describe various ways to organize data within a program. Some common data structures include arrays, records, trees, linked lists, and anything else the programmer cares to invent. (See *algorithm.*)

Sentence: "Programs consist of algorithms that tell the program what to do and *data structures* that hold the information for the program to use."

database

Pronunciation: *day-tah-bay-se.*

Meaning: An organized collection of information (data). (See also *data.*)

Sentence: "I stored all my clients' names, addresses, and phone numbers in a *database.* Now I can't find where I put the disk."

DATE

Pronunciation: *Dayt.*

Meaning: An MS-DOS and OS/2 command that displays the computer's date. DATE gives you the chance to type the correct date, if necessary.

Sentence: "Type **DATE** at the DOS prompt and press Enter. On computers without an internal clock, the date is probably 1/1/80. On computers that have an internal clock, the date is usually anything but the correct date."

datum

Pronunciation: *day-tum.*

Meaning: The singular of "data," seldom used except by extremely socially backward programmers who wish to impress others with their useless technical knowledge. (See also *data.*)

Sentence: "Maybe Data, the android in *Star Trek: The Next Generation,* should have been named *Datum* because there's only one of him."

daughterboard

Pronunciation: *dah-ter-bored.*

Meaning: An optional circuit board that can plug into the main circuit board of the computer. Because the main circuit board of the computer is called a *motherboard,* this optional circuit board is called the *daughterboard.* (See also *motherboard.*)

Sentence: "Every computer has a motherboard, but mine has special superhero qualities because I installed a *daughterboard.*"

DDE

Pronunciation: *Dee Dee Eee.* (Just imagine a baby saying this.)

Meaning: An acronym that means *Dynamic Data Exchange.* Used with Microsoft Windows and OS/2. DDE lets two Windows or OS/2 programs share data, such as numbers stored in a spreadsheet and word processor report.

Sentence: "If it wasn't for *DDE,* I'd have to type these numbers twice in my word processor report and spreadsheet. With DDE, I simply type the numbers in my spreadsheet, and they magically appear in my word processor. Every time I change the numbers in the spreadsheet, the numbers automatically change in my word processor report."

DDT

Pronunciation: *Dee Dee Tee.*

Meaning: A pesticide used in the '60s and '70s to wipe out insects, crops, small animals, and people wherever it appeared.

Sentence: "*DDT* keeps bugs out of my garden, so I sprayed some on my computer, hoping it might get rid of the bugs in WordPerfect."

debug

Pronunciation: *dee-bug.*

Meaning: To eliminate problems (bugs) in a program. Programmers try to debug a program while they are developing it, but often they miss things. (See also *bug.*)

Sentence: "Version 1.0 of any program usually has many bugs that the programmers haven't found yet. Once the program starts messing up lots of customers, the programmers *debug* the program and release it as version 2.0."

debugger

Pronunciation: *dee-bug-er.*

Meaning: A special program with a sole purpose in life to help programmers track down and eliminate bugs in a program.

Sentence: "With my *debugger,* it's much easier to check for problems in my programs before I release them for sale. Then again, I make more money selling buggy programs and then charging customers an update fee for the debugged version."

decimal number

Pronunciation: *deh-sim-mall num-ber.*

Meaning: A number that uses the digits 0, 1, 2, 3, 4, 5, 6, 7, 8, 9 in ordinary base-ten notation. (See also *binary, hexidecimal,* and *octal.*)

Sentence: "Most people use *decimal numbers* for counting, but computers can use binary or hexadecimal numbers as well. Sometimes this is more convenient for the computer, but it's always a royal pain in the neck for the programmer."

decryption

Pronunciation: *dee-crip-shin.*

Meaning: To convert indecipherable gibberish into plain English that everyone can understand. (See *encryption.*)

Sentence: "Everything that computer people write sounds like it has been encrypted by the CIA. But reading *DOS For Dummies* seemed like reading the *decryption* of all the normal computer terms."

dedicated

Pronunciation: *ded-i-ka-ted.*

Meaning: An adjective describing a piece of equipment that performs only one function.

Sentence: "I have a separate phone line *dedicated* to sending and receiving FAXes. I also have a collie dedicated to retrieving my slippers every Sunday morning."

default

Pronunciation: *dee-falt.*

Meaning: An assumption the computer makes to perform a certain action unless the user specifies differently, such as using a predetermined value for an option.

Sentence: "If you try to quit a program without saving your file, the computer asks whether you really want to do that. By pressing the Enter key, you choose the *default* command of saving your file (and in some cases, thus saving your life)."

default directory

Pronunciation: *dee-falt dir-ek-to-ree.*

Meaning: The directory on a hard disk that the computer uses to perform commands if it isn't given specific instructions to use a different directory. (See also *default drive* and *directory.*)

Sentence: "The *default directory* for my computer is C:\DOS. Any time I type a command, my computer looks in this directory for the files."

default drive

Pronunciation: *dee-falt drive.*

Meaning: The disk drive the computer looks for if it isn't given specific instructions to look anywhere else.

Sentence: "The *default drive* for most computers is the C: drive, which is the hard drive. So if you save a file on a floppy disk but can't find it again, chances are you stored it on the C: drive instead of the floppy drive."

Del key

Pronunciation: *Dell kee.*

Meaning: The Delete key, sometimes abbreviated on computer keyboards as DEL.

Sentence: "In some programs, pressing the *Del key* erases the character to the left of the cursor. In other programs, pressing the *Del key* erases the character to the right. This is like driving one car where the accelerator pedal is on the right and driving your other car where the brake pedal is on the right."

DES

(See *Data Encryption Standard.*)

descender

Pronunciation: *dee-sen-der.*

Meaning: The part of a letter that falls below the imaginary line on which the letter rests. For example, the letters *p, y,* and *q* have descenders, but the letters *t, u,* and *o* do not. (See also *ascender.*)

Sentence: "If you make the line spacing too small, the *descenders* from the top line get in the way of the letters on the next line."

deselect

Pronunciation: *dee-sell-ect.*

Meaning: To change your mind after selecting an item, such as by unhighlighting an item or by removing the X in an option box. (See also *select.*)

Sentence: "George Bush selected Dan Quayle for his vice president. After so much bad publicity surrounding Quayle, many people wondered whether Bush would have liked to *deselect* Quayle and choose someone else."

desk accessory

(See *DA.*)

desktop

Pronunciation: *desk-top.*

Meaning: The blank screen (background) that appears on programs that use a *graphical user interface* such as the Macintosh, Windows, or OS/2. (See *graphical user interface.*)

Sentence: "Whenever I start my Macintosh, I see a menu bar at the top of the screen and a big gray screen underneath cluttered with icons and windows. This gray screen is my *desktop* because it looks as disorganized as the top of my real desk."

desktop PC

Pronunciation: *desk-top Pee-See.*

Meaning: A type of computer that's way too heavy to move more than once in a lifetime and that uses up more than half of the space on an ordinary desk. (Contrast with *portable, laptop,* and *notebook computers.*)

Sentence: "I don't need to take a computer when I travel, so I bought a *desktop PC* and left it at home instead."

desktop publishing

Pronunciation: *desk-top pub-li-shing.*

Meaning: To combine text and pictures on a computer screen to create neat-looking newsletters, books, or brochures. (See also *DTP.*)

Sentence: "With my *desktop publishing* program, I can create and publish my own book. Now I just need to get someone to buy it."

device

Pronunciation: *dee-vice.*

Meaning: Any type of equipment, such as a printer, modem, monitor, disk drive, or mouse that can send or receive data.

Sentence: "Hard-core computer people like to call my printer a *device.* I just call it a printer."

device driver

Pronunciation: *dee-vice driv-er.*

Meaning: A special program that provides specifications for the operation of a device connected to a computer, such as a printer or CD-ROM drive. Sometimes just called a *driver.*

Sentence: "Before I could get WordPerfect to print documents, I had to install the right printer *device driver.* This special program told WordPerfect exactly how to print stuff on my printer."

device name

Pronunciation: *dee-vice name.*

Meaning: An abbreviation that refers to a device connected to the computer.

Sentence: "MS-DOS uses the *device name* of PRN: to refer to the printer. I don't know how this is any easier to understand, but at least my computer seems happy."

dialog box

Pronunciation: *die-a-log box.*

Meaning: A window that pops up to ask for more information from the user. (See also *list box.*)

Sentence: "Whenever I choose the Save As command, my word processor pops up a *dialog box* on the screen, asking me to type the file name I want to use."

digital

Pronunciation: *di-jit-al.*

Meaning: A way of representing objects using two distinct states such as On or Off, Low or High, Good or Bad, or Republican or Democrat. All computers are digital computers because they consist of millions of On and Off switches. (See also *analog* and *binary.*)

Sentence: "Computers often seem cold and forbidding to liberal arts majors because computers are *digital* and see the world in terms of black and white. Liberal arts majors tend to see the world in shades of gray, which explains why most of them don't have jobs after graduation." (Relax, it's just a joke!)

dimmed

Pronunciation: *dim-da.*

Meaning: When an object or word appears on the screen in a soft, fuzzy color that's easy to overlook. In Windows, for example, options that do not apply in the current context are dimmed so that you can tell that they are not available.

Sentence: "To prevent you from choosing certain commands by mistake, these commands may appear *dimmed* on your screen."

dingbats

Pronunciation: *ding-batz.*

Meaning: A font consisting of bizarre characters made up of bullets, Greek and Egyptian hieroglyphics, and geometric figures. Also a slang term made popular by the '70s hit show *All in the Family,* when describing people that Archie Bunker didn't like.

Sentence: "When I chose the *dingbat* font on my word processor, all sorts of weird symbols appeared instead of my letters."

DIP switch

Pronunciation: Just like it sounds, like an insult.

Meaning: Tiny little switches that are almost impossible to find, let alone use properly. DIP is an acronym for *Dual-Inline Package* (as if that clarifies matters any). Mostly, you use DIP switches with modems to select COM ports or with printers to select options for output. Printed circuit boards can have them, too.

Sentence: "When I added more memory to my computer, I had to change the *DIP switch* settings with a real sharp pencil point."

DIR

Pronunciation: *Der.*

Meaning: An operating system command that displays a directory listing when typed at the DOS prompt, such as in C:\>DIR.

Sentence: "I typed **DIR** at the DOS prompt and all the file names scrolled so fast across the screen that I still couldn't read them. Boy, am I glad I spent $3,000 on a computer to make my life easier."

directory

Pronunciation: *der-ek-tor-ree.*

Meaning: A way of dividing a floppy or hard disk for organizing files. Every disk has at least one directory called the *root directory.* You can create other directories and label them to keep your files that relate to different programs, data, and projects separated.

Sentence: "I created a bunch of *directories* to organize the files on my hard disk. Now I can't remember in which directory I stored all my files."

directory list box

Pronunciation: *der-ek-tor-ree list box.*

Meaning: A display that lists directories and subdirectories in a hierarchical tree structure. You use these boxes in Windows and OS/2 programs.

Sentence: "Whenever I press the Save command in my word processor, the program pops up a *directory list box* so that I can choose which directory to save the file in."

disk

Pronunciation: *disk.* (How tough can this be?)

Meaning: A magnetic storage device shaped like a pizza and encased in a plastic case. Hard disks are encased in a box. The two most popular sizes for floppy disks are 5¼-inch and 3½-inch. Floppy disks may be double-density or high-density. High-density floppy disks can store two to four times as much information as double-density disks. (See also *floppy disk* and *hard disk.*)

Sentence: "After storing all my files on floppy *disks* for several years, I finally bought a hard disk. So now I'm using my old floppy disks as frisbees."

disk cache

Pronunciation: *disk cash.*

Meaning: A portion of memory in which the computer stores frequently used information. By copying information from the floppy or hard disk and storing it in a disk cache, the computer can access the information faster. Some computers have a built-in disk cache. Some utility programs create a disk cache out of the computer's main memory. Generally, the larger the disk cache, the faster the computer runs.

Sentence: "My computer runs really fast because I have a large *disk cache.* I still, however, run slow."

disk operating system

Pronunciation: *disk op-er-rate-ting siss-dum.*

Meaning: The main program that tells your computer how to work. Often abbreviated as DOS. On IBM and compatible computers, the disk operating system is called *MS-DOS* or *PC-DOS,* although many people have their own favorite four-letter word adjectives for it. The Mac operating system is often called something similar to *System 7.* (See also *operating system.*)

Sentence: "My computer had an old version of the *disk operating system,* so I couldn't run the latest programs. Once I upgraded to the new version of MS-DOS, my computer worked perfectly."

disk partition

Pronunciation: *disk par-tish-shin.*

Meaning: The division of a hard disk into two or more sections. Some people partition their disk so that one half of their hard disk runs MS-DOS and Windows and the other half runs OS/2.

Sentence: "Someone *partitioned* my hard *disk* into three separate partitions. One partition runs MS-DOS, one runs OS/2, and one runs Windows NT. Now, I'm three times as confused when I try to use my computer."

display

Pronunciation: *dis-play.*

Meaning: The monitor or screen of a computer that actually shows you something interesting such as a word processor, spreadsheet, or digitized picture of bathing suit-clad models. (See also *monitor.*)

Sentence: "The *display* on my computer is in color but the display on my laptop is only black and white. I'd like to buy a laptop with a color display, but then I'd have to take out a second mortgage on my home."

dithering

Pronunciation: *dith-er-ring.*

Meaning: Although it sounds like something drunk people might mumble in their sleep, dithering is the substitution of black and white dots for shades of gray in computer graphics. It can be used to make curving patterns less jaggy. (See also *aliasing* and *jaggies.*)

Sentence: "Because some displays and printers can't display the high-resolution quality of a graphic image, they use *dithering* to show you that the graphic still exists but that they can't show you the exact image."

DLL

Pronunciation: *Dee Ell Ell.*

Meaning: Acronym used in Windows and OS/2 that stands for *Dynamic Link Library.* DLL files contain commonly used routines that two or more programs can share.

Sentence: "I wrote a *DLL* file that takes care of printing. That way all the guys at work can just use my *DLL* file instead of writing their own printing routines for their programs. Let's just hope my DLL file really works."

DOC

Pronunciation: *Dock, as in "Hickory Dickory Dock."*

Meaning: An abbreviation for DOCument. Often used as a file extension for word processor files. (See also *BAK.*)

Sentence: "Check the hard drive for all the *DOC* files you can find. Then erase them so that the police won't find evidence that we're not honest guys after all."

document

Pronunciation: *dock-u-mint.*

Meaning: A file created by a word processor or desktop publisher, containing words or pictures. (See also *file.*)

Sentence: "He gave me all his *documents* on disk. Now I just need to figure out which word processor he used to create them all."

documentation

Pronunciation: *dock-u-mint-tay-shin.*

Meaning: The fat instruction manuals that everyone pays money for but no one bothers to read. Usually full of instructions that don't work, don't make sense, or are just plain wrong.

Sentence: "Many people pay for software so that they can get the *documentation.* Then they spend an extra $50 on third-party books, many of which give them almost the same information that the documentation gave."

DOS

Pronunciation: *Daw-ess.*

Meaning: Acronym that stands for *Disk Operating System.* By the way, if you have Windows, you still have DOS. (See also *disk operating system.*)

Sentence: "I use *DOS* on my laptop computer but Windows on my desktop. I don't know how to use either one, but at least I know the right words to sound intelligent."

DOS prompt

Pronunciation: *Daw-ess prom-ta.*

Meaning: When you're not in a program, you'll see this cryptic little signal that the computer displays on the screen that essentially says, "This is the computer. What do you want me to do?" Typical DOS prompts look like C:\>, A:, or C:\WINDOWS\SYSTEM>. (See also *$.*)

Sentence: "Type **DEL *.*** and press Enter at the *DOS prompt* if you want to erase all the files in your current directory."

dot matrix

Pronunciation: *daht may-tricks.*

Meaning: A type of printer or printout that creates letters and graphics by using lots of tiny dots. The more dots used, the sharper the image. The fewer the dots used, the more the printing looks like a cheap printer printed it. (See also *laser printer* and *daisy wheel.*)

Sentence: "Most magazines don't like submissions printed on *dot matrix.* They'd rather have submissions printed on laser printers."

dot pitch

Pronunciation: *daht pit-cha.*

Meaning: The smallest size dot that a monitor can display, usually measured in millimeters (mm). Typical dot pitches for monitors are .41mm, .31mm, and .28mm. The smaller the dot pitch, the sharper the resolution on the monitor. Also used to describe the distance between two color dots of the same color on a color monitor.

Sentence: "I had an old VGA monitor with .41 *dot pitch,* but it was too hard on my eyes. Thank goodness my new monitor has a .28mm *dot pitch.* I don't know what it means, but it's easier to read."

dots per inch

Pronunciation: *daughtz purh eenshch.*

Meaning: Sometimes abbreviated as DPI, dots per inch describes how sharp a printed image appears. The more dots per inch used, the sharper the image looks.

Sentence: "My laser printer has a maximum resolution of 300 *dots per inch,* but typesetting machines have 2400 dots per inch. That's why stuff printed on a laser printer still looks cheap compared to a typeset book or magazine."

double-click

Pronunciation: *dub-bull-klik.*

Meaning: To press the mouse button twice in rapid succession without moving the mouse between clicks. (See also *click.*)

Sentence: "To run the program, simply move the mouse cursor over the program's icon and *double-click.* If that doesn't work, put your fist through the monitor."

double-density disk

Pronunciation: *dub-bull-den-city disk.*

Meaning: A floppy disk that stores twice as much information in the same amount of space as a single-density disk (which is no longer sold). Double-density disks are abbreviated as DD. A 5¼-inch double-density floppy disk can hold 360K of data. A 3½-inch double-density floppy disk can hold 720K (800K for a Macintosh) of data. (See also *high density.*)

Sentence: "Hardly anyone uses *double-density disks* any more. Everyone uses high-density disks. I use double-density disks as coasters for drinks."

down

Pronunciation: *down.* (Just like it looks.)

Meaning: When a piece of computer equipment temporarily stops working.

Sentence: "We can't take your reservation because the computer is *down,* and we're too lame to figure out how to work without it."

download

Pronunciation: *down-lode.*

Meaning: To copy files through a modem from a distant computer to the one you're working on. (See also *upload.*)

Sentence: "I like to dial into CompuServe or GEnie and *download* programs from their computers. After downloading all the programs I want, I can start playing with them on my computer instead of doing any real work."

downward compatible

Pronunciation: *down-word kom-pat-i-bull.*

Meaning: The capability of software or hardware to work with earlier versions of the same software or hardware. (See also *upward compatible.*)

Sentence: "WordPerfect 7.0 is *downward compatible* with WordPerfect 5.1. This means any files I created with WordPerfect 5.1 can still be used with WordPerfect 7.0. Too bad I don't want to use WordPerfect anymore."

dpi

Pronunciation: *dee pee i.*

Meaning: Acronym for dots per inch. (See also *dots per inch.*)

Sentence: "My printer has 300 *dpi.* I guess that's good, but what the heck do I know? I'm just the CEO of a Fortune 500 corporation."

drag

Pronunciation: *drah-ga.*

Meaning: To use the mouse for moving an object across the screen. First, you have to highlight (select) the object you want by pointing to it with the mouse. Then hold down the mouse button and move the mouse. This drags the object.

Sentence: "To delete a file on the Macintosh, just *drag* it to the trash."

drag and drop

Pronunciation: *drah-ga and draw-pa.*

Meaning: To use a mouse for moving an object across the screen as a shortcut for copying or moving a group of objects.

Sentence: "The latest spreadsheets let you *drag and drop* entire rows and columns from one place to another. Spreadsheets without drag and drop force you to select the row or column you want to move, choose the Move command from the menu, and then click to the location to which you want to move it (or use cut and paste). *Drag and drop* is much easier to use."

DRAM

Pronunciation: *D-Ram*

Meaning: Acronym for *Dynamic Random-Access Memory.* Computers can use two types of RAM chips: DRAM and SRAM. DRAM chips are less expensive because the computer periodically has to put the information back into the DRAM chips or else the DRAM chips forget. (See also *RAM.*)

Sentence: "Every five minutes I have to stop and tell my kids not to run around the house. Now I know how a computer with *DRAM* chips must feel."

draw program

Pronunciation: *draw pro-gram.* (Well, can you think of a better pronunciation guide?)

Meaning: A type of program that lets you draw objects on the screen, such as lines, boxes, or circles.

Sentence: "A *draw program* turns your $2,500 computer into the equivalent of a $2 box of crayons and a sheet of paper."

drive list box

Pronunciation: What's the matter? Can't you say simple words?

Meaning: A list that displays the number of disk drives on the computer. Often used with the File Save command. The drive list box lets you decide which drive to save a file on.

Sentence: "To tell my word processor to save a file on a floppy disk in the A: drive, I have to use the *drive list box* and select the A: drive."

drop-down list box

Pronunciation: *drawp-down list box.*

Meaning: A combination of two boxes. One box lets the user type information. The second box underneath lists names that the user can choose from instead.

Sentence: "I like using *drop-down list boxes* because they give me the option of typing in a name or choosing one from a predefined list. Now we just need a way for the computer to do what I want without me doing a thing."

DS/DD

Pronunciation: *Dee Ess/Dee Dee.*

Meaning: Abbreviation for double-sided/double-density. (See also *double-density disk* and *high density.*)

Sentence: "Whenever I buy a box of floppy disks, I look to see whether they are labeled *DS/DD* or *HD.* Because my old computer uses only double-density floppy disks, I have to buy the DS/DD disks."

DTP

Pronunciation: *Dee Tee Pee.*

Meaning: Acronym for *DeskTop Publishing.* (See also *desktop publishing.*)

Sentence: "If it weren't for my *DTP* program, making counterfeit money would be a lot tougher."

DTR

Pronunciation: *Dee Tee R.*

Meaning: Acronym for *Data Terminal Ready,* a signal used by a computer to tell its modem that it's ready to start receiving information.

Sentence: "My modem has a special *DTR* light that lets me know that everything will work if I dial into another computer."

dumb terminal

Pronunciation: *dum ter-min-al.*

Meaning: A unit consisting of a keyboard and video display connected to a main computer (such as a mainframe). Dumb terminals don't have disk drives or their own processors, so they can't store files or do anything else on their own. Personal computers, on the other hand, can act as autonomous units which can be networked together.

Sentence: "Because they think they are saving money, many buyers in companies purchase a mainframe and install *dumb terminals* instead of personal computers. Also, this way, the people using the terminals have no choices in life whatsoever."

dump

Pronunciation: *dum-pa.*

Meaning: To copy information from one location to another without regard for its appearance or format. Often used for printing information that is temporarily useful.

Sentence: "I had to *dump* the file to the printer so that I could see what type of information was stored in it. Now I'll dump the printout in the trash can so that some hacker can find it and use everyone's secret passwords."

duplex

Pronunciation: *doo-plex.*

Meaning: A term used in telecommunications to describe how signals are sent. *Full duplex* means that signals can be sent simultaneously back and forth. *Half duplex* means signals can go only in one direction at a time.

Sentence: "With my communications program, setting ECHO ON means using full *duplex.* Setting ECHO OFF means using half duplex. Sometimes if I type, the computer repeats my typing so that my words look like tthhiiss. Then I have to turn ECHO OFF, so I use half duplex to fix the problem. Isn't learning about computers fun?"

Dvorak keyboard

Pronunciation: *Dee-vor-rak kee-bored.*

Meaning: A specially designed keyboard that organizes keys on the keyboard for maximum efficiency. Although known to be more efficient than current keyboards, hardly anyone uses them. So much for efficiency. (See also *QWERTY* and *keyboard.*)

Sentence: "The only reason I don't use the *Dvorak keyboard* is because everyone else uses the inefficient QWERTY keyboard, which has been around for a century."

dweeb

Pronunciation: *dwee-ba.*

Meaning: A person who may be technically competent but is socially a jerk that no one wants to hang around with after work.

Sentence: "Bob would make a great manager if he wasn't such a *dweeb.*"

DWIM

Pronunciation: *Dwim,* rhymes with *swim.*

Meaning: Acronym that stands for Do What I Mean, Not What I Say. Often used when people want the computer to read their minds and ignore the commands they're typing in.

Sentence: "I saw a father using *DWIM* on his daughter when he told her not to smoke, while he was puffing on a cigar and blowing smoke in her face."

dynamic allocation

Pronunciation: *di-nam-ik al-o-kay-shin.*

Meaning: To store information in the computer's memory (called the *heap*) while the program is running. Unless you plan on writing your own programs, you can safely ignore this definition. (See also *static.*)

Sentence: "My programs run slower because they use *dynamic allocation,* but at least they're more flexible than programs that use *static allocation.* By the way, do I know what the heck I just said?"

dynamic RAM

(See *DRAM.*)

e-mail

Pronunciation: *ee-may-ell.*

Meaning: Stands for *electronic mail.* Messages created, sent, and read completely on computers without ever being printed on paper. Electronic mail usually involves sending messages to other users on some kind of network.

Sentence: "With rising postal rates, it's cheaper to use a computer to send *e-mail* than to use an envelope and a stamp. Of course, you have to buy a computer first."

e-mail address

Pronunciation: *ee-may-ell add-ress.*

Meaning: An identifying number or word assigned to one person for sending and receiving electronic mail. A server acts as a post office, holding messages until users call in to retrieve them.

Sentence: "Whenever I send e-mail to my friend, I have to tell the computer which e-mail address to send it to. Once, I typed the wrong *e-mail address* and sent a love letter to my ex-wife."

E-notation

Pronunciation: *Ee no-tay-shin.*

Meaning: Abbreviation for *exponential notation,* a way that scientists express large and small numbers.

Sentence: "My spreadsheet lets me store numbers in *E-notation*. That way it doesn't look as if the company is losing millions of dollars."

EBCDIC

Pronunciation: *Eee Bee See Dee I See.*

Meaning: Acronym for *Extended Binary Coded Decimal Interchange Code.* A standard way of representing characters on a computer. Some mainframes use EBCDIC. (See also *ASCII.*)

Sentence: "IBM tried to get everyone to follow the *EBCDIC* standard, but everyone else followed the ASCII standard instead. It doesn't really matter which standard your computer uses as long as it works."

echo

Pronunciation: *ek-o.*

Meaning: When communicating through a modem, an echo displays every character you type on your computer screen. If you can't see what you're typing, echo is said to be off. If you see double words such as tthhiiss, you have to turn echo off. Echo also is an MS-DOS and OS/2 operating system command. Entering ECHO OFF in a batch file keeps the computer from displaying commands on the screen (as the computer is carrying them out). (See also *duplex.*)

Sentence: "Each time you dial into a computer using your modem, you may have to turn the *echo* on or off so that you can see what you're trying to do."

edit

Pronunciation: *ed-it.*

Meaning: To modify data (text, graphics, and so on) in a file.

Sentence: "I wrote a 20-page letter, but I had to *edit* the part about kicking my sister because I didn't think my mom would appreciate it."

editor

Pronunciation: *ed-it-or.*

Meaning: A program specifically designed for modifying files. The two types of editors are *line editors* and *full-screen editors.* A line editor lets you change one line at a time. A full-screen editor lets you change multiple lines that appear on the screen. Word processors, such as WordPerfect or Word for Windows, are much more sophisticated than simple editors. But sometimes an editor is all you need, especially if you are using it to edit programming code. (See also *line editor* and *full screen.*)

Sentence: "I had to use an *editor* to modify the programs that I wrote earlier. The programs still don't work, but at least I can keep changing them with my editor."

EDLIN

Pronunciation: *Ed-Lynn.*

Meaning: A line editor that came with MS-DOS versions 5.0 and lower. EDLIN was pretty much a useless program that nobody but the most nerdy people used. MS-DOS version 6.0 and higher no longer include EDLIN.

Sentence: "I tried using *EDLIN* to modify a file, but it was too much trouble editing a line at a time. Who was the bozo who invented EDLIN in the first place?"

EEPROM

Pronunciation: *Eee-Prom.*

Meaning: An acronym that stands for *Electronically Erasable Programmable Read-Only Memory.* An EEPROM chip can be reprogrammed through electrical signals that zap its contents and replace them with something else. EEPROM chips can hold their contents without power. (See also *PROM.*)

Sentence: "Many computer parts use *EEPROM* chips. Instead of yanking out the chips and replacing them with new ones, you can just zap them with electricity and reprogram them without even touching them."

EGA

Pronunciation: *Eee Gee A.*

Meaning: Acronym for *Enhanced Graphics Adapter,* a graphics standard once used for IBM computers and now remembered solely by trivia buffs. Instead of using the EGA standard, most computers use the newer VGA or SVGA standards, which display more colors with sharper resolution. (See also *CGA, VGA,* and *SVGA.*)

Sentence: "Don't buy an *EGA* monitor unless you want to waste your money. Most programs need a VGA monitor or else they won't even work."

EIEIO

Pronunciation: *Eee-I-Eee-I-O.*

Meaning: Nonsensical but rhythmic phrase used by farmers when they forget the rest of the words to a song. It's probably an acronym for something.

Sentence: "Old McDonald had a farm, *EIEIO!*"

EISA

Pronunciation: *Eee-Suh.*

Meaning: Acronym for *Extended Industry Standard Architecture.* ISA is the standard bus design for the older IBM computers. EISA is the new proposed standard for IBM-compatible computers. Instead of following the EISA standard, IBM's PS/2 computers follow their own *MCA* standard. (See also *architecture, bus, ISA,* and *MCA.*)

Sentence: "For a while, people wondered whether they should buy a computer with an *EISA* bus or an MCA bus. Then people got smart and figured that it didn't really matter after all."

eject

Pronunciation: *ee-jekt.*

Meaning: To remove a floppy disk from a floppy disk drive. (See also *disk.*)

Sentence: "If you want to save your files on this floppy disk, you first have to *eject* the disk that's already in your computer."

elite

Pronunciation: *ee-lee-ta.*

Meaning: Leftover from the typewriter days, elite refers to typefaces that print as 12 characters per inch. Often appears on printers as one of many choices to make for printing documents. (See also *pica.*)

Sentence: "If you want to squeeze more words on a page, use *elite* type. Otherwise, you can use pica type, which appears as 10 characters per inch."

ELIZA

Pronunciation: *EL-Li-Za.*

Meaning: A famous artificial intelligence program that mimicked a psychotherapist. Users typed their problems into the computer, and ELIZA parroted back empty phrases to give the appearance of deep thought (and then bill them $200 an hour). (See also *artificial intelligence.*)

Sentence: "Whenever I'm feeling down, I just load *ELIZA* on my computer and talk to it. Right now my biggest problem is talking to my computer instead of people."

ellipsis (. . .)

Pronunciation: *ee-lips-eez.*

Meaning: Three tiny dots that appear next to commands on pull-down menus. The ellipsis tells you that when you choose a command that ends with (...), the program will ask you for more information (via a dialog box).

Sentence: "When you choose a command such as Open from the File menu, the program does something right away. But when you choose a command such as Save As..., which has an *ellipsis,* the program bothers you with a dialog box before doing anything else."

em dash

Pronunciation: *em dah-sha.*

Meaning: A special character used in typography, approximated by typing two hyphens (such as --), which is as wide as the letter *M.* Often used for added emphasis in text. (See also *en dash.*)

Sentence: "Here is an example of an *em dash:* 'Don't touch that — oh well, you have another hand anyway.'"

EMM

Pronunciation: *Ee Em Em.*

Meaning: Acronym that stands for *Expanded Memory Manager,* which is a utility program that helps computers use memory more efficiently. Most often used on computers with 80386 or 80486 processors.

Sentence: "My computer has 16MB of RAM, but it doesn't use it very efficiently. That's why I bought an *EMM* program so that I can get maximum use of my computer's resources. Now if I only knew how to type, I'd be all set."

EMS

Pronunciation: *Eee Em Ess.*

Meaning: Acronym for *Expanded Memory Specification.* Sometimes called LIM-EMS, which stands for Lotus-Intel-Microsoft Expanded Memory Specification. EMS defines a specific way for 8088 processors to use more than 640K of memory. Originally developed so that users could load huge Lotus 1-2-3 spreadsheets into memory.

Sentence: "In the old days, IBM computers used only 640K of memory. If you added memory beyond this 640K range, you had to run a special *EMS* program so that the computer would recognize this extra memory. Boy, computers are kind of dense at times, aren't they?"

emulation

Pronunciation: *em-you-lay-shin.*

Meaning: To mimic the appearance and functionality of another program, computer, or computer accessory such as a printer or modem. Many printers offer Epson or Hewlett-Packard LaserJet emulation. Most modems offer Hayes emulation.

Sentence: "My Amiga computer has IBM *emulation*, so I can run any IBM program I want."

en dash

Pronunciation: *en dash,* just like it looks.

Meaning: A single dash that is the width of the letter *N.* En dashes are used to represent *to,* such as pages 64–98. (See also *em dash.*)

Sentence: "Here is an example of how to use an *en dash:* 'I stuck my leaf collection between pages 56–64 because that's the only use I could find for my MS-DOS user manual.'"

encryption

Pronunciation: *en-krip-shin.*

Meaning: To scramble information with a code or password so that other people can't read it. Often used to protect sensitive files, electronic mail, or legal documents so that the general public can't understand what they really mean. (See also *Data Encryption Standard.*)

Sentence: "I used *encryption* on all my important word processor documents. Now I forget the password to read them again."

End key

Pronunciation: *En-da kee.*

Meaning: The key on the keyboard with *End* printed on it. (What a remarkable coincidence!) It is often a neighbor of the Delete key or living with the number 1.

Sentence: "Press the *End key* to move the cursor to the end of the line. Press Ctrl-End to move the cursor to the end of the document."

end user

Pronunciation: *en-da yoo-zer.*

Meaning: The person who winds up using a computer or program that someone else designed. (See also *programmer.*)

Sentence: "Most programs are hard to use because programmers keep forgetting that the *end user* isn't as experienced with computers as they are. That's the same reason why so many people buy additional computer books."

End-Of-File

Pronunciation: *En-da-Of-Fi-ella.*

Meaning: Sometimes abbreviated as *EOF,* this is a special symbol that marks the end of a file. In MS-DOS, Control-Z creates the EOF symbol. Usually, the marker is placed automatically by the application. (See also *EOL.*)

Sentence: "Every time your word processor loads a document off the disk, it keeps reading information in until it reaches the EOF marker. Without this *End-Of-File* marker, the program doesn't know when the file ends, and it keeps trying to read everything else on the hard disk."

endless loop

Pronunciation: *end-less loop.*

Meaning: When a program keeps repeating the same instructions over and over again without stopping. Just think about what your record player used to do when the needle got stuck in a scratch (that is, if you can remember record players). A program that is stuck in an endless loop appears to be doing absolutely nothing, yet doesn't let you type any commands (sort of like endless love). (See also *infinite loop* and *loop.*)

Sentence: "I think this program's stuck in an *endless loop.* It hasn't done a thing in three days. Then again, neither have I, but at least I know how to pretend that I'm working."

enhanced keyboard

Pronunciation: *en-han-zts kee-bored.*

Meaning: A keyboard that provides a numeric key pad and cursor keys separate from the main typewriter keys. Enhanced keyboards usually contain 101 keys and also are called 101-key keyboards. The function keys go across the top of the keyboard. (See also *101-key keyboard.*)

Sentence: "Nearly every IBM-compatible computer comes with an *enhanced keyboard,* making this term pretty much meaningless today."

ENIAC

Pronunciation: *Ee-Nee-Ack.*

Meaning: Acronym for *Electronic Numerical Integrator And Calculator,* the name of an early computer built out of vacuum tubes in the '40s. (See also *ABC* and *vacuum tube.*)

Sentence: "In the computer museum, we saw a model of the *ENIAC* that took up a whole room and did as much useful work as a good pocket calculator of today."

Enter key

Pronunciation: *En-ter kee.*

Meaning: Sometimes called the *Return key,* the Enter key tells the computer that you're finished typing commands. In a word processor, pressing the Enter key creates a new line. In some programs, the Enter key doesn't do anything at all. (See also *CR/LF, Return key,* and *newline character.*)

Sentence: "To see which version of MS-DOS your computer uses, type **VER** at the DOS prompt and press the *Enter key.*"

EOF

(See *End-Of-File.*)

EOL

Pronunciation: *Ee O Ell.*

Meaning: Abbreviation for *End-Of-Line,* as in the end of a line of text on the screen. Word processors usually provide a keystroke combination that you can use to quickly jump to the end of the line. (See also *End-Of-File.*)

Sentence: "Okay, buddy. It's the *EOL* for you." (Quote overheard between two computer nerds, fighting for control of the only working computer left in the office.)

EPROM

Pronunciation: *Ee-Prom.*

Meaning: Acronym for *Erasable Programmable Read-Only Memory.* A type of chip that can be erased by ultraviolet lights and the continuing depletion of the ozone layer. (See also *EEPROM* and *PROM.*)

Sentence: "If you look in your computer, some chips have metal foil covering the top of the chip. If you take this foil off and hit it with ultraviolet light, the chip will lose all its contents. That means it has *EPROM.*"

EPS

Pronunciation: *Ee Pee Ess.*

Meaning: Acronym for *Encapsulated PostScript,* which is a graphic image stored using instructions written in the PostScript page description language. EPS graphic files contain special effects along with high-resolution images. Most expensive desktop publishing and illustration programs can use EPS files. Unfortunately, most people can't afford these expensive programs and wind up storing files in other formats instead. (See also *PostScript.*)

Sentence: "I stored all my graphics as *EPS* files. If I wanted to print them, I'd need a PostScript laser printer or a typesetting machine."

erase

Pronunciation: *ee-ray-sa.*

Meaning: To remove a file from a disk. To erase a file in MS-DOS, you can use the DEL command or the ERASE command.

Sentence: "Make sure you don't *erase* your files, unless you're sure you don't need them anymore or you need to destroy vital evidence from the courts."

ergonomics

Pronunciation: *er-go-nom-iks.*

Meaning: The science of designing equipment for maximum human comfort and minimal chances of lawsuits in the future. Some people get *carpal tunnel syndrome* or *RSI* (Repetitive Strain Injury) from improper positioning of their wrists when they type or from working at computers too long without breaks. Ergonomics involves the study of how to prevent these (and other) problems from poorly designed equipment in the workplace. So tell your boss you need a better chair and more breaks!

Sentence: "My whole computer desk uses *ergonomics* to hold the monitor at the optimum height and distance from my eyes. Because I liked it so much, I replaced my computer with a TV, and now I just vegetate in comfort at my desk."

error message

Pronunciation: *air-er mess-uj.*

Meaning: A cryptic note that the computer displays to let you know that the program isn't working right (or that you've made a big mistake). If you're lucky, the manual will tell you what on earth the message means, and if you're really lucky, the computer won't beep rudely at you.

Sentence: "I tried to save a file, but I got an *error message* that told me I had to put a floppy disk in the drive first. I think I've seen every error message this computer can display."

Esc

Pronunciation: *Es-kape.*

Meaning: Abbreviation for the ESCape key. Almost every keyboard has a key off to one side labeled *Esc.* Pressing this key usually cancels whatever command you last gave the computer.

Sentence: "If you change your mind about deleting a file, just press *Esc* to cancel the command. I wonder whether the Air Force has an Esc key for launching nuclear missiles?"

ESDI

Pronunciation: *Ee Ess Dee I.*

Meaning: Acronym for *Enhanced Small Device Interface,* which is an interface standard for hard disks. (See also *IDE.*)

Sentence: "If you buy an *ESDI* hard disk, you must have an ESDI controller card to make it work. If this sounds confusing, get someone else to install it so that you won't have to take the blame."

Ethernet

Pronunciation: *Ee-ther-net.*

Meaning: A local area network standard that uses radio frequency signals carried by coaxial cables. Developed primarily by Xerox. (See also *LAN.*)

Sentence: "Our computers are connected through an *Ethernet.* That doesn't mean we know what we're doing, but at least we have the lingo down pat."

event-driven programming

Pronunciation: *ee-ven-ta-driv-en pro-gram-ing.*

Meaning: A style of writing programs that waits for the user to press a key or a mouse button before doing anything else. When the user presses a key or mouse, it's called an *event.*

Sentence: "Before *event-driven programming,* programs forced the user to do whatever the program wanted to do next. With event-driven programming, the program waits for the user to tell it what to do first. At least event-driven programming gives people the illusion that they're in control."

exclusive OR

Pronunciation: *ex-kloo-sive OR,* sometimes *Zor.*

Meaning: Often abbreviated as *XOR,* this is a term commonly used by programmers for displaying graphics. XOR is a dreaded *logical* operation, taking two binary numbers and calculating a new result. The result is always zero if the values are the same, 1 if they're different. Isn't this amazingly relevant information to know when you're trying to save a file using WordPerfect?

Sentence: "No, I'm sorry, sir; you're just a regular OR, and this club is for the *exclusive OR* only."

EXE

Pronunciation: *Ee Ex Ee.*

Meaning: Abbreviation for EXEcutable file. This three-letter file extension is found on programs for MS-DOS and OS/2. An .EXE file identifies an actual program that does something useful, such as run WordPerfect or Lotus 1-2-3. If you type the name of the .EXE file and press Enter, it runs. You don't need to type the extension (.EXE) for the program to work. (See also *BIN, COM, DOC,* and *extension.*)

Sentence: "If you're deleting files off the hard disk, don't erase any *.EXE* files unless you're sure you don't need them. Then again, do what you want — it's not my computer anyway."

Exit

Pronunciation: *Ecks-it.*

Meaning: An option that lets the user stop the program. This is the civilized way to end a program; it makes it quietly go away until the next time you need it. Contrast with *Ctrl-Alt-Del.* (See also *Quit.*)

Sentence: "To quit some programs, you have to choose the *Exit* command. To exit some programs, you have to choose the Quit command. Aren't computers wonderful?"

expand

Pronunciation: *ex-pan-da.*

Meaning: To decompress previously compressed files so that the computer can use them. On IBM computers, most files are compressed using the PKZIP program. On Macintosh computers, most files are compressed using the StuffIt program. (See also *explode, data compression, compression,* and *ZIP.*)

Sentence: "After copying (or downloading) a file through a modem, you'll probably have to *expand* it before it will run."

expanded memory

Pronunciation: *ex-pan-ded mem-or-ree.*

Meaning: Memory used by DOS computers, kind of like bonus memory beyond 640K. Sometimes called EMS or LIM-EMS. Expanded memory is not memory "above" the 1MB mark on a PC. It's more like "beside" it because data is swapped quickly into and out of a small region of memory in the computer. It's extra memory that some DOS programs can use only if they are designed to take advantage of it. (See also *EMS, XMS,* and *extended memory.*)

Sentence: "Lotus helped develop *expanded memory* so that people could load large 1-2-3 spreadsheets into memory. Then when the 80286 processors came out, everyone ignored this standard and went with extended memory instead."

expansion bus

Pronunciation: *ex-pan-shin bus.*

Meaning: The part of the computer's bus that enables you to plug in boards to give your computer more features. Nearly every computer sold these days has an expansion bus. In the old days, computers without an expansion bus could not be upgraded at a future date. (See also *bus, expansion slot,* and *expansion card.*)

Sentence: "Plug these boards into the computer's *expansion bus* and then tell me how to use this thing."

expansion card

Pronunciation: *ex-pan-shin kard.*

Meaning: A circuit board that is specifically designed to plug into a computer's expansion bus. Expansion cards usually give a computer more memory, an internal modem, or the capability to use a CD-ROM drive. (See also *expansion bus* and *expansion slot.*)

Sentence: "By the time I bought all these *expansion cards* to plug into my old computer, I spent more money than I would have spent on a new computer."

expansion slot

Pronunciation: *ex-pan-shin slot.*

Meaning: The physical opening in a computer's expansion bus that the expansion cards plug into.

Sentence: "Make sure your computer has enough *expansion slots* so that you can upgrade your computer at a future date. Of course, by the time you want to upgrade, it will probably be cheaper to buy a brand new computer instead."

expert system

Pronunciation: *ex-pert siss-dum.*

Meaning: A program that mimics the intelligence of a human expert in a specific field of knowledge, such as mining or medicine. The system includes a knowledge base of information that has been gathered from an expert, along with a set of rules for processing the information. Expert systems ask users questions and reach conclusions that are hopefully similar in quality to those that a human expert may reach. (See also *artificial intelligence.*)

Sentence: "Hey, honey, why don't we let the *expert system* choose our wine for dinner tonight?"

explode

Pronunciation: *ex-plo-wda.*

Meaning: Another term for decompressing previously compressed files. Rather than tell you they are expanding a file, some programs tell you that they're exploding them. (See also *expand, data compression, compression,* and *ZIP.*)

Sentence: "In the old days, I had to expand compressed files before I could use them. Today, I have to *explode* them. Maybe tomorrow, I'll have to blow them up."

exponential notation

(See *E-notation.*)

extended ASCII

Pronunciation: *ex-ten-ded As-kee.*

Meaning: A set of 255 characters that includes the normal 128 ASCII character codes plus foreign language, mathematical, and block graphic characters. Another improvement of a "standard" that defeats the meaning of having standards in the first place.

Sentence: "To print an *extended ASCII* character, hold down the Alt key and type the extended ASCII code number. For example, typing Alt-243 produces ."

extended memory

Pronunciation: *ex-ten-ded mem-or-ree.*

Meaning: Memory used by 80286, '386, '486, and Pentium processors (and better) that goes beyond 1MB. It's memory that is used by high-power programs in DOS or by operating systems such as Windows, OS/2, or UNIX. (See also *EMS, expanded memory,* and *XMS.*)

Sentence: "My PC has 16MB of *extended memory,* just enough to run Windows."

extended memory specification

Pronunciation: *ex-ten-ded mem-or-ree spes-if-i-ka-shin.*

Meaning: Sometimes abbreviated as *XMS,* this is a set of rules for programs to access extended memory. Before using extended memory, you must have the HIMEM.SYS device driver or something similar in your computer's CONFIG.SYS file. This specification was developed by Lotus Development, Intel Corporation, Microsoft Corporation, and AST.

Sentence: "I bought a special memory-management program that follows the *extended memory specification.* Not only can I use memory beyond 1MB in my computer, but now I understand all these cool acronyms like XMS."

extension

Pronunciation: *ex-ten-shin.*

Meaning: An optional three-letter addition to a file name. In MS-DOS and other operating systems, the extension often identifies the file type and appears after the file name, separated by a period. A Pascal file usually has the .PAS file extension, a BASIC file has the .BAS file extension, and backup files have the .BAK file extension. (See also *EXE, COM, BIN,* and *DOC.*)

Sentence: "If you look at the file extensions, you'll notice that this guy writes a lot of batch files because every file ends with the .BAT *extension.*"

facing pages

Pronunciation: *fay-seen pay-juz.*

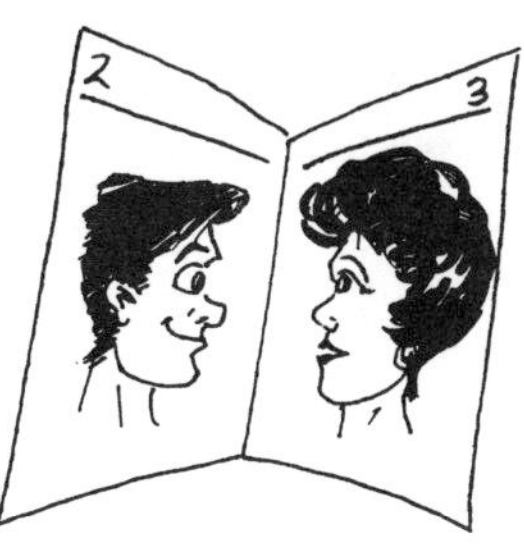

Meaning: Two pages of a bound document that face each other when the document is open. Usually the even-numbered page appears on the left; the odd-numbered page appears on the right. Most desktop publishing and word processing programs have a Facing Pages option that lets you see how two pages look side by side.

Sentence: "Many cookbooks show the recipe on one side and a picture of what you're supposed to be cooking on the other side. These *facing pages* show you that some of the best fiction writers today are writing cookbooks."

factorial

Pronunciation: *fak-tor-ee-al.*

Meaning: Take all the numbers from *1* to a specific number and multiply them together. This will give you the factorial for that specific number. So the factorial of 4 is 4 x 3 x 2 x 1 = 24. The factorial of a number is abbreviated with the exclamation point, such as 4!

Sentence: "The *factorial* of 4 is 24. The factorial of 3 is 6. Isn't this the most useful bit of information you've read in this book so far?"

fail

Pronunciation: *fay-ell.*

Meaning: When something no longer works the way it's supposed to. (See also *Abort, Retry, Fail, Ignore?*)

Sentence: "If you forget to make a second copy of your files, the computer will *fail* and you'll lose everything. That's Murphy's Law."

fail safe

Pronunciation: *fay-ell say-fa.*

Meaning: When something is so well designed that it's impossible for anything to go wrong, go wrong, go wrong....

Sentence: "Our computer is absolutely *fail safe.* But that's only because we never bother using it for anything important."

failure

Pronunciation: *fay-ell-ure.*

Meaning: When something goes wrong, usually something labeled as fail safe. (See *fail* and *fail safe.*)

Sentence: "We had a hard disk *failure* that wiped out all the company's data. Is it too late to find another job?"

fanfold paper

Pronunciation: *fan-fold pay-per.*

Meaning: Paper connected together with perforations and folded neatly in a stack, usually designed for tractor-feed printers. Also called *continuous paper.*

Sentence: "*Fanfold paper* looks a lot like toilet paper but with holes along the sides as well."

FAT

Pronunciation: *Fat.*

Meaning: A DOS acronym for File Allocation Table, which is a special part of every disk that stores sizes and locations for all the files saved on the disk.

Sentence: "Every time you erase a file, the computer modifies the FAT. If the *FAT* gets changed by accident, the computer won't be able to find your files even though they still exist."

fatal error

Pronunciation: *fay-tell air-er.*

Meaning: A problem that causes the program or computer to halt or crash completely. (See *crash.*)

Sentence: "We had a *fatal error* the other day, and the whole computer system shut down. I didn't mind because then I got to take the rest of the day off."

FatBits

Pronunciation: *Fat-Bits.*

Meaning: Individual pixels greatly magnified on the screen. Most paint programs (including MacPaint) enable you to zoom in on a picture so that you can edit individual pixels, called FatBits because they look so huge. (See also *pixel.*)

Sentence: "It can be tedious editing the *FatBits* of a picture, but if you have the patience, you can make that picture of your sister look as if she has three eyes and fangs sticking out of her mouth."

fax

Pronunciation: *fax,* rhymes with *axe.*

Meaning: Acronym for FAcsimile (but nobody tells you where the X comes from). A fax machine can send and receive text or images through the phone lines. You can even get a combination fax/modem board to stick in your computer. (See *modem.*)

Sentence: "I have a fax machine, call forwarding, call waiting, a beeper, a cellular phone, and an answering machine. And then I spend an extra $100 a year so that I can have an unlisted phone number."

FCC

Pronunciation: *Eff See See.*

Meaning: Acronym for Federal Communications Commission. This is a government agency that regulates all equipment (including computers) that produces radio-frequency signals. (See *Class A/Class B.*)

Sentence: "My computer has an *FCC* Class B rating, which means it shouldn't interfere with radio signals. Then again, the radio stations I listen to are probably worth jamming anyway."

featuritis

Pronunciation: *fee-chur-reye-tis.*

Meaning: The steady increase of program features that 90 percent of the people in the world will never use. Software companies often get carried away and brag about features that their programs offer that no other programs have. Naturally, these same companies never stop to question if anyone really needs these features that they're advertising.

Sentence: "I stopped buying WordPerfect, Microsoft Word, and Lotus 1-2-3 because they had creeping *featuritis.* Now I'm back to using a pad of paper, a pencil, and an adding machine."

feed

Pronunciation: *fee-da.*

Meaning: To guide something into something else, usually shoving paper into a printer. Printers often offer features such as tractor-feed, which are tiny spokes that poke through the holes along the side of computer paper, keeping the page perfectly aligned.

Sentence: "*Feed* the paper into the printer. Just make sure you don't feed your tie into the printer at the same time."

female connector

Pronunciation: *fee-may-ell kon-nek-tor.*

Meaning: A type of plug that consists of one or more holes that a corresponding male connector plugs in to. (See also *male connector.*)

Sentence: "When you buy a cable, look at the connector on your computer. If it's a male connector with pins sticking out, then you'll need a *female connector* to plug into it. Who'd have thought you could risk censorship while talking about electrical plugs?"

ferric oxide

Pronunciation: *fair-rik ox-ide.*

Meaning: The magnetic coating that gives hard disks, floppy disks, and tape cassettes their recording capabilities. (See also *floppy disk.*)

Sentence: "If you touch the surface of a floppy disk, you may rub the *ferric oxide* off. Then the disk is ruined and your fingertips are brown."

fiber optics

Pronunciation: *fi-ber op-tix.*

Meaning: Thin strands of glass used to carry light signals for communication purposes. A tiny strand of fiber optic cable can replace huge copper cables. Not only do fiber optics take up less space, but they can carry more information as well. Fiber optics are very popular for modern LANs because they are less susceptible to radioactivity and other types of interference. Fiber optics also has the potential for providing various types of interactive, information services. (See also *cable* and *LAN.*)

Sentence: "The phone company wants to replace their copper cables with *fiber optics.* That way they can send more data faster and justify charging us more to make a phone call."

Fibonacci numbers

Pronunciation: *Fib-o-na-chi num-bers.*

Meaning: Some sort of mathematical pattern where the third number is the sum of the previous two numbers: 4, 8, 12, 20, 32, and so on. These are used in some computer programs to speed up sorting and to quickly locate information. They may also help you win the lottery.

Sentence: "It took Lois forever to find her car keys, but then Ralph suggested she use *Fibonacci numbers.* Now we can't find Ralph."

field

Pronunciation: *fee-eld.*

Meaning: Space reserved for storing specific information in a database program. Fields may contain a person's name, address, phone number, age, Social Security number, sex, ZIP code or anything else you want, as long as all the items in a given field have a similar structure. A group of related fields make up a database record. (See also *database* and *record.*)

Sentence: "Type your name in the Name *field* and your age in the Age field. If you mix up the information, the database won't be accurate. Then again, that's a cool way to screw up somebody else's computer."

FIFO

Pronunciation: *Fi-fo.*

Meaning: Acronym for First In, First Out. A term used by programmers to describe a data structure called a *queue* where the first item stored is also the first item retrieved. Unless you plan to write your own programs, you can safely ignore this term. (See *LIFO, queue,* and *stack.*)

Sentence: "Lines at movie theaters or stadiums all use *FIFO.* The first person in line is the first person to get in. Unless, of course, everyone charges forward."

fifth-generation computers

Pronunciation: *fifth-jen-er-ra-shin kom-pu-ters.*

Meaning: A new generation of AI-based computers that manipulate data more efficiently (with massively parallel processing) and understand written and spoken human language. In 1981, the Japanese announced they wanted to be the world leaders in building fifth-generation computers. Ten years later, the only major Japanese contribution to computers has been Nintendo. (See *AI* and *artificial intelligence.*)

Sentence: "*Fifth-generation computers* will be so advanced that today's machines will look like Model Ts in comparison. Then again, a vintage Model T is worth a lot more than a brand new Ford Mustang of today."

file

Pronunciation: *fi-ell.*

Meaning: Information stored on magnetic media such as a floppy or hard disk. Files can be programs, data, or graphics. Text files consist solely of ASCII characters. Binary files consist of data stored in a proprietary manner, such as Lotus 1-2-3 .WK3 files or dBASE IV .DBF files. (See also *data.*)

Sentence: "If you erase all your *files,* you won't be able to use your computer any more."

file attribute

Pronunciation: *fi-ell at-tri-bute.*

Meaning: Information that defines the characteristics of a file. Some characteristics of a file may be hidden, read-only, locked, or archive. Changing a file's attributes does not affect the file's contents but does affect the computer's ability to modify or view the file. (See also *file.*)

Sentence: "I changed the *file attributes* on all of Bill's WordPerfect files to hidden and read-only. Not only couldn't he see them in his directory, but then he couldn't edit them either. I never knew computers could be such fertile ground for practical jokes."

file compression

Pronunciation: *fi-ell kom-press-shin.*

Meaning: To smash (or squish) a file into something smaller so that it takes up less disk space (or less time to transmit).

Sentence: "*File compression* comes in handy if you're running out of disk space or if you're just too lame to erase files you haven't needed since 1981."

file control block

Pronunciation: *fi-ell kon-troll blok.*

Meaning: Often abbreviated as FCB. It's a bunch of compu-cryptic information about a file — stuff only the programmer or DOS needs to know about.

Sentence: "I floored them at the cocktail party when I asked the rhetorical question, 'Then give me a proper reason why the *FCB* shouldn't be located at offset 1A-hex in the PSP header?'"

file conversion

Pronunciation: *fi-ell kon-ver-shin.*

Meaning: To translate one file format (that is, file structure) into another one. (See also *import.*)

Sentence: "I use WordStar, but Frank uses WordPerfect. So my documents are useless to Frank until I use a *file conversion* program that translates all my WordStar files into WordPerfect files."

file handle

Pronunciation: *fi-ell han-dell.*

Meaning: A shortcut code number used to access a file, primarily internal secret stuff known only to DOS and various programmer-types. When we — us, humans — open a file, we give it a name. In the computer, that name is translated into a number, which DOS uses to access the file. The number is called the *file handle.* (See also *handles.*)

Sentence: "No wonder you keep losing your files! The *file handle* is broken!"

file list box

Pronunciation: *fi-ell list box.*

Meaning: A box that lists all the files of a given directory. File list boxes are usually found in dialog boxes such as the ones in Windows. (See also *dialog box.*)

Sentence: "Whenever I choose the Save As command, a dialog box pops up and displays a *file list box.* By looking at this list, I can see the names of files already in use."

file server

Pronunciation: *fi-ell serv-er.*

Meaning: A network computer that stores all of the users' programs and data files on its own hard disk. Most large networks have at least one file server. File servers are particularly useful for acting as post offices for electronic mail messages or other applications where users need to share files or send them back and forth. Because the file server spends its time running the network, nobody can use the file server computer to do anything else. (See also *electronic mail* and *network.*)

Sentence: "We connected all our computers to a network, but we had to buy a really fast computer to use for the *file server.* Our network runs great, but all our computers connected to it run like turtles stricken with arthritis."

file sharing

Pronunciation: *fi-ell shar-ing.*

Meaning: When two or more computers have access to the same hard drive, such as when you run a network. This works like it did in kindergarten, when there were only so many toys available and everyone had to share. Only one person may make changes to a file at a time. Without file sharing, many people could modify the same file at once with potentially disastrous results.

Sentence: "My name is Billy Cartwright and this is my file, OOBADOOB.DBF. Please, everyone pass it around and take a look at it, but only one of you may make modifications at a time, in accordance with the rules of good *file sharing.*"

file size

Pronunciation: *fi-ell size.*

Meaning: The amount of disk space that a file requires for its existence, usually measured in bytes.

Sentence: "You can't copy that file onto that disk because the *file size* is 451,092 bytes and the disk only has 46,782 bytes free."

fill

Pronunciation: *fill* (rhymes with *hill, pill,* and *kill*).

Meaning: A command used by paint and draw programs that mimics spilling a bucket of paint inside a closed shape such as a circle or rectangle. If you want to create a black circle, you would first draw an empty circle and then use the Fill command to fill the circle with black. Also, in a spreadsheet, you use the Fill command to repeat values in a predefined cell area.

Sentence: "Plain black and white is boring. That's why I always draw blocks and *fill* them with neat colors and patterns."

filter

Pronunciation: *fil-ter.*

Meaning: An operating system command that processes data before passing it on to something else. MS-DOS filters include MORE, FIND, and SORT. MORE scrolls long output screen by screen, FIND searches for text, and SORT sorts ASCII files. Unless you're a die-hard operating system nut, you'll probably never need to know about this type of filter. In databases, another type of filter is used to select data (that is, to allow only data that matches certain conditions to pass on to the next step).

Sentence: "Some word processors have built-in file conversion programs called *filters.* These filters translate a file into another format before giving the file to the word processor."

Finder

Pronunciation: *Find-her.*

Meaning: The part of the Apple Macintosh operating system that provides cute little icons, menus, and windows for copying, moving, and deleting files. Most Macintosh programs require a certain version of the Finder, such as Version 6.02 or Version 7.01, before they will work.

Sentence: "If it wasn't for the *Finder,* the Macintosh would be as clumsy to use as MS-DOS. In fact, Microsoft Windows mimics the Finder, which is why IBM-compatible computers are finally getting easier to use."

firmware

Pronunciation: *firm-ware.*

Meaning: Software embedded into a chip as opposed to being stored on disk and loaded into memory.

Sentence: "Every computer has *firmware* that tells the computer how to start itself up. Too bad every person doesn't have firmware to tell him or her how to use a computer."

fixed disk

Pronunciation: *fixed disk,* just like it looks.

Meaning: Another name for a hard disk. You can't remove the disk from the computer, hence the name *fixed.*

Sentence: "This computer has 4MB of RAM and a 60MB *fixed disk.* That doesn't mean the disk works, but that if it does, it can hold up to 60MB of data."

fixed pitch

Pronunciation: *fi-xed pit-cha.*

Meaning: Type with all letters the same width — also called *monospaced.* Computer screens, typewriters, and cheap dot-matrix printers display type using fixed pitch. In comparison, fancier printers use proportional pitch, in which letters such as *i, l,* and *t* have different widths than letters such as *c, q,* and *m.*

Sentence: "If you're really fussy about how your printing looks, insist on proportional pitch (or *spacing*). But if it's not that important, then *fixed pitch* will do."

fixed-point number

Pronunciation: *fi-xed-poin-ta num-ber.*

Meaning: A number where the decimal point displays a specific or fixed number of digits to the right. In comparison, floating-point numbers display any amount of digits to the right of the decimal point that's needed.

Sentence: "Currency values are usually represented by a *fixed-point number* where only two digits appear to the right of the decimal point. But if you're weighing gold where fractions of an ounce are critical, you would want to use a floating-point number. Unless, of course, you wanted to round off values and short-change someone."

flag

Pronunciation: *fla-ga.*

Meaning: A term used by programmers for a status indicator within in a program (or hardware). Most flags use Boolean true or false values. For example, a flag may be used to keep track of whether or not a certain input has been received from a user, and if it has been received, to output an error message.

Sentence: "In your program, set to true a *flag* that assumes your program won't work. After you've made sure it actually will work, set the flag to false."

flame

Pronunciation: *flay-ma.*

Meaning: An angry, often nasty, brutal, and unsportsmanlike letter found only on electronic mail messages.

Sentence: "No matter what you do, someone will criticize you for it. Today I checked my e-mail and got a lot of *flames* for not living up to my campaign promises. Hey, now that I've been elected, what do they expect?"

flame wars

Pronunciation: *flay-ma wars.*

Meaning: A series of angry electronic mail messages, usually between two people who sincerely hope the other person gets run over by a train as soon as possible. (See also *flame.*)

Sentence: "The first time I got a flame, I ignored it. But the guy pestered me so much that I got into a *flame war* with him. Trust me, it's worse than paint ball."

flat-file database

Pronunciation: *flat-fi-ell day-ta-bay-sa.*

Meaning: A program for storing and retrieving information that someone thinks is important. Flat-file databases can use only one file at a time and usually cannot be programmed. In comparison, a relational database can use two or more files at the same time and can be programmed by people who think they know what they're doing. (See also *relational database.*)

Sentence: "I just need to store names and addresses, so I use a *flat-file database* instead of a relational one. Not only is it easier to use a flat-file database, but it's cheaper to buy."

flatbed scanner

Pronunciation: *flat-bed scan-er.*

Meaning: A device that lets you lay full-size (8.5" x 11") paper face-down on its surface to be electronically "read." Flatbed scanners look like photocopying machines and usually don't work as well as the manufacturer's claims lead you to believe.

Sentence: "I don't like typing stuff that's already printed, so I bought a *flatbed scanner.* This way I can just lay the page on top and have the computer scan in the words automatically."

floppy disk

Pronunciation: *flo-pee disk.*

Meaning: A magnetically coated disk you use to store information for a computer. Floppy disks come in two sizes: 5¼-inch and 3½-inch. Floppy disks also come in two formats: double-density (DD) and high-density (HD).

The following chart shows how much information each type of floppy disk can hold.

	5¼-inch	**3½-inch**
Double-density	360K	720K
High-density	1.2MB	1.44MB
Extended-density	—	2.88MB

Sentence: "My older IBM computer can use both 5¼-inch and 3½-inch *floppy disks,* but my laptop uses only 3½-inch floppy disks. That means I can store the same information on two different disks and double my chances of losing everything altogether."

flowchart

Pronunciation: *flo-char-ta.*

Meaning: A diagram consisting of lines and boxes that programmers use to represent the way their programs are supposed to work. Programmers who spend their time creating flowcharts have an unusually high propensity for writing fiction, telling fairy tales, and working as double agents for the CIA.

Sentence: "Before you start writing your program, decide how it's going to work by drawing a *flowchart* first. Then as you write your program, you can modify your flowchart so that it matches the way your program really does work."

flush

Pronunciation: *fluh-sha.*

Meaning: (1) To empty out the contents of a data structure or buffer. (2) To align text either flush left or flush right.

This is an example of flush left.	This is an example of flush right.

(See also *justify.*)

Sentence: "Load a program and then start banging on all the keys on the keyboard. If all these keystrokes don't bother the program, then the program *flushes* out the keyboard buffer before it's ready to start."

folder

Pronunciation: *fol-der.*

Meaning: Another name for a subdirectory; used on Macintosh computers.

Sentence: "On my Macintosh, *folders* appear as little paper folder icons on the screen. To copy a file from one folder to another, I just drag it from one folder to another."

font

Pronunciation: *fawn-ta.*

Meaning: A collection of characters with predefined sizes and style. Most word processors and desktop publishing programs let you choose different fonts to make your writing prettier. If you don't like the fonts you have, you can buy more.

Sentence: "When you have nothing important to say, put it in writing and use lots of fancy *fonts.* People will think it must be important if it looks good."

font cartridge

Pronunciation: *fawn-ta kar-trid-ja.*

Meaning: A device that plugs into a printer, giving it the ability to print a greater variety of fonts. (See also *font.*)

Sentence: "My laser printer can't print all the fonts I use in my word processor. That's why I had to plug a *font cartridge* into my laser printer. Now it can print all the fonts I use, until I decide to use some different ones again."

font family

Pronunciation: *fawn-ta fam-i-lee.*

Meaning: Much like the Partridge Family or the Swiss Family Robinson, a font family consists of a group of related fonts.

Sentence: "Use fonts from the same *font family* so your printing doesn't clash and look like something from outer space."

font size

Pronunciation: *fawn-ta si-za.*

Meaning: The height and width of specific fonts. Most fonts look smooth and attractive at fixed sizes such as 10-point or 24-point. If you display fonts at unusual sizes like 11-point or 23-point, they look jagged and frayed.

Sentence: "Make sure you use the appropriate *font sizes* for your fonts. Otherwise, your résume headings will look like a cheap dot-matrix printer printed them, even though they came out of an expensive laser printer."

Font/DA Mover

Pronunciation: *Fawn-ta/Dee A Moo-ver.*

Meaning: A utility program provided with Macintosh computers that enables users to add fonts and desk accessories to their computers.

Sentence: "I bought all these fonts, but my computer still didn't know how to use them. Then I used the *Font/DA Mover* and installed them so everything works fine. Aren't computers wonderful?"

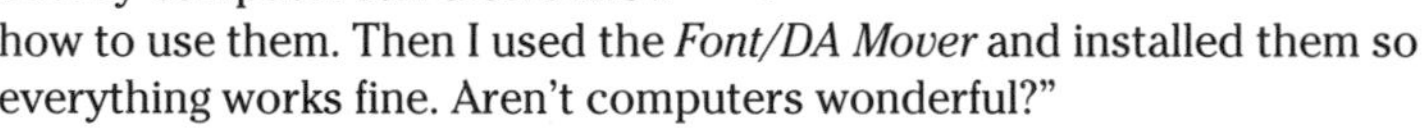

footer

Pronunciation: *fuh-ter.*

Meaning: A short title, word, or phrase that appears at the bottom of a page in word processors or desktop publishing programs.

Sentence: "Lots of people use *footers* for printing the page number on each sheet. I use footers to print the same rude message to people I don't like."

footprint

Pronunciation: *fut-print.*

Meaning: The physical size of an object, such as the footprint of a computer or printer. The smaller the footprint of an object, the less room it takes up on a desk.

Sentence: "My last computer had a *footprint* as large as Bigfoot because it took up my entire desk. My new computer has a much smaller footprint. In fact, I can't find where I put it."

foreground

Pronunciation: *for-grown-da.*

Meaning: When two or more windows appear on the screen, the active screen is considered to be in the foreground. Only one window may be in the foreground at one time, although any number of windows may be in the background at the same time. (See also *background.*)

Sentence: "With multitasking, I can run my word processor, spreadsheet, and database at the same time and move each one to the *foreground* when I need it. After I learn to use my computer, maybe all of this will even help me do something useful."

form feed

Pronunciation: *for-ma fee-da.*

Meaning: Sometimes abbreviated as FF, *form feed* means to advance the paper in a printer by one sheet. Most printers have a form feed button. To use this button, you have to take the printer off-line (by pressing the on-line button — makes sense) and then press the form feed button.

Sentence: "Sometimes, it's easier to press the *form feed* button so that you can tear your report out of the printer, and sometimes it's easier just to pull on the paper until the sheets come out."

format

Pronunciation: *for-mat.*

Meaning: To prepare a floppy or hard disk for storing information for a specific type of a computer. A floppy disk can be used by any type of computer. Formatting a disk on a Macintosh prepares that disk for storing Macintosh data. Formatting a disk on a DOS machine prepares that disk for storing IBM-compatible data.

Sentence: "If you want to erase a floppy disk quickly, you can just *format* it again."

FORMAT

Pronunciation: What? Didn't you see the pronunciation guide from the previous entry?

Meaning: An MS-DOS command for formatting a floppy or hard disk. The most common FORMAT commands are as follows:

Command	What it does
FORMAT A:	Formats a floppy disk in drive A.
FORMAT A: /S	Formats a floppy disk in drive A and makes it bootable.
FORMAT B: /F:360	Formats a 5¼-inch double-sided/double-density floppy disk in a high-density drive B:.
FORMAT B: /F:720	Formats a 3½-inch double-sided/double-density floppy disk in a high-density drive B:.

Sentence: "The *FORMAT* A: /F:720 command only works with MS-DOS version 4.0 and greater. But at least the FORMAT C: still formats your hard drive if you're not careful."

FORTH

Pronunciation: *For-th.*

Meaning: A unique programming language that enables programmers to define their own statements in terms of previously defined simpler statements. FORTH is not widely used, although the language has an almost cult-like following. You can often find FORTH programmers dancing in airports, chanting FORTH statements as mantras, and wearing chiffon bathrobes in their quest for truths from the computer.

Sentence: "*FORTH* programs can rival the best C++ programs in terms of speed and efficiency. Too bad hardly any schools teach FORTH in programming courses."

FORTRAN

Pronunciation: *For-tran.*

Meaning: An acronym for FORmula TRANslator, this was one of the first programming languages that enabled programmers to write mathematical formulas normally, such as X = (A * B) * 2. FORTRAN was one of the first high-level languages able to run on different types of computers with little or no modifications. Until FORTRAN appeared, programmers had to use assembly language.

Sentence: "When I was going to school, they made me learn *FORTRAN*. Now that I've graduated, everyone wants programmers who know C. Isn't higher education wonderful?"

fractals

Pronunciation: *frak-tellz.*

Meaning: A mathematically generated geometric shape that contains an infinite amount of detail. If you take a portion of the shape and magnify it, the same complex image begins to re-emerge. Fractals are commonly used to create computer-generated art or to draw objects such as mountains or clouds in flight simulator games. Closely associated with chaos theory, which is starting to show that there is more order in the universe than any of us expected.

Sentence: "Having your computer create *fractals* on the screen is like having a $3,000 lava lamp from the '60s sitting on your television. It's interesting at first, but after ten minutes most people are ready to look at something else."

fragmentation

Pronunciation: *frag-men-tay-shin.*

Meaning: A condition you find on hard disks that have been used for long periods of time. Every time you save a file to a hard disk, the computer stores the file as a continuous strip for fast and easy access. Eventually, as you erase, modify, and add new files, there won't be enough room to store every file as a continuous strip. Instead, the computer must break up individual files and store the separate parts in various places around the hard disk. This is called fragmentation. (See also *hard disk.*)

Sentence: "My hard disk runs so slowly that I think it's suffering from *fragmentation.* Fortunately MS-DOS version 6.0 has a special DEFRAG program that corrects any fragmentation on my hard disk. Too bad MS-DOS doesn't have a similar command to do the rest of my work for me, too."

frame

Pronunciation: *fray-ma.*

Meaning: A rectangular area used by word processors and desktop publishing programs for arranging text or graphics on a page.

Sentence: "My newsletter consists of two *frames.* One frame holds the newsletter headline, and the second frame holds the text. I'm thinking of adding a third frame to hold a picture of my dog's face."

freeware

Pronunciation: *free-wair.*

Meaning: Software that's copyrighted but allowed to be copied and given away freely without cost. In comparison, public domain software is not copyrighted and can be copied freely, and shareware is copyrighted and can be copied freely but must be paid for if used regularly. The most popular freeware program is LHarc, a file compression program written by a Japanese programmer named Haruyasu Yoshizaki. (See also *public domain* and *shareware.*)

Sentence: "I just paid $200 for WordPerfect, and now you're telling me I could have paid $50 for a shareware copy of a similar word processor? I wish someone would make a *freeware* word processor. That way I could use it and not pay a thing for it."

friction feed

Pronunciation: *frik-shin feed.*

Meaning: A method of moving paper by pressing rollers against the page and spinning them. Friction feed is the way typewriters (remember what those are?) advance paper a line at a time. Most inkjet and laser printers use friction feed.

Sentence: "Any printer that doesn't need paper with those silly little holes on the side probably uses *friction feed.*"

front end

Pronunciation: *front end.*

Meaning: A program or computer that hides the details of accessing data or another computer. In a sense, every program is a front end that prevents users from knowing the actual details of the computer's intricate workings. Most of the time, a front end simplifies using a computer more than most programs. One example of a front end processor is the kind used as a communications link to a mainframe.

Sentence: "To access my dBASE files, I avoid using a database program. Instead I use a *front end* that gets me the data I need without knowing any specific dBASE commands."

FUBAR

Pronunciation: *Foo-bar.*

Meaning: An acronym for what delicately could be called Fouled Up Beyond All Recognition or sometimes Fouled Up Beyond All Repair. It's actually an old military term but eventually wound its way into the early days of computing where it was used as a subtle expletive. A derivative term, FOO, is still popular with UNIX people.

Sentence: "Sad to say, your hard drive is completely *FUBAR.*"

FUD

Pronunciation: *Fud.*

Meaning: Acronym that stands for Fear, Uncertainty, and Dread. Propaganda created by one company in hopes of preventing people from buying a competing product.

Sentence: "I'm thinking about buying an IBM or a Macintosh, but there's so much *FUD* in the marketplace that I'll wait a little longer."

full duplex

Pronunciation: *full doo-plex.*

Meaning: The simultaneous transmission of data in both directions, used when communicating between two computers. Full duplex is sometimes called Echo On by some communications programs. (If you've ever read *A Wrinkle In Time,* you know that it's kind of like the way one of the characters talks.) (See also *duplex* and *half duplex.*)

Sentence: "Every time I used my modem and computer, I started seeing ddoouubbllee, like that. Then someone told me to turn off *full duplex,* and everything's working just fine."

full pathname

Pronunciation: *full path-nay-ma.*

Meaning: The name of a file plus the drive and directory where the file is located. Examples of a full pathname are C:\WINDOWS\SYSTEM\WIN.INI, D:\UTIL\ZIP\PKZIP.EXE, and A:\HELP\LOST\BYE.BAT. (See also *pathname.*)

Sentence: "When you want to save an existing file under a different name, type the *full pathname.* Otherwise, the computer will store the file in the current directory, which may or may not be where you want it to go."

full screen

Pronunciation: *full skreen.*

Meaning: The ability to type characters anywhere on the screen, provided you're using a computer, of course. A full-screen terminal displays information using the full screen (duh). A full-screen editor lets you type anywhere on the screen.

Sentence: "Using a line editor is like peeking out through venetian blinds. Using a *full-screen* editor is like looking out through the whole window."

full-height drive

Pronunciation: *full-hiyt drive.*

Meaning: A disk drive that's approximately 3¼ inches in height, or twice the height of a half-height drive. (What a concept!)

Sentence: "I yanked out one *full-height drive* from my computer and added two half-height drives: one for a 3½-inch floppy disk drive and the other for a hard disk."

function

Pronunciation: *funk-shin.*

Meaning: A computer language subprogram that performs some calculations and returns a single value to the main program. There are two types of subprograms: functions and procedures. In comparison, a procedure performs some calculations but can return zero or multiple values back to the main program.

Sentence: "I wrote a *function* in C++ called CUBE(x), which returns the cube of an integer such as x = CUBE(5)."

function keys

Pronunciation: *func-shin kees.*

Meaning: Special keys along the top or side of a keyboard that are specifically designed for giving commands to the computer. Most computer keyboards have 10 to 12 function keys, labeled F1 through F12. Function keys are shortcuts for pressing a variety of other keys such as Ctrl-S-D. Different programs use the function keys to perform different operations. That's why function key templates are so popular.

Sentence: "I like using *function keys* because it's easier than remembering which keystrokes or menus I need to choose for a specific command. Now I just have to remember what each function key does."

fuzzy logic

Pronunciation: *fuz-zee lo-jik.*

Meaning: The type of logic that avoids taking a stand, often used by expert systems, neural networks, and politicians running for higher office. Instead of using values such as True or False, fuzzy logic uses a range of values that includes True, False, Maybe, Sometimes, and I Forget. Fuzzy logic is often used when answers don't have a distinct true or false value or when programmers don't even know what they're doing.

Sentence: "Artificial intelligence and neural networks seek to make computers mimic the thought processes of human beings. Because people rarely see the world in terms of black and white, computers have to use *fuzzy logic* instead."

Fuzzy Wuzzy

Pronunciation: *Fuz-zee Wuz-zee.*

Meaning: The lightheaded feeling you get if you stare at your computer screen too long.

Sentence: "*Fuzzy Wuzzy* was a bear. Fuzzy Wuzzy had no hair. Fuzzy Wuzzy wasn't fuzzy, was he?"

Note: Now remember when you look at the picture, he's not supposed to be fuzzy 'cause he has no hair. . . .

gallium arsenide

Pronunciation: *gall-ee-um ar-suh-nyde*

Meaning: An alloy used for chip manufacturing that's faster than silicon — not that anyone other than chip manufacturers would care. (See also *germanium, semiconductor,* and *silicon.*)

Sentence: "I sure am glad my computer uses *gallium arsenide* chips. Last month alone I saved 3.8 seconds in computing time."

game

Pronunciation: *gay-ma.*

Meaning: The only type of program that people really buy a computer for. Game programs fall into three categories: arcade, strategy, and board. Arcade games, such as PacMan, Mario Brothers, or Flight Simulator, emphasize hand-eye coordination. Strategy games are often wargames where players control entire armies and attempt to conquer Europe or some other piece of high-rent property. Board games are computer versions of games such as chess, checkers, Monopoly, Go, Backgammon, or Risk.

Sentence: "I tell everyone that I spent a fortune on a computer so that I can balance my budget and teach myself programming. But the real reason is so that I can play a $50 *game* at home."

game control adapter

Pronunciation: *gay-ma kon-troll ah-dap-ter.*

Meaning: A special adapter card (or *board*) with a port for plugging a joystick into your computer. (See also *joystick.*)

Sentence: "Because I use my $3,000 computer just for playing flight simulator games, I had to buy a $20 *game control adapter* so I could use my joystick with my game as well."

Gantt chart

Pronunciation: *Gan-ta chart.*

Meaning: A diagram, often used in project management software, that purports to show the tasks and deadlines necessary for completing a specific project, such as eliminating the national deficit, raising the Titanic, or sending humans to Mars. Some of the best fiction writers today got their start designing Gantt charts for the government.

Sentence: "The Department of Defense asked me to create a *Gantt chart* for building a laser-based orbiting weapons system. My Gantt chart shows just two tasks: cash the government's check by next week and then run away to Argentina so that I won't get caught."

garbage

Pronunciation: *gar-bage.*

Meaning: Useless or indecipherable information. Some computers create garbage; others merely accept it from people who don't know what they are doing. (See also *GIGO.*)

Sentence: "Every time I tried to use my modem, I got *garbage* on the screen. Then I realized I had to adjust my monitor."

gas plasma display

Pronunciation: *gas plah-sma dis-play.*

Meaning: A special screen, designed for laptops, that glows orange and looks radioactive. Gas plasma screens use high voltage to ionize gas, a procedure that causes the screen's bright orange appearance. Few laptop computers use gas plasma displays because they are more expensive, consume a great deal of power, and won't display color. (See also *monitor.*)

Sentence: "My old 386 laptop had a *gas plasma display* that looked really nice if you liked looking at differing shades of orange."

gateway

Pronunciation: *gay-ta-way.*

Meaning: The connecting computer link that translates between two different kinds of computer networks. (See also *network.*)

Sentence: "To separate two networks, just turn off the computer that is acting as the *gateway.*"

GB

Pronunciation: *Gig-uh-Bite.*

Meaning: Abbreviation for gigabyte, which is approximately one billion bytes. (See also *gigabyte, hard disk, megabyte,* and *memory.*)

Sentence: "My 120MB hard disk is too small. I think I need a 5*GB* hard disk instead. That way I can save more useless files on my computer that I still won't know how to use."

geek

Pronunciation: *geek* (like it looks).

Meaning: A highly knowledgeable but obnoxious person who knows more about computers than about his or her own mother.

Sentence: "I'd ask Joe for help, but he's such a *geek.* I'd rather just suffer and read the MS-DOS manual instead."

geekus maximus

Pronunciation: *geek-us max-i-muss.*

Meaning: A highly knowledgeable but really obnoxious person who knows a lot about computers but who repels everyone with his or her personality or lack thereof.

Sentence: "Tom is a *geekus maximus.* The company can't get along without him, but nobody wants to talk to him, let alone work with him."

gender bender

Pronunciation: *jen-der ben-der.*

Meaning: A special plug, also called a *gender changer,* that turns a female connecting cable into a male connecting cable, and vice versa.

Sentence: "The salesman sold me the wrong cable. Instead of buying the right cable, I just bought a *gender bender* and now everything works fine."

GEnie

Pronunciation: *Jee-nee.*

Meaning: GEnie stands for the General Electric Network for Information Exchange, an on-line service that provides programs for copying, games for playing, and message conferences (called RoundTables) for chatting with other people about specific topics. GEnie is less expensive, but also more limited in scope, than the main on-line service called CompuServe. (See also *CompuServe, Internet,* and *Network.*)

Sentence: "It's too expensive to subscribe to CompuServe, so I use *GEnie* instead."

geranium

Pronunciation: *jer-ain-ee-um.*

Meaning: A pretty little flower with a name that looks like germanium, which is a material used to make semiconductors.

Sentence: "I blew my post-graduate thesis about semiconductors when I tried using *geraniums* to conduct electricity. Boy, do I feel stupid, but at least my workshop smells and looks good."

germanium

Pronunciation: *jer-mane-ee-um.*

Meaning: The second most popular material for making semiconductors, after silicon.

Sentence: "Some of my computer's semiconductors use *germanium* instead of silicon. Who cares, just as long as the stupid thing works?"

GIF

Pronunciation: *Jiff* (some people say Giff; rhymes with Biff).

Meaning: Acronym for Graphics Interchange Format. A special file format developed by CompuServe to store graphics that all computers can use.

Sentence: "A lot of pictures are stored in *GIF* format so that someone with an IBM, Macintosh, or Amiga can all look at the pictures."

gigabyte

Pronunciation: *gig-uh-bite.*

Meaning: About one billion bytes, often abbreviated as GB.

Sentence: "A hard disk with one *gigabyte* doesn't impress me. A hard disk with 100 gigabytes does."

GIGO

Pronunciation: *Gi-Go.*

Meaning: Acronym for Garbage In, Garbage Out. Used to explain to novices that if you put worthless information into the computer, the computer can only spit worthless information back out. In other words, the computer can't magically create wonderful new information on its own. (See also *garbage.*)

Sentence: "I can't get this computer to do anything useful. Then again, maybe I should turn it on first. I guess this is just another example of *GIGO* in action."

glitch

Pronunciation: *gli-tcha.*

Meaning: A problem (sometimes temporary) that causes a program to work erratically or not at all. Glitches can also be called bugs. Bugs can also be called insects. Insects can also be called squishy little things that squirt out yellow guts if you step on them.

Sentence: "Watch out. You may see some *glitches* every time you use any type of disk-compression program."

googleplex

Pronunciation: *goo-gull-plex.*

Meaning: A number so large that it can make your head dizzy just thinking about it. (See also *Avogadro's Number.*)

Sentence: "That new color laptop Macintosh costs a *googleplex.* It better not use geranium semiconductors."

GOTO

Pronunciation: *Go-Too.*

Meaning: A command used in many programming languages and batch files that tells the computer to "go to" another part of the program and run the instructions over there. Most programmers look down upon the GOTO command because it tends to create spaghetti code, which is a program where the structure is all but lost.

Sentence: "Early BASIC programs tended to use the *GOTO* command so much that you couldn't understand how the program worked, even if you had a Ph.D. from MIT. That either teaches you not to use the GOTO command or not to get a Ph.D. from MIT in computer science."

graceful exit

Pronunciation: *gray-sful eck-sit.*

Meaning: When a program stops running but doesn't freeze up your computer, crash your hard drive, or do anything else that prevents you from using your computer immediately afterwards. All programs should offer a graceful exit. (See also *crash* and *lock.*)

Sentence: "When you choose the Exit command from a program and it actually works, that's a *graceful exit.* When you choose the Exit command and your computer blows up in your face, that's a bug or a glitch."

grammar checker

Pronunciation: *gram-er che-ker.*

Meaning: A special program or built-in feature that examines a text document for grammatical errors and offers possible corrections. Most grammar checkers correct misspellings, incorrect grammar usage, and potentially confusing or obscure sentence structure. On the other hand, most grammar checkers offer to correct perfectly good sentences, don't work 100 percent accurately, and lead you to doubt that you can even write in English. Most word processors come with grammar checkers built in, although you also can buy grammar checkers separately.

Sentence: "After writing my report with a word processor, I use a spelling checker to check my spelling. Then I use a *grammar checker* to tell me whether my writing is as strong as it could be. Finally, I rewrite and edit my original document based on the grammar checker's report. By this time I'm usually past my deadline and fired from my job for being too slow."

WHAT DO YOU MEAN, IT'S IN PASSIVE VOICE?

graphic layout

Pronunciation: *gra-fik lay-out.*

Meaning: Designing text and graphics on a page for maximum aesthetic appeal, if you have nothing else to do. (See also *desktop publishing.*)

Sentence: "I need to learn more about *graphic layout* so that I can become an advertising director for a big agency and make a lot of money peddling products that nobody really wants."

graphical user interface

Pronunciation: *gra-fi-kal yoo-zer int-er-face.*

Meaning: Abbreviated as GUI, a graphical user interface provides people a way to communicate with the computer through icons and pull-down menus — in other words, pictures. (See also *icon* and *pull-down menu.*)

Sentence: "Windows and the Macintosh offer *graphical user interfaces* that provide icons instead of words. This is like the old days when shopkeepers had signs of their products because most people couldn't read. Say, you don't think there's a correlation between the growing use of graphical user interfaces and the growing rate of illiteracy in this country, do you?"

graphics

Pronunciation: *gra-fiks.*

Meaning: The capability of a computer to display pretty little pictures on the screen. Most new computers have monitors that can display graphics, but some older computers had monitors that could not. If you tried to run a program that required graphics, such as a game, the program wouldn't work (or you would get garbage on your screen).

Sentence: "I first bought a monochrome monitor that just displayed text. Then I spent more money to get a *graphics* monitor. Now I can play games and draw all sorts of misleading bar graphs and pie charts."

graphics adapter card

Pronunciation: *gra-fiks ah-dap-ter kard.*

Meaning: A circuit board that plugs into a computer so that the monitor will have something to plug into. The common graphics adapter cards for IBM-compatible computers include CGA, EGA, VGA, and Super VGA, although most newer computers use VGA or Super VGA graphics adapter cards. (See also *CGA, EGA, VGA,* and *SVGA.*)

Sentence: "I built my own computer, but I couldn't plug my monitor in until I bought a *graphics adapter card.* Then I had to make sure my graphics adapter card would work with my monitor. I have a headache now. Can I go home yet?"

graphs

Pronunciation: *grafs* (rhymes with "giraffes that laugh").

Meaning: A visual representation of numeric quantities such as costs, distances, or speeds. Common types of graphs include bar graphs, line graphs, pie graphs, and scatter graphs. Most spreadsheets enable you to create graphs from your data, or you can buy a separate presentation graphics program that does a much better job.

Sentence: "My boss is impressed with lots of *graphs,* although he doesn't know what any of them really mean. That's okay because this new graph shows all the cutbacks we need to make, and his job is one of them."

gray scale

Pronunciation: *gray skay-ell.*

Meaning: Differing shades of gray ranging from black to white. Gray scale often refers to the capability of scanners, laser printers, or laptop computer screens that don't know how to use color.

Sentence: "This laptop offers a screen with 64 *gray scales.* That means its screen is sharper than one with 32 gray scales, but not as good as a color screen."

greeking

Pronunciation: *gree-king.*

Meaning: The use of nonsensical characters and symbols to represent the overall appearance of a page without showing the actual text. Often used with the Print Preview feature used by word processors or desktop publishing programs to show an entire page on your tiny little computer screen.

Sentence: "To see how my margins will look, I'll shrink the entire page so that I can see the whole thing. Although I can see how the page will look if printed, I can't read or edit the text because my program uses *greeking.*"

grid

Pronunciation: *grid* (rhymes with id).

Meaning: A series of dots that helps users align drawings precisely on the screen. Grids are often used in desktop publishing, drawing, and painting programs for creating straight lines and perfectly aligned angles that people think are important for advancing their careers.

Sentence: "Don't struggle with drawing lines. Just use the *grid* and connect the dots to make your lines look good."

GUI

Pronunciation: *Goo-Ee.*

(See *graphical user interface.*)

guru

Pronunciation: *goo-roo*

Meaning: Someone who is very knowledgeable about computers and therefore able to help fix problems, answer questions, and give worldly advice when your whole world seems like it's starting to fall apart.

Sentence: "I was working in UNIX when all of a sudden the computer beeped at me and said something about me having mail from somebody named Zoe. I didn't know what to do, so I got our local guru, Simon from accounting, to help me out. He said not to worry about it, that it was probably a glitch or something."

hack

Pronunciation: *ha-ka.*

Meaning: To modify a program, usually illegally or poorly.

Sentence: "This game used to be copy-protected, but someone *hacked* it, so now you can copy it easily and illegally."

hacker

Pronunciation: *ha-ker.*

Meaning: A person highly skilled with computers who can do seemingly magical things. Often used derogatorily to describe someone who uses a computer for illegal activities such as breaking into other people's computers or stealing funds electronically. (See also *guru.*)

Sentence: "A lot of *hackers* try to break into our computer every night. The only thing saving us is that our computer has nothing worthwhile in the first place."

HAL

Pronunciation: *Ha-ell.*

Meaning: The super-intelligent computer that played the bad guy in Stanley Kubrick's science fiction classic, *2001: A Space Odyssey* (based on a short story by Arthur C. Clarke).

Sentence: "Because *HAL* was an evil computer, people were worried when they realized that if you take the next corresponding letter of each letter in HAL, you get IBM."

half card

Pronunciation: *haf kard.*

Meaning: An expansion card that takes up half the amount of space usually required by an expansion card. Half cards usually perform one function, such as adding a game port or a modem to a computer. Some older computers had expansion slots in which only a half card can fit. (See also *expansion card.*)

Sentence: "*Half cards* look like someone cut them in half, but they work just as well as full-size expansion cards."

half-duplex

Pronunciation: *haf-doo-plex.*

Meaning: The transmission of data in one direction at a time through a modem. Sometimes called *Echo Off* by communications programs that refuse to use standard terms for the same thing. (See also *duplex, echo,* and *full duplex.*)

Sentence: "If you connect to a BBS through your modem and can't see anything you're typing, you're probably using *half-duplex.* To fix this problem, turn Echo On. If this doesn't work, make sure your monitor is on."

half-height drive

Pronunciation: *haf-hi-ta dri-va.*

Meaning: A disk drive that's half the size of a full-size disk drive (duh). Half-height drives are usually 1⅝-inches high. Most computers have enough space only for two full-height drives or four half-height drives. Using half-height drives increases a computer's capabilities. Some computers have ⅓-height drives.

Sentence: "My old computer came with two full-height drives. I yanked out one and put in two *half-height drives.*"

halftone

Pronunciation: *haf-toe-na.*

Meaning: A black-and-white copy of a photograph where dark shades are represented by thick dots and light shades are represented by tinier dots. Halftones reproduce better than ordinary photographs because copying photographs over and over again tends to blur images into one blob of gray.

Sentence: "Whenever I take pictures of my sister, I use *halftones.* Not that anyone really wants to see her clearly, but at least the image is sharper than copying an ordinary photograph."

handles

Pronunciation: *han-dulls.*

Meaning: In graphics and desktop publishing programs, handles are small black squares that appear around any object you have selected. Dragging the handle with a mouse lets you change the size or position of the object. When using modems, on the other hand, your handle is your name.

Sentence: "After you draw an object, click on it and a dotted rectangle appears with *handles.* Four handles appear on the corners and four in the middle of each line. Isn't this interesting?"

hands-on

Pronunciation: *hand-za-on.*

Meaning: To teach by having the end user physically type on the keyboard or use the mouse of a computer. (See also *end user.*)

Sentence: "You can't learn anything by listening to someone speak all day. You have to get *hands-on* experience and wipe out a few hard disks by mistake before you'll realize how destructive the ERASE command really can be."

handshake

Pronunciation: *hand-shay-ka.*

Meaning: The exchange of signals between two connected computers, indicating that data transmission can safely take place.

Sentence: "When everything works, my modem gets a *handshake* from the other computer, and I can start copying files. If something goes wrong, my modem usually just gets a rude gesture from me."

hard copy

Pronunciation: *har-da kop-ee.*

Meaning: Information printed by the computer.

Sentence: "Sure, our computer can store billions of names and addresses, but until I have a *hard copy* in my hands, I can't use the information the next time I'm stuck in the deserts of Saudi Arabia."

hard disk

Pronunciation: *har-da dis-ka.*

Meaning: A magnetically coated metal disk, hermetically sealed in a box and used to store massive amounts of information. Sometimes called a fixed disk, a Winchester disk, or a four-letter expletive if something goes wrong. (See also *disk* and *floppy disk.*)

Sentence: "For the longest time, I just used floppy disks. Then I finally broke down and bought a *hard disk.* Now I have to buy another hard disk because my first one is running out of room."

hardware

Pronunciation: *har-da-wayr.*

Meaning: The physical parts of a computer, printer, modem, monitor, and keyboard that you can touch. In comparison, software are programs that tell your hardware what to do next. (See also *software.*)

Sentence: "Some people say the *hardware* is more important because a fast computer can get your work done quicker. Others say software is more important because a well-designed program can make your work easier. I say hiring a high school kid at minimum wage is easier because then you don't have to do anything at all."

hashing

Pronunciation: *haa-shing.*

Meaning: A programming method used to store information based on a mathematical calculation. If you plan on writing your own programs, you need to know that hashing can make a program store data quickly. If you just want to use a computer, you don't have to know a single thing about hashing.

Sentence: "I'm writing my own database using C. To store data efficiently for fast retrieval, I'm using a *hashing* algorithm. That doesn't mean I know what I'm doing, but at least it sounds impressive to others."

hat

Pronunciation: *hat* (rhymes with *The Cat in the Hat*).

Meaning: The character ^ is called a hat. Often used by spreadsheet programs as a symbol for exponentiation and by computer manuals as a substitute for the Control key. Instead of writing, "Press the Control key

and then press X," manuals abbreviate it such as "Press Ctrl-D" or "Press ^D". (See also *caret.*)

Sentence: "In Lotus 1-2-3, typing **5^3** means raising 5 to the third power. Remember this because it's on the test at the end of this book."

Hayes compatibility

Pronunciation: *Hayz kom-pat-i-bill-i-tee.*

Meaning: The capability for a modem to mimic the operation of a Hayes brand modem. (See also *modem.*)

Sentence: "Because Hayes modems are the most popular in the world, nearly every modem in the world must mimic the Hayes modem and thus offer *Hayes compatibility.* Otherwise, modems would have as much trouble talking to each other as international leaders have talking to each other."

HD

Pronunciation: *A-cha Dee.*

Meaning: Acronym for *High-Density.* High-density 5¼-inch floppy disks can hold up to 1.2MB of data. High-density 3½-inch floppy disks can hold up to 1.44MB of data. When you buy a box of floppy disks, the high-density ones have HD printed somewhere on the box. (See also *high-capacity.*)

Sentence: "Here's 10 bucks. Buy me a box of *HD* floppy disks for my Macintosh or else I'll erase your hard disk."

head

Pronunciation: *hed.*

Meaning: The part of any floppy or hard disk drive that reads data off the spinning disk. For those of you old enough to remember what turntables are, heads are like the needles of a record player. (See also *floppy disk* and *hard disk.*)

Sentence: "Don't blow smoke in my floppy disk drive or you might contaminate the *heads.* Then the computer won't be able to read data off the floppy disk correctly."

head crash

Pronunciation: *hed kra-sha.*

Meaning: When the heads of a disk drive fail to work properly. Head crashes usually occur when the disk drive is old or dirty, or when something jolts your machine. (See also *hung.*)

Sentence: "I told my boss I couldn't get any work done because my computer suffered a *head crash.* He told me to suffer and write my report using a typewriter."

headache

Pronunciation: *hed-ay-ka.*

Meaning: An intense pain in the skull caused by trying to use and understand personal computers. See also *pain in the **!&.* (Just kidding.)

Sentence: "After reading 20 pages in my MS-DOS manual, I got a *headache.* Can I kick something now or do I have to wait until I get better?"

header

Pronunciation: *hed-er.*

Meaning: Repetitive text (such as a page number, chapter title, or rude message) which appears at the top of each page in a document. In comparison, footers are repetitive text which appears at the bottom of each page in a document. (See also *footer.*)

Sentence: "I created a *header* to print the page numbers in the right-hand corner of each page."

heavy iron

Pronunciation: *heh-vee i-yern.*

Meaning: Slang term for a mainframe computer or other type of computer that looks about the size of a small car. (See also *boat anchor* and *mainframe.*)

Sentence: "Our department refuses to use personal computers for anything. We're sticking with our *heavy iron* because we don't have the slightest idea how to use MS-DOS."

Hello, Larry

Pronunciation: *Hell-o Lair-ree.*

Meaning: A failed situation comedy back in the '70s that starred McLean Stevenson, the former star of the hit sitcom *M*A*S*H.*

Sentence: "Whenever anyone thinks of bad situation comedies that never made it, someone always remembers *Hello, Larry.*"

help

Pronunciation: *hel-pa.*

Meaning: Information that's supposed to show you what to do next, but usually just confuses you even more. Help can come in the form of printed manuals, on-screen information displayed in pop-up windows, or spoken words by well-meaning people.

Sentence: "When I tried using WordPerfect, I didn't know how to print my document. I tried getting *help* by reading the manual, but finally I had to call the company and ask for help. I still don't know what I'm doing, but at least I can keep calling for help whenever I need it."

help system

Pronunciation: *hell-pa sis-dum.*

Meaning: A predefined way for displaying help on the screen. Microsoft Windows offers a help system, which explains why commands for using help in any Windows programs look so similar.

Sentence: "In the old days of MS-DOS, programmers had to write the help text plus their own *help system* for displaying the information on the screen. Nowadays, Windows programmers can just write the help text and use the built-in help system."

Helvetica

Pronunciation: *Hell-vet-i-ka.*

Meaning: A common sans serif font that looks clean and professional (to most of us, anyway). Windows and the Macintosh have Helvetica as a built-in font. (See also *dingbats* and *font.*)

Sentence: "I formatted my document using *Helvetica* because it looks nicer than Courier or Times Roman. Then again, I just like playing around with different fonts."

Hercules Graphics card

Pronunciation: *Herk-yoo-leez Gra-fiks kar-da.*

Meaning: In the old days of IBM computers, a Hercules Graphics card (or "adapter") gave a monochrome monitor the capability to display a limited form of graphics but only in one color, usually green or orange. Nowadays, almost everyone uses VGA or Super VGA graphics cards, so Hercules Graphics cards are an interesting antique. (See also *graphics, Super VGA,* and *VGA.*)

Sentence: "My first computer couldn't display graphics because I had a monochrome monitor and a monochrome graphics card. Then I threw out the monochrome graphics card and put in a *Hercules Graphics card.* I could see some graphics but nothing in color. Boy, do I feel like I got ripped off."

hertz

Pronunciation: *hurts.*

Meaning: A unit of measurement for electrical vibrations, usually used in large quantities to measure the speed of a computer and abbreviated as megahertz (MHz). One hertz is equal to the number of cycles per second. So if you're standing on the street corner and three bicyclists pedal by in a second, you have three hertz. In China, they have billions of hertz. (See also *megahertz.*)

Sentence: "When I arrived at the airport, I got a *Hertz* rental car and borrowed a laptop computer that runs at 16 M*Hz.*"

heuristics

Pronunciation: *her-ris-tics* or *hyer-ris-tics.*

Meaning: A method for solving problems that don't have a clear-cut solution, such as playing chess, recognizing visual images, or avoiding income taxes. Heuristics provide instructions that essentially tell the computer to guess as best it can and pray that the results come out right.

Sentence: "Computer scientists planned to use *heuristics* for shooting down nuclear missiles."

hexadecimal

Pronunciation: *hex-a-des-i-mull.*

Meaning: A number that uses base 16 as opposed to base 10 (decimal) or base 2 (binary). Programmers often use hexadecimal numbers as a shortcut to represent binary numbers. (See also *binary.*)

Sentence: "My paycheck says I made $100 last week. But if I use *hexadecimal* notation, my paycheck would state I made $64. Are you confused yet?"

hi, hi, hi

Pronunciation: *hi, hi, hi.*

Meaning: A repetitive greeting given by programmers after spending all night trying to get their program to work. Also the name of a song by Paul McCartney that was banned in England for its drug references.

Sentence: "*Hi, hi, hi.* Don't mind me, I'm just working on my program that I'll never get done."

hidden files

Pronunciation: *hid-den fi-ells.*

Meaning: MS-DOS files that do not show up when you use the DIR command. Some programs create hidden files to keep users (or viruses) from copying them illegally or from erasing or altering them by mistake. (See also *file attribute.*)

Sentence: "Every time I tried to erase my directory, the computer kept saying that I couldn't because the directory wasn't empty. I used The Norton Utilities to find and erase the *hidden files,* and then I could erase my directory with no problem."

hierarchical file system

Pronunciation: *hi-er-ark-i-kal fi-ell siss-dum.*

Meaning: Sometimes abbreviated as HFS, this is the feature on Macintosh computers that lets you store files in separate subdirectories called *folders*. The directory/subdirectory structure of DOS is analogous to this system.

Sentence: "After using MS-DOS for so long, I find the Macintosh's *hierarchical file system* a lot easier to use because all those cute little folder icons make computing fun again."

hierarchical menus

Pronunciation: *hi-er-ark-i-kal men-yoos.*

Meaning: A menu that displays more menus when you choose certain options.

Sentence: "*Hierarchical menus* sometimes make you feel like you're endlessly choosing menus, and by the time you find what you want, you forget why you wanted it in the first place."

high-capacity

Pronunciation: *hi-ka-pah-si-tee.*

Meaning: Another term for high-density floppy disks. (See also *HD.*)

Sentence: "Don't buy double-density disks. Buy these *high-capacity* floppy disks instead because they hold more information."

high-density

(See *HD.*)

high memory

Pronunciation: *hi mem-or-ree.*

Meaning: On IBM-compatible computers, the memory between 640K of conventional memory and 1MB, more commonly referred to as *Upper Memory.* Do not confuse *high memory* with the *HMA (the High Memory Area)*, which is actually above the 1MB mark. This gap is reserved for running special system programs. To maximize the amount of conventional 640K memory for programs, memory-management programs move programs such as mouse or video drivers into high memory. (See also *conventional memory, HMA, Upper Memory,* and *UMB.*)

Sentence: "My old computer had only 483K of memory for running programs. After I used a memory-management program to take advantage of my *high memory,* I had 520K of memory to use."

high resolution

Pronunciation: *hi rez-o-loo-shin.*

Meaning: An overused adjective that describes the capability of a monitor to display crisp text and graphic images that won't give you headaches to stare at all day. (See also *low resolution.*)

Sentence: "I bought a *high-resolution* monitor so that I could see the screen better."

high tech

Pronunciation: *hi tek.*

Meaning: Overused adjective that tries to evoke images of the latest laboratory creations now available for your consumption and pleasure.

Sentence: "All this *high tech* stuff doesn't help if the power ever goes out."

high-level language

Pronunciation: *hi-lev-el lan-gwa-ja.*

Meaning: A programming language that enables you to write commands without knowing the internal structure of the computer. Some popular high-level languages include C, BASIC, and Pascal. Assembly language is often called a *low-level language* because you have to know how the computer works before you can write an assembly language program.

Sentence: "You can't write an assembly language program for Windows. Make it easy on yourself and use a *high-level language* such as BASIC before your brain explodes."

HMA

Pronunciation: *Ay-cha Em Ay.*

Meaning: Acronym that stands for *High Memory Area,* the first 64K of extended memory beyond 1MB in MS-DOS computers.

Sentence: "Programs that follow the extended memory specification (XMS) can use *HMA* as an extension of conventional 640K memory. This means your programs have more memory than they ordinarily have."

Home key

Pronunciation: *Ho-ma kee.*

Meaning: The key on the keyboard that usually moves the cursor to the beginning of a line or the top of a document, depending on the whims of the program at the time. The Home key usually has the word *Home* printed on it, which is probably the last straightforward guidance you'll get from computers. (See also *End key.*)

Sentence: "Press the *Home key* and then the left arrow key to move the cursor to the beginning of a line if you're using WordPerfect."

horizontal scroll bar

Pronunciation: *hor-i-zon-tal skroll bar.*

Meaning: A thin strip that appears on the right side of a window, used for scrolling the contents of a window up or down. At the very top and bottom of the scroll bar are arrows. Clicking these arrows scrolls the window contents up or down. Between these arrows is a scroll box. Moving the scroll box up or down also scrolls the window contents. (See also *vertical scroll bar.*)

Sentence: "Instead of pressing the Page Down key multiple times until your fingertips turn blue, just use the mouse and the *horizontal scroll bar* instead. That way you can browse the document without touching the keyboard."

host

Pronunciation: *ho-sta.*

Meaning: (1) In networks, the host computer is the one that controls the network and stores the programs and data that the other computers on the network use. (2) In telecommunications, it's the host computer that you have dialed and are connected to. (3) At parties and social gatherings, the host is the person who offers the twinkies. (See also *server* and *network.*)

Sentence: "This network wouldn't be so bad if the *host* computer were faster. Right now, I have to wait 10 seconds longer than I want to."

hot key

Pronunciation: *hot kee.*

Meaning: Any key or combination of keys that performs a special action in a program. This term applies usually to memory-resident programs. (See also *memory-resident programs* and *hot spot.*)

Sentence: "Don't worry about saving your file before quitting the program. Just press this *hot key* and the computer saves the file every time you take a break to regain your sanity."

hot link

Pronunciation: *hot ling-ka.*

Meaning: When two programs share data and when changing data in one program automatically changes the same data in another program. An example of a hot link is a word processor document with spreadsheet data. If you change the spreadsheet data using a spreadsheet, the data automatically changes in the word processor document as well. Yet another amazing technological breakthrough inspired by humankind's inherent laziness. (See also *DDE* and *link*.)

Sentence: "*Hot links* really save time and ensure accuracy. In the old days, we had to type the data separately and then check to see whether we made any mistakes."

hot spot

Pronunciation: *hot spot*

Meaning: An area on the screen where you can click the mouse to make something happen instead of issuing the conventional command. Hot spots usually appear in multimedia programs such as those found in HyperCard or the Windows Help System. (See also *hot key*.)

Sentence: "I you click *this hot spot*, you'll see a list of all the people who worked on the program. If you click *this* hot spot, the program will show you a neat visual effect. If you click this hot spot, you'll declare war on our enemies and launch a nuclear missile in their direction."

hourglass icon

Pronunciation: *ow-er-glass i-kon.*

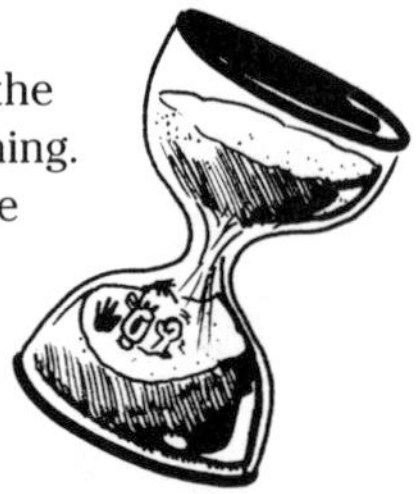

Meaning: A symbol of an hourglass that appears on the screen whenever the computer is busy doing something. The hourglass icon tells you to wait patiently, and the name alone (it's not a minuteglass!) means you may have a longer wait than you expect. (See also *beachball pointer*.)

Sentence: "Every time I save my file, I see an *hourglass icon* on my screen. After a few minutes, it goes away to let me know I can start using my computer again. I wonder how much time I waste staring at this stupid little icon every day?"

housekeeping

Pronunciation: *hows-kee-ping.*

Meaning: Organizing (backing up and deleting) files so that you can find them again. (See also *backup*.)

Sentence: "Every now and then you have to do some *housekeeping* on your computer. Otherwise, you'll have stuff all over the place, and you'll never be able to find it again. By the way, does anyone know what this disk is for?"

hue

Pronunciation: *hyou* or *Hugh.*

Meaning: A tint or shade of a specific color.

Sentence: "You can always tell the people who work on that faulty computer monitor because it leaks lots of radiation and turns people's faces various *hues* as the day wears on."

hung

Pronunciation: *hung.*

Meaning: When your computer stops working for some unknown reason and smashing on the keyboard or kicking the computer doesn't have any effect. (See also *crash* and *head crash.*)

Sentence: "I wrote a program to calculate the best way to steal a million dollars. Unfortunately, the program *hung* the computer and I had to start all over again."

HyperCard

Pronunciation: *Hi-per-Kard.*

Meaning: A "software erector set" for the Macintosh, designed to let nonprogrammers create their own programs, which makes as much sense as General Motors selling toolkits with the promise that nonmechanics can make their own transmissions. Although revolutionary when first introduced, HyperCard inherits the worst of both worlds. HyperCard proved too difficult for most nonprogrammers to use, and the programs people finally did create didn't run as quickly as those created using traditional languages such as C or Pascal. HyperCard helped introduce the idea of hypertext, and just as quickly, its fading popularity helped drag hypertext back down to obscurity. (See also *Hypertext.*)

Sentence: "Because programming the Macintosh is so difficult, I tried writing my own program using *HyperCard* instead. Then my program ran so slowly that I went back to writing my own program in C. Now nothing works, and I've wasted three years of my life."

hypermedia

Pronunciation: *hi-per-me-dee-ya.*

Meaning: Sometimes called *hypertext* or *multimedia,* it's the combination of text, graphics, sound, and video to present information. (See also *multimedia* and *hypertext.*)

Sentence: "I made up a *hypermedia* presentation to lobby for additional funds. Then my boss told me to sell my computer and that would be the source of my additional funds."

hypertext

Pronunciation: *hi-per-text.*

Meaning: The nonlinear display and retrieval of information. Hypertext can consist of text, graphics, video, sound, and animation. One example of the use of hypertext is the following: Imagine that you are reading along about a topic and you come across a term that you want to know more about because it is unfamiliar. You simply select the term and more detailed information emerges for you to read. If you want less information, you simply step back a level. (See also *HyperCard.*)

Sentence: "The help windows used by Windows programs use *hypertext.* By clicking a specially highlighted word, the computer instantly displays that bit of information on the screen."

hyphenation

Pronunciation: *hi-fin-ay-shin.*

Meaning: The ability to divide long words in half (across two lines) when the entire word doesn't fit in the given margin. Most word processors and desktop publishing programs let you turn hyphenation on or off.

Sentence: "The trouble with *hyphenation* is that it breaks up all your words. The advantage is that it keeps all your margins from having huge white gaps where words should be."

Hz

(See *Hertz.*)

I-beam pointer

Pronunciation: *I-beem poin-ter.*

Meaning: The shape of the cursor when the computer is waiting for you to type letters and numbers. Depending on the program you're using and the situation you're in, the cursor can change shape to a hand, an arrow, an hourglass, or a crosshair. Various religions have been popping up lately, worshipping each symbol as a special sign from the heavens above. (See also *crosshairs, cursor, hourglass icon,* and *pointer.*)

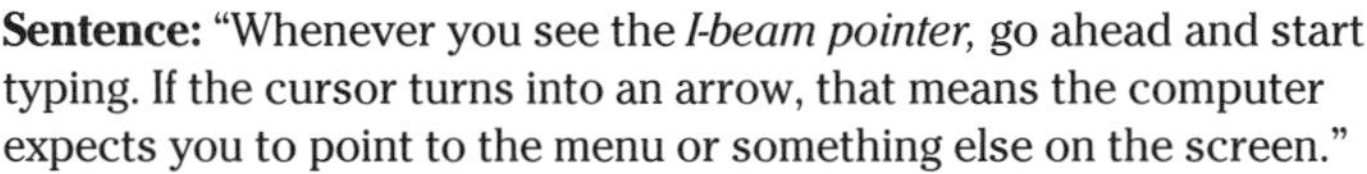

Sentence: "Whenever you see the *I-beam pointer,* go ahead and start typing. If the cursor turns into an arrow, that means the computer expects you to point to the menu or something else on the screen."

I/O

Pronunciation: *I Oh.*

Meaning: Acronym for Input/Output, which is the interface of every computer that lets data move from one part to another. (See also *input* and *output.*)

Sentence: "There's so much garbage going through the *I/O* that I'm surprised the ecologists don't declare our computer a source of pollution."

i486

Pronunciation: *I for-ay-tee-six.*

Meaning: Acronym for the Intel 80486DX microprocessor. (See also *386, 486, microprocessor,* and *Pentium.*)

Sentence: "This computer has an *i486* in it, but that one over there has only a 386 processor. Now if I had enough money to buy one, I might actually care to know the difference between the two."

IBM

Pronunciation: *I Bee Em.*

Meaning: Acronym for International Business Machines, sometimes called Big Blue. One of the largest computer companies around, IBM made a fortune leasing expensive mainframe computers to unsuspecting and captive customers. After setting the standard for personal computers, IBM promptly lost its lead through high prices and more efficient competition.

Sentence: "Don't buy an *IBM* computer unless you want to pay a lot more than you should. Then again, if it's not your money, who cares?"

IBM AT

Pronunciation: *I Bee Em Ay Tee.*

Meaning: Introduced in 1984, the first IBM personal computer to use the 80286 microprocessor. The AT stands for Advanced Technology.

Sentence: "Sure, we have an old *IBM AT* still chugging away at the office. We paid $3,000 for it new, but now it's worth about $200."

IBM PC

Pronunciation: *I Bee Em Pee See.*

Meaning: The first IBM personal computer introduced in 1981. The PC stands for Personal Computer. Today, PC refers to any personal computer that's IBM compatible. (See also *clone* and *PC.*)

Sentence: "I found an *IBM PC* at a garage sale last week. I paid $50 for it, and in ninety more years, it will be an antique."

IBM XT

Pronunciation: *I Bee Em Ex Tee.*

Meaning: The first IBM personal computer to have a built-in hard disk. The XT stands for eXtended Technology. (See also *AT, hard disk,* and *XT.*)

Sentence: "My first computer was an *IBM XT* with a 10 megabyte hard disk. My latest computer is an IBM compatible with a 452 megabyte hard disk."

icon

Pronunciation: *i-kon.*

Meaning: A symbol that looks like Egyptian hieroglyphics, often used in place of actual words. Many programs display icons as shortcuts to choosing commands through menus. Instead of choosing a menu command, you can just click on the icon, as long as you remember which icon represents which command. (See also *crosshairs, cursor, hourglass icon, I-beam pointer,* and *pointer.*)

Sentence: "*Icons* are easier to use than typing in specific commands. Maybe in the future, everything will use icons and reading will become obsolete."

IDE

Pronunciation: *I Dee Ee.*

Meaning: Acronym for Integrated Drive Electronics (or Intelligent Device Electronics), which is a type of interface for controlling hard disks. Other types of hard disk controller interfaces include SCSI, ESDI, and ST-506. IDE is also an acronym for Integrated Development Environment, which relates to programs that share a common user interface.

Sentence: "I bought a new hard disk, but it won't work because my hard disk controller card uses *IDE* but the hard disk needs SCSI. I hate computers."

idle

Pronunciation: *i-dull.*

Meaning: When a computer or user sits around doing nothing. (See also *screen saver.*)

Sentence: "We have four computers that are *idle* and three people. How come nobody's using the computers to at least play video games?"

IEEE

Pronunciation: Usually pronounced as *"I triple E."*

Meaning: Acronym for Institute of Electrical and Electronic Engineers, yet another organization dedicating its life to peace, freedom, and defining standards in the electronics industry.

Sentence: "I went to an *IEEE* conference last fall where they defined the standard for networks. Of course, it's one thing to define a standard and an entirely different thing to get people to follow it."

IF

Pronunciation: *If* (can't get much easier than that).

Meaning: A keyword used in programming languages so that computers can make decisions provided certain conditions are true. In BASIC, an IF statement might look like this:

```
IF X = 5 THEN PRINT "The value of X is five."
```

(See also *keyword.*)

Sentence: "If only I knew how to use the *IF* statement correctly, then I could write better programs that worked."

import

Pronunciation: *im-port.*

Meaning: To load a file created by another program.

Sentence: "Many word processors let you *import* WordPerfect files. Almost every spreadsheet can import Lotus 1-2-3 files, and nearly every database lets you import dBASE files. Too bad if you want to import a file created by VisiWord, Office Writer, or any other program that's no longer around."

inclusive OR

Pronunciation: *in-kloo-sive Or.*

Meaning: A programming operator used to manipulate individual bits of data, often used for creating graphics. The result of an inclusive OR is always 1 (which represents true) unless both operands are 0 (false). If you have no idea what this means, you probably don't need to use inclusive OR in your everyday life. (See also *exclusive OR.*)

Sentence: "For those of you who want to see a truth table for *inclusive OR,* this is it, where the '|' symbol represents an inclusive OR:

Value of A	*Value of B*	*A | B*
0	0	0
1	0	1
0	1	1
1	1	1"

incremental backup

Pronunciation: *ink-kreh-ment-al bak-up.*

Meaning: The process of copying files that have been newly created or modified since the time of the last full backup. (See also *backup.*)

Sentence: "Once you've done a full backup on your hard disk, just do an *incremental backup* once a week. No sense copying files over again if they haven't changed, unless you like wasting time."

incremental compiler

Pronunciation: *ink-kreh-ment-al kom-pi-ell-ler.*

Meaning: A special program that converts programming language statements into machine code each time the programmer types a complete line. Incremental compilers work without interfering with your work. That way, when you get done typing your final program, it seems to compile almost instantly. In comparison, most compilers wait for you to type an entire program before they start compiling. This makes you wait a long time until the entire program finishes compiling. Unless you're a programmer, you can safely ignore this definition. (See also *compile, compiler,* and *interpreter.*)

Sentence: "I like programming with an *incremental compiler* because I don't like waiting for my program to compile. Of course, the drawback is that on a slow computer, the incremental compiler may get in your way while you're writing your program."

indentation

Pronunciation: *in-den-tay-shin.*

Meaning: The alignment of paragraphs within the margins of a page. Usually, the first line of every paragraph is indented several spaces to make the text easier to read, whether or not the text is worth reading in the first place. (See also *word processor.*)

Sentence: "Use the Tab key for *indentation.* If you use the spacebar, it's harder to adjust the indentation later, and it's more time-consuming, too."

index

Pronunciation: *in-deks.*

Meaning: In many word processors or desktop publishing programs, a feature that creates a list of important words, phrases, or ideas in

alphabetical order, along with the page numbers where those items appear. This feature creates the index after key terms and phrases are first marked manually.

Sentence: "Any good desktop publishing application will have an *index* feature. This is especially important if you are laying out a computer book. Because computer books can be as dry as dust, indexes make them useful."

indexed file

Pronunciation: *in-deks-ed fi-ell.*

Meaning: In database programs, the index is usually a separate file containing information about the physical location of records stored in a database file. Instead of searching the actual database file, database programs use indexes to run faster. This works as long as the index is accurate, and we all know what the chances of that are. (See also *database.*)

Sentence: "Keep your *indexed files* up to date so that your database program will run faster. An inaccurate indexed file may confuse your database and keep it from working. (So what else is new?)"

inference engine

Pronunciation: *in-fur-ren-sa en-jin.*

Meaning: The part of an expert system that calculates results based on stored facts and information supplied by the user. An expert system consists of three parts: the user interface, the knowledge base, and the inference engine. (See also *expert system, interface,* and *knowledge base.*)

Sentence: "The so-called intelligence of an expert system resides almost solely in the accurate reasoning of its *inference engine.*"

infinite loop

Pronunciation: *in-fin-it loop.*

Meaning: When a computer keeps running the same instructions over and over again without stopping. To better understand the sense of futility that an infinite loop can create, think of driving in circles, trying to find a parking space in a major shopping mall the day before Christmas. (See also *endless loop* and *loop.*)

Sentence: "This is my example of an *infinite loop.* If you don't like it, keep reading it until you do like it."

inheritance

Pronunciation: *in-hair-rah-tan-sa.*

Meaning: Used in object-oriented programming languages. Inheritance is when one object copies the features of another object (where an "object" refers to a block of code with a specialized task). Programmers like the idea of inheritance because it keeps them from typing the same lines of code over and over again. (See also *base, child process, object code file, object-oriented,* and *parent/child.*)

Sentence: "Using C++, I created an object to display a window. Bob's object *inherited* my object's features and added the ability to display a message in the window. Now I'm suing Bob for copyright infringement."

initialize

Pronunciation: *in-i-shal-lize.*

Meaning: To prepare a piece of equipment (computer, printer, modem, and so on) to get ready to do something important. Initializing clears the equipment of any old data still stored in it. (See also *boot, cold boot,* and *warm boot.*)

Sentence: "Every time you turn on your computer, it *initializes* itself by loading the files it needs to get ready to run. If everything goes well, you can start using the computer as soon as it's finished. If something goes wrong, you'll probably be out of luck."

inkjet printer

Pronunciation: *inkjet prin-ter.*

Meaning: A type of printer that sprays ink on paper, instead of smacking an inked ribbon against the page like a dot-matrix printer does. Inkjet printers are quieter than dot-matrix printers, produce better quality printing than dot-matrix printers (but not as good as laser printers), and cost less than laser printers (but more than dot-matrix printers). (See also *dot-matrix, laser printer,* and *printer.*)

Sentence: "For a good laugh at the office, you actually can adjust your *inkjet printer* so that instead of spraying ink on the page, it sprays ink in the face of the person standing right in front of it."

input

Pronunciation: *in-put.*

Meaning: Information fed into the computer for processing. Comput-

ers can receive input from a variety of sources, including the keyboard, mouse, modem, touch screen, or mad scientists bent on the destruction of the entire human race as we know it. (See also *I/O* and *output.*)

Sentence: "Give that poor computer some *input* so that it will have something to do such as print mailing labels. I hate to see a computer sitting idle."

input/output

(See *I/O.*)

Insert key

Pronunciation: *In-sert kee.*

Meaning: The key on the keyboard that has the word *Insert* or *Ins* printed on it (Wow, what an amazing fact!). The Insert key is often used to change the insert mode of a program. (See also *insert mode.*)

Sentence: "If everything you type starts erasing all your existing information, you're probably in insert mode. To turn this off and turn on overwrite mode, press the *Insert key.*"

insert mode

Pronunciation: *in-sert mow-da.*

Meaning: Programs have two modes for entering data: insert mode and overwrite mode. Insert mode means that if you type something, the letters will not harm any existing letters on the screen. Most word processors have insert mode as the default mode. (See also *Insert key.*)

Sentence: "Most of the time, you don't want to erase the words already on your screen. So make sure your word processor is in *insert mode* or you might accidentally overwrite your previous text. If that happens, it's time for a good cry."

insertion pointer

Pronunciation: *in-ser-shin poin-ter.*

Meaning: The cursor shape that shows you where letters will start appearing on the screen if you start typing on the keyboard. Most programs display the insertion pointer as a thin vertical line or as an I-shaped icon. (See also *crosshairs, cursor, I-beam,* and *pointer.*)

Sentence: "If you want to type your name in the right-hand corner of the screen, you have to move the *insertion pointer* there first. See? Computers really are dumber than you think."

install

Pronunciation: *in-stall.*

Meaning: To prepare equipment or software for use for the first time. (See also *initialize.*)

Sentence: "I bought WordPerfect, and the program came on seven floppy disks. Before I could even run the program, I had to *install* it on my hard disk. Oops. I guess that means I should install my hard disk first."

instruction

Pronunciation: *in-struk-shin.*

Meaning: A statement, written in a programming language, that can be converted into a machine language so that the computer can understand and run it. (See also *code.*)

Sentence: "If you ever decide to lose your mind, try writing an entire program using assembly language. Just to multiply two numbers, you'll have to write a page full of *instructions.*"

integer

Pronunciation: *int-ah-jer.*

Meaning: A whole number, which is any positive or negative number without fractions or decimals.

Sentence: "Your age can be a fractional number, but the number of people in this room is an *integer.* Unless, of course, you chop somebody in half."

integrated software

Pronunciation: *in-teh-gray-ted soft-wair.*

Meaning: A single program that performs multiple functions, usually none very well. Most integrated software includes a word processor, spreadsheet, database, and communications program rolled into one. (See also *communications, database, spreadsheet,* and *word processor.*)

Sentence: "I didn't want to bother learning WordPerfect, Excel, and FoxPro, so I bought some *integrated software.* Now I just have to learn one program, but it's still so confusing that I can't do very much."

interactive

Pronunciation: *in-ter-ak-tive.*

Meaning: A program or computer that responds immediately whenever the user presses a key or does something else that the computer should respond to. Using interactive software is similar to carrying on a conversation; the user's responses change the way the system functions. In comparison, non-interactive computers tend to just sit there and do something only when they feel like it.

Sentence: "I liked learning BASIC because every time I typed a command, the computer immediately told me I did something wrong. With such an *interactive* system, it was only a matter of time before I got discouraged from using the computer altogether."

interface

Pronunciation: *int-er-fay-sa.*

Meaning: The connection between the computer and the person trying to use it. A keyboard is an interface and so is a monitor. Putting your fist through the computer can also be considered an interface. (See also *graphical user interface, user-friendly,* and *user-hostile.*)

Sentence: "This program is hard to use because the *interface* is poorly designed. I'd rather use a Macintosh because the interface is easier for me to understand."

interlacing

Pronunciation: *int-er-lay-sing.*

Meaning: When the cathode-ray tube (CRT) of a monitor scans every other row to display information on the screen. TVs use interlacing, but computer monitors that use interlacing tend to flicker. The best computer monitors use non interlacing. (See also *monitor.*)

Sentence: "My eyes are going to explode from my head if I keep using this lousy *interlacing* monitor. Tomorrow I'm going to buy a noninterlacing monitor or else I'll refuse to work any more."

interleaving

Pronunciation: *in-ter-lee-ving.*

Meaning: The ratio of disk sectors on a hard disk that are skipped for every sector actually used. For example, an interleave of 3:1 means the disk writes to a sector, skips three sectors, and writes to the other sector. The interleave is usually set by the hard disk manufacturer, and you can change it with special programs if you know what you're doing. (See also *fragmentation.*)

Sentence: "My hard disk uses an *interleaving* of 4:1, but my friend's hard disk uses an interleaving of 5:1. The optimum ratio of interleaving depends on the hard disk, so a 5:1 interleave factor isn't necessarily faster than 3:1 interleaving."

Internet

Pronunciation: *Int-er-net.*

Meaning: A worldwide computer network available via modem that connects universities, government laboratories, and individuals around the world. Users of Internet can send each other electronic mail, copy files from one another, break into other people's computers, and electronically transfer funds from poorly defended computers owned by worldwide banks. (See also *CompuServe, network,* and *user group.*)

Sentence: "I use *Internet* to contact friends as far away as Australia and Thailand. Fortunately, I don't have to make a long distance call each time because I can connect to the Internet through a local number."

interpreted language

Pronunciation: *in-ter-preh-ted lan-gwage.*

Meaning: A programming language where the computer reads the program statements one at a time and then follows the instructions. Common interpreted languages are BASIC, LISP, Prolog, and LOGO; although C and Pascal also can be interpreted. (See also *compile, compiler, interpreter,* and *language.*)

Sentence: "*Interpreted languages* run slower than compiled languages because the computer has to read each statement, follow its instruction, and then read the next statement. This is like trying to read a French novel by reading a word to a translator, waiting for her to tell you what it means in English, and then reading another word."

interpreter

Pronunciation: *in-ter-pret-ter.*

Meaning: A program that reads statements written in a programming language, such as BASIC, and immediately follows the instructions. An interpreter is usually easier for learning a language because it gives you immediate feedback. The disadvantage is that other people can't use your programs unless they also have a copy of your program's interpreter. (See also *compile, compiler, interpreted language,* and *language.*)

Sentence: "MS-DOS comes with a BASIC *interpreter* called QBASIC. You can write and run BASIC programs, but nobody else can use your program unless he also has a copy of QBASIC."

interrupt

Pronunciation: *in-ter-rup-ta.*

Meaning: An instruction that rudely butts in, stops the computer from whatever it's doing, and makes it do something completely different. Whenever you press the Ctrl-Alt-Del key combination, you're causing an interrupt that restarts the computer. People also talk about hardware interrupts on DOS machines, particularly in terms of interrupt requests (IRQs). Trust us, you don't want to get into this on your own; consult your local guru for help. (See also *warm boot.*)

Sentence: "Don't *interrupt* me while I'm writing my program. It works by waiting for an interrupt from the keyboard and then it shows a calendar of appointments on the screen."

invalid

Pronunciation: *in-val-id.*

Meaning: Not valid. Not true. No way. No how. Uh-uh. I mean, not only are you wrong, but your intention is misguided and possibly diabolical. Don't get ridiculous on me, now.

Sentence: "The notion that the IRS owes you money is *invalid.*"

inverse text

Pronunciation: *in-ver-sa tex-ta.*

Meaning: Letters that appear white against a dark background. In comparison, normal text appears as black letters against a light background. (See also *text.*)

Sentence: "I like using *inverse text* for special emphasis, like when I'm writing blackmail notes to my enemies."

ISA

Pronunciation: *I Ess Ay,* or *I-suh.*

Meaning: Acronym for Industry Standard Architecture, which is the type of bus originally used in the IBM AT. Most IBM-compatible computers use either an ISA, an EISA, or an MCA bus. (See also *bus, EISA, IBM AT,* and *MCA.*)

Sentence: "If you buy an expansion board for IBM computers, make sure it follows the *ISA* standard. Otherwise, it won't work in my computer, and then I'll make you buy me another one."

ISAM

Pronunciation: *I Ess Ay EM* or *I-Sam.*

Meaning: Acronym for Indexed Sequential Access Method, which is a technique for storing and retrieving data efficiently using "tables" and "indexes." ISAM is often used by database programs. (See also *database.*)

Sentence: "If you're writing your own database program using C or Pascal, use *ISAM,* or else your program wastes too much time sorting and searching for information. Then again, who in his right mind would want to write his own database program?"

ISDN

Pronunciation: *I Ess Dee En.*

Meaning: Acronym for Integrated Services Digital Network, a very futuristic, international telecommunications standard. An ISDN phone line enables you to send data, video, and voice over the same phone line.

Sentence: "With so many modem standards and speeds on the market these days, I'm looking forward to the day when every phone will follow the *ISDN* standard. That way I won't have to use a modem to connect my computer to another one"

ISO

Pronunciation: *I Ess Oh.*

Meaning: Acronym for International Standards Organization, which is a group that tries to set standards for lots of different industries. In the computer world, the ISO has defined the standard for the Pascal language, often called ISO Pascal. Unfortunately, the most popular version of Pascal, Turbo Pascal, ignores the ISO standard altogether. So much for standards. (See also *Pascal.*)

Sentence: "Turbo Pascal can't run programs that follow the *ISO* Pascal standard. Then again, who cares?"

italic

Pronunciation: *i-tal-ik.*

Meaning: A type style that slants text to the right for special emphasis. (See also *font, text,* and *typeface.*)

Sentence: "I like using *italics* in my letters because it emphasizes the four-letter words I want the reader to see. Of course, I only use italics sparingly so that the italics I do use stick out even more."

iteration

Pronunciation: *it-er-ray-shin.*

Meaning: The repetition of a statement in a program, often called a loop, or, if something goes terribly wrong, an endless loop. (See also *endless loop, infinite loop,* and *loop.*)

Sentence: "The most useless statements in a program are those that are never used. The most valuable statements are those used in several *iterations,* because if something is wrong with those statements, your program has more than one chance to crash."

jack

Pronunciation: *ja-ka.*

Meaning: A place to plug in electrical wires.

Sentence: "Hey, Jack, plug that red wire into the *jack* over there. And don't electrocute yourself in the process."

jacket

Pronunciation: *ja-ket.*

Meaning: The plastic, square case that protects a floppy disk from dirt, fingerprints, and other forms of physical damage short of gunshots, fire, or hydrochloric acid. (See also *floppy disk.*)

Sentence: "When you hold a floppy disk, grab it by the *jacket.* If you touch the actual floppy disk surface, you may ruin the disk (and possibly go to jail)."

jaggies

Pronunciation: *jag-gees.*

Meaning: When curved drawings or letters look like tiny little steps that combine to give the illusion of a curve. (See also *alias, aliasing,* and *dithering.*)

Sentence: "If you make the letter *O* too big, you'll notice little *jaggies* all around the edges."

job

Pronunciation: *jawb.*

Meaning: A task that the computer is supposed to do whenever it gets around to doing it. (See also *queue.*)

Sentence: "This computer's running so slowly because it has so many *jobs* backed up in the queue. Let's unplug it and start the whole thing over again."

join

Pronunciation: *joyn.*

Meaning: A term used when a relational database cross-references two files. (See also *database* and *relational database.*)

Sentence: "Instead of typing the same information over and over again, just store it in separate files and *join* them when you need them. If that doesn't work, then type the same information over and over again."

joystick

Pronunciation: *joy-stik.*

Meaning: A little stick that swivels around in a base. Moving the stick moves the cursor around the screen.

Sentence: "When you buy a flight simulator program, you have to buy a *joystick* so that it feels like you're really flying the airplane. After all, how many pilots fly an F-16 using a keyboard?"

Julian

Pronunciation: *Joo-lee-on.*

Meaning: A method to simplify computing dates. In the Julian system, every day has a unique number. Day 1 represents January 1, 4713 B.C. Day 2448299 represents February 11, 1991. Programmers often use the Julian system for representing dates because it's easy for computers to handle. If you try guessing the date 100 days from January 23, 1964, you'll see how clumsy our ordinary calendar system can be.

Sentence: "My brother was born on February 11, 1991, or 2448299 if you use the *Julian* system."

jump

Pronunciation: *jumpa.*

Meaning: When a program follows a series of instructions one by one and then suddenly starts following instructions somewhere else. If someone drops an ice cube down your shorts, you'll jump too. (See also *GOTO.*)

Sentence: "If you're programming in assembly language, you have to use the *jump* command a lot, abbreviated as JMP. In other languages, a jump often is called a GOTO command."

jumper

Pronunciation: *jum-per.*

Meaning: A small, plastic, rectangular-shaped plug found on circuit boards. Usually, a two- or three-prong pin sticks out of the circuit board, and the jumper slides over these pins. (See also *DIP switch.*)

Sentence: "You can modify your computer by changing one or two *jumpers.* Just make sure you know what you're doing and how to reverse anything you do."

junk

Pronunciation: *junk.*

Meaning: The stuff that seems to pop up magically around every computer.

Sentence: "How come I have so much *junk* around here? Last week I got so fed up I even threw away my computer."

justify

Pronunciation: *just-i-fi.*

Meaning: To align text within the margins of a page, either left, right, center, or justified. Many people call alignment *justification*.

This is text	This is	This is
using left	text using	text using
alignment.	center alignment.	right alignment.

Sentence: "It's hard to *justify* the use of right justification in any document because it looks so strange. In most documents, you left align text and center align headlines."

This is text that is justified. This ridiculous illustration, however, is unjustified.

K

Pronunciation: *Kay* or *Kill-a-Bite.*

Meaning: An acronym for kilobyte (or 1,024 bytes) — sometimes abbreviated as *KB.* Used as a measure of the storage capacity of disks and memory. Because one byte equals one character, 1K of memory stores 1,024 characters. (See also *MB.*)

Sentence: "My floppy disk can hold 360*K* of data, and my computer's memory is only 640K. Obviously this is either a very old computer or a crippled one."

K&R

Pronunciation: *Kay and Ar.*

Meaning: Abbreviation for Brian Kernighan and Dennis Ritchie, authors of the book *The C Programming Language.* For the longest time, this book was the only specification for the C language. Many C compilers used to claim to follow the K&R language specification. Later, ANSI came up with a new standard. (See also *C* and *ANSI.*)

Sentence: "I bought a *K&R* C compiler in 1981. Since then, newer C compilers have been claiming ANSI C compatibility, and none of them mention K&R compliance any more. Just goes to show you that even specifications don't remain standard for very long."

Kermit

Pronunciation: *Ker-mit.*

Meaning: A method (or *protocol*) for transferring files that sounds like it was named after Miss Piggy's boyfriend, Kermit the Frog. Kermit is slower than XMODEM but often is used when transferring files from mainframes because no other protocol may be available. (See also *XMODEM* and *protocol.*)

Sentence: "After I broke into the Pentagon's computers, I had to use *Kermit* to copy all their secrets to my computer."

kernel

Pronunciation: *ker-null.*

Meaning: A term used by programmers to describe the main or core part of a program.

Sentence: "The operating system *kernel* takes up only one megabyte of hard disk space. The rest of the operating system takes up the other four megabytes."

kerning

Pronunciation: *ker-ning* (rhymes with burning).

Meaning: To adjust the spacing between letters so that they look nice together. Certain letters look better closer together than others, such as putting *T* and *y* together so the upper part of the *T* hangs slightly over the *y*. Kerning is used most often in word processors and desktop publishing programs when exact spacing of letters is important or when the boss just wants to give people something tedious to worry about.

Sentence: "Most people may not notice *kerning* in a paragraph, but when it's absent, they'll think the letters look funny, although they don't quite know why."

key

Pronunciation: *kee.*

Meaning: (1) The buttons on the keyboard. (2) A password needed to decrypt or encrypt a file. (3) The item used for searching and sorting a database. If you're searching for all the names and addresses of everyone who lives in California, California (CA) is the key.

Sentence: "Press this *key* and then type the password key to unlock this file. Once you've unlocked this file, search the database using ZIP codes as the key. Then sing 'The Star Spangled Banner' in honor of Francis Scott Key."

Key Caps

Pronunciation: *Kee Kaps.*

Meaning: A Macintosh program that shows you the characters you can produce by typing different keystroke combinations. The Key Caps program appears in the Apple menu and displays the keyboard along with any characters you type.

Sentence: "Sometimes when I don't feel like doing any real work, I'll experiment with the *Key Caps* program to see what odd keystroke combinations I can hit to create unusual characters. And to think I get paid to do this, too."

keyboard

Pronunciation: *kee-bored.*

Meaning: A device that looks like a typewriter and that is connected to the computer. When the user presses a key, the keyboard sends a signal to the computer, which displays the corresponding character on the screen.

Sentence: "Too many computer *keyboards* feel like a cheap toy typewriter. Others feel so mushy that it seems like you're typing on a spoiled banana."

keyboard buffer

Pronunciation: *kee-bored buf-fer.*

Meaning: An area of memory set aside to hold a specified number of keystrokes in case you type faster than the computer's response time. Once you stop typing, the keyboard buffer feeds the computer the remaining keystrokes stored in the buffer. (See also *buffer* and *print buffer.*)

Sentence: "I like a big *keyboard buffer* because sometimes if I type too quickly, the computer beeps and makes me stop and wait. With a big keyboard buffer, I can keep typing until my fingers fall off."

keyboard cover

Pronunciation: *kee-bored kuh-ver.*

Meaning: A clear, flexible, plastic sheet that fits over a keyboard, allowing you to type while protecting the keyboard from liquid spills, cookie crumbs, dirt particles, or crawling insects.

Sentence: "Good thing your computer had a *keyboard cover* on it because I just spilled my coffee all over it. Unfortunately, I also spilled my orange juice in your floppy drive. Maybe I shouldn't use your computer as a coaster."

keypad

Pronunciation: *kee-pad.*

Meaning: A related group of keys placed together for convenience. The most common keypads are the *numeric keypad* and the *cursor keypad.*

Sentence: "If you type numbers a lot, use the numeric *keypad* because the number keys are arranged close together. Otherwise, you'll have to use the number keys at the top of the keyboard, and then you'll have to do finger gymnastics."

keyword

Pronunciation: *kee-werd.*

Meaning: A word that has special meaning in a programming language. For example, CALL is a BASIC keyword, CASE is a Pascal keyword, and int is a C keyword. Also, in word processing, a keyword can be the word you use in a text search.

Sentence: "*Keywords* have special meaning in programming languages just as certain four-letter words have special meaning in the English language."

KHz

Pronunciation: *Kay Ay-cha zee or kill-a-hurtz-a.*

Meaning: Abbreviation for kilohertz. The word *kilo* means 1,000 of something. So kilohertz must mean 1,000 hertz. And *hertz* is a term for the number of cycles per second, so a kilohertz is the number of thousands of cycles per second. This must have something to do with computers, somewhere.

Sentence: "Killa the Gorilla was a primate so fine, eating peanuts and banana creme desserts. Yet one day Killa chewed on a telephone line, so now we can say *kilohertz.*"

kill

Pronunciation: *kill* (rhymes with *Bill, pill,* and *Jack and Jill*).

Meaning: To do something destructive, such as erasing a file or crashing the computer. In UNIX, to kill a process means to end it (as in to stop a program from running). (See also *Ctrl-Alt-Del, Quit,* and *Exit.*)

Sentence: "After reading my electronic mail, I usually *kill* all the files to free up space on the computer."

kilo-

Pronunciation: *kee-lo.*

Meaning: A prefix used in the metric system that means 1,000. So kilobyte means 1,000 bytes, kilogram means 1,000 grams, and kiloliter means 1,000 liters. But just to confuse matters: due to the binary (and onerous) nature of computers, when talking about memory, 1K actually refers to 1,024 bytes.

Sentence: "I like measuring my weight in *kilo*grams because it makes me seem lighter than I really am."

kilobyte

(See *KB.*)

kludge

Pronunciation: *kloo-j*

Meaning: A temporary but poorly designed solution that actually works and solves a problem. Another name for software.

Sentence: "My computer didn't work, so I started soldering wires everywhere, and now it works again. It's just a *kludge,* but what the heck, it works."

knowledge base

Pronunciation: *naw-ledge bay-sa.*

Meaning: The part of an expert system that stores facts about solving a particular problem. Most knowledge bases consist of IF-THEN rules for reaching an answer. A well-designed expert system should let you change knowledge bases whenever you need to solve a different type of problem. (See also *expert system* and *artificial intelligence.*)

Sentence: "For an expert system to be trustworthy, its *knowledge base* must be current and accurate. Because even human experts can't keep up with everything, how can you expect someone to keep updating a knowledge base regularly?"

label

Pronunciation: *lay-bull.*

Meaning: An identifying name used in spreadsheets for a heading, and in DOS and OS/2 batch files to mark the destination of a GOTO command. Also the name of a disk volume in MS-DOS. (See also *volume label.*)

Sentence: "In my Lotus 1-2-3 spreadsheet, I put *labels* such as TAXES OWED, MONEY STOLEN, and COST OF OVERSEAS AIRLINE TICKET to identify the meaning of the numbers listed underneath."

LAN

Pronunciation: *Lan* (rhymes with *ran*, *ban*, and *can*).

Meaning: Acronym for Local Area Network, which is a group of computers connected together to share information. Some popular LANs are Novell, LANtastic, and Banyan. (See also *network* and *wide area network.*)

Sentence: "The best part about having my computer connected to a *LAN* is that I can send messages to my coworker's computer and ask where he wants to go for lunch, all without leaving my desk. LANs certainly have made my life easier, that's for sure."

landscape orientation

Pronunciation: *land-skape or-ree-in-tay-shin.*

Meaning: Printing as if the page were turned sideways so that its width is longer than its height. In comparison, most printing is done where the width of the page is shorter than its height. This is known as portrait orientation. (See also *portrait orientation.*)

Sentence: "Maps are usually printed using *landscape orientation,* but brochures and letters usually use portrait orientation. When your printer totally screws up and chews your page into gibberish, that's known as Picasso orientation."

language

Pronunciation: *lan-gwage.*

Meaning: A specified way of using words and symbols to give the computer instructions and tell it what to do. All software is created by using a programming language. (See also *program, programmer,* and *programming language.*)

Sentence: "I tried learning to program in C, but it's much easier to use the BASIC *language* instead. Then again, it's even easier to have someone else do my work altogether."

laptop

Pronunciation: *lap-top.*

Meaning: A computer small enough to fit in your lap and not crush your kneecaps in the process. (See also *notebook computer* and *PC.*)

Sentence: "I like *laptop* computers because I can use them anywhere. Then again, why would I want to do work while vacationing in Hawaii?"

laser printer

Pronunciation: *lay-zer prin-ter.*

Meaning: A type of printer that uses a laser beam to generate an image and then electronically transfer it to paper. The speed of laser printers is measured in how many pages per minute (ppm) it can produce. The printing quality of laser printers is measured in dots per inch (dpi). (See also *dot-matrix, dots per inch, inkjet printer,* and *letter quality.*)

Sentence: "I use my *laser printer* for printing brochures, flyers, and fake college diplomas that I sell to people all over the country. Isn't technology terrific?"

launch

Pronunciation: *lawn-cha.*

Meaning: To start a program, usually directly from an operating system. Also used in place of the terms *load* and *run.* (See also *load* and *run.*)

Sentence: "From Windows I can *launch* several programs at once and switch among all of them. Now if I only knew how to use any of them, I might actually get some work done."

LCD

Pronunciation: *Ell See Dee.*

Meaning: Acronym for Liquid Crystal Display, which is a display commonly used in pocket calculators, watches, and laptop computers. LCD displays consume less power than normal monitors, but they tend to look as washed out as chalk drawings scribbled on the sidewalk in the rain. (See also *gas-plasma display* and *monitor.*)

Sentence: "My latest laptop computer uses a color *LCD* that looks almost as good as the color monitor on my desktop computer. Then again, Elvis impersonators look almost as good as the real Elvis, but it's still not the same."

leading

Pronunciation: *led-ding* (rhymes with *sledding*).

Meaning: Inserting extra space between lines of text for aesthetic purposes. The name comes from the days of printing presses when printers physically inserted thin strips of lead between lines. (See also *kerning.*)

Sentence: "Desktop publishing programs let you use *leading* to adjust your text. It's a subtle effect that hardly anyone notices until it's missing, or unless you have nothing better to do than measure lines of text on a page."

LED

Pronunciation: *Ell Ee Dee.*

Meaning: Acronym for Light-Emitting Diode, which is a device that lights up when an electrical current passes through it. Many digital clocks use LEDs to display numbers.

Sentence: "My alarm clock has a big, fat, red *LED.* I can see the numbers clear across the room without my glasses. I even think sleeping people can feel the numbers being burned into their eyelids."

left-justify

Pronunciation: *left-jus-ti-fi.*

Meaning: To align text flush against a left margin.

This is
an example
of left justification.

(See also *flush* and *justify*)

Sentence: "Most word processors *left-justify* text by default. Only if you're weird would you want to right-justify text."

letter quality

Pronunciation: *let-ter qua-li-tee.*

Meaning: Printed text that is clear enough that it looks like it came from a typewriter. Usually refers to printing that a dot-matrix printer produces. (See also *dot-matrix, laser printer,* and *line printer.*)

Sentence: "My dot-matrix printer can produce *letter quality* printing, so it looks like a typewriter printed it. Then again, how many people remember what a typewriter even looks like?"

LF

Pronunciation: *Ell Ef.*

Meaning: Acronym for Line Feed, which is a signal that tells a printer to start a new line. (See also *carriage return, Enter key, linefeed, newline character,* and *Return key.*)

Sentence: "Most dot-matrix printers have an *LF* and an FF button. If you press the FF button, the printer rolls a complete page out of the printer. If you just press the LF button, the printer just moves the page up one line."

LIFO

Pronunciation: *Li-fo* or *Ell I Ef O.*

Meaning: Acronym for Last In First Out, which describes a data structure used by programmers known as a stack. (See also *FIFO* and *stack.*)

Sentence: "*LIFO* is when you're in a cafeteria where the plates are stacked. The last plate the cooks put on the stack is the first one you have to take off. So if you're the last person to get a plate, your plate probably hasn't been washed since 1965."

light pen

Pronunciation: *lite pen.*

Meaning: A light-sensitive detector in the shape of a pen, which lets you draw pictures and give input to the computer from the screen. (See also *I/O, input, interface, keyboard,* and *mouse.*)

Sentence: "I use a *light pen* to draw pictures on my computer because it looks more natural than using a mouse. Then again, how natural is it to hold your arm straight out in the air for extended periods of time?"

line editor

Pronunciation: *lyne ed-i-ter.*

Meaning: A program that enables you to modify one line of a text file at a time, which is like trying to paint a wall through venetian blinds. (See also *editor.*)

Sentence: "The most infamous *line editor* of all time was one that came with MS-DOS called EDLIN. According to the manual, you could use EDLIN to write letters to other people. Good luck to those who tried."

line number

Pronunciation: *lyne num-ber.*

Meaning: A number used to identify lines in a document. The first line is number 1, the second line is number 2, and so on. To move to a specific line in a document, you would tell the computer to "Please show me line number 35."

Sentence: "Every word processor keeps track of *line numbers.* Then again, when was the last time you remembered that the information you need is on line number 35,819?"

line printer

Pronunciation: *lyne prin-ter.*

Meaning: A high-speed printer that can print an entire line at once. Line printers are great for printing quick drafts, but they're terrible for printing nice print. (See also *dot-matrix, laser printer, letter quality,* and *printer.*)

Sentence: "I bought a cheap dot-matrix *line printer* for fast printing. Then my friend showed me a fast laser printer that prints really nicely, too. Boy, do I feel like I got cheated by my computer dealer."

linefeed

Pronunciation: *lyne-feed.*

Meaning: Sometimes abbreviated as LF, this is a signal that tells the printer to advance the page one line. (See also *carriage return, Enter key, LF, newline character,* and *Return key.*)

Sentence: "If your program is lame, it isn't smart enough to send a *linefeed* signal to the printer, so your entire document prints on one line."

link

Pronunciation: *lin-ka.*

Meaning: (1) To connect two computers together through a modem, cable, or network. (2) Using Windows or OS/2, to connect two files together so that they share identical information. If you change data in one file, a hot link automatically changes the same data stored in the second file. With a cold link, changing data in one file does *not* automatically change the same data in a second file. (3) To combine multiple machine language files together to create a single program. (See also *network* and *serial communications.*)

Sentence: "After *linking* my computers with a serial cable, I linked a bunch of machine language files to make my own word processor. Then I used OS/2 to create a hot link between my word processor and my spreadsheet. Now I'm tired and need a nap."

linked list

Pronunciation: *lin-ked list.*

Meaning: A data structure used by programmers to store information. The size of a linked list can change as the program runs. A linked list consists of two parts: the data and a pointer that points to the next chunk of data. Think of a linked list as a train of cars connected together. Each car holds cargo (data) and each car is connected (linked) to the next car. (See also *data* and *stack.*)

Sentence: "Part of any programming language is learning how to make *linked lists.* That way your program can be more flexible and adapt to whatever amount of data it needs to hold."

linker

Pronunciation: *lin-ker.*

Meaning: A special program that combines one or more machine language files and converts them to a single executable file. (See also *link.*)

Sentence: "Instead of trying to create one huge program at once, write a bunch of little ones. Then use a *linker* to combine them all into one huge, unmanageable program loaded with bugs, and sell it for $495 like everyone else does. This is the secret of selling software."

Linotronic

Pronunciation: *Lyne-o-tron-ik.*

Meaning: The brand name for a typesetting machine used by many book and magazine publishers. A Linotronic printer produces extremely high-quality print and makes an ordinary laser printer look like trash. (See also *laser printer.*)

Sentence: "I like printing rough drafts on my home laser printer. Then for the final drafts, I print on a *Linotronic* machine."

LISP

Pronunciation: *Lisp* (rhymes with *crisp*).

Meaning: An acronym for LISt Processing, a language developed in the early '60s at MIT for artificial intelligence research. LISP code includes an incredible number of parentheses. Related dialects include Common LISP and Scheme. Typical LISP applications include computer learning, natural language processing, and understanding why people bother getting a Ph.D. in computer science when rock stars with third grade educations make millions by singing one hit single. (See also *artificial intelligence* and *language.*)

Sentence: "Unlike other languages, *LISP* programs can modify themselves while they're running, which means programs can really run completely out of control. And this is called artificial intelligence."

list

Pronunciation: *list* (rhymes with *mist*).

Meaning: A collection of data arranged in a certain order. Programs usually store lists as arrays or as a linked list. A phone book is a list of names and numbers. A grocery list is also a list. (See also *array, database* and *linked list.*)

Sentence: "My program reads names and addresses off the disk and stores it in a *list.* Good thing my computer isn't like me, or else it would lose it each time."

list box

Pronunciation: *list box.*

Meaning: A dialog box that displays a list of items. Items commonly found in a list box include filenames, printer names, directories, groceries, or anything else the computer thinks you might want. (See also *dialog box.*)

Sentence: "Whenever you choose the File Open command from the menu in Microsoft Word, the program displays a *list box* with all the filenames you can choose."

load

Pronunciation: *lode* (rhymes with *node*).

Meaning: To transfer data from storage to memory in the computer. (See also *launch* and *run.*)

Sentence: "Whenever I type **WP** at the DOS prompt, I can *load* WordPerfect onto my computer. Actually, the program loads into my computer's memory from the hard disk, but why bother with details just as long as it works okay?"

local bus

Pronunciation: *lo-kul bus.*

Meaning: A type of high-speed expansion slot for a PC, one that connects directly with the microprocessor. The advantage here is that devices connected to the local bus run much faster because they have a larger pipe through which they can yell at the CPU. Typical devices connected to a local bus include high-speed video cards and hard drives. (See also *bus* and *expansion slot.*)

Sentence: "Take a ride on the *local bus* and enjoy fast video, but only if you can afford it."

LocalTalk

Pronunciation: *Low-kul Tawk.*

Meaning: The connectors and cables that Apple Computer makes for AppleTalk networks. (See also *Apple Computer, AppleTalk,* and *network.*)

Sentence: "If you have a Macintosh network, just buy a *LocalTalk* cable and everything works fine. If you have a Novell network, then it costs you $125 an hour for a consultant, $200 per computer for a network card, $1,500 for installation...."

local variable

Pronunciation: *low-kal var-e-ay-bull.*

Meaning: An term that programmers use to describe data isolated in certain parts of a program. A variable is a fancy label, such as letters or numbers, for programs to assign to values. (See also *variable.*)

Sentence: "My program consists of one main program and three subprograms. Each subprogram has its own *local variables.* So if anything goes wrong, I can quickly find which variable is getting a wrong value and which subprogram I need to correct. Then I can spend the better part of an evening trying to track down the cause before I lose my mind."

lock

Pronunciation: *lah-ka.*

Meaning: To prevent access to something. Some computers have a key lock that you can use to prevent others from using your computer. Every 3½-inch floppy disk has a sliding tab that can prevent the disk from being written to. (See also *password.*)

Sentence: "As we sailed our tanker through the *locks,* I locked my 3½-inch floppy disk and turned my key in the computer lock so that no one would mess up my work until I returned. Then our ship sank and I lost everything anyway."

log

Pronunciation: *log* (rhymes with *dog, bog,* and *cog*).

Meaning: Abbreviation for LOGarithm, which is a mathematical function that fulfills an important role in some people's lives.

Sentence: "We learned about *logs* in math class, and after the test I promptly forgot all about them."

logic

Pronunciation: *lah-jik.*

Meaning: The main ingredient lacking in every computer manual in existence.

Sentence: "I tried to solve my problem using *logic,* but the computer still failed to work. That's when I decided to use a ball-peen hammer instead."

logic bomb

Pronunciation: *lah-jik bahm.*

Meaning: A secret part of a program that erases files or causes other destructive damage upon activation. Disgruntled employees wishing to wreak revenge on their former employers are usually the ones responsible for placing logic bombs. (See also *virus.*)

Sentence: "Can you believe I got fired? I got so mad that I put *logic bombs* in all my programs. One year from today, they'll erase everyone's hard disk."

logical drive

Pronunciation: *lah-ji-kal drive.*

Meaning: A way to partition a large single drive into smaller, "pretend" segments for the convenience of the user or the computer. Logical drives are rarely physical drives such as floppy or hard drives. Often, a single hard drive may be divided into two or more logical drives, such as drive C:, drive H:, and drive Z:. (See also *hard disk* and *partition.*)

Sentence: "To simplify my hard disk, I divided it in half and created a *logical drive* called drive S:. This is where I store all my the files that I don't want anyone else to see."

logical operator

Pronunciation: *lah-ji-kal op-er-ray-ter.*

Meaning: A symbol used in programming languages, spreadsheets, and databases for defining the relationship between two items. Examples of logical operators include AND, OR, and NOT. If you were using a database, you might want to find all the names of people who make over $50,000 a year AND who are interested in yachts. Or you might want the phone numbers of everyone in Wisconsin OR New York. Then again, you might want the ages of everyone who owns a car but NOT a foreign car. (See also *inclusive OR* and *operator.*)

Sentence: "The hardest part about using a database is searching for the information you need. If you can understand how *logical operators* can help you selectively sort a database, then you're halfway towards mastering databases or being further confused by the whole process."

log in

Pronunciation: *lahg in.*

Meaning: To connect to another computer or computer network to access its information. (See also *access time* and *log on.*)

Sentence: "Whenever I break into a secret bank computer, first I have to *log in* by typing an account name and a correct password. After that, I can do anything I want."

LOGO

Pronunciation: *Low-go.*

Meaning: A programming language specifically designed for teaching children how to use a computer. Users commonly write LOGO programs to control an imaginary turtle that moves around the screen and draws lines behind it. By writing LOGO commands to control the turtle, users can create neat little designs that impress adults as well. (See also *language.*)

Sentence: "When I was a kid, I learned about computers by learning *LOGO.* Then in elementary school, I learned BASIC. In high school, I learned Pascal. In college, I learned C. Now I don't know how to do anything. I'm so confused."

log on

Pronunciation: *lahg on.*

Meaning: To initially connect to a computer. (See also *access time* and *log in.*)

Sentence: "I can *log on* to any computer in the world with my modem. Of course, unless I have the right passwords, I can log in to only some of those computers."

loop

Pronunciation: *loop* (like Fruit Loops).

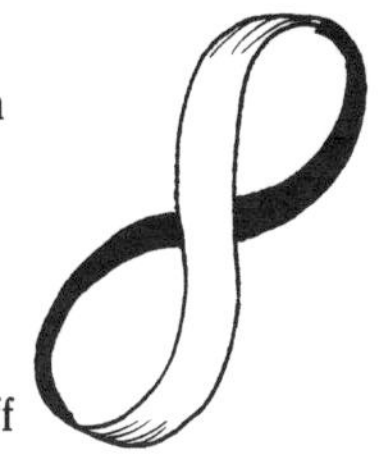

Meaning: A set of statements in a program that is run repeatedly. (See also *endless loop* and *infinite loop.*)

Sentence: "If the user doesn't type the correct password to log in, the program stays in the same *loop* and keeps asking for the right password until either the user gets it right or the user's fingers fall off from trying to guess."

lost cluster

Pronunciation: *law-sta klus-ter.*

Meaning: Part of a file that remains on the disk, even though the DOS file allocation table (FAT) has no record of its existence. Lost clusters usually occur when the computer is writing a file to the disk and the power fails. Sometimes lost clusters seem to occur without reason, which is the way most computer problems seem to appear. You can use the CHKDSK /F command in MS-DOS to convert lost clusters into files that you can delete to conserve disk space. (See also *FAT.*)

Sentence: "After I ran CHKDSK on my computer, I found a bunch of *lost clusters.* I turned them into files and erased them."

low-level format

Pronunciation: *lo-leh-vel for-mat.*

Meaning: To physically arrange the pattern of magnetic tracks and sectors of a hard disk. Low-level formats are only necessary when you are using a new hard disk for the first time. After performing a low-level format on a new hard disk, then you must use the MS-DOS FORMAT command to perform a high-level format. (See also *format.*)

Sentence: "You don't need to do a *low-level format* on a floppy disk. But a new hard disk requires it or else it won't work. Once you get your hard disk working, have fun trying to get the rest of your computer to work as well."

low resolution

Pronunciation: *lo re-zo-loo-shin.*

Meaning: On printers or computer monitors, low resolution is a mode that produces quick results but poorly drawn images that are likely to

hurt your eyes and give you headaches to boot. (See also *high resolution, monitor, printer,* and *resolution.*)

Sentence: "I have an old, *low resolution* monitor. The letters on the screen look jagged and fuzzy, but the money I saved by buying a cheap monitor is going to my doctor to pay for new eyeglasses."

lowercase

Pronunciation: *lo-wer-kase.*

Meaning: The opposite of capitalization. Most text appears with the initial letter of a word in a sentence in uppercase, and the rest of the text in lowercase. (See also *uppercase.*)

Sentence: "Don't type IN ALL UPPERCASE BECAUSE IT LOOKS OBNOXIOUS. Then again, don't type in all *lowercase* because it looks like you're trying to rip off e.e. cummings."

LPT

Pronunciation: *Ell Pee Tee.*

Meaning: In MS-DOS, the name given to the parallel ports of the computer. The first parallel port is called LPT1:, the second LPT2:, and so on. (See also *parallel port.*)

Sentence: "If you type **COPY AUTOEXEC.BAT LPT1:** and press the Enter key, your printer prints the contents of your AUTOEXEC.BAT file. Then again, if you don't have a printer connected to your first parallel port, your computer will hang temporarily, and you'll think that this book made you deliberately screw up."

M&Ms

Pronunciation: *Em-en-Emz.*

Meaning: Candy-covered chocolates with little *M*s on them that don't melt in your hand. Primary source of nourishment for programmers. Belongs to the food group: Candy. Other food groups include Pizza, Caffeine, and Processed Potato Foods (for example, chips).

Sentence: "Hey, isn't it about time for dinner? Pass me the *M&Ms,* will ya?"

Mac

(See *Macintosh.*)

machine independent

Pronunciation: *ma-sheen in-dee-pen-dunt.*

Meaning: Commonly used to refer to a program that runs on any computer without modification. A machine independent program can be developed on an IBM clone and used — without any modifications — on a Macintosh, for example.

Sentence: "*Machine independent* programs do not exist."

machine language

Pronunciation: *ma-sheen lang-wedge.*

Meaning: A "low-level" computer language that communicates directly to the computer hardware. Programs are written in secret code (binary); each instruction corresponds to a single computer operation. Often, an assembly language is used to make the machine language codes more

understandable by computer programmers — but that's not saying much because the whole thing is hard, hard, hard. Programming in machine language is not for beginners, no way! (See also *assembly language.*)

Sentence: "Real programmers use *machine language,* but they also tend to grunt and point at the dinner table. Therefore, when I learn to program, I'll do it in the BASIC programming language, which is more my speed."

Macintosh

Pronunciation: *Mak-en-tah-sha.*

Meaning: A family of personal computers created by Apple Computer in 1984 that features a graphical user interface. The Mac was the first computer to offer a 32-bit microprocessor. More importantly, the application program interface (API) gives users ease of use and reduced learning time. The Macintosh family is the largest non-IBM compatible personal computer series in use. (See also *Quadra, System 7, DA, API,* and *graphical user interface.*)

Sentence: "I always click the little apple menu option on my *Macintosh.* I don't always need to; I just think it's cute."

macro

Pronunciation: *ma-kro.*

Meaning: A "high-level" programming tool used to automate tasks or procedures within a program. Unlike standard programming languages, macros work only within specific programs. For example, an Excel macro works only within Microsoft Excel to automate complex, repetitious, or boring tasks. Users often can create macros without knowing any programming, by simply "recording" their actions (mouse movements, keystrokes, and so on) within the program. The macro command then "plays back" the recorded movements. Voilà. A macro! Advanced macros can be used to create custom applications that run within a program. For example, an Excel macro might provide custom commands and automate lengthy procedures for balancing your checkbook. A person using the checkbook macro does not have to know much about using Excel. (See also *macro instruction.*)

Sentence: "Hey, Phil, I finally finished that *macro* that automatically fouls up everyone's phone bill!"

macro assembler

Pronunciation: *mak-ro ah-sem-blur.*

Meaning: A program that lets you construct assembly language macros. An assembly language macro is an instruction that represents several other machine language instructions at once — like shorthand for programming geeks. By using the macro instruction, the programmer doesn't have to type as much, and it leaves one hand free to dive into the Doritos. (See also *machine language* and *assembly language.*)

Sentence: "I got a *macro assembler* to speed up my machine language programming. Now I can write my program in three years instead of five."

macro instruction

Pronunciation: *ma-kro in-struk-shun.*

Meaning: An individual command used in a macro. A collection of macro instructions is usually required for a complete macro. (See also *macro.*)

Sentence: "Do you know the *macro instruction* that tells this program to make toast?"

magnetic disk

Pronunciation: *mag-ne-tik dis-ka.*

Meaning: A medium (that is, a "flat round thing") on which computer data is stored. Often called floppy disks or hard disks, a magnetic disk is a surface coated with iron oxide and magnetically charged; bits (electronic charges) of computer data can be stored on the disk for future use. Floppy disks also make great cocktail coasters and impromptu frisbees. Never use a magnetic disk to play tug-of-war with your dog. Keep all magnetic disks away from magnetic charges, such as your stereo speakers and the planet Jupiter. (See also *disk, hard disk, floppy disk, double-density disk,* and *high density.*)

Sentence: "The instructions said to store my *magnetic disks* in an out-of-the-way place, so I put them in the toaster."

magneto-optical disk

Pronunciation: *mag-net-o op-ti-cal dis-ka.*

Meaning: A type of storage device that combines optical-disk technology with magnetic-disk technology to make a disk capable of storing lots

of information at incredibly slow speeds. These high-capacity disks require special disk drives and extra toil. (See also *disk* and *high density.*)

Sentence: "I am now on the cutting edge of technology with this new *magneto-optical disk.* My data will certainly survive a nuclear attack, but it may take that long for my program to load."

mail merge

Pronunciation: *may-l mur-ja.*

Meaning: A process by which names and addresses are combined with a form letter "master" to create those personalized form letters despised by all. When the master form letter is printed, names and addresses from the mail merge list are inserted into key locations. Each name and address creates a new form letter from the master.

Sentence: "I just got a personal letter from Ed McMahon. You don't suppose he has a *mail merge* program, do you?"

mailbox

Pronunciation: *may-l bok-sa.*

Meaning: An e-mail account or "address" to which you can send messages to people on networked or remote computers. An electronic mailbox can store your electronic mail, much the way the mailbox on the front porch stores your junk mail. (See also *e-mail, handle, network,* and *e-mail address.*)

Sentence: "I just got an electronic *mailbox;* now I can get bills on my computer, too!"

mainframe

Pronunciation: *may-na-fray-ma.*

Meaning: A powerful computer to which "dumb" terminals are often connected. A mainframe is identified by its storage and computing capacity; capability to create multiple, virtual computers; and its variety of input/output options. Mainframe computers also are called the dinosaurs of the computer industry. They require cool climates (air conditioning), open spaces, and plenty of electricity. (See also *VAX, PC, Cray, SQL,* and *dumb terminal.*)

Sentence: "We keep our company data on a *mainframe,* but all our employees want their own personal computers. So we got them each a mainframe."

male connector

Pronunciation: *may-l kon-nek-ter.*

Meaning: Any type of connector that inserts into a female connector. Male connectors are often located at the ends of cables and generally have prongs or wires that fit into the holes of the female connector (I'm blushing). After combining a male and female connector, you have a flow of electricity (occasionally accompanied by sparks flying), a surge of power, and, finally, a cigarette (cigarette optional). Please practice safe cable connection. (See also *female connector, serial, serial port, parallel,* and *parallel port.*)

Sentence: "You're trying to fit that serial *male connector* into a parallel female connector. It will never work out; they're not meant for each other."

mapping software

Pronunciation: *ma-ping soft-wayr.*

Meaning: Software that enables you to create and store maps. Maps can be viewed at different magnification factors and usually require a significant amount of disk space to store.

Sentence: "It's a good thing I brought my portable computer and *mapping software* on this road trip. Now I can get lost in half the time."

masochist

Pronunciation: *mas-o-kist.*

Meaning: (1) A person who inflicts pain on himself or herself. (2) Anyone who tries to use Windows with less than 4MB of RAM. (3) Anyone who uses WordPerfect for DOS.

Sentence: "They asked at the job interview whether I could use WordPerfect for DOS. I said, 'What do you think I am, a *masochist?*' I didn't get the job."

mass storage

Pronunciation: *mas stor-edge.*

Meaning: A high-capacity storage device. Because normal disk capacity has increased over the years, the definition of mass storage is somewhat loose. Typical hard disk drives store at least 80 megabytes of data; mass storage is generally considered to be at least 250 megabytes of data.

However, mass storage devices can hold over one *terabyte* (one trillion bytes) of data. Mass storage has nothing to do with Catholicism. (See also *high density, byte,* and *high capacity.*)

Sentence: "Father John is a computer enthusiast. He needs a *mass storage* device just to hold all his computer games."

master/slave arrangement

Pronunciation: *mas-ter/slayv ah-range-men-ta.*

Meaning: When one device (a slave) is controlled by another to which it is connected (a master). Master/slave arrangements are found in disk drive arrays and other hardware configurations and also with mainframes and dumb terminals. (See also *client, client/server network, network,* and *server.*)

Sentence: "When I push the remote control, the TV changes channels. It's a perfect *master/slave arrangement.*"

math coprocessor

Pronunciation: *math ko-pross-ess-er.*

Meaning: A separate circuit (or computer chip) that performs floating-point arithmetic to enhance the capabilities of the CPU (central processing unit). Math coprocessors are available for PC computers to perform math-intensive software procedures. Software is often written specifically to take advantage of a math coprocessor and may not run properly without it. (See also *central processing unit, microprocessor,* and *number crunching.*)

Sentence: "I just got a *math coprocessor* to perform floating point arithmetic on my computer. Now can somebody loan me a calculator so that I can balance my checkbook?"

matrix

Pronunciation: *may-triks.*

Meaning: A method of storing data in a grid-like thing so that each data element can be easily retrieved. To store the amount of your phone bill for each month of the year requires a one-dimensional matrix with 12 items; one item for each month of the year. To store the amounts of all your bills (phone, food, gas, and so on) requires a two-dimensional matrix, with bills down one side and months across the top. To store these values for several years requires a three-dimensional matrix, one separate grid for each year. (See also *array.*)

Sentence: "The Rubik's cube is the ultimate type of *matrix,* making computers relatively tame by comparison."

maximize

Pronunciation: *maks-im-eyes.*

Meaning: To increase to full capacity. When using Windows software, the term maximize refers to increasing the size of a window to fill the entire screen. You can do this by clicking the Maximize button or choosing Maximize from the window's control menu. (See also *minimize.*)

Sentence: "If I *maximize* the window on my checkbook program, will I maximize my income too?"

MB

Pronunciation: *Em Bee,* not pronounced *Mub.*

Meaning: An abbreviation for megabyte. 1,000,000 bytes of data. (See also *megabyte, byte,* and *bit.*)

Sentence: "My floppy disk holds 1.2*MB* of data, but my file is 3MB. It doesn't take a Ph.D. or M.D. to figure out that I need more MBs."

Mb (M-bit)

Pronunciation: *Em bee.*

Meaning: Acronym for megabit. 1,000,000 bits of data. Note the little *b.* Big *B* means bytes; little **b** means bits. There is a difference. (See also *megabit, bit,* and *nibble.*)

Sentence: "If 1,000,000 bits makes a *Mb* and 1,000,000 bytes makes an MB, what do I need to make a BMW?"

MCA

Pronunciation: *Em See Ay.*

Meaning: Acronym for *Micro Channel Architecture.* An expansion slot (bus) design that IBM developed for their PS/2 computers. The main idea behind the design was to enhance the speed of data transfer and to make plugging in expansion boards easier because the expansion board would automatically configure itself to the MCA slots. In reality, the purpose of MCA was to create a new bus standard that other computer manufacturers would have to pay massive royalties for if they wanted to develop MCA-compatible computers. (See also *expansion slot, expansion bus, expansion card,* and *bus.*)

Sentence: "The salesman told me if I bought an IBM PS/2 with an *MCA* bus that I would be all set for the future. He didn't know that five years later, hardly anyone would make expansion boards for the MCA standard."

MCGA

Pronunciation: *Em See Gee Ay.*

Meaning: Acronym for *Monochrome/Color Graphics Adapter.* The IBM graphics adapter used on the PS/2 computers. This is similar to combining an MGA and CGA adapter, but it also contains some special features of its own. MCGA adapters have generally been replaced by the more powerful EGA, VGA, and SVGA adapters. (See also *MDA, EGA, CGA, VGA, SVGA,* and *monochrome.*)

Sentence: "*MCGA* is a useless toad of a standard. Get Super VGA (SVGA) instead."

MDA

Pronunciation: *Em Dee Ay.*

Meaning: Acronym for *Monochrome Display Adapter.* The IBM adapter for monochrome monitors. This adapter does not provide graphics capabilities. (See also *monochrome, MCGA, EGA, CGA,* and *VGA.*)

Sentence: "*MDA* is boring black-and-white text, ladies and gentlemen. Major Yawn city."

media

Pronunciation: *mee-dee-ya.*

Meaning: Any kind of material used for data storage and communication, including magnetic media, optical media, print media, and so on. Plural of medium, a tiny lady who will cleanse your house of spirits and poltergeists. A *medium* is a carrier of information, much like your paper girl or that little voice telling you to go ahead and have a second piece of pie. (See also *disk* and *communications.*)

Sentence: "The stone tablet was among the first data storage *media.* Talk about a hard disk!"

meg

Pronunciation: *meg* (as in Ryan).

Meaning: Short for megabyte or Margaret. (See also *megabyte, MB, byte, or mega-.*)

Sentence: "My hard disk holds 120 *megs* of data."

mega-

Pronunciation: *may-ga.*

Meaning: Prefix meaning one million. A unit of measure in the metric system. Also a slang word to designate an abundance of something, as in *mega-fun.* (See also *megabyte*, *megahertz,* and *MB.*)

Sentence: "My 240 *mega*byte hard disk gives me mega-room for files and programs."

megabyte

Pronunciation: *may-ga-bite.*

Meaning: Approximately one million bytes. Actually a megabyte is equal to 1,024 kilobytes, or 1,048,576 bytes. You need only be this specific on your tax form. Outside the IRS, the government has passed numerous laws declaring a megabyte to be exactly one million bytes (the 48,576 extra bytes are kept "off budget"). (See also *MB, byte, Mb,* and *bit.*)

Sentence: "Back in the early days of computing, a *megabyte* was considered way, way too much storage space. Now I need six megabytes of space just to store my shoes."

megahertz

Pronunciation: *may-ga-hurt-sa.*

Meaning: One million hertz (MHz), or one million cycles per second. Microprocessor chips oscillate (wiggle) at a certain speed, measured in cycles per second, or hertz. Besides the clock speed, the internal design of the processor determines its overall speed. (See also *hertz, MHz,* and *mega-.*)

Sentence: "The People's Republic of China has over one billion bicycles. That's 1,000 *megahertz.*"

membrane keyboard

Pronunciation: *mem-brain kee-bord.*

Meaning: A keyboard that has a flat, plastic surface (called a membrane) with keys printed on it — like a cheap, flat calculator. This is keyboard that you probably don't want to use; a touch-typist's nightmare. (See also *boat anchor* and *heavy iron.*)

Sentence: "Yes, Jared, the *membrane keyboard* on your little Atari 400 makes it perhaps the silliest computer known to the human race."

memory

Pronunciation: *mem-o-ree.*

Meaning: Commonly refers to the chips inside a computer in which information is stored. Two types of internal memory exist: *read-only memory* (ROM) permanently holds information vital to the computer's operation, such as the BIOS. *Random-access memory* (RAM) holds information that you are currently using, such as your letter to the Editor or your genealogy chart. Whereas the information in ROM is permanent, the information in RAM goes away when you turn off the computer. Programs load information into RAM as needed for smooth operation. Generally, the more RAM you have, the better. If you use Windows software, you can't have too much RAM. (See also *RAM, random access, nonvolatile memory,* and *ROM.*)

Sentence: "My computer has 16 megabytes of *memory* inside. Now if only I could remember where I put the car keys."

memory map

Pronunciation: *mem-o-ree map.*

Meaning: A graphical depiction of how RAM is used in a computer. Actually, the memory map is for trivial purposes only, although some programmer types want to know "where in memory" some tidbit or secret switch is located. To us humans, the information is silly beyond all recourse.

Sentence: "After looking at my computer's *memory map,* I can find Detroit."

memory resident programs

Pronunciation: *mem-o-ree rez-i-dent pro-grams.*

Meaning: Programs that stay in memory that you can't see, laying low, when you are not using them. Memory resident programs also are called *TSRs* (*Tee-Ess-Ars* for Terminate and Stay Resident). Memory resident programs are often utilities that extend the basic functions of the computer, such as mouse drivers, fax software, and print spools. They're also often the cause of problems and conflicts in your software. (See also *terminate-and-stay resident programs.*)

Sentence: "My pop-up calendar is a *memory resident program* that helps me schedule my tasks; I can access the calendar whenever I need it by pressing Ctrl-Alt-C and . . . Oops! My system just crashed."

menu

Pronunciation: *men-yu.*

Meaning: A list of commands or options available within a program. When several options are available at a particular time, programs often present those options in menus. The menu shows each available option and, using the mouse or keyboard, you can choose a command from the menu. Such programs are often called *menu-driven programs.* Almost all Macintosh and Windows programs are menu driven. (See also *menu bar, menu item, pop-up menu,* and *pull-down menu.*)

Sentence: "When I want to change the fonts in my word processor, I just click the Format *menu* and choose the Font command. When I want to order lunch, I often use the Chinese menu and choose Chow Mein. You can't really get through life without knowing something about menus."

menu bar

Pronunciation: *men-yu bar.*

Meaning: An area, usually located at the top of the screen, that contains several menus listed across in a single line. It's from the menu bar that you can choose commands. You choose commands by using the keyboard, the mouse, or by asking the waiter for a translation. (See also *menu* and *menu item.*)

Sentence: "*Menu bars* usually include appetizers to make you thirsty so that you'll order more drinks."

menu item

Pronunciation: *men-yu i-tim.*

Meaning: An individual command or option that appears on a menu.

Sentence: "The File menu contains 14 *menu items,* including an Exit command. When I'm not sure which item to choose, I choose Exit."

menu tree

Pronunciation: *men-yu tree.*

Meaning: A diagram showing the menu structure within a program. Some menu items do not produce immediate results but "branch out" to more menus or dialog boxes. This creates a hierarchy ("Me first! No me!") of menu commands and options. A menu tree displays this hierarchy of

commands so that you can locate any command through the maze of menus. (See also *menu, menu bar,* and *menu item.*)

Sentence: "There are so many menus in this program that I need a *menu tree* to help me find the command I want."

message box

Pronunciation: *mess-ij boks.*

Meaning: A box or small window that appears on the screen and presents a message from the program you are using. Message boxes can appear as the result of your choosing a command or option. They often inform you of mistakes or provide warnings about your actions. (See also *dialog box* and *list box.*)

Sentence: "Last night I was working late on the computer, and I got a *message box* that said, 'Go to bed!'"

meta

Pronunciation: *met-uh* ("I meta on a Monday and my heart stood still, Da-do-run-run-run, Da-do-run-run.")

Meaning: Above and beyond, from the original meaning of meta, which meant *to change.* In computers, meta refers to a special character combination often associated with a specific key. For example, some weird keyboards may have a shift key named META. If a program asks you to press META-S, you press and hold the META key and press S.

Sentence: "The S key makes an S on the screen; Ctrl-S saves my file; Alt-S brings up the Silly menu; and *META-S* zooms me to outer space."

MHz

Pronunciation: *May-ga-Hurtz.*

Meaning: Abbreviation for megahertz. (See also *megahertz.*)

Sentence: "I gave my old 8 *MHz* computer to my kids and got a more powerful computer for myself. How come they can get more done than I do?"

Mickey Mouse

Pronunciation: *Mi-kee Mowss.*

Meaning: (1) A fictional character, created by Walt Disney, who talks in a high voice and goes easily through life with his wacky friends and his dog, Pluto. Best known works include "The Sorcerer's Apprentice" from *Fantasia* and regular appearances at Disneyland and Disneyworld. Also a popular export to Japan. (2) Something not quite up to snuff, or straying from the task at hand. (See also *mouse.*)

Sentence: "*Mickey Mouse* may be the world's most popular cartoon character. I like him because he doesn't take life too seriously."

micro-

Pronunciation: *my-kro.*

Meaning: A prefix that means one millionth. A microsecond is one millionth of a second. Micro is used also to imply a microscopic size, as in microorganism and microprocessor. Micro is also one of the most coveted words to use for computer companies and software product names (for example, Microsoft).

Sentence: "I use Microsoft Word on my *micro*computer and can type a letter in a microsecond."

Micro Channel Architecture

Pronunciation: *My-kro Chan-l Awr-ki-tek-chur.*

Meaning: A type of expansion slot design used in IBM PS/2 model 50 (and higher) computers, abbreviated MCA. Hardware companies design computer enhancement boards (or cards) that plug into the MCA bus. Boards designed for the MCA bus do not work with a standard bus. Among other enhancements, the MCA bus allows use of multiple CPUs within the computer, although I wouldn't try that at home. (See also *bus, expansion slot, expansion bus, expansion card,* and *MCA.*)

Sentence: "I bought a computer that uses the *Micro Channel Architecture.* Now everybody is talking about the EISA bus. The problem is that most of the enhancement cards are available for the ISA bus. By the way, what type of bus did Ralph Kramden drive?"

microcomputer

Pronunciation: *my-kro-kum-pew-ter.*

Meaning: Actually intended as a disparaging term for the new personal computers that started appearing in the mid-1970s. The term *micro* came from the microprocessor, the chip that provided the brains for these new computers. The term fell into disuse when PCs became popular in the mid-1980s. (See also *PC* and *mainframe.*)

Sentence: "Most *microcomputers* of today are far more powerful than the so-called 'real' computers of 20 years ago. So let's all give a Bronx cheer to our pals in mainframe and minicomputer land: Ptbtbtbtb!"

microfloppy disk

Pronunciation: *my-kro-flop-ee dis-ka.*

Meaning: Generally refers to a 3½-inch floppy disk, which is smaller than the widely used 5¼-inch floppy disk, which is smaller than the original 8-inch floppy disk. Actually, the original 8-inch floppy was called a *floppy* because it really had some flop to it. The 5¼-inchers were called minifloppies when they first appeared. This left microfloppy to describe the smaller 3½-inch floppy disks. A microfloppy disk holds either 720KB or 1.22MB of data, depending on whether it is a double-density or high-density disk (respectively). (See also *magnetic disk, floppy disk,* and *disk.*)

Where is that microfloppy?

Sentence: "I replaced my old 5.25-inch floppy disk drive with a *microfloppy disk* drive. Pretty soon, disks will be the size of a toenail and almost as chewy."

microprocessor

Pronunciation: *my-kro-pro-ses-er.*

Meaning: The central processing chip (the "brains") in a microcomputer. Common microprocessors include the Motorola 68000, 68030, 68040 used in Macintoshes, and the Intel 286, 386, 486, and Pentium chips used in DOS machines. The microprocessor controls most of the core functions of the computer but can be enhanced with coprocessor chips. (See also *central processing unit* and *math coprocessor.*)

Sentence: "When you upgrade from a '286 *microprocessor* to a '386 or better, you get enhanced features from your Windows software. For example, you can add virtual memory to your computer, which handles the overflow when you fill up your RAM. But most of all, the '386 microprocessor is a lot faster than the '286."

microsecond

Pronunciation: *my-kro-sek-und.*

Meaning: One millionth of a second. Also used as an exaggeration to imply something that happened very quickly.

Sentence: "If you do that again, I'll be out of here in a *microsecond!*"

Microsoft

Pronunciation: *My-kro-soft.*

Meaning: (1) A large software company, located in Redmond, Washington, that produces MS-DOS, Windows, and a suite of best-selling application programs for the PC and Macintosh computers. (2) Stock I never should have sold. (3) See OZ. (4) See Federal Trade Commission. (5) Rulers of the known world. (6) Microsoft has no meaning. (See also *IBM.*)

Sentence: "Almost every program you see these days is made by *Microsoft.*"

microspacing

Pronunciation: *my-kro-spay-sing.*

Meaning: The insertion of small spaces (smaller than one character) between words to aid in justification. Used in all laser printers and some dot-matrix printers. (See also *kerning* and *justify.*)

Sentence: "My first dot-matrix printer had a *microspacing* feature that made its justified documents look more professional. Now my laser printer uses this same technique — in a much more professional fashion."

MIDI

Pronunciation: *Mid-Ee.*

Meaning: Acronym for *Musical Instrument Digital Interface.* A protocol, or standard, for encoding musical sounds in digital form. The differences in sounds and musical voices can be measured and stored using the MIDI standard and then transferred digitally between computers and MIDI-equipped instruments. Electronic keyboards commonly use MIDI.

Sentence: "Using the *MIDI* port in my electronic synthesizer, I can play music on the keyboard, and my computer transcribes the music onto the screen. Imagine what Mozart could do today."

milli-

Pronunciation: *mil-ee.*

Meaning: A prefix meaning one thousandth. One milligram equals one thousandth of a gram. Also a good (or bad?) name for a dog.

Sentence: "A *milli*second is the length of time it takes for Bill Gates to earn one million dollars in interest."

MiniFinder

Pronunciation: *Mi-nee-Find-er.*

Meaning: A piece of software for the Macintosh that makes it easy to locate your programs. You can configure the MiniFinder to access your most commonly used programs so that you don't have to search through your folders to locate them.

Sentence: "Using *MiniFinder,* I can launch Microsoft Word instantly."

minimize

Pronunciation: *min-ee-mize.*

Meaning: (1) To shrink or reduce to minimum size or capacity. In Windows, minimize refers to shrinking a window to appear as an icon on the desktop. You can minimize a window by clicking the Minimize button or by using the Minimize command in the Control menu. (2) To do something unspeakable to Mickey's girlfriend. (See also *maximize.*)

Sentence: "I thought that when I *minimized* my programs, I would minimize my computer problems, too."

MIPS

Pronunciation: *Mips,* like *lips* or *hips* or chocolate *chips.*

Meaning: Acronym for *Million Instructions Per Second.* A measurement of the speed at which programs run on a particular microprocessor. Because programs are coded differently for different microprocessors, it's important to measure MIPS by using equivalent code on each machine. (See also *central processing unit* and *microprocessor.*)

Sentence: "If you toss the word *MIPS* around in conversation, as in 'my 386 is clocked at 200 *MIPS,*' people will think you know what you're talking about."

MIS department

Pronunciation: *Em-Eye-Es dee-part-mint.*

Meaning: An acronym for *Management Information System.* The employees in a big organization who are responsible for purchasing, running, and fixing the company's computers and software. Also called the *IS department.*

Sentence: "I called Jane from the *MIS department* to come fix my Macintosh. She told me it would work better if I would quit trying to install DOS on my machine."

mnemonic

Pronunciation: *new-mon-ik.*

Meaning: A way of naming something that helps you remember its purpose. For example, mnemonic commands can begin with the first letter of the command, as in Alt-F-S to represent the File Save command.

Sentence: "My program uses *mnemonic* commands to make it easier to remember important procedures. Now if only I could remember how to start the program."

mode

Pronunciation: *mode* (rhymes with *toad, explode,* or *freeload*).

Meaning: One of several distinct ways of running a program. For example, you can use many DOS programs either in text mode or graphics mode. In graphics mode, you can see fonts and graphics on the screen in a WYSIWYG fashion. In text mode, only the computer's built-in text characters appear. (See also *protected mode* and *WYSIWYG.*)

Sentence: "If you have a 286 computer, you can run Windows in standard *mode,* which eliminates the use of special 386 options."

modem

Pronunciation: *mo-dum* (short for *modulator-demodulator*).

Meaning: A device used by your computer to communicate to remote computers through the phone lines. Modems come in various speeds, or *baud rates,* such as 1200, 2400, 9600, and 14,400. To connect to an on-line bulletin board service (BBS), you need a modem and communications software. An internal modem can be inserted inside your computer's case. An external modem can be attached to a standard RS-232 serial port. (See also *BBS, baud, fax, modem,* and *Hayes compatibility.*)

Sentence: "I wanted to call GEnie and make a few wishes, but first I had to buy a modem."

modifier keys

Pronunciation: *mod-i-fi-er kees.*

Meaning: Keys that work with other keys to give commands to the computer. Examples of modifier keys are Shift, Ctrl, and Alt. (See also *function keys* and *key.*)

Sentence: "If you press F7, you can save your files. If you press Shift-F7, you can print your file. And if you press Alt-F7 plus all of the other *modifier keys* at once, a magic genie appears granting your every wish (or maybe your system crashes — I forget)."

Modula-2

Pronunciation: *Mod-yu-lah-Too.*

Meaning: A structured programming language, similar to Pascal, that encourages programmers to create programs in modules. Modules are linked when the program is loaded. Pascal and Modula-2 were both created by Niklaus Wirth. (See also *language, modular,* and *programming language.*)

Sentence: "If you know how to program in Pascal, you'll find *Modula-2* an easy transition."

modular

Pronunciation: *mod-u-ler.*

Meaning: Consisting of, or relating to, individual units, or *modules.* Programs are often written in modules, or separate pieces, to make programming easier. Modular programming also allows programmers to work on different aspects of the program simultaneously. Modular programming also can enhance memory management. (See also *Modula-2.*)

Sentence: "I think this program is *modular.* Each time I do something new, it goes back to the disk to read another program module."

molecular beam epitaxy

Pronunciation: *moll-eck-yoo-lar beem ep-i-taks-ee.*

Meaning: The process by which circuits are engraved on a piece of silicon to make a semiconductor — a computer chip. This is a big, hunky word you can toss around to really impress your friends. We're not kidding. (See also *semiconductor* and *central processing unit.*)

Sentence: "The *molecular beam epitaxy* certainly vaporizes the substrate layers to form nice, crisp semiconducting material. Yessiree."

monitor

Pronunciation: *mah-ni-ter.*

Meaning: Another name for a CRT, screen, or terminal — the thing that you stare into for hours on end when using your computer. There are several types of monitors, including TTL monochrome, RGB color, analog color, and multisync. (2) A verb meaning the act of checking the progress of an activity, such as snooping around inside your PC's guts to see how things work. (See also *CRT, RGB,* and *terminal.*)

Sentence: "I was playing Solitaire on my new color multisync *monitor* when my boss came in to monitor my progress. Luckily, Windows let me task switch to my word processor instantly."

monochrome

Pronunciation: *mah-no-krome.*

Meaning: An adjective meaning one color. Monochrome monitors display information in a single color— often green or amber — on top of black. Monochrome monitors are not capable of high-resolution graphics and are best used for text-based applications or boat anchors. (See also *MDA, EGA, CGA, VGA, MCGA, boat anchor,* and *heavy iron.*)

Sentence: "When I exit Windows to use a DOS command, my screen looks like a dull *monochrome monitor* for a while."

monospacing

Pronunciation: *mah-no-spay-sing.*

Meaning: Uniform and equal spacing between the letters of words. With monospacing, each letter of the alphabet uses the same amount of space as every other letter; an *i* uses a much space as an *m.* With proportional spacing, each letter uses only as much space as it needs. Monospacing is still used in some applications, such as business forms. Most fonts use monospacing also for numerals to aid in alignment of financial data. (See also *proportional pitch.*)

Sentence: "Lois, darling, that *monospaced* letter you did, it's *tres gauche.* Get with the time, girl. Everyone is going proportionally spaced now."

MOS

Pronunciation: *Moss* (as in slimy green fungus).

Meaning: Acronym for *Metal Oxide Semiconductor.* A type of semiconductor used in computers. (See also *semiconductor* and *CMOS.*)

Sentence: "See *MOS.* CMOS Run. Run, MOS, Run."

motherboard

Pronunciation: *muh-ther-bored.*

Meaning: The main circuit board of a computer, to which most devices connect. The motherboard is the real estate upon which the computer's CPU, ROM chips, and often the RAM chips sit and work. It also contains the expansion slots and other electronic doodads, making it look like an electronic sushi display. (See also *daughterboard, expansion slots,* and *central processing unit.*)

Sentence: "Always do something nice for your *motherboard* on Mother's Day."

mount

Pronunciation: *moww-nt.*

Meaning: A term used to describe that something, usually a disk drive, is being used. In a networking context, *mounting a volume* means to connect to a remote disk drive, making it accessible from your computer. This comes from the olden computer days when they physically had to mount a reel of computer tape on the machine before anyone could access it. Nowadays, the mounting takes place through software commands that make the connections over various wires and hoses. (See also *hard disk.*)

Sentence: "Jump through the fiery network hoop, and then you can *mount* the remote H: drive and access your files."

mouse

Pronunciation: *mows.*

Meaning: A pointing device used to provide input for the computer. Most graphical user interfaces (Windows and the Macintosh) use mouse input devices. When you move the mouse on your desk, the mouse pointer on the screen mimics its movement. This allows you to control, point at, grab, and manipulate various graphics goodies (and text) in a program. (See also *track ball, joy stick, mouse button, mouse pad,* and *Mickey Mouse.*)

Sentence: "Units of *mouse* movement are measured in Mic-Keys."

mouse button

Pronunciation: *mows butt-on.*

Meaning: An area on the mouse that you press in order to make things happen. When pressed, a button makes a clicking sound. Mice have from one to three buttons, each performing different functions. The Macintosh uses a one-button mouse. By holding certain keys down as you click the button, you can perform different options — just as if you had a two-button mouse. (See also *mouse* and *mouse pad.*)

Sentence: "The program says to click the *mouse button* twice. So I figured that if I click it ten times, it'll really work great (kind of like the TV remote)."

mouse pad

Pronunciation: *mows pad.*

Meaning: A flat surface, usually padded, used to roll your mouse around. The ball on the mouse operates best on a clean, flat surface; a mouse pad is better than most people's desktop for rolling your mouse around. (See also *mouse* and *mouse button.*)

Sentence: "When finished making movies for the day, Mickey Mouse returns to his *mouse pad* to party with Minnie."

move

Pronunciation: *moov.*

Meaning: (1) A command in many software products that lets you transfer objects or text from one location to another, as in Excel's Edit-Move command. (2) What you do when your accountant discovers a bug in his tax software that results in an extra $20,000 you owe to the IRS. (See also *drag.*)

Sentence: "My spreadsheet calculated a negative cash flow in my budget, so I *moved* the expense column to next year's worksheet. Now I can move to a bigger house."

MPC

Pronunciation: *Em Pee See.*

Meaning: Acronym for *Multimedia Personal Computer.* A set of minimal requirements a computer system needs in order to create or use multimedia software. All MPC products are designed to work together so that you can create multimedia presentations. (See also *multimedia* and *PC.*)

Sentence: "I wanted to create a hypertext manual, so I bought an *MPC* computer, an MPC sound board, and an MPC hypertext word processor."

Mr. Data

Pronunciation: *Mis-ter Day-tah.*

Meaning: A fictional character from the television series *Star Trek: The Next Generation.* More frequently called Commander Data, Mr. Data is an android officer on the Starship Enterprise. He has a charming, innocent personality and is a fine example of artificial intelligence at work. (See *data, Star Trek,* and *Star Trek: The Next Generation.*)

Sentence: "I hear *Mr. Data* just installed Stacker, and he now can remember twice as many things."

MS-DOS

Pronunciation: *Em-Es-Doss.*

Meaning: Acronym for *Microsoft Disk Operating System.* The most widely used operating system for personal computers, sold also as PC-DOS by IBM. Also called simply DOS. MS-DOS is the reason why Macintosh users avoid IBM and compatible computers. To organize disks and data, it uses a tree-like directory structure wherein files can be stored inside directories and subdirectories. DOS commands include DIR, CD, COPY, DEL, RD, and so on.

For more information on MS-DOS, refer to your friendly "dummies" book: *DOS For Dummies* by Dan Gookin, available in most 7/11 Convenience stores. (See also *disk operating system, DOS,* and *Microsoft.*)

Sentence: "When I start my computer, the screen says `Starting MS-DOS....` Then I get the DOS prompt and I type **WIN** to go right into Windows and avoid using DOS altogether."

MTBF

Pronunciation: *Em Tee Bee Ef.*

Meaning: Acronym for *Mean Time Between Failure,* used to tell someone the average life of a product such as a hard disk or laser printer.

Sentence: "This laser printer has an *MTBF* of 35,000 pages, which means if I print page 35,001, the printer should statistically blow up on me."

MultiFinder

Pronunciation: *Mul-tee-Fine-der.*

Meaning: A part of the Macintosh operating system that organizes and provides access to your files and folders. MultiFinder is a hierarchical filing system (HFS). (See also *Chooser, Finder, hierarchical file system,* and *Macintosh.*)

Sentence: "My Macintosh is equipped with *MultiFinder*, and I still can't find a thing on my disk drive."

multimedia

Pronunciation: *Mul-tee-mee-dee-ya* (geek pronunciation: *Mul-tie-mee-dee-ya*).

Meaning: Relating to video, audio, and graphics. Multimedia software combines two or more media for presentation or analysis purposes. For example, many packages let you combine graphics with sound. Large multimedia applications are often stored on CD-ROM devices due to their incredible size and memory requirements. Multimedia will likely be common in the future for all sorts of information retrieval. (See also *communications* and *MPC.*)

Sentence: "I have a *multimedia* version of the encyclopedia. To explain the topics, the software plays movie clips, plays music, and shows graphics and artwork. Some day, it will write my term papers for me, too."

multiplexing

Pronunciation: *mul-tee-plex-ing.*

Meaning: The simultaneous transmission of multiple messages in one channel over a network. This is the equivalent of watching both CNN and C-SPAN at the same time as the local station. In a computer, multiplexing lets more than one computer access a network at the same time. (See also *network.*)

Sentence: "Before we got *multiplexing,* it seemed stupid that only one person could use the network at any give time. Now with multiplexing, everyone can use the network, everyone can get more work done, and everyone has cleaner, whiter teeth in less than three weeks!"

multiprocessing

Pronunciation: *mul-tee-pros-ses-sing.*

Meaning: The use of multiple microprocessors in the same computer. A computer that uses any type of coprocessor is a multiprocessing computer. (See also *coprocessor* and *central processing unit.*)

Sentence: "When I run my CAD program, the *multiprocessing* powers of the computer are fully used. The multiprocessing powers of my brain are used when I run my CAD program while I'm talking on the phone."

multisync monitor

Pronunciation: *mul-tee-sink mon-i-ter.*

Meaning: A computer monitor that can scan the screen (display data) at different rates, due to different video modes and hardware configurations. Also called multiscan monitors. (See also *monitor* and *graphics.*)

Sentence: "I bought a *multisync monitor* so that I could see incredible graphics in sharp resolution. Then I realized I needed to buy an expensive video board to go along with it. How come I feel like I'm being ripped off each time I upgrade my computer?"

multitasking

Pronunciation: *mul-tee-tas-king.*

Meaning: The capability for one machine to run two or more programs at the same time without knowing how to use any of them. Multitasking is commonly used for background operations, such as printing, fax and data communications, and complex calculations. While the background operation (or task) is running, you can perform other tasks with other software. Multitasking slows down computer operation. (See also *protect mode.*)

Sentence: "When I print using the Windows Print Manager, I can switch to another application or continue working while the document prints. This *multitasking* feature cuts down on the idle time spent on meaningless tasks, such as thinking, while you wait for your document to print."

multiuser

Pronunciation: *mul-tee-yu-zer.*

Meaning: Relating to multiple users. A program or operating system that supports more than one user at the same time. A multiuser database, for example, allows numerous computers to access the data at the same time. Multiuser software uses a network to connect users to the data. (See also *network.*)

Sentence: "If you have a *multiuser* database, you can have several employees typing the wrong information simultaneously."

Murphy's Law

Pronunciation: *Mer-Fees Lah.*

Meaning: (1) A universal law, or truth, that states: If anything can go wrong, it will. A subset of Murphy's Law is embodied in Parkinson's Law, which states that your clutter will expand to fill the space allotted for it. Another subset of Murphy's Law is Smucker's Law, which states that if you drop your bread, it will always land with the jelly side down.

Sentence: "Never forget to back up your computer data because the one time you forget, *Murphy's Law* goes into action and lightning strikes your computer."

n

Pronunciation: *en.*

Meaning: An unknown value, typically the largest value possible. Computer people say "from 1 to *n* things can go wrong." Or they'll use the *nth* value to mean the highest, last — nay, umpteenth — value. (See also *variable.*)

Sentence: "This is the *nth* time that I've been put on hold for n minutes when calling tech support."

nano

Pronunciation: *na-no.*

Meaning: A prefix meaning one billionth. For example, a nanogram equals one billionth of a gram. A nanosecond is one billionth of a second, or the amount of time it takes for the U.S. Government to spend $40. (See also *nanosecond.*)

Sentence: "Computer book authors make about a *nano*portion of Bill Gates' income."

nanosecond

Pronunciation: *na-no-sek-und.*

Meaning: One billionth of a second. Also used to measure the speed of chips. The amount of time it takes users to find an error in the software documentation. (See also *nano.*)

Sentence: "I always wondered how anyone measures a *nanosecond.* There can't be much of a margin for error."

natural language processing

Pronunciation: *na-chur-role lang-wedge pro-se-sing.*

Meaning: The use of natural languages by computers for processing information. Today, computers use artificial languages, such as BASIC and C++, which are limited in syntax and vocabulary. Natural language processing would enable computers to understand and process languages such as English and Zulu. Although much progress has been made, natural language processing is many years away from reality. Problems with syntax, pronunciation, and vocabulary have not been completely solved. A complex set of rules is required to decipher the simplest sentences; as language gets more complex, the rules become colossally difficult to construct. (See also *artificial intelligence, language, BASIC, C, C++,* and *syntax.*)

Sentence: "My dog must use *natural language processing* to understand what I mean when I say, 'Where's your ball?' I guess dogs are more intelligent than computers."

navigation

Pronunciation: *nav-i-gay-shun.*

Meaning: The act of finding your way through data, a program, a disk, or a network. In a software application, navigation refers to moving the insertion point (or cursor) around the document. Proper navigation lets you edit and manipulate a document more efficiently. Most programs, for example, have sophisticated navigation keys and procedures. For example, in Microsoft Word for Windows, you can press Ctrl-Home to move instantly to the top of a document. (See also *cursor.*)

Sentence: "Microsoft Word provides numerous *navigation* options, allowing even an amateur to become completely lost in a matter of nanoseconds."

near-letter quality

Pronunciation: *neer let-tur kwal-i-tee.*

Meaning: Letter-quality printing is produced by typewriters and daisy-wheel printers. A hammer, containing the impression of a character, strikes an inked ribbon, which in turn strikes the paper. Letter-quality type has no rough edges and is used for professional documents, such as business letters and contracts. Near-letter quality printing is produced by dot-matrix printers. By condensing the dots to a high resolution, the rough edges around the characters are minimized and a near-letter quality is achieved. Fact is, you can always tell the difference. And laser printers, with their resolution and graphics capabilities, send near-letter quality printers to the cleaners. Often abbreviated as *NLQ.* (See also *laser printer, letter quality, dot matrix,* and *daisy wheel.*)

Sentence: "When I got my laser printer, the *near-letter quality* printer wasn't very useful. It makes a pretty good footstool, though."

nerd

Pronunciation: *nerd* (rhymes with *pilchard, thitherward,* and *whirlybird*).

Meaning: Someone who is very wrapped up in computers — and often him or herself as well. There are actually several degrees of nerdhood. At the very top are the elitists, often members of the *Programming Priesthood.* They're nice and understanding but still dedicated to computers. Nerds include those who love the computers because nothing else loves them back; the geeks who are into it just because a good "Dungeons and Dragons" game isn't going on anywhere nearby; and the dweebs, whose idea of being socially acceptable is brushing their teeth *and* applying deodorant. Nerd also can be a charming term, applied to anyone who's hopelessly involved with computers yet still remains a vibrant part of society. (See also *hacker, geek,* and *dweeb.*)

Sentence: "I knew Milton was a *nerd* and socially awkward. I couldn't understand why he was so popular. That was until someone told me that he pulls down six figures — plus stock options — writing software at Microsoft."

nested

Pronunciation: *nest-ed.*

Meaning: A programming term that means to include a procedure within another, similar, procedure. For example, nested FOR/NEXT loops can look like this:

```
FOR E=1 TO 10
 FOR F=1 TO 3
 NEXT F
NEXT E
```

In this example, the F loop is nested inside the E loop. Nesting can be constructed several levels deep to create a complex procedure. (See also *loop, infinite loop,* and *endless loop.*)

Sentence: "My programs use a lot of *nested* loops. It must be my nesting instinct."

NetBIOS

Pronunciation: *Net-By-Oss.*

Meaning: Abbreviation for *Network Basic Input/Output System.* The BIOS tells a computer what types of devices and memory are connected to the computer and how to find them. A network BIOS includes basic information about the network to which a computer is connected. When you load your network operating system, the NetBIOS loads into the computer to supplement the standard BIOS. (See also *BIOS* and *network.*)

Sentence: "When I log on to the network, my *NetBIOS* tells the computer where to locate the other computers."

network

Pronunciation: *net-werk.*

Meaning: (1) A system of autonomous computers connected to each other for data transfer and communications. A network requires two or more computers, networking software (also called the network operating system), network adapters, and cables. Examples of networks include Ethernet, Token Ring, and AppleTalk. Examples of network operating systems include Novell NetWare and Windows for Workgroups. Networks are useful when several users must share resources, such as data or printers. (2) The source of most computer problems in business computer systems. (See also *LAN, wide area network,* and *node.*)

Sentence: "When I log on to the *network,* I can send e-mail and files to my coworkers without leaving my office. If only I could network my laundry to the cleaners."

network adapter

Pronunciation: *net-werk uh-dap-ter.*

Meaning: A hardware device (or *card*) that establishes a network and enables a computer to connect to another computer with a similar device. All computers in a network should use compatible adapters. (See also *network, LAN,* and *wide area network.*)

Sentence: "Our office purchased Ethernet *network adapters* for our computers. After installing and configuring the adapters, we can then install and configure the network software. I think I like the old-fashioned way of communicating around the office; it's called the phone."

network hose

Pronunciation: *net-werk hoh-za.*

Meaning: The cable that connects your computer to other computers in the network. It's too thin to be a wire, so we call it a hose.

Sentence: "The data starts in my computer, then it's squirted out the *network hose,* down the hall and into Phil's computer, and then he totally fouls up my report."

network operating system (NOS)

Pronunciation: *net-werk op-er-ate-ting sis-tem.*

Meaning: The software used on a *local area network* (LAN) that includes the network's hardware components. A NOS is made up of the file server software and workstation software and is responsible for maintaining the "conversation" between the two. (See also *local area network, network, server,* and *workstation.*)

Sentence: "We use Windows for Workgroups as our *network operating system* and connect to a file server with a Novell NOS. I guess our computers are working NOS to NOS."

neural network

Pronunciation: *ner-roll net-werk.*

Meaning: A computer system that mimics the activities of the human brain's neurons. In the human brain, a very large number of neurons (billions, in fact) process information in a parallel fashion, all working on one problem at the same time to produce a single answer. Based on established patterns (learned processes), certain connections are made across a network to produce repeated results. In this way, neural networks can learn to process complex information over time — recognizing patterns of data. Because of this learned behavior, neural networks, like humans, produce only approximate results based on large amounts of input. Neural networks are useful for specific types of problems, such as processing stock market data or finding trends in graphical patterns. (See also *artificial intelligence*.)

Sentence: "Dave! Have you seen our gas bill? I guess the gas company has installed that darn new *neural network* computer!"

New command

Pronunciation: *Nu ko-mand.*

Meaning: A software command that produces a new document or file, as in the File New command in Microsoft Word. Most application programs have a New command used to produce new documents.

Sentence: "I used the *New command* in the File menu to start a new document. I wish there was a New command that would find me a new job."

newline character

Pronunciation: *nu-line kare-akt-er.*

Meaning: The character you type that makes a new line of text on the screen. This is the character produced when you press the Enter key. Many word processors use the term newline character because pressing the Enter key starts you off writing stuff on a new line. (See also *Return key, carriage return, linefeed,* and *Enter key*.)

Sentence: "Pity poor Alice. She did a search and replace, searching for the *newline character* and replacing it with nothing. Now she has one four-page paragraph in her document. Pass it on."

nibble

Pronunciation: *nib-ol.*

Meaning: One half of a byte, or four bits. (See also *byte* and *bit*.)

Sentence: "I can't get a *nibble* or a bite with this two-bit bait."

NiCad

Pronunciation: *Nigh-Kad.*

Meaning: Abbreviation for *Nickel Cadmium,* a type of battery used in notebook and portable computers. You can recharge NiCad batteries frequently, but you have to drain them of power first; otherwise, they forget how much energy they hold and begin to hold only the amount you've recharged. NiCad batteries are sort of stupid.

Sentence: "My laptop computer uses two rechargeable *NiCad* batteries to provide a full six hours of use, but they take 12 hours each to charge!"

nil

Pronunciation: *nil,* like *Bill, still,* or *pill.*

Meaning: Nothing, zero, zilch. (See also *null.*)

Sentence: "I've been working with this income spreadsheet all day; every way I look at it, my profits are *nil.*"

NLQ

(See *near-letter quality.*)

no-op

Pronunciation: *no-op* (Like, "The op was here just a second ago.").

Meaning: A type of computer instruction that does nothing. Although you may think there are lots of no-ops in your software; alas, there may be only a few. It seems silly, but your car as a "neutral" gear and many people stare at the TV slack-jawed for hours. No-op is the same thing, but for a computer.

Sentence: "I don't know how many *no-ops* this computer is doing, but it's doing them quite fast."

node

Pronunciation: *no-ed.*

Meaning: A single computer or terminal in a network. Networks can consist of numerous nodes, each operating independently. Also the way *note* sounds when you have a cold. (See also *network* and *server.*)

Sentence: "Our Ethernet network has 20 *nodes,* which means 20 of us won't have anything to do when the network stops working."

nondocument

Pronunciation: *non-dok-yu-ment.*

Meaning: A nondocument is a word processing text file or ASCII file that contains no formatting, such as underlining. This term originated from the Nondocument mode in WordStar, which was commonly used to write programs.

Sentence: "I wrote that program using the *nondocument* mode of my word processor. I'm going to run it using the noncomputer mode of my computer. I hope all the nonusers like it."

noninterlacing

Pronunciation: *non-in-ter-lays-ing.*

Meaning: Not interlacing, as in no overlap or twisty-tangly things. Noninterlacing monitors are standard for computer graphics because of their consistency and lack of flicker. (See also *interlacing* and *NTSC.*)

Sentence: "My new monitor is a *noninterlacing* type. It scans the screen over 50 times per second but still hasn't found my car keys."

nonvolatile memory

Pronunciation: *non-vul-li-tile mem-or-ree.*

Meaning: The memory in your computer that holds information even when you turn off your computer (whew!). Read-only memory is nonvolatile, as are disk drives. (See also *RAM* and *memory.*)

Sentence: "I wrote a story called 'The Violent Vibrations of a Volatile Vocalist' and saved it on my hard drive, so now it's in *nonvolatile memory* and I can finally turn off my computer."

NOP

Pronunciation: *En Oh Pee.*

Meaning: Abbreviation for *Not Operating Properly.* A program that is not working. A computer that is not working. An employee who is not working. Also used to describe accidental "features" in software (*Not On Purpose*).

Sentence: "This program is *NOP.* Let's ship it anyway."

notepad

Pronunciation: *note-pad.*

Meaning: A small application or accessory commonly found in graphical user interfaces (such as Windows and the Macintosh System) that you can use to type simple notes. The Windows notepad is a simple, text-only word processor that lets you write, edit, and print notes without having to use the more complex word processors. A notepad is useful also for editing DOS batch files, such as AUTOEXEC.BAT. (See also *graphical user interface.*)

Sentence: "I keep the *notepad* accessory handy so that I can jot quick notes while I'm working on the computer. It's easier than switching back and forth between my application and a word processor."

notebook computer

Pronunciation: *note-book kum-pue-ter.*

Meaning: (1) A compact computer, about the size of a three-ring binder. Notebook computers are commonly used while traveling. They operate on both AC and DC power. You can also use notebook computers on the desktop by "docking" them to a larger computer or by attaching a desktop monitor and keyboard. A practical notebook computer should weigh between 3 and 5 pounds. (2) A good excuse to get out of the office. (3) Something a computer book author takes on her honeymoon.

Sentence: "I'm so glad I brought the *notebook computer* on this trip. I haven't used it yet, but just carrying it around saves time going to the gym."

notwork

Pronunciation: *not-werk.*

Meaning: A task performed at your desk or on the computer that is not work. Notwork includes playing computer games, arranging your Windows or Macintosh desktop, organizing files on the computer, installing new software that you're not really going to use, faxing your lunch order to the corner deli, and sending e-mail to Bill Clinton (even if you are a politician).

Sentence: "When the boss came in, I was doing a lot of *notwork.* Then she told me I was doing a good job and left. I guess I'll keep up the good notwork."

NTSC

Pronunciation: *En Tee Ess See.*

Meaning: Acronym for *National Television Standards Committee.* A committee that determines standards for television broadcast and reception, influencing most of the known world, except Europe and Asia. The NTSC standard for broadcast is 125-line frames scanned at 30 per second using noninterlaced video. The European PAL standard produces a much higher resolution and quality of color than the NTSC standard used in the United States.

Sentence: "Americans have been trying to upgrade the *NTSC* standard for years. We watch the most television in the world and have the worst quality. We want HDTV!"

NuBus

Pronunciation: *Noo-Bus.*

Meaning: A Macintosh bus that provides faster data transfer than the older S-bus and has support for multiple CPUs. (See also *bus, expansion slot,* and *expansion card.*)

Sentence: "Those Mac people always have splashy new hardware with much more interesting names than PC people. They have names like *NuBus,* Local Talk, and System Error."

NUL

Pronunciation: *Nul,* like *dull.*

Meaning: The name of a DOS "device" that doesn't exist and is no good, which means this is probably the first thing the programmers at Microsoft did because it works very well at doing nothing.

Sentence: "Go to *NUL,* go directly to NUL, do not pass Redmond, do not collect stock options."

null

Pronunciation: *nul.*

Meaning: An empty set. Nothing. Unlike the number zero, null has no value whatever, like Donald Trump's estate. (See also *nil.*)

Sentence: "Programmers often use a *null* character to cancel a numeric variable because the number zero has a value."

null modem

Pronunciation: *nul mo-dum.*

Meaning: A connection between two computers that does not include a modem. A null modem is usually accomplished with a cable connection, such as between a notebook computer and a desktop for direct data transfer. (See also *modem* and *cable.*)

Sentence: "I use a *null modem* to download my calendar information to the notebook computer before a business trip. After the trip, I upload the calendar from the notebook back to the desktop computer."

NumLock

Pronunciation: *Num-Lok.*

Meaning: A key on standard PC keyboards that toggles the numeric keypad between numbers and direction keys. When NumLock is on, the numeric keypad produces numbers. When NumLock is off, the numeric keys act as direction keys. Many keyboards include a second set of direction keys, so you can use the numeric keypad for numbers and still have direction keys available. (See also *numeric keyboard* and *CapsLock.*)

Sentence: "When I press the *NumLock* key, I can enter large amounts of numeric data into my spreadsheet program by using the numeric keypad. If only I could figure out how to get the cell pointer to move down when I press Enter."

number crunching

Pronunciation: *nuhm-ber krun-ching.*

Meaning: The act of performing numerous calculations and computations on a computer. Number crunching is common in financial and engineering applications.

Sentence: "After six days of *number crunching,* we discovered that the human brain cannot survive on coffee and Twinkies, so we went out for lunch."

numeric format

Pronunciation: *nu-mair-ik for-mat.*

Meaning: A visual style of displaying numbers. Different numeric formats display numbers for different purposes. For example, a currency format displays the number 567.899 as $567.90, and a percent format displays the number .25 as 25%. Numeric formats are commonly found in spreadsheet programs so that you can display numbers for special purposes without actually changing the value or "true form" of the number.

Sentence: "I used Excel's custom *number format* feature to add a few extra zeros to each number in my Net Worth report. Because number formats don't actually change the underlying values in the spreadsheet, you couldn't call this dishonest . . . could you?"

numeric keypad

Pronunciation: *nu-mair-ik kee-pad.*

Meaning: A set of keys, often adjacent to the standard keyboard keys, that include numbers and symbols for 10-key operation. A numeric keypad displays numbers just as a 10-key calculator does and lets you enter large amounts of numeric data into your applications. Notebook computers often insert the numeric keypad into the standard keys, requiring that you use the NumLock function to access them. (See also *NumLock.*)

Sentence: "My keyboard includes a *numeric keypad* to the right of the standard keys. Because I'm left handed, I had to purchase a separate numeric keypad that I could place on the left side of the keyboard. Everything is all right (left?) now."

object code file

Pronunciation: *ahb-jekt kode fi-ell.*

Meaning: The middle step when writing a program. It's not exactly the final program, more like the slimy pod-person thing that eventually turns into the program, thanks to another program called a Linker.

Sentence: "We are waiting for Susan to complete her *object code file* so that we can package this program and get it out on the market before we test-run it to see if it works."

object-oriented

Pronunciation: *ahb-jekt o-ree-unt-ed.*

Meaning: A style of programming where you bundle sets of instructions into packages known as objects, similar to the way you can bundle pieces of paper into objects called wads. In the old-fashioned kind of programming, known as procedural programming, the writer would just write instructions one after the other, one thing leading to the next. Object-oriented programming squishes the instructions into self-sufficient modules. Thus, if you've written an code object that displays the date and time in a box on your screen, you merely toss that wad of code into your program and, lo, it works. You can even take that whole chunk and transplant it into another program, rather than having to rewrite the second program from scratch. Object-oriented programming is favored for this kind of versatility.

Object-orientedness also applies to graphics. A graphic element, say a circle, is called an object and is created by a formula in the program that calculates and "draws" the object onto the screen. Individual objects can then be manipulated without messing up the rest of what you've drawn.

Sentence: "I was trying to manipulate an *object* on the screen and then realized that it was a piece of spaghetti stuck to the screen. I guess I shouldn't work and eat at the same time."

occasional irregularity

Pronunciation: *oh-kay-zhun-uhl e-reg-yoo-lar-i-tee.*

Meaning: Times when a computer — or the software program it's running — messes up or shuts down. The symptoms can't be repeated so that you can try to fix the problem — they just happen for no apparent reason, like being late for work, forgetting your spouse's name, or UFOs. The solution is to shut down completely and reboot (probably true for humans as well). Another solution is to have anyone else look at the problem; these problems only occur when you are by yourself and will not repeat for others.

Sentence: "My computer's problem is worse than *occasional irregularity,* so I am taking it to see a specialist in Singapore."

OCR

Pronunciation: *Oh See Ar.*

Meaning: Abbreviation for Optical Character Recognition. The ability of a computer (via special software) to look at a page of text and recognize letters and words and translate them into a computer file so that you don't have to retype anything. The OCR software sees that an *A* is an *A,* rather than a collection of dots making a picture. This is important at certain times, for example, if you have a fax modem inside your computer, and somebody faxes you a document. If you have OCR software, then the FAX is a document you can edit. If you don't have OCR software, your computer just thinks the document is one big picture. OCR also stands for Obvious Candidate for Rehabilitation, a term used fondly to describe some programmers.

Sentence: "Using *OCR,* someday computers will even be able to decipher a doctor's prescription."

octal

Pronunciation: *ok-toll.*

Meaning: Base eight, where the numbers range from zero to 7 and then the value eight is represented by the number 10. Weird? Yes! We humans count in base 10, probably because we have ten fingers. Base

10 uses numbers zero through 9 and then 10 to represent the value ten. Octal, hey — it's just weird. And no one uses it any more, at least no one you'll have to deal with unless you get lost somewhere at a university or nuclear plant.

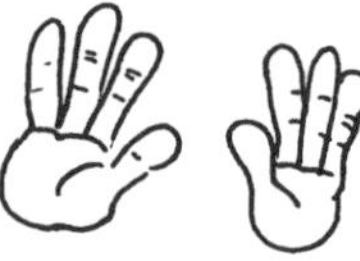

Sentence: "If an octopus could count, it would probably do so in base 8, *octal.*"

OEM

Pronunciation: *Oh Ee Em.*

Meaning: Abbreviation for Original Equipment Manufacturer. The company that makes the parts that go into machines assembled and sold by somebody else. For example, Joe Blorf may make disk drives which are then installed into your computer and sold by Milo Cooper. Joe is the OEM for Milo's hard drives. Very few computer manufacturers make all of their own stuff.

Sentence: "Although American computers are the most advanced in the world, most of the parts come from Japanese *OEMs.*"

off-line

Pronunciation: *awf-li-na.*

Meaning: Not connected to a computer, or more probably not really bothering with the computer. There's a difference between off-line and un-plugged. If you yank out the printer cable, then you've unplugged it. But if the printer is plugged in, you may have to turn it on to make it on-line. Further, you may have to punch another button that tells the printer to obey the computer, which is also "putting it on-line."

Sentence: "Sometimes I have to take my printer *off-line* to advance a sheet of paper. Sometimes I have to take my brain off-line to get some peace and quiet."

offset

Pronunciation: *awf-set.*

Meaning: To allow extra room for inner margins on a word-processed document so that it can be bound in book form. This book has an offset of an inch or so, which allows for the pages to be bound together. If you were to yank a page out, you would see more blank space on one side than the other, which is the offset.

Sentence: "We *offset* the document six inches in case we made a mistake in the binding."

OK button

Pronunciation: *Oh-Kay butt-en.*

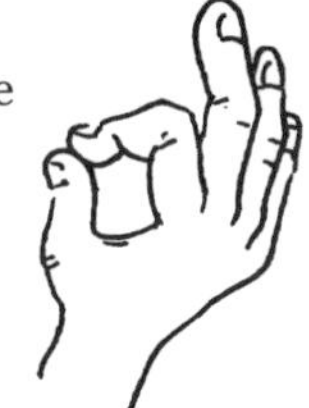

Meaning: The letters "OK" inside a little rectangle, inside a dialog box. You use your mouse to click on the OK rectangle and, voilá, you "press" the button. You can also "click" the OK button by pressing the Enter key.

Sentence: "I think the *OK buttons* I use should be renamed 'Oh, well.'"

OK Corral

Pronunciation: *Oh-kay Ko-ral.*

Meaning: The place where you hang your hat, where the Naughahydes roam, where the skies are not cloudy or gray, where the only time you hear about is suppertime, where... Doggone it! Wrong dictionary! See *Cowherding For Dummies.*

Sentence: "It's suppertime at the *OK Corral.* Click the OK button."

OLE

Pronunciation: *Oh El Ee,* also pronounced *oh-lay,* as in bullfighting.

Meaning: Acronym for Object Linking and Embedding, an activity carried out while you are in Windows. OLE means that you can insert a document (or part of a document) created by one application inside of a document created by another application, and maintain a live link between the two. For example, suppose you're in Windows. (Now, please stop screaming!) You have a chart in Excel that you want to include in a business letter in Word. With OLE linking, you can paste the chart from Excel into the letter in Word. Every time you make a change in the chart in the original Excel document, it automatically updates the chart in the Word document. Likewise, if you clicked the chart while you were in the Word document, you could make changes in Excel, and it would update both the original and the linked version. With embedding, you are placing a severed copy of the original document in the destination document.

Sentence: "And now Miguel will paste the picture of the bull into his document about bullfighting. Here he goes. Click *OLE!*"

on-line

Pronunciation: *ahn-lyne.*

Meaning: Hooked up to a specified computer, usually said of the printer when it's connected to your PC and ready to print. You see, it's entirely possible to have a computer and a printer, both are plugged into the wall and each other, and both are turned on. Yet they won't talk until you punch that special button on the printer that makes it go on-line. In a way, on-line means "no earplugs."

On-line may also refer to the state of "being connected" to a national modem service, such as Prodigy or CompuServe or even a local BBS. Though your computer, modem, and software are all running, you aren't on-line until you're connected with the service. Some of these systems are called on-line services because they want you to believe that they're "on" all the time.

Sentence: "I use the CompuServe *on-line* service to get answers to all my odd software questions. It's a warehouse o' computer geeks."

OOP

Pronunciation: *Oop*

Meaning: Abbreviation for Object-Oriented Programming. A method of programming that creates individual software objects that can be used again and again in other programs. Although it takes more time to create objects, the ability to reuse them in other programs reduces programming time.(See also *object-oriented.)*

Sentence: "Programming languages such as C++ and Pascal are now designed to provide *OOP* capabilities. So you can write one part of a program and use it in several other programs. Just don't leave the parts lying around your desktop, or you're liable to step in the *oop.*"

open

Pronunciation: *oh-pen.*

Meaning: To access a program or file, just as you would open a book if you wanted to read it, a notebook if you wanted to write in it, a car door if you wanted to hit your knee with it, or a can of tuna fish if you wanted to eat out of it. So if you last saved that BLOTCH.DOC file and want to work on it again, you start the program that created BLOTCH.DOC and then use that program to open the file, loading it in for editing or other ridicule.

Sentence: Please don't *open* the file called "WORMCAN.DOC."

open architecture

Pronunciation: *oh-pen ar-ki-tek-chur.*

Meaning: The philosophy and practice of building computers and making the design and engineering public knowledge. It invites other manufacturers and developers to augment the computer with peripherals, software, and internal components. The theory is, the more doodads and gizmos available on the market to work with a given machine, the more tricks a user can do with it, and the more the machine will sell.

IBM has practiced open architecture with its PCs, and Sun Microsystems has practiced it with its workstations. Apple Computer is famous for NOT practicing it. And in fact, Apple has become notorious for doing exactly the opposite, for shouting "Off with their head!" when anyone else builds something that looks remotely like an Apple product. Although, the Macintosh *is* getting to be a rather "open" machine these days. (See also *architecture.*)

Sentence: "Although IBM had the foresight to create an *open architecture* PC, they didn't have the foresight to realize that clone manufacturers would take most of their business away from them."

operand

Pronunciation: *ah-per-and.*

Meaning: A value, variable, or doodad in an equation that gets operated on by an operator. In the statement 2 + 3 = 5, *2* and *3* are operands. The plus and equal signs are operators. (See also *operator.*)

Sentence: "If you take away the symbols, all you have left in a mathematical equation are the *operands.* This doesn't sound very useful, which is why it's a mathematical concept."

operating system

Pronunciation: *ah-per-ay-ting sis-tim.*

Meaning: The software that controls the hardware, and which also runs your programs. Some common operating systems include DOS, System 7 for the Macintosh, OS/2, and UNIX. (Windows is not an operating system by itself because it must run "on top of" DOS.)

Sentence: "Some people who use the DOS *operating system* add Windows to avoid having to use DOS commands. Some of those people use programs such as Norton Desktop to avoid using Windows commands. Avoidance is a big part of computing."

operator

Pronunciation: *ah-per-ay-ter.*

Meaning: A symbol representing a mathematical operation. The usual context is within a software program or programming language. Typical operators are

+	Addition
-	Subtraction
*	Multiplication
/	Division

In addition to these mathematical operators, many other types exist. Relational operators, for example, test the relationships between values, as in the following:

<	Less than
>	Greater than
=	Equal to
<=	Less than or equal to
>=	Greater than or equal to
<>	Not equal to

Sentence: "In the spreadsheet, I use mathematical *operators* to produce a budget worksheet. Then I use other operators to cover up the funds I'm embezzling."

optical

Pronunciation: *ahp-ti-kul.*

Meaning: In general, refers to light or vision. For instance, when you are having an optical illusion, it means you are seeing something that's not there, such as national health care.

Sentence: "The other day Windows just came up — splat — right there on the screen. I'm certain I experienced an *optical* illusion."

optical disk

Pronunciation: *ahp-ti-kul dis-ka.*

Meaning: A computer storage medium (a disk drive) that operates by digitized beams of light or lasers. That sounds so cool that there must be a catch — and there are two: speed and price; the optical disks are expensive and slow, though they hold lots of information. Optical disks are somewhat akin to CD-ROM technology. The claim to fame of the optical disk drive is that its storage capacity is much greater than that of a magnetic disk drive, which is your typical type of disk.

Sentence: "I don't like the way that new *optical disk* is looking at me."

optical mouse

Pronunciation: *ahp-ti-kul mows.*

Meaning: The distant cousins of the three non-optical, or "blind," mice who got their tails.... Oops, wrong dictionary! See *Nursery Rhymes For Dummies.* In computer terms, an optical mouse is a pointing device that uses a light beam to track the position of the cursor or pointer on the screen. Normal mice use a mechanical ball that rolls to detect movement. The light beam type of optical mouse is used with a special grid type of mouse pad that reflects the beam. (Actually, the mechanical type of mouse also uses some optical technology, but internally. An electronic eye watches the ball roll around and this is how the mouse detects movement. Cool, huh?)

Sentence: "If your *optical mouse* gets loose, you need a special optical mousetrap to catch it."

optimize

Pronunciation: *ahp-tim-eyes.*

Meaning: To customize software or hardware so that it will serve the user to its utmost capacity. The goal is to have the machinery run faster and more efficiently. This could include shuffling parts of the software into different parts of the computer's memory, rewriting chunks of software applications, or even just tweaking the controls on your desktop control panel.

Sentence: "Microsoft Windows gets its bloated reputation partly because it loads your hard drive with graphic images you can use for 'wallpaper.' If you think you can do without these images, you can *optimize* Windows by getting rid of all the picture files."

Option key

Pronunciation: *Ahp-shun kee.*

Meaning: A key on any Apple keyboard. You can use it in conjunction with a number of other keys on the keyboard to execute special functions, such as you would use the Alt, Shift, or Ctrl keys. Like the Shift key, the Option key doesn't do anything if you press it by itself. An example: in Word on the Mac, pressing the Option key and the numeral 8 key will give you a bullet character. Option-* gives you a little bad guy character. And Shift-Option-Enter shoots the bad guy character with the bullet character. Ctrl-Option-B cleans up the mess character afterwards.

Sentence: "If I press *Option*-S, I save my document. If I press Shift-Option-S, I save all open documents. If I press Ctrl-Shift-Option-S, I get a cramp in my hand."

orphan

Pronunciation: *or-fun.*

Meaning: The first line of a paragraph abandoned at the bottom of one page, while the rest of the lines continue on the following page. The dimensions of this tragedy have attained to such proportions that developers of page layout software have included social service capabilities in their programs to rescue orphans from this plight. The term also applies to a computer, usually one of the early models, that is no longer made or supported by the company that heralded it as a "technological revolution" just a few years back. This happens to all computers, sooner or later.

Sentence: "Pity, ye, O Osborne owners. And ye Adam and Atari and owners of old Radio Shack stuff. Fare thee well old Apple II, Apple III, and Lisa owners. Big adieu to the long throng of forgotten PCs, nay the *orphans* of the electronics age."

OS/2

Pronunciation: *Oh-Es-Too* (trademarked acronym standing for Operating System/2).

Meaning: An operating system developed jointly by IBM and Microsoft for PC computers. It was to be the next operating system, the one that would take over and succeed in DOS's footsteps. That prediction and $75 buys you swampland in Florida. Despite the initial fanfare, few software developers came out with applications for OS/2, so when Windows appeared, it stole the show. It's as if IBM gave a party and nobody came. Now Windows NT promises to nail the OS/2 coffin shut. OS/2 can run both DOS and Windows applications. OS/2 has gained some popularity among business users, but it's nowhere near taking over DOS's shoes.

Sentence: "Someday, perhaps, *OS/2* will replace the term 'white elephant' as something big and well-intended but utterly useless."

outline font

Pronunciation: *owt-lihn fawn-ta.*

Meaning: A typeface that is solid around the edges and hollow in the middle. It's used for posters and headlines but not so much for regular typing. Some font families give you a choice of making an outline typeface out of a regular one. For example, Times Roman can become Times

Roman Outline. The outline fonts keep the styles and proportions of the regular fonts they come from. (See also *font family*)

Sentence: "Kids love *outline fonts* because they can color in the middle with crayons."

outliner software

Pronunciation: *owt-lihn-er soft-waer.*

Meaning: Software that can make the kind of outline you used to make in high school on 3x5 cards when you were learning how to organize your writing compositions. Those roman numerals followed by uppercase letters followed by Arabic numerals followed by lowercase letters will really take you back. In the old days — not quite as old as your high school days — this kind of software was a separate application from word processing. In these enlightened times, you can make outlines in the same software program as you can write letters and novels in. For example, WordPerfect includes an outlining feature, though few bother with it.

Sentence: "We used *outlining software* to organize the outline for this new dictionary. Dan and Wally came up with all the letters, but it was Chris who deftly suggested we use the alphabetizing feature to organize. Thanks, Chris."

output

Pronunciation: *owt-put.*

Meaning: What the computer spits out after it churns through the information you put into it. Output can be in the form of characters on your screen, sounds out of speakers, or printed paper out of a printer. The machines that give us the output are called output devices. (See, learning about computers is way easier than you thought!) (See also *Input, BIOS,* and *BUS.*)

Sentence: "When your input is poorly conceived, you shouldn't be surprised when your *output* is garbage."

overflow

Pronunciation: *oh-ver-flo.*

Meaning: This is to memory as a swollen river is to a dam. Only, water finds its own level, whereas a memory overflow will stop a computer dead in its tracks — or worse, the excess bits may flood out the back of your PC, drop to the floor, and run up your legs and start byting you! The overflow happens because what you put in is bigger than the space the programmer has set aside for it. So the programmer wanted 10 characters for your last name, and your last name is Zinzinburger. Too many characters equals overflow. Solution: make the thing you're trying to do smaller or make the space in the program bigger. (Mostly this is a programmer's problem, not our problem.)

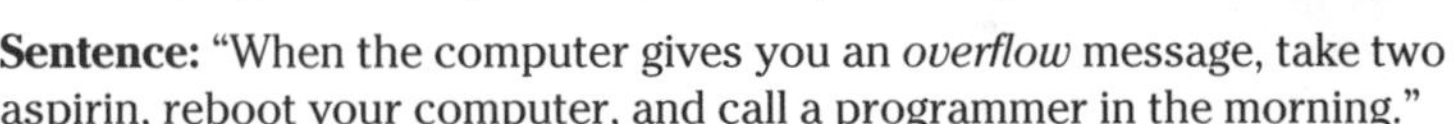

Sentence: "When the computer gives you an *overflow* message, take two aspirin, reboot your computer, and call a programmer in the morning."

overhead

Pronunciation: *oh-ver-hed.*

Meaning: Similar to what it means in real life: the resources you need just to stay operational — in this case, measured in RAM, megabytes, processing speed, and I/O capacity. Mostly this refers to the requirements of a program just to run on your PC. Some programs may require 640K of RAM, 5MB of hard disk space, plus special graphics cards and printers.

Sentence: "Working with graphics requires a lot of *overhead.* Do you think there's a conspiracy going on between the stores that sell the hardware and the guys who write the software?"

overlay

Pronunciation: *oh-ver-lay.*

Meaning: This is a sophisticated form of program juggling, where the whole program is just too darn big to fit into memory at once. So what they do is split the program into modules and overlay them into memory, swapping parts of the program back and forth between RAM and a disk. (See also *Murphy's Law.*)

Sentence: "They used *overlay* technology to overcome limitations in RAM. Now we can use Parkinson's law of programming: 'expand your program to fill as much RAM as you have available.'"

owner

Pronunciation: *oh-ner.*

Meaning: The person who paid for the software, as opposed to the two dozen people using the pirated copy. If you had to look this word up, turn to the word *Pirate* to find your picture.

Sentence: "If you're the *owner* of this software package, how come the startup screen says 'Bill Clinton, The White House?'"

p-code

Pronunciation: *pee-cohd*

Meaning: P-code is relevant only to the old p-system operating system, which we'd bet $10 right now half of you have never heard of. With the p-system, a programmer would compile a program, usually written in Pascal, into p-code, which is short for *pseudocode*. The p-code could be interpreted by the p-system's interpreter into the language understood best by the PC's microprocessor. This meant, theoretically, that p-code could run on any computer, as long as that computer was running the p-system. P-get it? (See also *pseudocode.)*

Sentence: "Since the p-system went defunct in the early '80s, *p-code* is no longer a useful term, unless you redefine it to mean *problem code* or programming instructions the dog mistook for the newspaper."

paddle

Pronunciation: *pa-dul.*

Meaning: Input device, like a joystick, that is frequently used for computer and video games. The paddle is a knob you twist, rotating it one way or the other. (See also *joystick*.)

Sentence: "My flight simulator program lets you use a *paddle* to control the plane, but I still can't get the plane off the ground."

page

Pronunciation: *paej.*

Meaning: (1) Like in regular English, the electronic unit of text that corresponds to a page in real life. The default mode is 8½ x 11 inches, and you can change these measurements in your word processing or page layout software. Even if your monitor is too small to fit a page of this size on the screen all at once, the computer still knows where the page starts and ends and will communicate this to the printer. (2) A chunk of RAM which acts as a unit that can be swapped back and forth to disk or to another spot in memory. (See also *expanded memory, printer,* and *page break.*)

Sentence: "One handy thing about *pages* on the computer is that you can recycle them over and over and over again. Al Gore would be pleased. Hug a tree."

page break

Pronunciation: *paej braek.*

Meaning: In word processing, the point at which one page leaves off and another begins. There are two ways to accomplish this: *soft* page breaks and *hard* page breaks. A soft page break happens automatically as soon as you get to the last character of the last line on a page. If you add or delete text (or graphics, for that matter) from the page, the page break will change accordingly, adding room for the new text. A hard page break is one you put in yourself at a precise location. A new page will always start at that point even if you add or delete material before the hard page break. (See also *page* and *printer.*)

Sentence: "Because I wanted my term paper to come out to 20 pages and I only had 7 pages to start with, I made the type bigger and put in a lot of extra hard *page breaks.*"

Page Down key

Pronunciation: *Paej Down kee.*

Meaning: A glorified cursor key that moves you forward (down) in the document the exact length of a page every time you press it. Depending on the program, a "page" can either be the amount of information that fits on a screen or the size of a real page. Often abbreviated PgDn. (See also *Page Up key.*)

Sentence: "Page, off my knee. Off! Now! Down Page! *Page Down*!"

page frame

Pronunciation: *paej fraem.*

Meaning: The page frame is a place in memory where a bunch of memory pages are kept, like storing blocks of ice in a freezer. This happens on a

PC when you use expanded memory. To access the extra memory, a page frame is created. Through that frame, individual pages of memory are stored that can access expanded memory. Is this complex or what? DOS lacks a true memory-management solution, so the Geeks That Be introduce obscure concepts like pages and page frames. Here are some more vitals:

A page is 16K of memory.

The page frame contains four 16K chunks of memory. Or sometimes it contains lots more chunks of memory.

The page frame is located in "upper memory."

The page frame is driving everyone nuts.

You don't need a page frame if none of your programs use expanded memory. (See also *expanded memory*.)

Sentence: "That memory looks bleak and ugly sitting there. *Frame* it and tell me what you think."

page layout

Pronunciation: *paej lae-out.*

Meaning: The design of text and graphics on a printed page and the software that you create it with, typically called *Desktop Publishing* (DTP) software. Most software programs that you can print from, such as word processors, databases, and spreadsheets, include some page layout capabilities. In word processing, you can set margins and specify typefaces; in a database, you can select where fields will be positioned in relation to each other; and in spreadsheets, you can adjust column widths and row heights. That's page layout.

For the ultimate in page layout, however, you would go to desktop publishing software, such as PageMaker, Ventura Publisher, or QuarkXpress. Applications like these give you precision control over the elements of your design in relation to each other, such as wrapping text around a graphic, or reducing or magnifying the size of an element in relation to elements around it. Most DTP programs let you "import" previously created word processing, graphics, database or spreadsheet files to polish up your presentation. (See also *desktop publishing software*.)

Sentence: "I want to start my own newspaper called *The Computer Chronicle For Dummies*, but I will need some *page layout* software and about 40,000 years to learn how to use it."

Page Up key

Pronunciation: *Paej Up kee.*

Meaning: The opposite of the Page Down key. This key moves you, page by page, backward through your document to the top. Often labeled PgUp on the keyboard. (See also *Page Down key.*)

Sentence: "If you're already at the top of the document, pressing the *Page Up key* won't take you anywhere."

pagination

Pronunciation: *pa-jin-ae-shun.*

Meaning: The act of making pages where there were none. Because everything you print eventually appears on a piece of paper — a *page* — the art of pagination shows you where those pages will be, right on the screen, before printing. It also allows you to see where various sections and titles appear in your document and make minor layout adjustments to see if everything will look hunky-dory when printed.

Sentence: "If I can't figure out how the *pagination* works in my word processing program, I'll have to print my novel as one long scroll."

paint

Pronunciation: *pain-ta.*

Meaning: Just like in real life, only on the computer, paint is not wet, which also means that it doesn't need to dry when you're done with the picture. Paint programs give you "tools" that let you draw electronically on the computer screen for different effects, like different size brushes, a roller (for large areas), a spray can, and so on. Artists are sometimes dismayed at how little precision control they have with a graphical paint program and a mouse. It feels like painting with ski gloves on. If you're not already an artist, you will be amazed at how easy it is to use a computer to paint — you can make endless mistakes and do endless fine-tuning without wearing holes in your paper or mucking it up with "colors" like *mud bath brown* or *murky gray*. Paint programs range from the simple Paintbrush program that comes bundled with Windows, all the way up to professional packages like Aldus Freehand and CorelDraw!

Sentence: "With that new black velvet mode in the Adobe Illustrator *paint* program, we're going to put the Tijuana Elvis Painting Society out of business."

palette

Pronunciation: *pal-et.*

Meaning: The selection of colors available in a paint or drawing program. The palette is somewhat limited by your hardware, specifically your monitor and graphics card. Some paint colors are given to you; others you can mix yourself. Palettes can also hold fill patterns, border styles, and other types of painting stuff.

Sentence: "There are so many colors in this *palette* that they take up the whole screen, and I have only 2 square inches to paint my picture in."

pane

Pronunciation: *paen.*

Meaning: A portion of a window that has been split into multiple parts. For example, in Excel you have a single window and can see your spreadsheet inside that window. Further, you can create up to four panes in the window by splitting it vertically and horizontally. Different parts of your spreadsheet or document can be displayed in the different panes. The end result is probably like what those independent-eyed iguanas see, but it helps you scope out big documents and spreadsheets easily. (See also *window.*)

Sentence: "I've traveled on the ocean, I've tramped upon the plain, but I've never seen a Window cry because it had a *pane.*"

paper-white B/W VGA monitor

Pronunciation: *pae-per wiht Vee-Gee-Ae mahn-i-ter.*

Meaning: A VGA monitor whose display approximates the whiteness of paper and provides black text and graphics to go with it. But wait! There's more! Because the paper-white screen also gives you shades of gray, from 4, 8, 16, or up to 32 shades, it's much more true-to-life than a monochrome monitor, which usually gives you amber on black or green on black. Yawn! Paper-white monitors are a good value and are often clearer and easier to read than bad color monitors, such as the one you have now! (see also *VGA Monitor.*)

Sentence: "Now that I've upgraded to a *paper-white monitor,* I can get the same kind of writer's block that I get when staring at a blank piece of paper."

parallel

Pronunciation: *pare-ell-ell.*

Meaning: Two lines that never touch, unless you're not looking or your name is Albert Einstein. What's parallel? Two lines that travel in the same direction, but never the twain do meet. With your PC, the term comes into play in the *parallel port*, which is covered just a few parallel inches below this term.

Sentence: "Actually, the universe isn't *parallel.* If a train travels along parallel rails that encompass the universe, and you're waiting to catch the 4:15 to Philly, eventually you'll see yourself get off the same train with a strange woman, ask yourself for $40, and then you'll never see yourself again."

parallel port

Pronunciation: *pare-ell-ell port.*

Meaning: A jack on the back of your computer that you can plug something into, especially a printer. The other kind of port is "serial." When a device is hooked up to the parallel port, it means that data is traveling at high speeds along parallel circuits in the innards of your computer. Parallel ports are known for their high-speed data transfer, but they poop out over long distances. (See also *printer* and *serial port.*)

Sentence: "The manual said to plug the printers into the *parallel ports,* so I arranged them neatly so that they each faced the door."

parallel processing

Pronunciation: *pare-ell-ell prah-sess-ing.*

Meaning: Having the computer be able to think about more than one thing at a time, which can cause neurotic behavior, as it does in humans. Technically, parallel process-ING comes from having parallel process-ORS, which is essentially only the case in computers far mightier than the average desktop PC or Mac. The top performers of any kind of computer can use several thousand processors in parallel, whereas the lowly desktop computer typically has only one. Parallel processing is the basis of artificial intelligence, or those computers that really can say "duh!"

Sentence: "Supercomputers, which are incredibly fast and powerful, use something called massively *parallel processing.* I never thought that one thing could be more parallel than another."

parameter

Pronunciation: *puh-ram-e-ter.*

Meaning: A value — which could be numbers, letters, or other characters — that you enter into an equation or statement, like an option. For example, the DOS FORMAT command is followed by a "drive" parameter. That's a drive letter telling the FORMAT command where the disk is that you want formatted. Parameter is just a fancy way of saying "option-thing that goes on the end of a command." You can also use parameters when searching for information. For example, Cornelia could enter the parameters "tall," "ugly," and "hairy" into the computer dating database to look for her dreamboat. (See also *option.*)

Sentence: "How about this error message: `optional required` *`parameter`* `missing`. How can something that's required be optional?"

paren (s)

Pronunciation: *pare-enz.*

Meaning: Slang for parenthesis (-theses). Sometimes you have to use a lot of them, so you don't want to waste your breath on extra syllables. They're used in mathematical calculations in programming, among other things. Paren is *not* the singular version of parentheses.

Sentence: "I don't know why the equation didn't work. Stick some *parens* in there and maybe it will."

parent/child

Pronunciation: *pare-ent-chil-da.*

Meaning: This describes the relationship (how cute!) between categories of information, which could be files, directories, levels of an outline, or families. The *child* is a subcategory of the parent. (See also *child process.*)

Sentence: "In my outline, 'Things to Eat' is the *parent* topic of the 'Candy' topic. 'Candy' is a *child* of 'Things to Eat.' This more than justifies what I put into my mouth for nourishment."

parity

Pronunciation: *pare-i-tee.*

Meaning: A way of testing whether data is OK or not by counting the number of bits (such as during data transmission). The number can be either odd or even, and that information is saved and compared with

subsequent calculations that also see if the number is odd or even. If it isn't, then there is no parity and the computer will pout. (See also *parity bit.*)

Sentence: "Okay, Ivan, if you have enough nukes to blow up the world 530 times and we have enough to blow up the world 488 times — not counting subs, of course — then we've reached *parity.* Nyet?"

parity bit

Pronunciation: *pare-i-tee bit.*

Meaning: An extra bit included to check the parity in data bytes. The arrangement is specified, say, that a parity bit set to 1 means that the parity is odd (there is an odd number of 1s in the eight bits that it's monitoring), 0 if it's even. (See also *parity.*)

Sentence: "I made fun of the word *parity* by writing a *parody*, but then my modem bit me."

park

Pronunciation: *park* or *pahk.*

Meaning: To immobilize the heads of your hard drive so that they don't rattle around and do damage if the computer is moved. Not to be confused with parallel parking — an easy mistake to make because so many things are parallel in computers. Nowadays, most hard drives park themselves automatically when you turn off the computer. (See also *head* and *head crash.*)

Sentence: "In most of the country, when you want to make sure your computer is secure, you would *park* the hard drive. In Hahvuhd Squai-uh, however, you would pahk your hahd drive."

parse

Pronunciation: *pars.*

Meaning: (1) In programming, when a compiler specifies what "part of speech" each component of an instruction is and acts on it accordingly. (2) In spreadsheets, the function used to distribute data imported from other applications into separate fields in your new spreadsheet. (3) Generically, the act of splitting up a group of items (such as a sentence of words) into individual components. (See also *compiler.*)

Sentence: "I tried to *parse* the spreadsheet I imported from Lotus, but the program couldn't figure out where to separate all the numbers — so I now have number soup."

partition

Pronunciation: *par-ti-shun.*

Meaning: A section of a hard disk set aside for use with a specific operating system, or the act of separating the hard drive into such sections (one of those devious nouns-turned-verbs). (See also *hard disk* and *logical drive.*)

Sentence: "It took so much disk space to set up the *partitions* on my hard drive that I now have no room left to install the operating system."

Pascal

Pronunciation: *Pass-kal.*

Meaning: A programming language used mainly for teaching programming concepts, with commands that look like regular English words — although they aren't strung together that way. Named after the 17th-century philosopher-mathematician Blaise Pascal, the language was created by Niklaus Wirth in the early '70s.

Sentence: "Even a beginning programmer can write programs in *Pascal.*"

password

Pronunciation: *pass-werd.*

Meaning: Exactly like saying "Open sesame" to the computer. Usually encountered on a computer network, where a password is required to access certain parts of the network or on BBSs, where it is required to gain access to a forum. However, you can also use passwords to protect individual files.

Sentence: "Peggy wanted to make sure she would be able to remember her *password*, so she wrote it on a sign in big letters and stuck it on the wall next to the computer." (Tip for power users: This defeats the purpose of having a password.)

paste

Pronunciation: *paest.*

Meaning: To insert an item previously cut or copied from elsewhere. The item can be text, graphics, records from a database, a column of numbers from a spreadsheet, and so on. The item has been cut or copied into a mystical no-man's-land called the *clipboard* until the next Cut or Copy event. Later, you can paste information from the clipboard into a document. (See also *clipboard, copy, cut,* and *cut and paste.*)

Sentence: "If you want to *paste* some of my term paper into your term paper, make sure that the fonts match so the teacher doesn't suspect."

path

Pronunciation: *path.*

Meaning: Otherwise known as *path statement*, the *path* is inserted into DOS's AUTOEXEC.BAT file, followed by names of whatever directories the user specifies. You can then start those applications from within any subdirectory in DOS without having to type the entire path name. Here's a typical PATH statement:

```
PATH=C:\DOS;C:\WINDOWS;C:\WINWORD;C:\EXCEL
```

(See also *path statement* and *path name*.)

Sentence: "When I said I could access my accounting program only from within the C:\PROGRAMS\ACCT directory, I was told to update my *path.* Now my front yard looks great, but I still can't access the accounting program from any directory."

path name

Pronunciation: *path naem.*

Meaning: The route the computer takes to get to a specified file, spelled out in excruciating detail. Sometimes programs require that you spell out the path name in this same kind of excruciating detail. You include the letter designating the drive, followed by a colon, followed by a backslash, followed by the directory, followed by any and all subdirectories, followed by the actual name of the file. Like this:

```
C:\PROGRAMS\GRAPHICS\PAINT.EXE
```

When you open or save files, you are usually required to specify the directory path (or path name) for the file to identify where the file is coming from or going. In Windows, you can specify a path name by typing it as shown or by working your way through folders that represent directories in a path statement. On a Macintosh, paths are not an issue, although an intricate maze of folders takes its place. (See also *path*.)

Sentence: "The *path name* that gets you to the file containing the manuscript for this book could be `C:\WINWORD\DUMMIES\P.DOC`. But it's not; it's something else, so don't go looking for it there."

Pause key

Pronunciation: *Paws kee.*

Meaning: A key that is often used to pause screen output, such as directory listings. Used within DOS and DOS applications, pressing Pause once usually freezes the display; pressing it again returns normal behavior.

Sentence: "The *Pause key* is on my keyboard, but what does it do? It seems to pause Windows when it's in the midst of opening but doesn't seem to have any effect elsewhere. Why would I want to wait any longer for Windows to open, anyway?"

PC

Pronunciation: *Pee See.*

Meaning: (1) Acronym for Personal Computer. Technically refers to any stand-alone computer that fits on a desktop and is configured to address the computing needs of one user at a time. This format includes Macintoshes, IBM-compatibles, Commodores, and others. In ordinary usage, though, refers to only an IBM-compatible computer, as opposed to a Macintosh. (2) Acronym for politically correct.

Sentence: "Some would say it's more PC to buy a *PC* rather than a Mac because Apple is so proprietary in its business practices."

PC-DOS

Pronunciation: *Pee See Doss.*

Meaning: Acronym for Personal Computer-Disk Operating System. The version of MS-DOS that is bundled with IBM-PCs. Either way, it's the most commonly used operating system on PCs. (See also *DOS* and *MS-DOS.*)

Sentence: "Do the upgrades for *PC-DOS* correspond to the upgrades for MS-DOS? I think not."

PC-XT

Pronunciation: *Pee See Ecks Tee.*

Meaning: Abbreviation for Personal Computer - eXtended Technology. A very early (relatively speaking — 1983) personal computer manufactured by IBM that used the Intel 8088 microprocessor. The XT, as it was called, was superior to previous PC computers. Now, you can't give one away. (See also *boat anchor.*)

Sentence: "You don't have to go to a computer museum to find a *PC-XT;* the technology changes so fast that most users can't afford to keep up with it."

PCL

Pronunciation: *Pee See Ell.*

Meaning: Acronym for Printer Control Language. A set of instructions used to control a specific brand of printer — not to be confused with *page description language*, nor with a *printer driver*. The printer driver might contain instructions written in a printer control language, but the PCL is germane to the printer itself. Also used commonly to refer to HP LaserJet compatibility.

Sentence: "I have a *PCL* printer that acts just like a LaserJet III, but it's a lot less expensive. It's called a LaserJet II."

PCX

Pronunciation: *Pee See Ecks.*

Meaning: A graphics file format (and therefore a file extension) for the PC. Originally developed for the PC Paintbrush program, PCX is supported by almost every program on the PC, both Windows and DOS. PCX files are bitmapped graphics files. (See also *bitmapped.*)

Sentence: "When you capture the screen by pressing Shift-Print Screen, you get a *PCX* file, which you can open and examine in Windows Paintbrush."

PDL

Pronunciation: *Pee Dee Ell.*

Meaning: Abbreviation for *Page Description Language*. A programming language, such as PostScript, that is processed by a CPU in the printer itself. The PDL, through its particular statements and commands, "describes" the information on a page of printed output, generally through vector graphics calculations. Although it may take thousands of lines of PDL code to describe a page, the result prints much faster than the previous method of sending information to the printer: bitmapped graphics. The PDL is independent of the particular kind of printer you're using — as long as the printer has the capability of understanding the language. (See also *PostScript* and *Vector Graphics.*)

Sentence: "PostScript is a *PDL* commonly used with Macintosh computers. TrueType is now the primary PDL for PCs. TrueType is PostScript-compatible, but PostScript is not TrueType-compatible."

peek

Pronunciation: *peek.*

Meaning: A BASIC command that lets the user "peek" at the contents of a precise address in memory. The user can then *poke* a new value into the address if desired. (See also *poke.*)

Sentence: "I took a *peek* into Santa's sack and saw that he was going to bring me a super duper Fax Modem for Christmas!"

peer-to-peer

Pronunciation: *peer-too-peer.*

Meaning: A democratic arrangement in networking technology where all nodes are created equal. The other kind of network is a *client-server* arrangement, where one machine is specially designated as a file server that can allocate resources not available to the "client" nodes. A peer-to-peer relationship has no shared resources on a server. You can have a peer-to-peer relationship between computers in a network that contains servers. A *peer-to-peer file transfer* is the technology for accessing the available files of other members along the network. (See also *client-server, network, nodes,* and *server.*)

Sentence: "*Peer-to-peer* means that our computers communicate on a network without a file server. Pier to peer means that we go to the end of the dock and peer over the edge."

pen

Pronunciation: *pen.*

Meaning: (1) Long, thin device used for writing, ranging from quills to felt-tip. (2) A computer that receives input from a stylus similar in shape to the above, but which registers signals electronically so that users can write in their own handwriting, rather than enter information on a keyboard or with a mouse. Pen-based input must be neatly printed. Hence, an ironic turnaround: when we lost touch with paper and became dependent on keyboards, our handwriting became a casualty of technological development. Now that the technology has advanced even further, tidy handwriting is once again becoming a necessity — to be able to take advantage of the technology! Industry analysts predicted that pen-based computing would be the hottest new technology in years. In reality, the pen has had little impact on the industry thus far. (See also *light pen.*)

Sentence: "The *pen* is mightier than the keyboard."

Pentium

Pronunciation: *Pent-ee-um.*

Meaning: A brand new chip (microprocessor) for personal computers, manufactured by Intel. It is the successor to the 486 chip, and even people who don't write ad copy for Intel consider it revolutionary because of its speed and efficiency. Intel was going to call this the 586 chip, but they couldn't copyright the term, so they called it the *Pentium.* As this book is being written, the first of the Pentium chips are being shipped, so currently, no known human beings are actually reaping the benefits of this technological advance. (See also *coprocessor, Intel, microprocessor,* and *processor.*)

Sentence: "The *Pentium* is a hot new gift idea when you don't know what else to get the friend who has everything. This Christmas, get her a Pentium."

peripheral

Pronunciation: *per-if-er-ul.*

Meaning: Any machinery connected to the computer, including monitors, printers, scanners, mice, external hard or floppy drives, CD-ROM drives, speakers, and keyboards.

Sentence: "We are going to get so overwhelmed with *peripherals* that we won't be able to find the center anymore."

peripheralitis

Pronunciation: *per-if-er-ul-ih-tis.*

Meaning: A disorder characterized by having too many peripherals and nowhere to plug them in. Another problem is that you'll have a hard time getting them to talk to each other.

Sentence: "A very effective cure for *peripheralitis* is poverty."

permanent storage

Pronunciation: *perm-e-nent stor-ej.*

Meaning: Any data or means of storing it that is bolted down and won't go ka-blooie when you turn the computer off. Hard drives, floppy drives, and ROM are examples of permanent storage. RAM is the opposite — anything in RAM will go ka-blooie when you turn off the computer. (See also *nonvolatile memory.*)

Sentence: "I put all the names in my little black book into *permanent storage* on my computer."

PERT

Pronunciation: *Pert.*

Meaning: Acronym for Program Evaluation and Review Technique (or Peripheral Envy Regression Training, for all you closet New Agers out there). An approach to project management that doesn't necessarily need the computer to implement it. You can perform PERT equally well on paper. PERT involves charting out the time and other resources needed to complete various components of a project. Project management software programs usually contain PERT charting features. (Isn't PERT a shampoo, too?)

Sentence: "I used a *PERT* diagram to show the vice president the schedule we intend to follow. He liked it so much that I'm now the official PERT manager at the company."

phosphor

Pronunciation: *fahs-fer.*

Meaning: The material used inside the CRT (cathode ray tube) to create the display. It works by being stimulated by an electron beam and emits the energy it absorbs in the form of light patterns that the user sees.

Sentence: "The *phosphor* in my monitor must be stimulated by now because I've been typing love poems all day."

phosphor burn-in

Pronunciation: *fahs-fer bern-in.*

Meaning: A ghost image that appears on the screen — and stays there — as a result of having the same particles activated for too long a time. Akin to sunburn of the monitor, phosphor burn-in occurs when you leave the same image on the screen for several hours. When you turn the screen off, you can still see an outline of the image. Screen savers help prevent this burn-in. (See also *screen saver.*)

Sentence: "When you get screen savers to prevent *phosphor burn-in,* they should have protection factor numbers like sunscreen."

physical device

Pronunciation: *fiz-i-kul dee-vis.*

Meaning: An actual, physical, touch-and-feel device associated with your computer. *Physical device* would not require defining if it weren't for virtual devices, which are imaginary, make believe, can't-touch-them devices. (See also *virtual device*.)

Sentence: "I put my virtual file, which contains my virtual income projection, onto a *physical device* for storage. I'm hoping it will become real."

physical drive

Pronunciation: *fiz-i-kul drih-va.*

Meaning: The actual floppy disk a user is writing to or reading from, with all its uniqueness, brand identity, and idiosyncrasies, as opposed to the *logical drive*, which is strictly an electronic concept, or the *virtual drive*, which is really just a file on a physical drive that acts like a separate drive. (See also *logical drive*.)

Sentence: "If you dissect the *physical drive* while saving data, you will have a virtual disaster."

pica

Pronunciation: *pih-ka.*

Meaning: An old-fashioned typographical measurement that rivals the English system (inches, pounds, and so on) for obsolescence. One pica equals 12 points, which is the measurement used to define typefaces. A pica equals *approximately* ⅙ of an inch, and each page layout program might have a different version of what this amounts to. Pages and parts of pages are measured in picas.

Sentence: "We'll make the gutters between those columns three *picas* wide."

pico-

Pronunciation: *pee-koh* or *pih-koh.*

Meaning: A prefix meaning one-trillionth.

Sentence: "Give me a couple of *pico*seconds to back up my hard drive, and I'll be right with you."

PIF

Pronunciation: *Piff.*

Meaning: Acronym for *Program Information File*. PIF files are used by Windows to define parameters for DOS programs. A PC-type file that contains information about the logistics of running the application to which it corresponds.

Sentence: "Windows has a *PIF* editor that lets you create and change PIF files. Does anyone really use this utility?"

pin

Pronunciation: *pin.*

Meaning: The doohickeys in a dot-matrix printer that make an impression on the ribbon which in turn makes an impression on the paper. The more pins, the sharper the image. Also, the doohickeys within a parallel or serial port that help configure the flow of information.

Sentence: "I have a 24-*pin* printer, but it takes forever to print out a simple letter."

pin feed

Pronunciation: *pin feed.*

Meaning: Not the same kind of pins as above. This kind of pin is located on the sprocket wheel, and it's not as sharp as the other kind. It's the mechanism found on dot-matrix printers that use tractor-feed computer paper, the kind with the tear-off margins that have holes in them. The pins grab onto the holes and propel the paper through the machine. (See also *dot-matrix printer.*)

Sentence: "Sometimes the *pin feed* mechanism jams, and my document comes out looking like a Chinese paper fan."

pipe

Pronunciation: *pihp.*

Meaning: In UNIX and DOS, the technology for naming and connecting two or more programs so that the results of the first one named in the statement are fed as input to the second one named, and so on, ad infinitum. It's like sending water through a series of pipes. (See also *filter* and *pipe character.*)

Sentence: "This first program logs into my bank's computer database and locates my checking account to see how much money I need. This

second program funnels the required money into my account. I use a *pipe* to connect these two programs."

pipe character

Pronunciation: *pihp kar-ek-ter.*

Meaning: A character found on the keyboard that you never see in real life, that looks like this: |. Sometimes it's one long line, and sometimes it's split in the middle. This character is usually found above the backslash, another character found only on computers. (See also *pipe*.)

Sentence: "I access the *pipe character* by pressing Shift and the Backslash key."

piracy

Pronunciation: *pih-re-see.*

Meaning: Copying software without the permission of the writer or publisher, and, if you're really bad, distributing it as well. It is estimated that for every copy of a program that is purchased legitimately, two copies are pirated. Most pirates justify this practice by explaining that the software companies are making too much money on the products they sell and that pirated copies do not really take away revenue from the publishers because pirates would not have purchased the product anyway. Efforts to squelch this plague have included copy protection, registration of legal owners, and Just Saying No — besides the fact that you could also go to jail for it.

Sentence: "Software *piracy* has generated a whole new field of legal activity and income for attorneys."

pitch

Pronunciation: *pich.*

Meaning: Number of characters per inch, as on old-fashioned typewriters. Some old word processing software still uses this type of measurement, and will, for instance, give you a choice of printing in 10-pitch or 12-pitch.

Sentence: "Printing in 12-*pitch* saves space and looks classier. Printing in 10-pitch takes up more paper, so this is probably the way you want to go when writing term papers — or when writing for money, when you're getting paid by the page."

pixel

Pronunciation: *piks-ell.*

Meaning: Acronym for PICture ELement. As atoms are to molecules, pixels are to pictures. They are the smallest un-break-down-able units of a picture on the monitor's screen. When the image quality is poor, you are painfully conscious of looking at a bunch of square dots.

Sentence: "When the *pixels* are too large, it's hard to navigate the curves in a picture with any precision."

PL/1

Pronunciation: *Pee Ell Won.*

Meaning: Abbreviation for Programming Language One, an early programming language mostly used on IBM mainframes.

Sentence: "Not too many people use *PL/1* anymore, but it's still cool to have on your résume."

plasma

Pronunciation: *plaz-ma.*

Meaning: The type of display or monitor used in laptop and notebook computers — adapted from LCD technology. Plasma monitors are flat, do not require tubes, and are therefore smaller and lighter than CRT monitors. The image is produced by stimulating a gas trapped between two panels. Also known as *flat panel display*. (See also *gas plasma display* and *monitor*.)

Sentence: "If I look at the *plasma* display on my laptop computer at just the right angle, I can see the ocean."

platen

Pronunciation: *play-ten.*

Meaning: In dot-matrix and daisy wheel printers, the roller that guides the paper through the printer. The character keys strike against the paper while it's rolling over this surface.

Sentence: "Do not let your *platen* get scratched or notched because that could make the letters come out looking funny."

platform

Pronunciation: *plat-form.*

Meaning: The hardware foundation on which an operating system sits, or the operating system on which a software application sits. For example, the Intel X86 processors constitute a platform on which operating systems are built. DOS/Windows is a platform on which application programs are built.

Sentence: "My friend told me he really likes the Macintosh *platform.* I told him to stop putting it on a pedestal."

plotter

Pronunciation: *plah-ter.*

Meaning: A type of printer that draws pictures with one or more pens, based on instructions fed to it from the computer. Especially useful with graphics or CAD applications.

Sentence: "When the ink jams up in a *plotter*-type printer, do you say, 'The plotter thickens?'"

plug

Pronunciation: *plug.*

Meaning: The thing at the end of a wire or cable that you stick into a jack to make information or electricity flow. Synonymous with *male connector.* (See also *male connector.*)

Sentence: "Sometimes when you can't get your computer to work, it's because you need to *plug* it in."

PMMU

Pronunciation: *Pee Em Em You.*

Meaning: Abbreviation for *Paged Memory Management Unit.* A chip or circuit in some later model computers that enables them to invoke virtual memory. (See also *virtual memory.*)

Sentence: "I just love thinking about all the things in my Mac that are virtual rather than real, like *PMMU.*"

point

Pronunciation: *poynt.*

Meaning: (1) A move that the user makes with the mouse or "pointing device" that simply involves moving the mouse so that the mouse pointer moves to the desired location on the screen. (2) A measurement for typefaces. It's easy to specify or to change the point size in a typical word processing program, but if you want to measure text on a page, you need a special ruler. A point is equal to one-sixth of a pica, which makes it equal to *approximately* 1⁄72 of an inch. The exact measurement varies with each word processing or page layout program. Typical point size for books is around 11- to 12-point type. Display type, used for advertising, can get up to 72-point or larger. (See also *pica*.)

Sentence: "If you want your résume to fit on one page, you can make the *point* size smaller."

point-of-sale system

Pronunciation: *poynt-uv-say-ell sis-tem.*

Meaning: Computer hardware and software for retail sales operations. The type of hardware can range from a personal computer to a mainframe, but its function is the same: it registers prices for individual items, gathers data from sales, tracks inventory, and maintains a customer database. It can include peripherals like a receipt printer, a bar code scanner, and a credit card verification capability.

Sentence: "We installed an expensive new *point-of-sale system* in our store. Now if we only had some customers."

pointer

Pronunciation: *poynt-er.*

Meaning: A symbol that appears on the screen and corresponds to the movement of the mouse or other pointing device. The pointer doesn't always look the same. It can take on different guises in different applications or even in different functions within the same application. A pointer is also a programming term relating to a variable that keeps track of an object (such as the next item in a linked list). (See also *I-beam pointer, linked list,* and *mouse*.)

Sentence: "On the Mac, the *pointer* changes from an arrow to a watch when the computer is busy doing something. That means you can't do a thing until it's finished."

pointing device

Pronunciation: *poynt-ing dee-vihs.*

Meaning: An input device like a mouse, trackball, joystick, or stylus that lets you move the cursor around the screen.

Sentence: "On a touch-sensitive monitor, your finger becomes a *pointing device.* As if a mouse is too difficult to use!"

poke

Pronunciation: *pohk.*

Meaning: A BASIC command that allows you to place a specific value into a precise memory address. (See also *peek.*)

Sentence: "What is a *pig in a poke*, anyway? Does it have anything to do with BASIC?"

polymorphism

Pronunciation: *pahl-ee-morf-iz-um.*

Meaning: In the context of object-oriented programming, this means using the same name to specify different procedures within different contexts. A good analogy is the word *cook.* This term can involve a different method for bread, for pasta, for vegetables, and for meat. You can define *display*, for instance, to apply to text, graphs, pictures, spreadsheets, movies, sound effects, and anything else you choose to associate with the term. (See also *object-oriented programming.*)

Sentence: "I think I have a *polymorphism* problem on my computer; when I issued the Exit command, the computer walked out of the room."

pong

Pronunciation: *pawng.*

Meaning: (1) Say you're working on a computer that's part of a network. You want to tap into another computer on the network. There's a way to send out a signal (other than e-mail) to find out if that computer is available to connect with or not. Your status check is the "ping;" the other computer's response is the "pong." (2) The original computer game developed by Atari in the mid-70s, now found in museums.

Sentence: "We used to play *Pong* when I was a kid. Now computer games are so complicated that I prefer to just go to work."

pop

Pronunciation: *pahp.*

Meaning: When data is arranged in a stack (like a stack of dishes), to retrieve the next record (or piece of data that is sitting on top of the stack) is to *pop* it. This doesn't happen much in an end-user situation but is more likely to happen within a programming context.

Sentence: "I tried to play *Pop Goes the Weasel* on my sound board, but it was a no-go."

pop-up menu

Pronunciation: *pahp-up men-yoo.*

Meaning: Essentially the same idea as a pull-down menu, only it appears someplace other than the menu bar itself and is often the result of a keyboard command. In a Mac environment, a pop-up menu can appear when you highlight one of the choices on a pull-down menu. (See also *pull-down menu.*)

Sentence: "A *pop-up menu* is a little different than a pop-up book. You do not get a picture of the item in question sticking up from the surface of the screen."

port

Pronunciation: *port.*

Meaning: (1) A jack in back of the computer where you can plug in a peripheral device. Ports are usually either serial or parallel. (2) To convert a software application to an operating system other than the one it was originally written for — that is, to *port* the application to another platform. (See also *printer.*)

Sentence: "Many software companies just *port* their applications from the PC to the Macintosh rather than rewriting the application from scratch on the Macintosh. Then they often discover that the problems associated with porting applications often take longer to resolve than just writing the program from scratch."

portable computer

Pronunciation: *port-e-bull cum-pyoo-ter.*

Meaning: A computer that you can carry around with you without making yourself a candidate for the trauma ward. Classifications include laptops, notebooks, and hand-held computers. A portable computer that is really too heavy to lug around regularly may be called "transportable" or "a brick on a leash."

Sentence: "I have a portable notebook computer, a hand-held calculator, a portable printer, and a new PIM device. I have so many *portable computer* devices that I need an extra suitcase to take them on a trip."

portrait orientation

Pronunciation: *por-tret aw-ree-en-tae-shun.*

Meaning: An amazingly convoluted way of saying "the usual direction" when discussing which way to turn the paper or which way the paper gets printed on. It means more vertical than horizontal, or "the long way," as opposed to "landscape orientation," or "the wide way." Usually you find this terminology in graphics applications. Like many other professionals, graphic artists seem to have an irresistible need to mystify even the simplest things. (See also *landscape orientation.*)

Sentence: "If you didn't print that picture of President Clinton with *portrait orientation,* you would be making the expensive mistake of cutting off the top of his hair."

POS

Pronunciation: *Pee Oh Ess.*

Meaning: Abbreviation for Point of Sale. (See also *point-of-sale system.*)

Sentence: "Our *POS* system was just installed. It consists of a receipt book, a pen, and a cash drawer."

POSIX

Pronunciation: *Pos-icks.*

Meaning: Acronym for Portable Operating System Interface for UNIX. A version of UNIX developed by the Institute of Electrical and Electronics Engineers. (See also *UNIX.*)

Sentence: "IEEE tries again, with POSIX, to impose some standardization on the many implementations of UNIX."

POST

Pronunciation: *Po-sta.*

Meaning: Acronym for Power-On Self-Test, a rigorous battery of tests the PC subjects itself to when first started. Rumor has it that if the computer fails any of the tests, it displays a cryptic error message and pouts in the corner until you call someone to tell you what to do.

Sentence: "Before I leave the house, I perform a personal *POST.* I check to see if I have my wallet, my keys, my glasses, that my hair is combed, and that I have my important stuff with me. Oh, and I check to ensure that I'm wearing pants."

PostScript

Pronunciation: *Pohst-Skript.*

Meaning: A page description language developed by Adobe Systems, used with laser printers and other high-resolution machines. To make PostScript work, you need to have a PostScript printer driver included with either the software application or the operating system. One of the great benefits of this technology is that you can create a document with an ordinary desktop computer, but the file can be read by very professional typesetting machines, like a Linotronic. Thus, if you wanted to make a brochure or poster or print advertisement, you could do *all* of the design on your end and just take the disk to a print shop that would generate the output required by the printer. (See also *Linotronic.*)

Sentence: "If you need typeset-quality printouts, take your *PostScript* files to a laser bureau for output."

power down

Pronunciation: *pow-er down.*

Meaning: (1) To turn off the electric supply to the computer and/or peripherals. (2) To eat quickly and with vigor.

Sentence: "We have 30,000 more lines of code to write by 5:00; *power down* that Twinkie and get back to work!"

power supply

Pronunciation: *pow-er sup-plih.*

Meaning: The gizmo within the computer that changes the AC (alternating current) that comes out of your wall to the DC current that the computer actually uses. It's not a one-to-one correspondence. You need to make sure that your computer's power supply is adequate to cover the needs of all the machinery it's serving. (See also *AC* and *alternating current.*)

Sentence: "My computer's *power supply* gets so hot that I now use it to cook my breakfast in the morning."

power surge

Pronunciation: *pow-er serj.*

Meaning: You might think that because the shape of your plugs doesn't change, and the size of your wires doesn't change, if you keep the same thing plugged into the same outlet you get the same amount of electric-

ity. If only that were true. The amount of power flowing through your wires can vary considerably, and having it increase drastically and suddenly can cause damage to your computer's innards. Most of this surge (or spike) is beyond your control, but regardless of the cause, every computer user needs to install a device called a *surge protector* between the computer and the wall. This offers full protection against power surges but offers no protection against other communicable diseases. (See also *surge protector.*)

Sentence: "I read a science fiction story about a *power surge* that caused a computer to come alive. In reality, *power surges* are more likely to kill your computer."

power user

Pronunciation: *pow-er yoo-zer.*

Meaning: Somebody who's totally hip, adept, and cool in every way when it comes to doing things with computers. Power users not only know what to do to get something to happen, but they know *why* the thing works, as well. They can figure out shortcuts. They can hold down more than one key at a time with one hand. While munching on cocktail wieners, they can dazzle a roomful of people at a party with discussions of leveraged software, object-oriented programming, and cross-platform porting technologies.

Sentence: "When I was having problems with my computer, I asked our company's hottest *power user* what to do. He told me to turn the computer off and then turn it back on again. Can a person get paid to be a *power user?*"

PPM

Pronunciation: *Pee Pee Em.*

Meaning: Abbreviation for Pages Per Minute. The number of pages that come out of a printer in each minute. "In each," in this case, is the same as "per," so it's OK to say "Pages PER Minute" or PPM. Don't get stuck on the numbers, though. Eight pages per minute to one manufacturer might mean something different to another manufacturer (even if they both know how to count). You need to know whether that's eight pages of text only, eight pages of the printer's favorite font, eight pages with four-color graphics, eight pages only when the sun is shining, there's a gentle breeze, and the federal budget deficit is under control....

Sentence: "When you are talking about buying a printer, ask about the *PPMs* as well as PCLs and PDLs. And while you're at it, ask about printers you can use with PIMs or PDAs. Whatever you end up getting, make sure to treat it with TLC."

precedence

Pronunciation: *pre-se-dens.*

Meaning: The order in which things are done in a mathematical operation. If operation A gets done (on purpose, mind you) before operation B, then operation A has *precedence* over operation B. An operation in the innermost parentheses in a statement has precedence over those in the outer parentheses. If there are no parentheses, the order of operations is determined by the natural order of operation.

Sentence: "Calculating the subtotal must take *precedence* over calculating the total."

precision

Pronunciation: *pree-si-zhun.*

Meaning: Exactness of a number, in terms of how many decimal places you take it out to. For instance, 3.17259324867 has a greater precision than 3.17. Precision is an area that triggers people's obsessive/compulsive tendencies, but fortunately, computers have more of a sense of self-restraint than that.

Sentence: "My spreadsheet program calculates to 16-digit *precision.* I suppose that's enough to balance my checkbook."

presentation graphics

Pronunciation: *prez-en-tae-shun graf-icks.*

Meaning: A branch of software geared to creating impressive visual components that are used for speeches and other presentations. Essentially, such software translates data from a database or spreadsheet into a chart or graph, as well as being able to integrate text, titles, art, sound, and even multimedia activities. The end result is a high-tech slide show that can be viewed on a monitor or projected onto a screen from slides. (See also *graphics.*)

Sentence: "I have a *presentation graphics* package that I use to create graphs for my board of directors meetings."

Presentation Manager

Pronunciation: *Prez-en-tae-shun Man-a-jer.*

Meaning: A GUI and API for OS/2, or, in other words, a graphic user interface and application programming interface for IBM's Operating System 2. (See also *OS/2.*)

Sentence: "*Presentation Manager* gives OS/2 its look and feel."

print

Pronunciation: *print.*

Meaning: To generate output from the computer onto pages of paper or mylar via any number of fascinating technologies. Also, a very standard command for any program or programming language, one of the few that are universally understood and not called by weird names in different programs in an effort to create brand identity. There are some choices involved in each print job. You can specify, for instance, how many copies, which pages of the file you want printed (if you don't want the whole file printed), whether the machine should collate the pages, and so on.

Sentence: "I used the *Print* command to print my document to the Print Manager, which holds it in a print queue while the printer completes its current print job. Do you think I'll ever see my document again?"

print buffer

Pronunciation: *print buf-er.*

Meaning: A portion of memory that temporarily holds the print queue. The printer needs an area like this because its processing is much slower than the computer's, and this "holding cell" prevents a traffic jam. The computer sends information to the printer only as fast as the print buffer accepts it. (See also *buffer* and *screen buffer.*)

Sentence: "I expanded the *print buffer* on my printer to 4 megabytes."

print head

Pronunciation: *print hed.*

Meaning: The part of a dot-matrix printer's mechanism that contains the pins. The print head scans the paper while the pins strike the ribbon, creating images. (See also *dot-matrix.*)

Sentence: "The guarantee on my dot-matrix printer said that the *print head* will last for 300 million impressions. I'm sure I wasn't past one million impressions by the time I upgraded to the laser printer."

print job

Pronunciation: *print jahb.*

Meaning: An order to print certain material in a certain way at a certain time. Every time you hit the final OK key (or the equivalent) after making all your print specifications, that constitutes a print job — no matter how many times you might create an exact duplicate of that same order. A print job is also the unit you can cancel, delay, or perform other operations on. (See also *queue.*)

Sentence: "I sent a *print job* to the network printer where it is waiting in queue to be printed."

Print Screen

Pronunciation: *Print Skreen.*

Meaning: An instruction to the computer to print the screen exactly the way it is, weird formatting commands and all. Also a key on your keyboard which, in some applications, prints the screen.

Sentence: "In Windows, I can press Shift-*Print Screen* to capture the screen in a PCX file."

print spooler

Pronunciation: *print spool-er.*

Meaning: Software that manages a print queue and lets print jobs line up one after the other — as if they were wrapped around a spool — patiently feeding them to the printer in the background while the user is busy writing novels, crunching numbers, playing Tetris, or doing other productive things in the foreground. (See also *background, foreground, queue,* and *printer buffer.)*

Sentence: "The Windows *print spooler* is called the Print Manager, which manages your print jobs and sends them to the printer in a queue. You can bypass the print spooler by taking the check mark off the Use Print Manager option in the Printer Setup options."

printer

Pronunciation: *print-er.*

Meaning: An output device that translates signals from the computer into text and graphics on paper (or mylar, or any of a number of other materials, for that matter). Types of printers range from the old-fashioned dot-matrix printers that are so noisy their owners sometimes

put boxes over them in a futile attempt to muffle the racket, to the wondrously, whisperingly quiet professional laser printers. Printers, like xerox machines, are subject to the most ultimate extrapolations of Murphy's Law. Not only will anything that can go wrong actually do so, but it will go wrong more persistently and with less feedback than almost any other machine you've grown to love. The principal types of printers include *dot-matrix, daisy wheel, LED* and *LCD, inkjet*, and *laser*. (See also *Murphy's Law.*)

Sentence: "My laser *printer* cranks out eight pages a minute. That's a little bit faster than I can type, so I guess it's worth it."

printer driver

Pronunciation: *print-er drih-ver.*

Meaning: The software that acts as an interpreter between the operating system or application software and the particular make and model of printer you're trying to talk to. In most cases, the set of printer drivers is written into the operating system, but in some cases, like DOS, each application has to have its own printer driver.

Sentence: "I can't seem to get the right *printer driver* for my printer. Maybe because it's from Korea, the instructions need to be in Korean."

printer font

Pronunciation: *print-er fahnt.*

Meaning: In the old days, fonts that the printer was capable of printing out but that the computer was *not* capable of displaying on the screen. This is rarely the case in these enlightened times. In fact, sometimes it's the other way around, where you can get fonts to show up on the screen that the printer can't necessarily produce. The term *printer font* also applies to a font that is created for the printer's PDL and that, hopefully, matches a screen font so you can see something close to what the printer will print. (See also *font.*)

Sentence: "Because I couldn't see any of my *printer fonts,* I rolled the dice to decide which font to use for my presentation."

printer port

Pronunciation: *print-er port.*

Meaning: The jack on the back of your computer that you plug your printer into — usually a parallel port. (See also *parallel port.*)

Sentence: "I'm waiting for the ultimate portable computer that will let me plug my electric razor into the *printer port.*"

processor

Pronunciation: *prah-sess-er.*

Meaning: The brains of the computer, the sine qua non of the computer experience. Generally, the processor of note is the CPU, but there are other kinds, second most notably the math coprocessor. Also, there are processors in probably every single type of consumer electronics. The hallmark of a processor is that it acts on instructions: sorting them, filtering them, or performing mathematical operations on them. (See also *microprocessor* and *coprocessor.*)

Sentence: "The *processor* in most PC computers is of the X86 family. Macintosh computers use 680X0 processors."

Prodigy

Pronunciation: *Prah-di-jee.*

Meaning: An on-line service for computer users that offers electronic shopping, securities trading, games, downloadable files, and electronic mail, to name a few. Anybody can join; all it takes is a relatively new computer, a modem, and an indifference to the high cost of communications.

Sentence: "I went to Sears to buy the software for Prodigy, but the salesman didn't know what I was talking about. He asked me if it was some kind of Mozart thing."

program

Pronunciation: *proh-gram.*

Meaning: A set of instructions written in a programming language. Software is the same thing as a program. Also called an *application.* Either way you express it, a program is composed on a keyboard and assembled by machines or underpaid technicians. The most familiar types of programs on the consumer or end-user market are application programs, like word processing, databases, spreadsheets, graphics programs, games, and educational programs. However, there are other types of programs less visible to the naked eye, which can be thought of as the computer talking to itself (in a roundabout way). These include operating systems, communications software, and utilities — the ultimate computer navel-gazing program being the Norton Utilities where the computer gazes inward to detect and repair problems on the hard and floppy drives. In a way, a computer can also imagine itself: you can get programs that can simulate the performance of a chip or other piece of hardware. (See also *application program.*)

Sentence: "I just purchased a new *program* for my computer. Can someone tell me what to do next?"

programmer

Pronunciation: *proh-gram-er.*

Meaning: Someone who writes programs. This involves designing the program — what it should accomplish and how — writing the code in a programming language, putting the source code through a compiler, which translates it into a form the machine can understand, and debugging it, or fixing any errors. Programmers come in three types: Geeks, Wizards, and Hackers. (See *programming language*.)

Sentence: "I went to school for eight years to become a doctor, but now I'm a *programmer.* And to think, it took no education at all!"

programming language

Pronunciation: *proh-gram-ing lang-wij.*

Meaning: A way of talking to the computer, analogous to the ways humans have evolved in talking to each other. Like natural languages, programming languages include grammar, syntax, and vocabulary, as well as style and organization. Some programming languages are not too far removed from English (called *high-level languages*), while others are more like hieroglyphics (called *low-level languages*). Some languages are more suited to specific vertical markets, like Ada to the defense industry, FORTRAN to business, and C++ to applications building.

The lower the level of language, the closer it is to the guts of the machine, and therefore, the most efficient, such as assembly language. But when you're talking to a machine in a low-level language, you're talking to a specific machine, and your work can't be reused on a different platform. Higher level languages, which include just about everything from BASIC to C++, approximate human languages more closely. (See also *Ada, BASIC, C, C++, Fortran, LISP,* and *Pascal.*)

Sentence: "When I first started programming, I used the BASIC *programming language.*"

progress indicator

Pronunciation: *prah-gres in-di-kae-ter.*

Meaning: A graphic element that displays the progress of an event, such as opening a file or sorting a database. Progress indicators are often called *thermometer bars.* As an event progresses, the "level" of the thermometer rises until the entire bar is full, indicating that the event is 100 percent complete. Progress indicators can also be simple `percent complete` counts.

Sentence: "When I save a file, the *progress indicator* shows me how long it will take. When the progress indicator is full, it disappears and I have to wait some more."

PROLOG

Pronunciation: *Proh-log,* short for PROgramming in LOGic.

Meaning: A programming language of special interest to mathematicians and computer science researchers. In real life, useful in diagnostic-type applications and expert systems, where the procedure involves proving or disproving that x is the case.

Sentence: "I use *PROLOG* to figure out whether my x will get off my case."

PROM

Pronunciation: *Pee-Rom.*

Meaning: Acronym for Programmable Read-Only Memory. A semiconductor chip that allows a program to be written onto it once — and only once — by the computer manufacturer. This type of chip sits in the middle of the spectrum between the two extremes: chips that come with the programming etched in by the semiconductor manufacturer, and EPROM chips, which can be erased (that's what the "E" stands for) and reprogrammed. (See also *EPROM, EEPROM,* and *ROM.*)

Sentence: "Instead of letting me go to the Junior Prom with Luke Perry, my dad made me finish assembling the *PROM* chips I had started."

prompt

Pronunciation: *prahmpt.*

Meaning: A little character that appears on the screen to let you know the ball is in your court. In DOS, it often looks like the symbol for "greater than." In CompuServe, it is an exclamation point. In other programs, it may appear as a flashing underline or flashing pipe character. Sometimes it's just a question mark. Whatever the form, a prompt tells you that the program is waiting for you to enter something. Usually, you must type something and then press Enter. You can change the appearance of the DOS prompt by typing the PROMPT command, like this:

```
PROMPT = $p "What do you want now?"
```

Sentence: "When the Pentagon computer *prompted* me for a high-security password, I typed **HILLERYISQUEEN** and it gave me access."

proportional pitch

Pronunciation: *pre-por-shun-ul pich.*

Meaning: The practice of letting a letter take up as much room as it needs to. If this sounds obvious, consider that older printers and typewriters did not use proportional pitch. On such typewriters, an *i* would be allotted the same amount of space as a *w*, even though it had no need for it. You can pretty well expect the newer, more advanced printers to offer proportional pitch, as our sensibilities have gotten used to this aesthetic.

Sentence: "My new laser printer is so advanced, it can print my reports so they look like an old typewriter typed them without *proportional pitch.*"

proprietary

Pronunciation: *pro-prih-e-tare-ee.*

Meaning: "Mine, all mine, and no one else's," to quote my favorite 7-year-old. Proprietary means the company that developed the design owns the design, and no one may duplicate it or distribute it without that company's permission. (See also *open architecture.*)

Sentence: "The Macintosh System 7 is a *proprietary* operating system developed by Apple Computer Inc. But then, Apple considers everything it does to be proprietary. Apparently, they don't know how to share."

protect mode

Pronunciation: *pro-tekt mohd.*

Meaning: Used most notably in reference to 386 PCs or better. It means that each program is allotted its own niche in memory (RAM) so that, if you run more than one program at a time, the processing of one program is easy to keep separate from the processing of the other program. Without this capability, programs being multitasked could enjoy all the simple elegance and delicate choreography of rush hour in Boston. Protect mode is not accessed by DOS or any DOS programs, including Windows. However, new operating systems are available that take advantage of the protect mode of X86 processors. Such operating systems include Windows NT and OS/2. (See also *multitasking.*)

Sentence: "The ability to use the microprocessor's *protect mode* allows OS/2 to run Windows software better than Windows. If you could just get the darned thing installed."

protocol

Pronunciation: *proh-te-kahl.*

Meaning: A set of standards that enables communication or file transfers between two computers. In a communications context, for instance, parameters need to be set for baud rate, parity, the number of data bits, the presence or absence of a stop bit, and type of duplex. Without such agreement, the two computers might as well be speaking different languages.

Sentence: "It's important that the computers in a network use the same network *protocol.* Otherwise, no one nodes what's going on."

prototype

Pronunciation: *proh-toh-tihp.*

Meaning: A model for later/more advanced versions of a piece of hardware of software. A prototype typically embodies the intentions of the designer but hasn't worked out all of the details.

Sentence: "My communications hardware is so difficult to use that I wonder if the manufacturer just shipped me the *prototype.*"

PrScr

(See *Print Screen*)

PS/1

Pronunciation: *Pee Ess Won.*

Meaning: Abbreviation for Personal System 1. A PC actually made and marketed by IBM itself. The PS/1 computer was designed for personal/home use and is IBM's second attempt at entering the home computer market. (See also *Bozo.*)

Sentence: "I got a *PS/1* computer to use at home. It's great for playing computer games."

PS/2

Pronunciation: *Pee Ess Too.*

Meaning: Abbreviation for Personal System 2, an IBM PC featuring a proprietary 32-bit expansion bus called the Microchannel bus. PS/2

computers are often shipped with the OS/2 operating system. The PS/2 continues to be a major player in computer wars. (See also *expansion bus, MCA,* and *OS/2.*)

Sentence: "The prices of computers like the *PS/2* are so low that I'm tempted to purchase a better clone."

pseudocode

Pronunciation: *soo-doh kohd.*

Meaning: The flow of a program expressed in fractured English — that is, part ordinary English, part programming language — so that the programmer can map it out without getting stuck in the details. (See also *p-code.*)

Sentence: "I wrote this program in *pseudocode* so that my mother could understand it. She's now a high-paid programmer in the Silicon Valley."

public domain

Pronunciation: *pub-lik doh-maen.*

Meaning: Software that has no copyright and can be copied and distributed without ramification. There are hundreds of public domain programs available through catalogs and PD distributors. Public domain is also called *freeware*. However, *shareware* is not public domain. Generally, public domain software is "at your own risk" stuff. If it makes your disk drive smoke and gives your computer a wet, hacking cough, that's your tough luck. (See also *freeware* and *shareware.*)

Sentence: "I got a great *public domain* program that lets me arrange my furniture on the computer. Now if only I could take out the trash on the computer, I would never have to get up out of my chair."

pull-down menu

Pronunciation: *puhl-down men-yoo.*

Meaning: In a software application, a pull-down menu is a list of intriguing possibilities that appears when you select an option on the menu bar. To choose an item from the list, you drag the mouse down to it and let go, or use the appropriate keyboard strokes. The Macintosh popularized pull-down menus in its original operating system back in 1983. Now, pull-down, pop-up, and tear-off menus are commonplace.

Sentence: "The *pull-down menu* for the Format function in Microsoft Word offers these choices: Character, Paragraph, Tabs, Border, Language, Style, Page Setup, Columns, Section Layout, Frame, and Picture. Something for everyone at this restaurant!"

punched card

Pronunciation: *punchd kard.*

Meaning: Old-fashioned, unwieldy style of data processing which used a separate heavy-stock card to transmit information. The computer would translate a hole pattern punched in the card — or the light coming through them — into electronic signals. This author prefers to think they're obsolete.

Sentence: "Many eons ago when I went to college, we registered for our courses by using *punched cards.*"

purge

Pronunciation: *purj.*

Meaning: To get rid of unwanted/unneeded stuff, preferably in an automated fashion, like with a global search-and-delete operation or a PURGE command.

Sentence: "When I *purged* my hard drive, I deleted my address book by mistake. Now I have an excuse for not calling my mother!"

push

Pronunciation: *push.*

Meaning: Related to the stacking of data, which usually happens far from the watchful eye of the end-user, somewhere in the bowels of a program. Stacked data may be envisioned like a stack of dishes, and it refers to the way data is stored in a part of computer memory. To *push* a record onto the stack means to install it at the top of the stack, where it will be the first one *popped* when the stack is addressed. (See also *stack* and *pop.*)

Sentence: "When I *pushed* that data onto the stack, I got a `Stack Overflow` error, and the computer pushed me back."

Quadra

Pronunciation: *kwa-drah.*

Meaning: A fast, high-end (expensive) Macintosh with a 68040 processor. Ideal for use as a file server, for desktop publishing, for image processing, or for complex number-crunching.

Sentence: "I bought a new *Quadra* because I wanted to outdo Joe, the manager in the next department. He only has a Classic. Besides, Quadras have such a cool name, and the company was paying for it anyway."

query

Pronunciation: *kwr-ee, kweer-ee,* or *kway-ree.*

Meaning: To inquire of. To ask a database for specific information. For example, to find all records containing *Padlevski* in the Last Name field, you use a query such as this:

```
Last Name = Padlevski
```

The database then searches every record until it finds a match. Database queries can become rather complex and intricate, such as the following:

```
Last Name = or (ZIP > 80000 and < 99999)
```

This makes no sense, but queries the database to locate all records containing a Padlevski in the Last Name field or a ZIP code between 80000 and 99999. (See also *database.*)

Sentence: "That last customer started yelling when I couldn't find his record in our database; so I *queried* the database for all records containing 'Jerk' and found him!"

queue

Pronunciation: *kyoo* (as in the dreaded Q on *Star Trek:TNG*).

Meaning: A collection of documents or files waiting as patiently as they can in turn for printing or some other form of processing. For example, a *print queue* is a collection of documents waiting to be printed. In England, the word queue means *a line,* such as a line of people waiting to buy tickets. They say, "Queue up and buy your tickets. Jolly good. Tut-tut."

Sentence: "My document is waiting in the network *queue* to be printed. It's number four. And I'm still waiting. Yessir. I'm waiting. Here I sit. Waiting for that document. It's number four. Wait! Wait a sec. Look! Everything is moving up. Now it's document three in the queue. Okay. Pretty soon now. Just keep standing here patiently. Waiting for my document to print. Just waiting here. Looking at the queue on the screen. There's my document. It's number three now. Used to be number four. Waiting in the queue . . ."

Quit

Pronunciation: *Kwit.*

Meaning: (1) What to do if your company makes you work on a Macintosh Plus computer or on a 286 PC with 2MB of RAM. (2) A command that exits a program. Quit. Done. Kapeesh. All finished. All gone. Going bye-bye. (See also *exit.*)

Sentence: "The *Quit* command is one of the first commands you should know. There's nothing worse than getting into a program and not knowing how to get out again (total 'Hotel California')."

QWERTY

Pronunciation: *Kwer-Tee.*

Meaning: The name commonly given to a standard keyboard layout. The name comes from the combination of the first six keys on the keyboard in the third row. (See also *Dvorak keyboard* and *keyboard.*)

Sentence: "Several attempts have been made to replace the old *QWERTY* keyboard with something more sensible. It's like trying to switch the entire United States to the metric system. Can't be done."

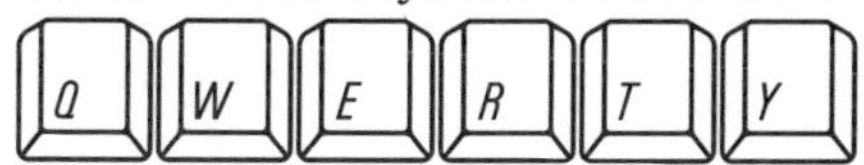

radiation

Pronunciation: *ray-dee-ay-shin.*

Meaning: An invisible form of energy that kills nuclear power plant workers, blows up hot dogs in microwave ovens, and smacks you in the face every time you look at a computer screen. Completely harmless.

Sentence: "Treating eye surgery with acupuncture is like treating hair loss with *radiation.*"

radio button

Pronunciation: *ray-dee-oh butt-on.*

Meaning: A type of mouse-clickable button in a graphical user interface. Radio buttons are grouped together and only one of the group can be "on" at a time. The name comes from the type of buttons that used to be on car radios; when you press a button to select a station, the other buttons all pop out. The same logic is applied to radio buttons, which are used to select only one of a group of options at a time. (See also *button* and *graphical user interface.*)

Sentence: "When I use the Format-Tabs command in Microsoft Word, a set of *radio buttons* assaults me with several alignment options."

ragged justification

Pronunciation: *rag-ed jus-ti-fi-kay-shun.*

Meaning: An oxymoron that really means you have no justification at all. Ragged justification means that both the left and right margins in a document aren't lined up against anything. Specifically, it's usually applied to either the left or right margins individually. Ragged right justification, for example, refers to a paragraph of text that has an uneven right edge. (See also *justify.*)

Sentence: "When I asked John why he took a two-hour lunch, he gave me a *ragged justification* for his actions."

RAM

Pronunciation: *Ram.*

Meaning: Acronym for Random-Access Memory, a type of computer memory that can be written to and read from. The "random" means that any one location can be read at any time; it's not necessary to read all of memory to find one location. RAM commonly refers to the internal memory of your computer, supplied by microchips and measured in kilobytes or megabytes. However, RAM can refer to any random-access memory medium, including magnetic disks and the human brain. RAM is usually a fast, temporary memory area where your data and programs live until you save them or the power is turned off on your computer. (See also *ROM* and *WORM.*)

Sentence: "The best way to improve the performance of Windows is to increase the *RAM* in your computer. Follow this formula: Figure out how much RAM you can buy without going over your credit card limit. Then buy that much RAM and install it in your PC."

RAM disk

Pronunciation: *Ram disk.*

Meaning: A portion of the computer's internal memory (RAM) that is configured to behave like a disk drive. You can use a RAM disk as you would use any normal disk drive — storing and retrieving files — but a RAM disk is significantly faster than a standard disk drive because it's all electronic and has no moving parts. The drawback is that everything stored on the RAM disk disappears when you turn the computer off or reset. RAM disks are useful for storing some disk-intensive programs because RAM drives are so much faster than regular disks. The drawback here is that you usually need a large RAM drive to store the program, which means there's less RAM available for programs that need it.

Sentence: "The astrologer down the street says it's best to create a *RAM disk* under the sign of Aries."

RAM drive

(See *RAM disk.*)

random access

Pronunciation: *ran-dum ak-ses.*

Meaning: The ability to access any piece of information from a storage medium, such as a disk or RAM. The idea here is that random access gives you the ability to access any ol' information without having to read everything that comes before it. The opposite of Random Access is Sequential Access. Sequential Access works like a videotape. If you want to watch the second half of a movie, you must fast forward to that spot in the tape. Random Access works more like a laser disk (or a record player, if you're an old fogey). On the laser disk you just tell the laser beam to "point to the second half of the movie," and it instantly goes there, no fast-forwarding involved. With RAM, random access means you can access any byte in memory any time you want. On a disk, random access means you can access any files without having to churn through all those written to disk before it. (See also *sequential access.*)

Sentence: "My uncle Marty tells jokes with *random access.* You give him a topic, and he'll have a joke."

random numbers

Pronunciation: *ran-dum nuhm-bers.*

Meaning: Numbers that are generated randomly (that is, without any particular aim, order, direction, or sequence), such as when you throw dice.

Sentence: "Due to new theories on the nature of chaos and randomness, many people argue that there is no such thing as a *random number.* These people have not seen my checking account."

range

Pronunciation: *rayn-ja.*

Meaning: A term used to describe a series of things, from a low-numbered thing to a high-numbered thing. For example, a range could be a block of cells in a spreadsheet. A range could also mean a span of values, such as the range between 1 and 10. Also a place where the dear and antelope play. (See also *block* and *cell.*)

Sentence: "A *range* can range from one cell in a spreadsheet to another, hither to thither, or to Amana Radar."

raster

Pronunciation: *rast-er.*

Meaning: A frame or pattern that an electron beam sends to the screen on your monitor. Scan patterns are sent to the screen continuously, a line at a time, to create the images and motion you see. The patterns displayed on the screen are sent using an electron "gun" that wipes the inside of your monitor like a firefighter's hose. The patterns are sent from top to bottom and each new pattern is sent before the last one is finished. This creates "bands" of images, called raster images. If you look out of the corner of your eye at the computer screen, you can see a pulsating effect that the raster images cause. (See also *graphics.*)

Sentence: "It's the *raster* scan line you see when you look at a computer monitor on TV. Ugly, aren't they?"

RCA connector

Pronunciation: *Ahr See Ay kon-nek-ter.*

Meaning: A standard type of connector used for stereo headphones and speakers. They have a long metal tip or prong surrounded by a quarter-inch in diameter plastic jacket. The type of connector is used for some video systems but mostly for computer audio equipment.

Sentence: "Nothing will brighten your guru's heart like referring to the 'connector doohickey' properly as an *RCA* jack."

read

Pronunciation: *reed.*

Meaning: The act of transferring data from a storage medium to the internal RAM of a computer. For example, a computer "reads" information from a disk and then stores it into memory. If your disk drive were a video or cassette tape, "read" would be equivalent to "play."

Sentence: "My computer is not *reading* the file from this floppy disk: it says, '`Cannot read from Drive A`.' Maybe the computer needs glasses."

read only

Pronunciation: *reed ohn-lee.*

Meaning: A type of medium from which you can read data but not write data to it. CD-ROM disks are read only media, as are LP phonograph records; you can read from them (play), but you cannot write (record). Also a file attribute in DOS. (See also *file attribute* and *write-protect.*)

Sentence: "*Read-only* media are used for information that you would not want to change, such as your weight when you were 18."

read/write head

Pronunciation: *reed/riht hed.*

Meaning: The mechanism in a disk drive that accesses and stores information on the disk. The "head" is usually a ceramic material that floats, or hovers, above the disk surface, creating a magnetic field that is charged by the magnetic impulses on the disk. When it writes information to the disk, the head changes the magnetic particles instead of being affected by them. This is how information is read from and written to a disk. (See also *head* and *head crash.*)

Sentence: "A *read/write head* is a delicate thing; small particles of dust between the read/write head and the disk surface can cause errors. This is why you don't go slamming melted cheese sandwiches into your disk drives."

README

Pronunciation: *Reed-mee.*

Meaning: (1) A name typically given to a text file that contains up-to-date information about a program, such as changes to the documentation, information about last-minute additions, and explanations of errors that were not fixed before the product shipped. When a program differs from the documentation, software developers turn to the README file to explain what happened. README files are usually text-only files, so they can be read with any text editor or word processor. (2) A file that nobody reads.

Sentence: "I was having some trouble with a new software package. When I looked at the *README* file, it said that a last-minute change prohibited the software from working on my system. When the company sent me the bill, I sent them a copy of my SUEME file."

real mode

Pronunciation: *reel mohd.*

Meaning: An operating mode of the 80286 and later microprocessors that operates just like the 8088 microprocessor in the first PC. DOS and all DOS applications use the real mode no matter which microprocessor lives inside your PC. (See also *protect mode.*)

Sentence: "Abigail wasn't sure if her virtual reality program would run in the *real mode.*"

real number

Pronunciation: *reel num-ber.*

Meaning: Basically, a real number is any value, usually a value that has some sort of fractional part. Contrast this with an integer, which is just a whole number, no fractions and no decimals allowed.

Sentence: "I gave my accountant a copy of my income projection, and he told me I should stop using imaginary numbers and try some *real numbers.*"

real time

Pronunciation: *reel tihm.*

Meaning: A measurement of time based on actual time elapsed, rather than computer time units. Real-time computer events can be measured with normal time-telling equipment. Many computer operations measure elapsed time based on computer processing time or other non-real systems, or they can simulate faster-than-normal or slower-than-normal time for experiments.

Sentence: "I'm sorry, Jenkins, but you can only clock in on *real time* here."

real-time clock

Pronunciation: *reel-tihm klok.*

Meaning: A computerized clock or timing device that tracks accurate time. For example, when DOS used to start, it would assume that "today" was January 1, 1980, at midnight. In those olden days, people would have to set the date and time manually whenever DOS started — unless they bought a device called a real-time clock, which would automatically keep track of the time and set DOS's clock every time the PC started.

Sentence: "The guy on the street corner told me it was a *real-time clock*, but when I installed it, the faceplate came off and a gum wrapper fell out."

reboot

Pronunciation: *ree-boot.*

Meaning: To restart the computer. Starting the computer is called "booting" or "booting up." There are two ways to reboot the computer: you perform a cold boot by switching the computer off, waiting and then turning it back on again. You perform a warm boot by pressing Ctrl-Alt-Del on a PC or by punching a reset button. Usually a warm

boot is all that's required, but occasionally, a cold boot is necessary to clear memory completely.

Sentence: "When the computer malfunctions, I usually *reboot* by pressing Ctrl-Alt-Del. When that doesn't work, I put my cold boots on and kick it."

record

Pronunciation: *reh-kord.*

Meaning as a noun: An individual unit of data stored in a database. A record consists of one or more related fields, which are the actual pieces of data being stored. Fields combine to create a record the way blanks are filled in on a sheet of paper. The blanks are the fields and the sheet of paper is the record.

Meaning as a verb: To write information, usually applied when recording sound information and storing it in a computer file on disk. Normally, the word "write" is used when you record information to a disk or to memory (RAM).

Sentence: "When that annoying Mr. Smith called, I searched for his *record* and found 200 Smiths in the database. Perhaps we should sort our records by customer IQ?"

recover

Pronunciation: *ree-kuhv-er.*

Meaning: (1) To restore a deleted file. You can often recover deleted files using an UNDELETE utility or command. (See also *undelete.*) (2) A program's ability to continue operating after any errors that would normally send it crashing into outer space.

Sentence: "Our database program is pretty sophisticated. It can *recover* from serious errors, such as when I kick the computer." (See also *reboot.*)

recursion

Pronunciation: *ree-ker-zhun.*

Meaning: This is an advanced programming concept, not required by mere mortals. But if you care to know, recursion is the process that occurs when a software routine (or procedure) calls itself while running. It would just blow your mind if we discussed this any further. Suffice it to say, the process keeps calling itself until it finds itself, and then it stops and the computer — miraculously — doesn't blow up.

Sentence: "I tried to write a program that used *recursion.* But every time the program called itself, it got a busy signal."

redirection

Pronunciation: *ree-dur-ek-shun.*

Meaning: The act of sending a program's output to a location other than the screen. Normally, output goes to the screen; you type it, you see it. Input normally comes from the keyboard. Using redirection, you can tell the computer where to send its output and from where to receive its input. For example, the following DOS command uses output redirection to send its output to the printer: `DIR > PRN`
The > symbol is the output redirection symbol for both DOS and UNIX. The < is the input redirection symbol. Use these things with caution; consult a good DOS text for the lowdown. (See also *output.*)

Sentence: "I used output *redirection* to have the computer send all my network memos to the trash can."

redundant

Same as *repetitive*.

reformat

Pronunciation: *ree-fohr-mat.*

Meaning: The act of formatting something again. You format it once; then the second (and any additional) time, it's a reformat. (See also *format* and *FORMAT.*)

Sentence: "You should never try to *reformat* a disk to a higher capacity. You'll get one of those '`Track 0 unusable`' errors."

refresh rate

Pronunciation: *ree-fresh raet.*

Meaning: The rate at which a screen refreshes, or redraws, its image based on new information. The faster the rate, the less likely the screen is to flicker, which saves the wear and tear on your eyeballs and brain. It also means you pay a lot more for your monitor.

Sentence: "Joe didn't pay much for his monitor. The *refresh rate* is so slow that it works more like a strobe light."

register

Pronunciation: *rej-iss-ter.*

Meaning: (1) Tiny storage places inside your computer's microprocessor. A register is a row or bank of what are called flip flops (binary storage units) that store bits of information for processing by the computer. This is something you'll never need to know unless you program a computer at a very low level. (See also *assembly language, bit, flip flop,* and *word.*) (2) What software publishers want you to do with your software products so they can sell you upgrades through the mail.

Sentence: "Isn't it ironic that you have to *register* a software product before you can get customer service, yet you'll never have to register a gun?"

relational database

Pronunciation: *ree-lae-shun-ul dae-tah-baes.*

Meaning: A database that consists of several, separate files that "relate" to one another through key words or values. Information stored in one file can be accessed through one or more of the other files because of the relations established in the database. For example, you might store customer address information in your Customer database and product order information in an Orders database. These two databases can relate to each other through the customer name. When you examine a customer record in the Customer database, you might, for instance, be able to view all orders associated with that customer. Similarly, when entering an order into the Orders database, you can type a customer name and the entire customer record automatically appears at the top of the order form. Another advantage of relational database design is that each field (type of information) in the database can be accessed individually (that is, you can search for an entry based on any field.) (See also *data, database, field,* and *record.*)

Sentence: "It's *relational database* management that explains why you constantly have to tell the support people your name and address each time you call."

relational operator

Pronunciation: *ree-lae-shun-ul ah-per-rae-ter.*

Meaning: A symbol, such as > or <, that defines a relational operation between two variables or operands. Relational operators are used by programming languages, spreadsheet products, and database management systems for testing the relationships between two values. (See also *operator.*)

Sentence: "I used a *relational operator* to calculate whether meatloaf was better than sushi for dinner tonight."

relative reference

Pronunciation: *rel-uh-tiv ref-rens.*

Meaning: A cell address (or reference) entered into a spreadsheet formula using relative row and/or column designations. When a formula containing relative references is copied to other cells in the spreadsheet, the references are automatically updated to reflect cells that are relative to the new location of the formula. Relative references are applied only during copy procedures. (See also *absolute reference.*)

Sentence: "When it comes time to tell old, spooky Halloween stories, we all use Aunt Shirley as a *relative reference.*"

REM

Pronunciation: *Rem.*

Meaning: Abbreviation for REMARK. REM is a statement, or command, used in many programming languages (including the DOS batch file programming language) that lets you add a line to the program without affecting the program itself. In other words, it lets you enter remarks or comments to help explain what the program is doing. Here's an example:

```
REM This is a typical batch file
PATH C:\DOS;C:\WINDOWS;C:\WINWORD
PROMPT $p$g
C:\MOUSE\MOUSE.COM
```

Above, the REM command is just a comment, and is ignored when the program runs.

Sentence: "Steve's really getting into programming. Last night I hear he even tried to *REM* his dog."

remote

Pronunciation: *ree-moht.*

Meaning: Something that is not within your near vicinity. A remote computer is one that is connected to your network from a distant location — like across the hall. Remote access means you're using a computer that's not within arm's reach.

Sentence: "When I log onto our network from another location, my chances of making a connection are *remote.*"

removable disk

Pronunciation: *ree-moov-ah-bul disk.*

Meaning: Any disk that can be removed from its drive or from the computer. However, the term is generally used to describe a type of high-capacity disk (such as a hard disk) that can be inserted and removed from its drive, as in a Bernouli disk drive. Another term for the unremovable disk is *fixed disk*, which means the disk is solidly attached to the computer—not that it was once broken.

Sentence: "Uh-oh, there goes Fred down the hall with the Jaws of Life. I guess we better tell him that his hard drive isn't a *removable disk.*"

repetitive

Same as *redundant.*

ResEdit

Pronunciation: *Rez-Edit.*

Meaning: Abbreviation for Resource Editor, a Macintosh utility that lets you access and edit system resources. ResEdit lets you mess with the various components of a Mac file. You can actually use it to rename menus, text in dialog boxes, buttons, copy or paste graphics and so on. It's a fun tool, which implies that it's also quite technical and using it is a sure key to goofing up your system.

Sentence: "That Johnson is such a card. He uses *ResEdit* to change all the Mac's error messages to dirty limericks. The problem is, no one noticed."

reserved word

Pronunciation: *ree-zerved werd.*

Meaning: Any word or code used for a special purpose that cannot be used for any other purpose. Reserved words happen in programming languages, operating system, and some applications. For example, in DOS the words COPY, DEL, and REN are all names of DOS commands and therefore reserved words. Other programs cannot use these names or DOS will, well, get mad.

Sentence: "Around our house, *blockhead* is a *reserved word.*"

reset

Pronunciation: *ree-set.*

Meaning: To restart the computer or restore previous settings. Reset is also a key on some Macintosh keyboards that performs a warm boot when you press it. (See also *warm boot.*)

Sentence: "There. I just finished the final page of my speech, and I must admit it's brilliant. Now I have a few idle moments to sit back and brain-relax and . . . hey? I wonder what this button labeled *Reset* does. . . ."

resolution

Pronunciation: *rez-oh-loo-shun.*

Meaning: A way of measuring the clarity of an image. Resolution involves the number of elements per inch — the number of pixels on your screen or dots your laser printer can produce — which indicates how clear and sharp an image is. For example, some laser printers produce 300 dots-per-inch (dpi) resolution. High-resolution printers display from 600 to 2400 dots per inch. Video graphics resolutions are measured horizontally and vertically. A resolution of 320 x 200 indicates large dots to create an image; a resolution of 1240 x 800 means smaller dots and finer image, and therefore a higher resolution. When examining the resolution of an image, your naked eye can discern the dots in resolutions below 600 dpi. However, 300 dpi laser printers are considered adequate resolution for most printing needs.

With color displays, the resolution is also tied to the number of colors that can be displayed at once. For example, a relatively low-resolution picture may be able to display several hundred colors at once. This gives an illusion that the image has a higher resolution, but that's only because the eye is tricked by the multiple colors. Higher resolution images generally use fewer colors. (Most computer games use a medium resolution as a trade-off.) Resolution may be abbreviated as *res* (pronounced *rez*). For example, "high res" or "low res" to indicate high or low resolution. (See also *pixel.*)

Sentence: "I made a new year's resolution that I'd get myself a high-*resolution* printer this year."

resource

Pronunciation: *ree-sohrs.*

Meaning: Just as humans have natural resources, a computer has its own resources. A resource may be memory, disk drive storage, the printer, a monitor, and so on. In Windows, and on networks you always want to watch that your resources aren't running out.

Sentence: "We were getting low on *resources,* running out of disk drive space and memory, and then all of a sudden Al Gore shows up all hopping mad and everything. He made us go down to the computer store and buy more resources, but we can only use 50 percent of them because we have to save the Spotted Disk Owl."

restore

Pronunciation: *ree-stohr.*

Meaning: (1) To return to normal, as in "Yes, Mary is fully restored after her conniption fit." (2) The act of copying files from an archive or set of backup disks or a tape drive to their original locations on the hard drive. This is the opposite of backing up, usually done after something bad has happened. For example, after losing all your data, you would restore your files from a recent backup disk. Or if you deleted a file, you could restore it from a backup disk. Needless to say, this only works if you back up frequently. (3) In DOS, the RESTORE command returns backed-up data to the hard disk.

Sentence: "Don't panic, Dave. You can *restore* the missing files from your backup diskettes. You do back up, don't you?"

retrieve

Pronunciation: *ree-treev.*

Meaning: (1) Fancy talk for accessing or opening a file, as in Lotus 1-2-3's Worksheet Retrieve command. (See also *open.*) (2) May refer to opening a file inside of another file as in WordPerfect.

Sentence: "Most people use the word *open* when they refer to getting a file from disk into a program. Some use *retrieve.* Old Microsoft Word fans may remember Transfer Load. Doesn't that bring back memories?"

Return key

Pronunciation: *Ree-tern kee.*

Meaning: Same as the Enter key, but it gets its name from the carriage return key on a typewriter. Currently found on some Mac keyboards.

Sentence: " Both Enter and *Return* generally perform the same function, but don't quote us on that."

reverse engineer

Pronunciation: *ree-vers in-jin-eer.*

Meaning: The process of decoding a program based not upon the program's code but what the program does and how it affects things. Also applies to the act of analyzing hardware to determine how it works. Reverse engineering is primarily performed when engineers want to figure out how a *black box* gizmo works, and they're either unable to take it apart or forbidden from taking it apart for legal motives. For example, the reason we all have "IBM-compatible" computers today is that someone somewhere reverse engineered the chips in the first IBM PC (the BIOS) and created a working counterpart without infringing upon IBM's copyrights.

Sentence: "I bet IBM really regrets not sicking their legions of lawyers on the first company to successfully *reverse engineer* the guts of the IBM PC."

revision history

Pronunciation: *ree-vi-zjun his-toh-ree.*

Meaning: A revision history tracks the various revisions of a program and what occurred in each. For example:

Version 1.0 Product introduced. They'll love this.
Version 1.1 Annoying "all files accidentally deleted" bug removed.
Version 1.2 Annoying "erased hard drive" thing fixed.
Version 2.0 Networking features added, flock sheared for $50 upgrade fee.
Version 2.1 Annoying "network not found" bug fixed.
Version 2.2 Support for tall people added.
Version 2.3 Support for left-handed people added.
Version 3.0 DOS 5 update, sheared flock for another $50.
Version 3.1 DOS bug fix.

Sentence: "Obviously, most major applications don't include a *revision history* because it would prove to be a source of embarrassment."

RF

Pronunciation: *Ar Ef.*

Meaning: Acronym for Radio Frequency, which includes a certain chunk of the electromagnetic spectrum that you would find terribly uninteresting. Mostly used with RFI, discussed below.

Sentence: "Tune to KRUD, that's 1240 AM on your *RF* dial."

RFI

Pronunciation: *Ar Ef Eye.*

Meaning: Acronym for Radio Frequency Interference. This is the type of interference that occurs when two devices emitting electromagnetic waves interfere with one another. Computers, radios, TVs, and many other radio transmission devices emit waves that can interfere with other devices' waves, causing fuzzy noise, snow on the monitor, an annoyed cat, and other anomalies. RFI is why you can't use your mobile phone on an airplane, and it's why notebook computers undergo monstrous testing for FCC approval. Proper grounding and quality cables help to minimize RFI in computers.

Sentence: "This *RFI* is causing some strange effects on my computer. I could swear I saw a fuzzy image of Bill Gates appear on my monitor."

RGB

Pronunciation: *Ar Gee Bee.*

Meaning: Acronym for Red Green Blue. A type of color process that involves mixing intensities of Red, Green, and Blue reflective (or additive) colors. Based on the mixture and intensity of these colors, you can produce many of the colors in the normal spectrum. TVs and computer monitors use RGB to produce color on the screen. You light individual red, green, and blue pixels to mix colors.

Sentence: "I have an *RGB* monitor, but in this case *RGB* stands for Randomly Goes Blank."

ribbon cable

Pronunciation: *ri-bun kay-bul.*

Meaning: A type of computer cable in which the wires are flat like a ribbon. Ribbon cables are often used for the printer and, inside the PC, disk drives. In the old Apple II days, the ribbon cables were multi-color — like rainbows. Today, they're usually all a pasty hospital-blue. (See also *cable.*)

Sentence: "Doris is so nice. She thought the office looked rather dreary, so she went around and tied bows in all our *ribbon cables.*"

Rich Text Format

Pronunciation: *Rich Teks-ta For-mat.*

Meaning: A type of document file format, usually readable by most major word processors. The Rich Text Format (RTF) file is basically a text file. However, included in the text are various instructions that describe the document's formatting. This looks utterly gross when you see it in the raw, text-only format. But word processors that understand RTF can read in the files and translate the ugly text into formatting codes, making the document look really nice.

Sentence: "The *Rich Text Format* was an attempt to create a common document file format compatible with all word processors and people living in Scarsboro."

RISC

Pronunciation: *Risk.*

Meaning: Acronym for Reduced Instruction Set Computer. A RISC system is a computer that runs very fast because the microprocessor can only do a limited number of things. The idea here is that those little things make the building blocks for larger things, so the RISC processor isn't hindered by its limited number of instructions.

Sentence: "I don't care how fast it is, putting something called *RISC* into my computer doesn't sit well with me."

RLL

Pronunciation: *Ar El El.*

Meaning: Abbreviation for Run-Length-Limited. A type of hard disk controller (now deceased) that increases the capacity of the hard drive by using disk-compression technology directly from the hard disk controller. An RLL controller can increase disk storage capacity by as much as 50 percent. (See also *IDE.*)

Sentence: "Wow! Where did you get the antique *RLL* drive?"

robot

Pronunciation: *roh-baht.*

Meaning: An automated mechanism that simulates or reproduces (or replaces) human activities, such as assembly-line work and deep space work. R2D2 from *STAR WARS* is an example of a robot. Robots are used in many applications, including computer assembly and testing.

Sentence: "Perhaps the most famous *robot* of all time is Robby the Robot from the film *Forbidden Planet.* He was charming, polite, a good friend, and could crush your head like a grapefruit."

robotics

Pronunciation: *roh-baht-iks.*

Meaning: (1) The study and application of robots. (2) Mechanical bugs that suck your blood (pronounced robo-ticks).

Sentence: "My nephew studied *robotics* in school. Now he's working in Burger King. I suppose he's experiencing what it's like to be a robot."

ROM

Pronunciation: *Rahm.*

Meaning: Acronym for Read-Only Memory. ROM is any type of memory that can be read but not written to. For example, compact discs (CDs) are ROM media. ROM is also used to describe the chip inside your computer that permanently contains basic information for the computer. (See also *RAM, PROM,* and *ROM BIOS.*)

Sentence: "I think 'crash randomly' is a special instruction in my computer's *ROM.*"

ROM BIOS

Pronunciation: *Rahm Bi-ahss.*

Meaning: Acronym for Read-Only Memory Basic Input/Output System. It's a BIOS that is stored in ROM. (See also *ROM* and *BIOS.*)

Sentence: "No, Mr. Pinkston, *BIOS* is not *ROM's* 'last name.'"

Roman

Pronunciation: *Roh-mun.*

Meaning: A classification of type styles (fonts), including Times and many others. Also refers to the normal, non-slanted version of type, as opposed to italic type. (See also *font.*)

Sentence: "A *Roman* man once said, 'Hello, my name is Gaius Julius Caesar, and I'm looking for a specific type of font, or do I need to ask?'"

root directory

Pronunciation: *root duh-rek-toh-ree.*

Meaning: The first and often only directory on a disk. The root directory doesn't become important until you have subdirectories and a disk tree structure. Then, the other directories — the subdirectories — branch from the root like a tree. In DOS, the symbol for the root directory is the single backslash. Under UNIX, the symbol is a single forward slash. (See also *tree structure, directory, subdirectory, path,* and *pathname.)*

Sentence: "I wrote this nifty program, DOG.COM, that instantly sniffs out the *root directory* of my hard drive's tree structure."

rounding error

Pronunciation: *rown-ding eh-rohr.*

Meaning: A one-cent error that occurs when the computer converts decimal numbers into binary code (for internal processing) and back again. This always happens, but it's nothing to be overly concerned about — unless you're doing nuclear physics or thousands of lives are at stake, in which case you can use the "blame Microsoft" defense at your U.N. Crimes of Humanity trial. The reason for the rounding error is that certain numbers can only be approximated in the computer's memory as binary digits. As a result, there is a little bit of a fudge factor as the computer's approximations are mathematically manipulated.

Sentence: "I tried to explain all the wrong answers on my math final were due to *rounding errors,* but the professor declines to believe that I'm a computer."

row

Pronunciation: *roh.*

Meaning: A horizontal array of data, as in a spreadsheet or table. Spreadsheets organize data into rows and columns to make totals and other calculations faster and easier. The row may also refer to a line of text in a word processing document or just a line of text across the screen.

Sentence: "The typical PC screen has 25 *rows* of text, only four of which may make sense at any one time."

RPM

Pronunciation: *Ar Pee Em.*

Meaning: Acronym for Revolutions Per Minute. A measurement of the number of times something turns around. Disk drives and phonograph records (remember those) spin at particular RPMs. Phonograph records spin at 33⅓ or 44 RPMs.

Sentence: "I like CD players because I don't have to worry about the *RPM.*"

RS-232C

Pronunciation: *Ar-ess-too-thur-tee-too-see.*

Meaning: Abbreviation for Recommended Standard-232C, also known as RS-232. This is not a Radio Shack part number. Instead, it's a standard method of transmitting data across serial cables and is used by modems, printers, and other serial devices. There's lots of technical stuff surrounding the standard and it can be boring, so that's all we're going to say here. (See also *serial* and *serial port.*)

Sentence: "If *RS-232* is the 232nd standard they came up with that year, then I'd hate to have sat through the first 231 meetings."

RTF

(See *Rich Text Format.*)

run

Pronunciation: *Ruhn.*

Meaning: (1) What to do when the computer starts to smoke. (2) To execute or use a program. Other terms for run are start, launch, execute, and initiate.

Sentence: "The customer service operator told me to *run* my program, but I couldn't find a leash to fit it."

run time

Pronunciation: *ruhn tihm.*

Meaning: (1) The time spent while a program is running. (2) A special version of a program, such as a database or spreadsheet, that performs a specific task. For example, a run-time version of Excel would let you use your Excel worksheets but would not let you use any Excel commands or options.

Sentence: "*Run time* is a misnomer when you work with Windows. Then, it's more like walk or crawl time."

S-100

Pronunciation: *Ess-won-hun-dred.*

Meaning: A type of expansion card and also the name of a CP/M computer from the late 1970s that used that type of expansion card. These systems would be called dinosaurs today. (See also *expansion card* and *CP/M.*)

Sentence: "During their heyday, the *S-100* systems were the Cadillacs of PCs."

SAA

Pronunciation: *Ess Ay Ay.*

Meaning: Acronym for Systems Application Architecture, a set of guidelines that IBM developed for standardizing the way computers work. Most people follow these guidelines and then add just enough "improvements" to destroy the whole purpose of a standard in the first place. (See also *IBM.*)

Sentence: "My computer follows IBM's *SAA* standard. That seems odd because my computer is a Macintosh."

sans serif

Pronunciation: *san ser-if.*

serif
sans serif

Meaning: A typeface that lacks *serifs*, which are tiny ornamental curves and such that appear at the edges of letters. Believe it or not, serifs actually make letters easier to read. Sans serif typefaces (*sans* from the French word for *without*) are harder to read. (See also *serif.*)

Sentence: "A simple desktop publishing rule is to use *sans serif fonts* for headlines or titles and serif fonts for the text. I once followed that

advice painstakingly in Microsoft Word for Windows, only to save and then reload my document and have WinWord switch everything around."

save

Pronunciation: *save* (rhymes with *shave, knave,* and *wave*).

Meaning: To store data (from RAM) on to a floppy or hard disk in hopes that you'll be able to find it again. Nearly every program has a Save command to store your work. (See also *RAM.*)

Sentence: "Use the *Save* command periodically to store your work in case the power goes out or the computer short-circuits itself."

save as

Pronunciation: *save as.*

Meaning: To store an existing file under a different name. The Save As command saves a file, but it allows you to change the file name and maybe also to save the format under which the file is saved.

Sentence: "All top-secret documents have file names like SECRET1 and SECRET2. So I just loaded each file into my word processor, used the *Save As* command, and saved each file under a different name. Now I can sneak out these secret files without the guard getting suspicious."

scalable font

Pronunciation: *skay-lah-bull faunt.*

Meaning: A type of font that can appear in different sizes and still look good. Non-scalable fonts can also appear in different sizes, but at certain sizes they look as horrible as seeing your skin pores through a magnifying glass.

Sentence: "I only use *scalable fonts* in my desktop publishing work, just in case some customer wants to change the type sizes at the last minute."

scan

Pronunciation: *skan.*

Meaning: To read text, images, or bar codes into the computer. Accomplished by a device called a *scanner.* (See also *scanner.*)

Sentence: "I brought a zebra to the supermarket, forced it to lie flat on the checkout conveyor belt, and *scanned* in its skin to see how much it was worth."

scan rate

Pronunciation: *skan ray-ta.*

Meaning: The speed at which a monitor constantly draws an image on-screen. Sometimes called the *refresh rate*, the scan rate is measured in hertz (Hz), which sounds like the name of a popular rental car agency found in airports near the baggage claim. The higher the scan rate, the more expensive your monitor. And, as anyone familiar with computers knows, the more you pay for it, the better it is. (See also *refresh rate.*)

Sentence: "My monitor has a *scan rate* of 72 Hz. Most clerks in the grocery store have a scan rate of about 18 items a minute."

scanner

Pronunciation: *skan-ner.*

Meaning: (1) A device that can electronically "read" printed text or images into a computer. Scanners come in two sizes: flat-bed and hand-held. Flat-bed scanners can scan an entire page at one time while hand-held scanners can scan in widths of approximately four inches. (2) In 1981, Hollywood released a bad horror movie called *Scanners,* where people could use mental powers to make other people's heads explode. (See also *scan.*)

Sentence: "While watching *Scanners* on TV and trying to concentrate hard enough to make my dog's head explode, I decided to buy a *scanner* so I wouldn't have to retype newspaper articles into my word processor."

scope

Pronunciation: *sko-pa.*

Meaning: (1) A mouthwash typically not used by halitosis-happy computer programmers. (2) A term used by programmers to describe the area within a program in which a variable can be used.

Sentence: "While rinsing my mouth out with Scope, I noticed that the *scope* of my subprogram's variables actually included my own subprogram and those subprograms written by Bob as well. But that subject is really beyond the scope of this book."

Scrapbook

Pronunciation: *Skrap-book.*

Meaning: A desk accessory found on the Macintosh that stores frequently used graphic images or text for pasting into documents.

Sentence: "Whenever I draw a picture of my sister shoving pencils in her ear using MacPaint, I store the images in the *Scrapbook* so that I can paste them into a PageMaker document and blackmail her later."

screen blanker

Pronunciation: *skreen blayn-ker.*

Meaning: A special program that periodically blanks out the screen and replaces it with utter darkness — on purpose. Screen blankers prevent the same image from appearing on your screen and being "burned-in" permanently. For example, a lot of older PCs have images of 1-2-3 or WordPerfect permanently etched into their monitors. Some screen blankers can be quite creative. Instead of just blanking the screen, they show images of some sort such as flying toasters, lightning flashes, or raindrops; these are called *screen savers.* (See also *phosphor burn-in* and *screen savers.*)

Sentence: "If I don't touch my keyboard or mouse for five minutes, my *screen blanker* shuts off my screen and displays fish in an aquarium to protect my monitor from burn-in. Then my stupid brother thought it was a real aquarium and poured water in the top, ruining my monitor anyway."

screen buffer

Pronunciation: *skreen buf-fer.*

Meaning: An area of memory used to store the graphic or text image displayed on-screen. Also called *Screen Memory* or *Video RAM.*

Sentence: "And all this time I thought a *screen buffer* was this thing from Ronco for only $19.95 that you used to clean your monitor."

screen dump

Pronunciation: *skreen dump.*

Meaning: A printout of the image that appears on-screen. The unflattering term *dump* is often used in computer lingo to mean a wholesale copying of information from one place to another. We could dwell on this for a long time and get very descriptive. But the editorial matron at IDG Books, Mary Bednarek, would doubtless frown upon such verbosity.

Sentence: "Whenever my computer crashes for no apparent reason, I try to get a *screen dump* so I can show the technician what happened and why his last solution didn't really work after all."

screen font

Pronunciation: *skreen fawnt.*

Meaning: A bit-mapped font that mimics the appearance of printer fonts. Because printers often print with a resolution of 300 dots per inch or more, the fonts tend to look better printed than they do on-screen. As a result, the fonts that appear on-screen may look plain and simple compared to the fonts that appear on the printer, resulting in confusion when you try to figure out what you're doing.

Sentence: "I hate *screen fonts* because you can never tell what they'll look like until you print them out and waste paper in the process."

screen saver

(See *screen blanker.*)

scroll

Pronunciation: *sk-roll.*

Meaning: To move text or graphics vertically or horizontally on-screen as if your monitor were a porthole, looking at a much larger image a little bit at a time.

Sentence: "With a 250-page document, your monitor can only show half a page at any given time. To see the rest of your document, you have to *scroll* up or down. Then again, you can just pretend that you only saw part of the document so you can't be held responsible for the rest of it."

scroll bar

Pronunciation: *sk-roll bar.*

Meaning: A horizontal or vertical rectangular strip that often appears at the right and bottom sides of a window. The scroll bar lets you use a mouse to scroll the image up/down or left/right. The scroll bar also shows you the approximate position of the current screen in relation to the beginning or end of the file.

Sentence: "Whenever I get bored doing my work, I stare at the *scroll bar* and guess how far I've gone since I started. Then I'll use the scroll bar to move to the beginning of my document so it looks like I know what I'm doing."

scroll box

Pronunciation: *sk-roll boks.*

Meaning: Sometimes called an *elevator box*, the scroll box appears in the middle of a scroll bar. By using the mouse, you can scroll through a file just by moving the scroll box within the scroll bar. By looking at the position of the scroll box within the scroll bar, you can see how close the current screen is to the beginning or end of the file. (See also *elevator.*)

Sentence: "Don't waste time pressing the Page Up/Down keys. Move the *scroll box* wildly up and down in the scroll bar and pretend there are people in there alternatively being slammed into the floor and ceiling."

Scroll Lock key

Pronunciation: *Sk-roll Lok kee.*

Meaning: (1) A key that appears on keyboards that appears to do absolutely nothing when you press it. (2) In some (but not all) programs, pressing the up/down cursor keys causes the cursor to scroll up or down. But if you press the Scroll Lock key and then press the up/down cursor keys, the cursor remains fixed on-screen, but the text or graphics appear to slide up or down underneath. If you try this with your program and nothing happens, then you know that your program ignores the Scroll Lock key.

Sentence: "Sometimes I like to press the *Scroll Lock key* while using different programs just to see which programs actually use the Scroll Lock key. I guess this key is the computer equivalent to wisdom teeth in people today."

SCSI

Pronunciation: *Scuz-zee.*

Meaning: Acronym for Small Computer System Interface, which is yet another standard for connecting tape drives, hard disks, and scanners to computers. This is a truly whimsical and easily pronounceable acronym, like WYSIWYG, but not like GUI.

Sentence: "I bought a *SCSI* hard drive and then found I couldn't hook it to my computer without a SCSI port. Now I have a SCSI port, a SCSI hard drive, and a $1,000 credit card bill I can't pay."

search

Pronunciation: *ser-cha.*

Meaning: To examine a file for specific data such as words, characters, or symbols. Word processors let you search for words, and databases let you search for specific records. (See also *sort.*)

Sentence: "Because the board can't decide who we should lay off, we're going to conduct a *search* of everyone's hard drive and fire all of those who have the words `I hate this company` in one or more of their files."

search and destroy

Pronunciation: *ser-cha and dee-stroy.*

Meaning: A military term made popular during the Vietnam war, which is a nice way of saying to look for someone so you can kill him. In computers, search and destroy is a form of search and replace when you replace what you found with nothing. The proper term is really *search and delete*, but no one would turn to that entry. (See also *search and replace.*)

Sentence: "Someone told me my computer program had bugs in it, so I spent the last few days on a *search and destroy* mission using pesticides long since outlawed by the government."

search and replace

Pronunciation: *ser-cha and ree-play-sa.*

Meaning: To look for specific characters in a file and substitute them for another character or group of characters. Every word processor offers a search and replace command so that you can quickly change multiple words or phrases at the touch of a button.

Sentence: "When Margaret Mitchell wrote *Gone With The Wind,* she originally named her heroine Pansy O'Hara. At the last moment she changed it to Scarlett O'Hara. If she had used a word processor, she could have just used the *search and replace* feature to make the changes instantly. Instead, some poor editor had to manually go through each page and change it by hand."

search string

Pronunciation: *ser-cha string.*

Meaning: The group of characters that the computer looks for when given the Search or Search and Replace command. A string is a group of characters. (See also *string.*)

Sentence: "If you want to replace all occurrences of *Pansy* with *Scarlett* in your word processor document, tell the computer to use *Pansy* as the *search string.*"

sector

Pronunciation: *sek-ter.*

Meaning: To store data, disks are formatted into concentric rings called *tracks*, and each track is further divided into sectors. When a disk gets screwed up to the point where the computer can't read information off it anymore, it's usually because one or two sectors are damaged. A damaged sector on a disk is like a book with one or more pages ripped out of it. (See also *track.*)

Sentence: "The technician said that I couldn't use my floppy disk because the boot *sector* was destroyed by a virus. He said this was like someone ripping out the battery and starter from my car to keep it from working. I thanked him for this analogy and took my computer to another technician who didn't aspire to lofty literary pretensions."

seek

Pronunciation: *seek* (rhymes with *geek, Greek,* and *reek*).

Meaning: To move the read/write heads of a disk drive so data and program instructions can be loaded, much the same way as you might move a needle over a record on your grandmother's old turntable. This is actually quite a religious term for a computer, don't you think? You'd expect a term like Go To or Find or Search. Seek, of course, always implies that there may be some chance at failure, which is probably why the computer gods selected it instead. (See also *read/write head.*)

Sentence: "I bought a Bible program and wanted to find the passage where `Seek and ye shall find` occurs. When I started looking, I could hear the disk drive heads sliding back and forth, seeking the information I wanted off the floppy disk."

segment

Pronunciation: *seg-ment.*

Meaning: A portion or part of something. With worms, a segment is like a new piece of the worm that makes it longer — a worm-slice, should the worm chance to crawl over an upended razor blade. In the PC, a *segment* refers to a 64K chunk of memory.

Sentence: "Programs generally run slow under DOS because they must fit their parts into puny little 64K memory *segments.*"

select

Pronunciation: *seh-lekt.*

Meaning: To highlight and choose text or graphics that appear on-screen, usually by dragging the mouse, using the cursor keys, or randomly punching keys while cursing intensely. Selecting is the same thing as "marking it as a block" or "highlighting it."

Sentence: "Before you can delete, copy, or cut anything off the screen, you have to *select* it first so the computer knows what you want to delete, copy, or cut."

select all

Pronunciation: *seh-lekt all.*

Meaning: To highlight and choose all text and graphic images on-screen or in your document at one time. This is a good command to use to erase everything at once, adjust everything on-screen, or copy everything at the same time. If used carelessly, this is also a good way to delete four years' worth of work at the touch of a button.

Sentence: "To reformat my 500-page report, I chose the *Select All* command, but then I hit the Del key by mistake and lost everything. Can I go home now?"

selected

Pronunciation: *sel-ekt-ed.*

Meaning: Highlighted text or graphic images that show you what objects will be affected by the next command you give (cut, copy, delete, and so on).

Sentence: "After I *selected* everything on-screen, I pressed Del to delete it all. It's so easy to wreck someone else's work."

self-modifying

Pronunciation: *self-mod-if-fi-ing.*

Meaning: When a program makes changes to itself while running. Many virus programs are self-modifying (also called *mutating*) to prevent detection by anti-virus software. Many artificial intelligence programs are also self-modifying, to give the illusion of correcting itself or adapting to outside stimuli like a living organism.

Sentence: "I wrote a chess program that's *self-modifying.* Each time it loses a game, it rewrites its own algorithms to correct its behavior. It still can't play chess very well, and you know something else? It also can't program itself very well either.

semiconductor

Pronunciation: *sem-i-kon-duk-ter.*

Meaning: A material that is neither a good insulator nor a good conductor of electricity. Semiconductors are used to make transistors, diodes, integrated circuits, and all the other neat stuff that make up the parts of a computer. Silicon and germanium are two popular materials used for semiconductors. (See also *silicon* and *germanium.*)

Sentence: "Before he got a job designing *semiconductors* in the electronics industry, George used to work part-time as a conductor on Amtrak."

separator bar

Pronunciation: *sep-er-ray-ter bar.*

Meaning: On pull-down menus, the separator bar appears between groups of commands, making it easier to see each command without your eyes going buggy. (See also *pull-down menu.*)

Sentence: "The File menu of my word processor has a *separator bar* between commands like Open, New, Save, and Save As and commands like Print, Print Setup, and Repaginate."

sequential access

Pronunciation: *see-quen-chal ax-sess.*

Meaning: To scan information starting from the beginning, such as a tape backup or a cassette tape on your stereo. In comparison, random access lets you scan for information anywhere, such as on a CD-ROM disk.

Sequential access is usually much slower than random access, although if you want to kill some time so that you can goof off for a while, it's a fine method for searching on your computer. (See also *random access.*)

Sentence: "Every time I want to play my favorite song stored on a tape cassette, I have to use *sequential access* by fast forwarding or rewinding. If I had the song stored on a CD-ROM disk, I could use random access and start playing the song immediately."

serial

Pronunciation: *cereal.*

Meaning: To transmit data, one bit after another, through a single cable. This is akin to marching single file. Serial contrasts with *parallel*, which is where data is sent eight (or more) bits abreast — like marching in a parade. The advantage of serial is that the information can be sent over longer distances. (See also *parallel.*)

Sentence: "Talking is a *serial* activity because you have to speak the words one after another. Arguing is more parallel in nature because nobody bothers listening to what the other person has to say before he starts shouting right back. What a nuisance. I think I'll go eat some Super Chompo Sugar Flakes cereal instead."

serial communications

Pronunciation: *cereal kom-mew-ni-kay-shins.*

Meaning: To transfer data one bit at a time through a single cable, usually through a modem. (See also *modem.*)

Sentence: "Ted's our *serial communications* expert. He knows all about modems, transmission protocols such as ZModem and Kermit, and who manufactured cereals such as Quisp and Quake."

serial mouse

Pronunciation: *cereal mow-sa.*

Meaning: A mouse that plugs into the serial port of a computer. The other type of mouse, called a *bus* mouse, plugs into a special expansion card which is plugged into the computer. (See also *bus mouse.*)

Sentence: "Most people use a *serial mouse* because it's cheaper than buying a bus mouse. I use a serial mouse because it is easier to move from one computer to another."

serial port

Pronunciation: *cereal port.*

Meaning: A port (connector on the back of a PC) that allows data transfer, one bit at a time. Serial ports are sometimes called *RS-232* ports or "that hole in the back of the computer." They come in 9-pin and 25-pin sizes. (See also *RS-232C* and *parallel port.*)

Sentence: "I bought an external modem and a mouse. Unfortunately, my computer only had one *serial port,* so I had to plug another serial port into my computer so I could use my modem and mouse simultaneously. Too bad I still don't know how to use my computer."

serial printer

Pronunciation: *cereal print-her.*

Meaning: A printer that plugs into the serial port of a computer. Most printers plug into the parallel ports for faster data transfer and easier setup. Some printers only plug into a serial or parallel port, some printers can plug into either a serial or parallel port, and some printers don't work at all. (See also *serial port* and *parallel port.*)

Sentence: "I decided to buy my boss the slowest printer possible, so I got him a *serial printer.* Now he has to buy another serial port so he can use his external modem, mouse, and serial printer simultaneously."

serif

Pronunciation: *ser-if.*

Meaning: Tiny ornamental curves on letters to make them easier to read. Most typefaces have serifs. (See also *sans serif.*)

serif
sans serif

Sentence: "This book uses a typeface with *serifs* so the printing won't strain your eyes and give you headaches while reading it. Too bad the same can't be said for legal documents, tax forms, or textbooks."

server

Pronunciation: *ser-ver.*

Meaning: Usually the most expensive computer that nobody can use because it's busy controlling the entire network. You would think that the server would be the "slave" on the network, but this isn't so. The server is really the "master computer," the one all the other computers hook into and beg for the use of disk drives and printers. This is the same evil concept that dominated main frame computing during the last three decades. (See also *client/server network.*)

Sentence: "If you want to sabotage a network, don't bother wrecking each computer. Just unplug the *server* and then the whole network will be down like the Titanic."

session

Pronunciation: *se-shin.*

Meaning: (1) A fifty-minute hour spent with a psychiatrist to help repair the mental trauma of having to use a computer. (2) An individual activity being carried out by a multitasking computer. (See also *multitasking.*)

Sentence: "I spent over $23,000 last year for *sessions* with my psychiatrist. Now I think I'm entirely cured from my addiction to computers. Too bad I'm now stuck on Nintendo."

setting

Pronunciation: *set-ting.*

Meaning: The configuration of a program that defines its appearance on-screen (color, window size, memory usage, and so on).

Sentence: "By the time the sun got done *setting* in the west, I had finished modifying the program's settings so it wouldn't keep appearing as hot pink on purple everytime you loaded it up."

setup

Pronunciation: *set-up.*

Meaning: The modification of a program or computer so it works in a particular way each time you use it. The first time you set up a program or computer is when you install it. Later, you can adjust the settings. (See also *configure* and *install.*)

Sentence: "I had to choose the Print *Setup* command so my computer would know how to use my printer. Now the computer and printer work great, but I still don't have the slightest idea what I'm doing."

shareware

Pronunciation: *shar-wear.*

Meaning: Software that you can legally copy and give away but must pay for if you use it regularly. Many shareware programs often rival the features of commercial programs but cost far less. Once you pay for shareware, you will get a printed manual, telephone support, and notice of future upgrades. (See also *freeware* and *public domain.*)

Sentence: "*Shareware* programs let you try before you buy, which is like asking your local Ford dealer if you could drive around the latest Mustang for a few weeks before deciding if you want to buy it."

sheet feeder

Pronunciation: *sheet feed-er.*

Meaning: A tray that holds paper and feeds it one page or a sheet at a time to a printer. Sheet feeders let you use special stationery or letterhead that you may have lying around instead of using computer paper every time.

Sentence: "Every time my boss hands me a memo, I just flip it over, store it in my *sheet feeder,* and print on the other side, thereby saving valuable computer paper."

shell

Pronunciation: *shell* (rhymes with *bell, sell,* and *well*).

Meaning: (1) A program that makes another program easier to use. DOS shells are the most common shell programs and often provide menus for choosing common DOS commands. (2) The name given to any program that someone uses to control a computer. In DOS, the shell is really a program called COMMAND.COM. That program displays the DOS prompt, interprets your commands, and runs other programs. (3) The name given to the command that runs another program from a first program. For example, the Shell command in WordPerfect allows you to run a second program without having to first quit WordPerfect. When you quit the second program, you're back in WordPerfect.

Sentence: "Sue sells sea shells by the sea shore, and uses a DOS *shell* for making her IBM computer easier to use. Sue likes using pull-down menus instead of memorizing cryptic DOS commands."

Shift key

Pronunciation: *Shift kee.*

Meaning: The key labeled Shift (really?) that you have to hold down to produce uppercase letters LIKE THIS. The Shift key can also be used with function keys for commands like Shift-F4.

Sentence: "Hold down the *Shift key* while tapping the F4 key once and then let both of them go. That's what Shift-F4 means when you see it printed in the manual. Shift-Tab means hold down the Shift key and press the Tab key."

Shift-Arrow

Pronunciation: Shift-Air-row.

Meaning: To hold down the Shift key, tap one of the arrow keys (up, down, left, right), and then let both of them go. This command is often used for moving the cursor to highlight text in a word processor.

Sentence: "Press *Shift-left arrow*, and the cursor highlights all the text you just wrote. Now if you press Del, you'll just wipe out all your valuable work in an instant."

shift-click

Pronunciation: *shift-klik.*

Meaning: To hold down the Shift key while clicking on the mouse button at the same time. Shift-clicking is used to select two or more objects on-screen. (See also *click.*)

Sentence: "In your drawing program, you can select two objects by clicking on the first object and then *shift-clicking* on the second one. If you just clicked on the second object, the first object would no longer be selected. If you turn off your computer at this point, you won't have to worry about anything at all."

Show Clipboard

Pronunciation: *Show Klip-bored.*

Meaning: A command that lets you see the last item that was Cut or Copied from the screen. By choosing the Show Clipboard command first, you can see what will appear on-screen if you choose the Paste command next.

Sentence: "I typed my entire résume, highlighted it, and then Cut it so it disappeared on to the Clipboard. For fun, I chose the *Show Clipboard*

command to see it on the Clipboard. Then I typed one sentence, Cut it, and chose the Show Clipboard command again. Boy, was I surprised when I didn't see my entire résume there any more. Now I've just learned something new but lost my résume forever, so I'll never get a decent-paying job again."

shrink wrap

Pronunciation: *shrink rap.*

Meaning: To cover a box completely with clear plastic, giving it the illusion that it hasn't been touched by the grubby little hands of other people before reaching your computer desk intact and pristine. Most software is sold in shrink-wrapped boxes for that sanitized look, much like finding a 'Sanitized For Your Protection' paper loop covering the toilet seat at a motel.

Sentence: "Buy only *shrink-wrapped* software to lessen the chances of getting programs that someone else returned and infected with a virus. Then again, if someone went through all that trouble, they could probably spend a little time shrink-wrapping the package again, so you better be careful anyway."

sidelit

Pronunciation: *siyd-lit.*

Meaning: Additional illumination from the side of a liquid crystal display (LCD) to make it easier to read. (See also *backlit.*)

Sentence: "If it weren't for my *sidelit* LCD, I wouldn't be able to see my laptop computer screen as well. Then again, if I really had problems, I'd just make my secretary do all my grunt work instead."

SIG

Pronunciation: *Sig* (rhymes with *big wig*).

Meaning: Acronym for Special Interest Group, which is a collection of people who share the same interest in computers such as using a specific computer like an Amiga, a type of program like dBASE IV, or a field such as Artificial Intelligence or Desktop Publishing.

Sentence: "Cool people say that they belong to a *SIG.* Uncool people say they belong to a Special Interest Group, because everyone knows that only cool computer people use acronyms whenever possible."

sign on

Pronunciation: *sine on.*

Meaning: To call another computer, such as a local BBS, CompuServe, or Prodigy, and type your name and password so that you can start using the services. (See also *logon.*)

Sentence: "Before breaking into the Pentagon's computers, we put the 'Do not disturb' sign on the motel door and then plugged our portable computers into the phone jack so we could dial out and *sign on* without anybody watching us."

silicon

Pronunciation: *sil-i-kon.*

Meaning: An element — sand — that's used in making glass and the ceramic wafers out of which computer chips are punched. Do not pronounce this "silly con."

Sentence: "The hors d'oeuvres wouldn't be complete at any computer party without a tray of *silicon* wafers."

Silicon Valley

Pronunciation: *Sil-i-kon Val-lee.*

Meaning: The place in Northern California that is world famous for making semiconductors, microprocessors, and other computer electronic circuitry. They also have a few good pizza parlors and take-out Chinese restaurants, too.

Sentence: "We drove through *Silicon Valley* to look for a job in the computer industry. But with computers so prevalent, we wound up getting a job with a computer company in Fresno instead."

silicone

Pronunciation: *sil-i-kown.*

Meaning: The stuff that plastic surgeons use to mold people's noses, cheeks, and body parts into different shapes and forms. This is not the same as silicon.

Sentence: "I thought *silicone* was the same stuff they made Silly Putty from."

SIMM

Pronunciation: *Sim* (rhymes with *rim* and *brim*).

Meaning: Acronym for Single In-line Memory Module, which is a tiny circuit board that holds several memory chips. Several SIMMs plugged into a computer look like headless cockroaches stuck face first in the surface of a Roach Motel. (See also *SIP.*)

Sentence: "*SIMMs* make it easier to install large amounts of memory. Instead of plugging individual memory chips in your computer, you can just plug in a couple of SIMMs."

simulation

Pronunciation: *sim-yoo-lay-shin.*

Meaning: A program or device that mimics the operation of something else. A flight simulation program mimics flying an airplane (although how many airplane cockpits do you know that use a keyboard to control the plane?), while a stock market simulation mimics the actual rise and fall of stocks on Wall Street. (See also *emulation.*)

Sentence: "To give my kids an idea what driving a real car is like, my computer has a driving *simulation* they can play with."

single-density

Pronunciation: *sin-gull-den-si-tee.*

Meaning: The earliest form of storage on magnetic media that has been replaced with double-density and quad or high-density. A single-density 5.25-inch floppy disk might contain 180K of data, a double-density 5.25-inch floppy disk might contain 360K, and a high-density 5.25-inch floppy disk might hold 1.2MB. (See also *high-density* and *double-density.*)

Sentence: "Don't buy *single-density* floppy disks because they're obsolete. Then again, so will be everything else in another month or two."

single-sided disk

Pronunciation: *sin-gul-si-ded disk.*

Meaning: A floppy disk that stores data only on one side. Sometimes you can cut a notch in the side of these disks, flip them over, and store data on the other side, although disk manufacturers recommend against this (because if you follow their instructions, you have to buy twice as many floppy disks).

Sentence: "Give me all your *single-sided disks* and I'll punch holes in them so you can use the other side. Better yet, why don't we just toss these disks and buy high-density ones instead?"

single-user

Pronunciation: *sin-gull yoo-zer.*

Meaning: Equipment that only one person can try to use at any given time. A laptop computer is a single-user computer, because if two or more people tried to type on the keyboard simultaneously, it might look obscene. Some database programs are single-user, meaning only one person can use it at a time. Multiuser database programs let two or more people use the program. (See also *multiuser.*)

Sentence: "Lots of companies want to eliminate *single-user* computers and connect everything in a network. That way they can watch what everyone's doing and keep people from playing games on their computers at work. Too bad that destroys morale and reduces productivity in the long run. And then people wonder why the Japanese are more productive than Americans."

SIP

Pronunciation: *Sip* (as in "I want a small drink of what you have but will gulp it anyway").

Meaning: Acronym for Single In-line Processor, a type of memory expansion card similar to a SIMM. The difference between a SIP and a SIMM is that the SIP uses a row of tiny pins as a connector — like a cheap comb. SIPs aren't generally user-upgradable and are usually installed at the factory only. (See also *SIMM.*)

Sentence: "I need more *SIPs* because my PC gulps down memory."

site license

Pronunciation: *siyt liy-senz.*

Meaning: A software agreement that lets you legally use multiple copies of the same program on several computers at the same time. Site licenses are cheaper than buying multiple copies of the same program and legal in comparison to software piracy.

Sentence: "We needed fifty zillion copies of WordPerfect for our company's computers, so I saved money by buying a *site license.* Too bad nobody in our company knows how to use our computers in the first place."

slot

Pronunciation: *slaught.*

Meaning: A long, thin hole into which an expansion card is plugged. These are usually called *expansion* slots, though in advertising you may see that a PC comes with "8 slots," meaning you can plug in up to eight expansion cards. The term *slot* is actually the easy term. Nerds call all the slots *the bus* and refer to it by terms such as MCA, ISA, EISA, and NuBus. (See also *expansion card* and *expansion slot.*)

Sentence: "Plugging things into your PC's expansion *slot* makes upgrading your hardware Tinker Toy-simple. Only remember to turn your computer off before you do this or your PC's guts will look like toast."

small caps

Pronunciation: *small kaps.*

Meaning: A text attribute or style where lowercase letters are replaced by capital letters of a smaller size. For example, the following title is in small caps:

BOSCO SLUGWORTH LANCES A BOIL

The first letter of each word is capitalized. That's called *initial caps.* The subsequent letters are still uppercase, but in a smaller size than the other letters. That's *small caps.* If all the letters were capitalized, it would be called *all caps.*

Sentence: "These seven guys came into the computer store looking for *small caps,* so I told them to go to the milliner instead."

Smalltalk

Pronunciation: *Small-tawk.*

Meaning: One of the first object-oriented programming languages in the world. Originally developed at the Xerox Palo Alto Research Center, the Smalltalk interface has been responsible for the graphical user interface ideas of the Macintosh and Microsoft Windows. So now you know who to blame.

Sentence: "Only cool programmers use a pure object-oriented programming language like *Smalltalk* instead of C++. But I guess I shouldn't talk because none of my programs have ever worked the way they're supposed to."

smart terminal

Pronunciation: *smart ter-min-al.*

Meaning: A computer, connected to a network, that can function independent of the network. Smart terminals are usually just personal computers with their own hard disk, disk drive, and memory. In comparison, *dumb terminals* are usually nothing more than a monitor and a keyboard. (See also *dumb terminal.*)

Sentence: "*Smart terminals* scare most managers because they can't control them as easily. Who knows if that employee is working on a report or his résume? Managers who distrust smart terminals are called 'dumb managers,' and managers who trust smart terminals are called 'smart managers'."

smoke and mirrors

Pronunciation: *smoke and mir-ors.*

Meaning: Slang term describing verbal special effects to make a product sound more enticing and powerful than it really is. Smoke and mirrors techniques are commonly used in advertising and sales. A great smoke and mirrors story has to do with the ancestor of the Macintosh, the ill-fated Lisa computer. (In many ways, the Lisa was the "father," or is it "mother," of the Macintosh and Windows, but in a way it isn't because they stole the idea from elsewhere.) When the original Lisa was demonstrated for the computer industry, it wasn't a computer at all! Instead, under the table, the designers had rigged several Apple II computers, which actually controlled the Lisa. This is classic smoke and mirrors.

Sentence: "Don't listen to that ad or that company salesman. It's just *smoke and mirrors* when he says that his sales program can make you money without working. If that's true, how come he's working as a salesman?"

SNOBOL

Pronunciation: *Sno-ball.*

Meaning: Specialized language for processing character strings (text). Developed at Bell Laboratories in 1962, SNOBOL is rarely used today, except as an answer for computer trivia questions.

Sentence: "*SNOBOL,* ALGOL, and FORTH are all programming languages that seem to be fading away from popularity. If you want to confuse a little kid learning computer programming for the first time, make him learn SNOBOL so he'll have a hard time understanding languages like BASIC or Pascal."

snow

Pronunciation: *sno.*

Meaning: Small flickering dots that sometimes appear on certain monitors, caused when the screen image changes too fast for a lame monitor to handle. Usually found only on CGA monitors or really bad VGA monitors. (See also *VGA.*)

Sentence: "This computer drives me crazy because every time I scroll through a document, I see all this *snow* on-screen. I hate computers."

soft hyphen

Pronunciation: *sof-ta hi-fen.*

Meaning: A hyphen in a word processing document that appears only when a word hangs precariously close to the right margin, in which case the hyphen hyphenates the word. At times, the term may also apply to any hyphen character, which is used to split a word. This contrasts with hard hyphens that are not supposed to split a word when that word is too close to the right margin.

Sentence: "No, if you poke a *soft hyphen*, you won't get gunk all over your fingers."

software

Pronunciation: *sof-ta wear.*

Meaning: Computer programs. Software generally refers to any type of computer program, from an operating system such as DOS, to a utility to an application to a program stored on a ROM chip. This contrasts with *hardware*, which is the physical side of computing. It's the software that makes the hardware go. Without it, the hardware would be nothing but potential — like an uneducated kid but minus the hyperactivity. (See also *hardware*.)

Sentence: "Og know difference between *software* and hardware. Hardware hard. Software soft."

sort

Pronunciation: *sort.*

Meaning: To organize according to some pattern or rule. The typical sort is alphabetical, though you can also have numeric sorts. Sorts can also be ascending or descending. An ascending sort is from first to last, smallest to biggest, or A to Z. Descending goes the other way.

Sentence: "Kinkaid should be busy for a while. I just told him to *sort* our list of Japanese clients — in Japanese."

source

Pronunciation: *sores.*

Meaning: The original or the location of the original, normally used when copying files. The source file is the original file; the *source* directory or disk drive is the place from where the files are being copied. The *target* is the final destination, the place to which files are being copied or moved. (See also *target*.)

Sentence: "The first *source* for anything has to be your brain. Or it could be the devil, if you were possessed."

source code

Pronunciation: *sores kohd.*

Meaning: The original file or instructions from which a program is created. A programmer, call him Melvin, starts by writing a computer program using a text editor. The text editor creates a file that contains source code. That's swallowed and manipulated in several mystical manners until another file is created, the final program itself.

Sentence: "Melvin is such a deft programmer that his *source code* reads like poetry. Okay, you have to be pretty weird to appreciate it."

space character

Pronunciation: *spa-sa kear-ik-tor.*

Meaning: The character, or blank, produced by pressing the spacebar. With computers, the space is actually a character on-screen, just like A or $ or the ~ thing.

Sentence: "I keep having to tell Tom that 'alot' is really two words. I told him to insert a *space character* and so he drew a picture of Captain Kirk."

spacebar

Pronunciation: *spa-sa-bar.*

Meaning: The longest key on your keyboard, the one that produces the space character.

Sentence: "Is it called the *spacebar* or the spacebar key? Is it a bar or a key? And, no, there will be no tired and obvious outer space cocktail lounge jokes here."

spaghetti code

Pronunciation: *spa-geh-tee kohd.*

Meaning: A program written so sloppily that it has no flow or logic to it. It's said of such a program that reading it is like following a noodle around a plate of spaghetti. Such programs are typically written by those new to programming or by a programming committee.

Sentence: "Well, I guess if Sergio Leone wrote a program, it could be called *spaghetti code.*"

SPARC

Pronunciation: *Spark.*

Meaning: Acronym for Scalable Performance ARCitechture. A RISC processor developed by Sun Microsystems for their line of workstations. It must be cool; we've never seen one. (See also *RISC.*)

Sentence: "This Sun workstation is running kind of slowly. Maybe it needs another *SPARC* plug."

special characters

Pronunciation: *spesh-el kar-ek-ters.*

Meaning: Any oddball or unusual characters or those characters that perform special functions. For example, the trademark character (™) is considered a special character because it's not found on the keyboard. Most characters that aren't alphanumeric or a handful of symbols are special characters. Other special characters may look like normal characters but carry out special functions. For example, a wildcard character, such as the ?, may be a special character.

Sentence: "Will you look at that J *character*? What's so *special* about him?"

speed

Pronunciation: *speed.*

Meaning: A measure of how fast something is. With microprocessors, the speed is measured in MHz (megahertz). Disk drive speed is measured in access time by the millisecond. Generally speaking, the larger the number, the faster the thing operates (and the faster the money comes out of your wallet). (See also *MHz.*)

Sentence: "I wouldn't say this new printer is fast. Its *speed* is probably one notch above stop."

spell checker

Pronunciation: *spell che-ker.*

Meaning: A program, usually built-in to a word processor, that examines every word you've typed for correct spelling and offers possible corrections when it finds a word it doesn't recognize. This is only really necessary in English, where spelling still remains a mystery some 150 years after Webster made up the whole idea."

Sentence: "I couldn't live without my word processor and *spell checker.* Now I never have to learn to spell because my computer does it for me. That's why my reports have sentences like 'Overrr tharr, I see tuy dogs trying ta get yorre food.'"

spike

Pronunciation: *spi-ka.*

Meaning: A power surge that can potentially fry electronic equipment but most likely does nothing other than cause the screen to flicker momentarily. Look out your window. Find a tall tree. If a bolt of lightning hits that tree, it will send a power spike through all the circuits in the room you're sitting in, making your PC's guts go pop. Also, the name of Joan Rivers' dog. (See also *surge suppressor.*)

Sentence: "I bought a surge suppressor to protect against power *spikes,* but I still unplug the computer during an electrical storm."

Spock

Pronunciation: *Spahk.*

Meaning: The character played by Leonard Nimoy on the original *Star Trek* television show. Spock is admired by the computer-loving crowd because he, too, enjoyed using computers. Some great Spock-computer *Star Trek* moments:

"This computer here is the key. Destroy this one and the whole planet goes."

"Computer? Compute to the last digit the value of pi." (The computer starts screaming here.)

"Landru is a computer."

"The computer lied."

Spock is also the name of a real doctor, well-known for his expert advice for caring for babies and for blocking trains carrying nuclear waste.

Sentence: "Okay, Mr. *Spock.* It's your turn to wear a red shirt and beam down to the planet."

spool

Pronunciation: *spool* (rhymes with *school, pool,* and *cruel*).

Meaning: To store data temporarily before printing it. The main reason for spooling files is to free up your computer so you can use it without waiting for the printer to finish printing it out. This feature is less important with multitasking operating systems such as OS/2 or Windows. (See also *buffer* and *print buffer.*)

Sentence: "Be sure to *spool* your document to a print buffer or else you'll have to wait until the printer is done before you can use your computer again."

spooler

Pronunciation: *spoo-ler.*

Meaning: A chunk of memory that's either built-in to a printer, carved out from the computer's main memory, or stored in a separate box connected between a printer and a computer. Sometimes called a *Print Spooler* or a *Print Buffer.*

Sentence: "If it wasn't for my *spooler,* I would have to wait until my printer got done printing before I could use my computer again. Now with multitasking, I don't really need a spooler. Come to think of it, with multitasking, I don't need anyone."

spreadsheet

Pronunciation: *spred-sheet.*

Meaning: A program that organizes numbers, labels, and formulas in rows and columns for calculating results. Spreadsheets rapidly and accurately calculate results using mathematical formulas. Accountants love spreadsheets, as do scientists, mathematicians, and people with nothing better to do on a Saturday night. Many spreadsheets have built-in statistical, mathematical, or financial equations (called *functions*) so users can focus more on entering in their numbers and less on creating the necessary equations. Some of the more popular spreadsheets are Lotus 1-2-3, Excel, Quattro Pro, and the backs of envelopes and cocktail napkins.

Sentence: "I wanted a *spreadsheet* to calculate all my illicit money laundering. It works perfectly, so now I know exactly how much I'm cheating the government out of taxes each year."

Sprite

Pronunciation: *Sprite* (rhymes with *right, kite*, and *bite*).

Meaning: (1) A moving element in a graphic display, such as those found in video games. (2) A sugar-flavored, carbonated beverage with exaggerated claims of refreshment that two out of three hard-core programmers and computer users prefer over Coke, Pepsi, or Kool-Aid.

Sentence: "Whenever I get tired of watching *sprites* on my computer, I drink Sprite and hope that twenty years from now, it won't rot out my teeth, give me cancer, or poison me with artificial flavorings that will forever lodge in my fat cells."

SS/DD

Pronunciation: *Ess Ess/Dee Dee.*

Meaning: Acronym for Single-Sided/Double-Density. This type of disk is obsolete, although older computers still use these disks. An SS/DD 5 ¼-inch floppy disk can typically store 180K of data.

Sentence: "Whenever you buy floppy disks, check for the *SS/DD* label. If you see it, then buy something else because you probably don't want these disks unless you use a really old computer."

SS/SD

Pronunciation: *Ess Ess/Ess Dee.*

Meaning: Acronym for Single-Sided/Single-Density. These types of disks are obsolete although some older computers still use them. An SS/SD 5 ¼-inch floppy disk can typically store 90K of data.

Sentence: "I found this old box of *SS/SD* floppy disks in my closet. I could use them, but I'd rather cut them open and toss them around the house as frisbees instead."

stack

Pronunciation: *stahk.*

Meaning: A data structure that programmers use to store and remove data in a last-in, first-out (LIFO) order (especially used in assembly language). (See also *LIFO* and *POP*.)

Sentence: "Programmers like using *stacks* because it makes them feel like they actually know what they're talking about."

standard

Pronunciation: *stan-dard.*

Meaning: A stubborn, mythical belief held by scientists that they can define specific methods, appearances, or equipment that everyone else in the world will voluntarily follow.

Sentence: "The American National Standards Institute (ANSI) keeps trying to define the C language. The International Standards Organization (ISO) keeps trying to define the Pascal language. Too bad the most popular C and Pascal compilers rarely follow either *standard* perfectly."

Star Trek

Pronunciation: *Star Trek* (just like it looks).

Meaning: A science fiction TV show, with a rabid following, that tells the story of a spaceship sent from Earth to explore the galaxy, confront alien life forms that look surprisingly like actors wearing lots of makeup and speaking perfect English, and earn residuals from the sales of *Star Trek* T-shirts, action figures, and annual conventions.

Sentence: "How come only the extras in *Star Trek* get killed? If some of the main characters got shot, maimed, or murdered once in a while, I'm sure ratings would go up."

Star Trek: The Next Generation

Pronunciation: Oh, give me a break; you can say this one.

Meaning: The very popular first sequel to *Star Trek* (see preceding). *ST:TNG* has several beloved characters, including an android named Commander Data, a Klingon named Worf, and the very poised, sophisticated Captain Picard. Some two-year-olds know who these guys are before they even recognize Ernie or Bert (we're not even going to discuss Barney). *ST:TNG* has now been joined by the new series *Star Trek: Deep Space Nine* (the jury's still out on this one.)

Sentence:"If you don't watch *Star Trek: The Next Generation,* you may have trouble conversing with nerds, geeks, and gurus. So, hey, start watching it."

star-dot-star

Pronunciation: *star-dot-star* (just like it looks).

Meaning: The *.* wildcard in MS-DOS that tells the computer to look for all files no matter what the filename or file extensions may be. Some less computer-literate people call it "asterisk-period-asterisk," but the cool people always say "star-dot-star." (See also *wildcard.*)

Sentence: "Type **DEL *.*** and press Enter to erase all the files on your disk. Oh, you mean you didn't want to do that? Oh well, that's what you get for asking me for help when I'm busy in the first place."

start bit

Pronunciation: *start bit.*

Meaning: The tiny chunk of information that signals the beginning of data transfer.

Sentence: "Before my wife starts yelling at me for spending too much time at my computer, she starts wringing her hands. To me, that's a *start bit* signalling she's about to start screaming again."

start-up disk

Pronunciation: *start-up disk.*

Meaning: The floppy or hard disk that the computer uses when you turn it on for the first time. The start-up disk differs from other disks because the start-up disk has special commands and programs that tell the computer what to do to wake itself up.

Sentence: "My hard disk is my *start-up disk.* But when the hard disk starts acting flaky, I have a special floppy disk that I use for my start-up disk. If that floppy disk doesn't work, then I start to cry."

static

Pronunciation: *stah-tik.*

Meaning: Random electrical noise that garbles voice and modem communication through the phone lines.

Sentence: "Every time I try to dial into NASA's computers, *static* interferes and I have to hang up. Every time my mother-in-law calls, I make crackling noises with my mouth and pretend that static is preventing me from hearing what she has to say."

stop bit

Pronunciation: *stop bit* (just like it looks).

Meaning: The tiny chunk of information that signals the end of successful data transfer. Hanging up the phone in the middle of a call is NOT an example of a stop bit.

Sentence: "Some communications programs let you choose between one or two *stop bits.* Most of the time, one stop bit is fine, unless the other computer specifically requires two stop bits."

storage

Pronunciation: *stow-r-age.*

Meaning: A place to put valuable information in the hopes you'll be able to find it again. Common storage devices are tape drives, floppy disks, hard disks, and CD-ROM discs.

Sentence: "To protect our records, we back up all of our hard disks onto tape drives and then make duplicate copies to keep for *storage.* Then our accountant embezzled all our cash, and we had to declare bankruptcy anyway."

string

Pronunciation: *string* (rhymes with *sting, sing,* and *ring*).

Meaning: A group of letters. Humans call groups of letters *words*, but computers call them *strings.*

Sentence: "I consider my name to be a representation of ancient history, but when I type it into my database, the computer just thinks of it as a *string* of meaningless characters."

string variable

Pronunciation: *string var-ee-ah-bull.*

Meaning: A symbol that a program uses to represent a group of characters. Most databases use the string variable NAME to represent a person's name.

Sentence: "If you're writing a program to steal other people's passwords, you need to use a *string variable* to capture each password when someone types it in."

structured programming

Pronunciation: *struk-sured pro-gram-ming.*

Meaning: A method for writing programs in small subprograms or modules so they are easy to read and understand. A myth pursued by computer scientists with the same vigor that early Spanish explorers had when they searched the New World for the Fountain of Youth and the Seven Cities of Gold. Structured programming emphasizes that programs can be written using three types of statements: sequential, conditional, and loops. Sequential program statements occur one after another. Conditional statements are IF-THEN or CASE statements. Loop statements are WHILE-DO, DO-WHILE, FOR-DO, and REPEAT-UNTIL statements. If you have no idea what this last paragraph means, you probably don't need to know anything about structured programming, except for the fact that it rarely works and that's why programs today have so many bugs in them.

Sentence: "In *structured programming,* I'm supposed to break a large program into several subprograms where each subprogram performs a single, isolated task. Because I usually don't know all the problems that will occur when I start planning, I have no idea how to properly define my subprograms. Hence, the flaw with structured programming."

style

Pronunciation: *stiy-el.*

Meaning: Text formatting and character attributes all combined into one. Style refers to the way text looks. In some programs, you can format your text using a Style command. Other times, Style may refer to a collection of formatting and character attributes that can be slapped onto text all at once.

Sentence: "This new word processor comes with three *styles* automatically: Ugly, Uglier, and Too Crude to Print."

stylus

Pronunciation: *stiy-less.*

Meaning: A long pointy thing, like a pencil. The stylus is a type of input device like a mouse. You use the stylus to draw on an electronic pad embedded with sensors. What you draw shows up on-screen. These things are more expensive than your typical computer mouse but offer a higher degree of control. (See also *digitizer.*)

Sentence: "If Baron Lytton had known computers, he might have said, 'The *stylus* is mightier than the mouse,' but he'd run the risk of being locked up for that."

subdirectory

Pronunciation: *sub-dir-ek-toh-ree.*

Meaning: A directory within or "under" the current directory. All disks have directories, in which they store files. The directories can also store other directories, which are then called subdirectories. Technically, the term applies only to directories "beneath" another directory. Generally, any directory on disk — save for the main or root directory — is called a subdirectory. The Macintosh operating system also uses the subdirectory concept, but they call subdirectories "folders" instead. (See also *tree structure* for more confusion.)

Sentence: "I'm sorry, Private, if you want to find a *subdirectory*, you'll have to look on the Navy's computers."

submenu

Pronunciation: *sub-men-yoo.*

Meaning: A menu below another menu. For example, if you're presented with a menu of choices and selecting one of them displays another menu, you have a submenu. In a GUI, a submenu is often a secondary or tertiary menu that hangs on to the main menu like an ugly piece of gum.

Sentence: "Today's *submenu* offers several items: Ham, Pastrami, Turkey, Provolone, Swiss, Cheddar, and a variety o' fixins."

subroutine

Pronunciation: *sub-roo-teen.*

Meaning: A miniprogram within a larger program. For example, a program may have a subroutine that displays text on-screen. The main program would "call" that subroutine any time it wanted to display text on-screen.

Sentence: "My son just can't seem to finish his homework. I think that he's missing some *subroutine*."

subscript

Pronunciation: *sub-skr-ipt.*

Meaning: Text that appears smaller and below the surrounding text. Subscript is a text formatting attribute available in word processors and other programs that let you manipulate text. The number 2 in H_2O is a subscript. (See also *superscript.*)

Sentence: "Jacob was trying to explain to me that the printer was broken, but it turned out he accidentally turned on *subscript* mode and didn't know it. Ah, the joys of WordPerfect. . . ."

Super VGA

Pronunciation: *Soo-per Vee Gee Ay.*

Meaning: Faster than regular VGA. More powerful than EGA. Able to leap puny old CGAs in a single bound. Look, up on-screen, it's high resolution, it's colorful — yes! — it's SuperVGA. IBM introduced its best PC graphics standard in 1987, the VGA. Other manufacturers liked it but offered an improvement called SuperVGA also known as SVGA. If you're buying a graphics card for your PC, Super VGA is the way to go. (See also *VGA.*)

Sentence: "*Super VGA* gives Phil the graphics horsepower he needs to see his golf tricks GIF collection at full resolution."

supercomputer

Pronunciation: *soo-per-kom-pyoo-ter.*

Meaning: Faster than a regular computer, a supercomputer is a very large, powerful, and fast computer. Supercomputers are used for important things like drawing dinosaurs in *Jurassic Park.* Unlike a mainframe, the super computer has an interesting design that makes it very, very fast. That's about all you need to know because you can't have a supercomputer in your house; turning it on would dim all the lights in the neighborhood.

Sentence: "I hear the boys in the lab just love the new *supercomputer.* They bow to it each time they enter the room."

superscript

Pronunciation: *soo-per-scr-ipt.*

Meaning: Text that appears smaller and above the surrounding text. Superscript is a text formatting attribute available in word processors and similar programs that manipulate text. The number 10 in 2^{10} is superscripted. (See also *subscript* unless you've already come here from there.)

Sentence: "Simon Nathaniel the Fourth thinks it's really nifty if he prints his name with a *superscripted* four: Simon Nathaniel^{4}."

support

Pronunciation: *suh-port.*

Meaning: (1) What you pay extra for when you pay extra. (2) What you don't get when you pay extra. (3) What you're supposed to get with each computer you buy, whether you pay extra or not. (4) Training or someone available for help with your new PC or a place to get it repaired. Support is the most important factor in buying a computer, one many people often neglect as a trade-off for a low price. Support includes service after the sale, as well as phone help, classroom help, and other assistance. Software vendors offer support in the form of phone lines, toll free or not, over which you can ask questions. Sometimes this actually works.

Sentence: "The only *support* that comes out of waiting on hold is support for the long distance phone company."

surge

Pronunciation: *serge.*

Meaning: An increase in the power level coming through the wall socket. Surges are gradual and build to a point where they may do some damage to your PC's components. Usually this is prevented by a circuit breaker or — sometimes in an utterly unbelievable twist of altruism — the power supply may actually give up its life to save the rest of the PC's components. A surge is the opposite of a brownout, when the power drops to low levels and your PC may not even start at all. (See also *spike* and *surge suppressor.*)

Sentence: "I was expecting the power *surge* to make my computer run faster. However, the circuit breaker popped and, though I lost my data, the computer is once again saved from the perils of the electric company."

surge protector

Pronunciation: *serge pro-tek-tor.*

Meaning: A device that guards against power surges (I think it kind of eats them) so that your computer doesn't blow up.

Sentence: "Although a *surge protector* is a good thing to have for your PC, it won't protect your computer against other power line nasties, such as spikes, line noise, and people who trip over cords."

suspend

Pronunciation: *sus-pend.*

Meaning: To temporarily halt — not completely stop, more like freeze.

Sentence: "When I answer the phone, I must *suspend* my dot-matrix printer. Otherwise, I can't hear a darn thing."

SVGA

Pronunciation: *Ess Vee Gee Ay.*

Meaning: An acronym for Super VGA, a PC graphics adapter standard. (See also *Super VGA.*)

switch

Pronunciation: *swi-cha.*

Meaning: (1) A knob or lever that has two positions, usually ON and OFF. It can also be a graphical representation of a knob or button in a GUI. (2) A command option or parameter. For example, the /F switch on DOS's FORMAT command is used to tell FORMAT how big of a disk to format. (3) To move from one program to another in a multitasking environment. In Windows and OS/2, you accomplish this by pressing the Ctrl-Esc key combination.

Sentence: "In IBM lingo, the Big Red *Switch* used to mean the on-off switch on the computer. Back in the early PC days, the switch was really big and red. Today, on-off switches are no longer red, nor are they necessarily big."

synchronous

Pronunciation: *sing-kro-nuss.*

Meaning: Happening at the same time, in synch. Usually this term applies to synchronous communications. In that mode, two computers communicate at a specific pace with each other, sending bits back and forth "on the beat." Microcomputer modems are asynchronous devices and do not send information at a specific pace. (See also *asynchronous.*)

Sentence: "No, Bob, *synchronous* communications doesn't mean we have to sing to each other."

syntax

Pronunciation: *sin-taks.*

Meaning: (1) A tax on beer, alcohol, or cigarettes. (2) The rules regarding the way a language is put together. This applies to programming languages as well as human languages.

Sentence: "Computers are persnickety. Disobeying their laws of *syntax* is akin to telling your neighbor, 'Day nice outside hot not it is.'"

syntax error

Pronunciation: *sin-taks air-or.*

Meaning: You have violated the rules of syntax. This usually happens when writing a computer program. If you flip-flop words or misspell something, the program compiler spits out a syntax error and then you're left scratching your head to figure out what you did wrong.

Sentence: "Computers say `Syntax Error` because the people who programmed them are too lazy to make the message any more precise."

sysop

Pronunciation: *siss-op* (not *sy-sop*).

Meaning: Abbreviation for System Operator, the head honcho in charge of the system. This term revolves primarily around computer bulletin boards (BBSs). The person who owns the computer and the BBS and in whose house it sits is the sysop. This is an exalted position among the modeming crowd. Everyone wants to be a sysop or be in the sysop's favor. (See also *BBS.*)

Sentence: "I begged the *sysop* for advanced access to his system; finally he gave me level six access. But the funny thing is, there's no one on level six."

system

Pronunciation: *siss-tim.*

Meaning: (1) A way of doing things. (2) The program that controls the entire computer. (3) The whole computer. (4) The network. (5) The Powers That Be. (6) What you can't fight.

Sentence: "Something has to be in charge, and that's the *system.* It rules the computer. In real life, there's a system too, but it doesn't rule anything. Instead, it's The Conspiracy who's in charge. And they watch everyone through cable TV and listen to our phone calls. And there's a helicopter over my head right now, and they're watching me type this. And that gnat is a spy for a terrorist group."

System 7

Pronunciation: *Sys-tem Seh-vin.*

Meaning: The operating system used on most Macintosh computers. System 7 is not the same thing as DOS on a PC. Most of the Macintosh's operating system is encoded in its ROM. System 7 provides the Finder interface, plus other extensions to the Mac's internal operating system.

Sentence: "I upgraded to *System 7* because I thought it would bring sanity to my Mac. Alas, the computer may be sane, but it's still as slow as ever."

system clock

Pronunciation: *sis-tim klaughck.*

Meaning: An internal time clock maintained by the operating system. This clock is primarily used to record the time when files were saved to disk.

Sentence: "I once reset my PC's *system clock* wrong on purpose to prove to the boss that I was getting work done way ahead of the deadline."

system disk

Pronunciation: *sis-tim dis-ka.*

Meaning: A disk that contains the system, or all the programs required to start your computer. For most of us, the system disk is our hard drive, which starts the computer each time we turn it on. You can also start your computer from a floppy drive, which some people do just to kill time.

Sentence: "You can't start your PC without a *system disk.* Because of this, we recommend that everyone create an 'Emergency Boot Floppy' with which you can start your PC in times of woe."

System Folder

Pronunciation: *Sis-tem Fold-her.*

Meaning: A special subdirectory on a Macintosh computer that contains all the system files. This is roughly equivalent to the DOS subdirectory on a PC. Into the System Folder you put (or have already installed) all the files necessary to make Mr. Mac boot up properly, special files and programs such as fonts, desk accessories, control panel thingys, and other stuff I can't think of.

Sentence: "The term *System Folder* makes it sound so neat and tidy. But the truth is that the System Folder is perhaps the junkiest folder on my disk."

system font

Pronunciation: *sis-tem fahnt.*

Meaning: A font built into the operating system or GUI. System fonts are those fonts that *must* be there. Text on menus and in dialog boxes is usually composed using the system font. Yes, there can be more than one system font.

Sentence: "Truly, the *system font* is the most boring font you have. I recommend buying other, more exciting fonts and doing your documents with those instead."

system unit

Pronunciation: *sys-tim yoo-nut.*

Meaning: The main computer box, also called the *console*. The system unit typically houses the computer's microprocessor, memory, and disk drives and usually contains expansion slots. All other items outside the system unit are peripherals.

Sentence: "Earl is such a card. He cleverly disguised his *system unit* in an old Philco TV box."

tab

Pronunciation: *tab.*

Meaning: A chunk of blank spaces created by pressing the Tab key. This chunk of spaces is treated as a unit so that if you wanted to delete the tab space, it would delete the whole thing, not one blank character at a time. In most database and spreadsheet programs, you move from one field or cell to another by pressing the Tab key. You can move backwards through the fields or cells by pressing the Shift key with the Tab key. This is known as a "back tab."

Sentence: "This is absolutely amazing. I pressed the *Tab* key and this diet beverage rolled out of my disk drive slot."

Tab key

Pronunciation: *Tab kee.*

Meaning: The key on the keyboard that produces the tab "character." In most programs, when you write something, pressing the Tab key moves you forward one tab stop, whether that's a chunk of spaces in word processing, a field in a database, or a cell in a spreadsheet.

Sentence: "On most PCs, the *Tab key* has two arrows pointing in opposite directions printed on it that leads me to believe the key doesn't know which direction is which."

table

Pronunciation: *tay-bull.*

Meaning: A way of organizing data or text into rows and columns, especially in a database context. You don't need a tablecloth for this kind of table, nor do you need good table manners. A data table is

simply a way to store information or, in word processors, to present text in a neat and tidy manner.

Sentence: "Tax *tables* list income on the left side and tax categories along the top. In the middle you can find out what outrageous amount the government would like you to pay."

tape

Pronunciation: *tay-pa.*

Meaning: A magnetic data storage medium (long, thin brown stuff), essentially the same material as audio and video cassettes. The advantages of this medium are its low cost and high density (ability to store lots of information). The disadvantage is that it offers only linear or sequential access, which means you have to rewind or fast forward through the whole tape in order to find what you're looking for. In contrast, disk drives offer random access so that you can get to any given point within a fraction of a second, no rewinding or fast forwarding involved. You generally only use tapes to store backup copies of data. (See also *sequential access.*)

Sentence: "Okay. Who's the joker who put the Scotch tape into the *tape* backup unit?"

tape drive

Pronunciation: *tay-pa dri-va.*

Meaning: A machine into which you insert a tape cassette that records data and stuff. The machine is like a tape recorder and player, reading and writing information to the tape. This is how sophisticated PC users back up their data. They buy these backup tape cartridges, slam them into the tape drive, and then run special tape backup software. There's no swapping involved (providing the tapes can hold enough data), and the backup takes only a few minutes. Tape drives are about as expensive as new hard drives. There are many formats available: ¼-inch cartridge, 8-mm VCR cartridge, 4-mm audio, and nine-track.

Sentence: "I'm sorry about the demotion, Jenson, but what you thought was a toaster oven was really our new $2,000 DAT *tape backup system.*"

task

Pronunciation: *task.*

Meaning: A task is something you do with a computer. For example, if you're word processing, the computer's task is word processing. This would be an utterly redundant thing if it weren't for multitasking, which is the ability of a computer to do several things — several tasks — at the same time.

Sentence: "Most of the time, my computer's main *task* is to ignore me."

task switching

Pronunciation: *tas-ka swi-ching.*

Meaning: When computers can multitask (run more than one program at a time), the art of switching between the running programs is called task switching. In Windows, you can do this by pressing Ctrl-Esc, Alt-Esc, Alt-Tab, or by clicking on a specific window that represents a program. When you move from one open application (task) to another, you are task switching.

Sentence: "The boss told me I was *task switching* too often between Word and Solitaire."

TCP/IP

Pronunciation: *Tee Cee Pee Ih Pee.*

Meaning: Take Caffeine Periodically/Intravenously, Preferably. Har, har. Actually, it stands for Transfer Control Protocol/Internet Protocol, and who knows or cares what it means? It's a protocol (a set of standards) that allows data connections between internet terminals or emulators. Only severe networking dweebs will use — and understand — what it's all about.

Sentence: "I went for a job interview that asked for *TCP/IP* knowledge. When I asked what it meant, they said, 'We were hoping you knew!'"

TeachText

Pronunciation: *Teech-Tekst.*

Meaning: A simple text-editing program that the Mac uses to read and display README files.

Sentence: "I don't think the *TeachText* program is teaching me anything."

tear-off menus

Pronunciation: *taer-off men-yoos.*

Meaning: Menus that you can actually tear off the menu bar (symbolically, of course) and place at any convenient location on the screen. For example, you might press Ctrl while clicking on the File menu to tear

it off. You can then drag it to any location on the screen. Tear-off menus are not widely used.

Sentence: "If you use a *tear-off menu,* do you use a BandAid to stick it back on again?"

techno weenie

Pronunciation: *tek-noh weenee.*

Meaning: Person who aspires to be a full-fledged geek, nerd, or dweeb, but either isn't smart enough about computers, isn't overly obsessed about computers, or has too many social skills. The guru at the office is a geek. Bill, your "computer literate" neighbor, is a techno weenie.

Sentence: "In college, you can tell who the *techno weenies* are because they take classes like Physics for Poets . . . and fail."

technology

Pronunciation: *tek-nal-uh-jee.*

Meaning: A stone used to shape another stone (as in the Stone Age) could be considered technology. You could say, in the broad sense, that technology means the use of tools. Power tools. Big anti-torque drills. Large dirt-moving vehicles. Ah, technology. More often, the word is used to refer to "high" technology, which is characterized by being abstract and not accessible to the naked eye. If you opened the hood of a vintage American car, you could tell exactly what was going on by seeing how the parts fit together and how they move. This is not-so-high tech. When you're talking about electronics, though, the relationships are not apparent. There could be millions of transistors on one silicon chip, and you would have no idea what the relationship of each was to its neighbors, nor where to fit the crescent wrench.

Sentence: "*Technology* actually comes from the ancient Greek term that roughly translates as 'If your VCR is blinking 12:00 all the time, you probably won't get any of this stuff.'"

telecommunications

Pronunciation: *tel-e-kom-yoo-ni-kae-shuns.*

Meaning: The field of technology dealing with communicating at a distance. It includes, but is not necessarily limited to, telephony, telegraphy, consumer radio, broadcast television, cable television, satellite television, radar, ham radio, CB radio, two tin cans connected by a string, and data transfer.

Sentence: "*Telecommunications* allows you to get confused at greater and greater distances."

telephony

Pronunciation: *tel-e-fohn-ee.*

Meaning: The art and science of making telephones happen. (Could just as well have been called "telephonology," but there was an editor on the loose that day, and the word got cut short.) Essentially what happens in the telephone process is that the voice — and all embarrassing or annoying background noises — get converted into electrical signals that travel through the wires and then get reconverted to sound at the other end. All this, even though Alexander Graham Bell used only two ordinary cups and a length of wire to make the World's First Telephone happen.

Sentence: "Using our new voice discriminator technology, it's easier to *telephony* call from a real one."

teletype

Pronunciation: *tel-e-tihp.*

Meaning: The old clunky typewriter-like things that typed "by magic" thanks to remote wires that controlled the keyboard. In the early days of computing, teletype machines were used to communicate with the behemoth computers of the time. You would type, Klunka-wunka, and then the computer would type back at you, Klunka-wunka-faster. All this would be transcribed on a long sheet of paper that fed into and out of the teletype machine. In these exciting, carefree computer days, teletype is used to describe the dumbest and least sophisticated way to connect one computer to another. The teletype is nothing more than a keyboard and monitor (also called a Dumb Terminal) that allows you to send and receive information from another computer. It's abbreviated TTY because most computer nerds can't remember if teletype has one or two L's in it.

Sentence: "In the early '80s, I used to communicate with my friends on home computers using then-speedy 2400 bps modems. At the same time, the 'hot line' connecting the White House with the Kremlin was run on a sluggish old *teletype* machine running at only 300 bps. That meant in the time Ronald Reagan could send 'Ivan, kiss your *@# goodbye,' I could have downloaded Tetris."

template

Pronunciation: *tem-plate.*

Meaning: A "master" document for a word processor, spreadsheet, or other application that is used as the starting point or rough draft for other documents. Generally, the template contains all the formatting, so all you have to do is fill in the blanks. Some software packages come with numerous templates so that you really don't even need to learn to use the software. Word for Windows, for instance, comes with 17 different templates that let you easily generate form letters, reports, memos, proposals, and fax cover sheets. You can create your own templates by performing the formatting and composing the text that will appear in every document of that type. Then, each time you need, say, an invoice, you open up the template file, fill in the blanks, and print out the document. Then you can either save the additions to the file (as a new file, now, so you don't mess up the template) or not.

Sentence: "I'm going to use a *template* to write a letter to Santa Claus this year."

tera-

Pronunciation: *ter-a.*

Meaning: A prefix meaning trillion (the same prefix from which we get the words *terrible* and *deficit*, by the way). Usually seen in computer use when talking about terabytes, which are pretty close to a trillion bytes (which is the same as 1,000 gigabytes, or a million megabytes). The actual measurement of a terabyte is 1,099,511,627,776 bytes.

Sentence: " If you had one dollar for each byte in a *tera*byte, it would take Bill Gates 134 years to catch up with you if he made 8 billion dollars a year (not including interest or subtracting taxes)."

terminal

Pronunciation: *term-un-nel.*

Meaning: A monitor hooked up to a mainframe computer, from the root of the Latin word for *death*. Like people, terminals can either be smart or dumb, and the only way to find out how smart or dumb they are is to check how they relate to the computer. If a terminal has a mind of its own, then it's a smart terminal. This means it has some processors, maybe even a CPU, and maybe even a disk drive so it can store its own data. With such capabilities, the terminal doesn't need to rely on the mainframe for all its operations. If all it's got is a monitor and keyboard (and/or similar peripherals), then it's pretty dumb.

Sentence: "People can get terminally ill from sitting at *terminals* their whole lives."

terminal emulation

Pronunciation: *term-in-el em-yoo-lae-shun.*

Meaning: The ability of an average, run-of-the-mill desktop computer to cleverly disguise itself as a certain type of terminal hooked up to a mainframe computer. This can only be done with the right software, called terminal emulation software. You only need to worry about this when you actually *want* to be hooked up to a mainframe computer — a rare circumstance for most of us mortals.

Sentence: "They've finally perfected Macintosh *terminal emulation* for the PC. Everything works really slow, and the system crashes just before you save your file to disk. (You think we're kidding.)"

terminate-and-stay-resident program

Pronunciation: *ter-min-aet-and-stae-rez-i-dent proh-gram.*

Meaning: A special type of program that always stays in RAM and can be easily activated by a keystroke or "hot key." Also known as a TSR or memory resident program. These programs became popular when Borland's SideKick was introduced in the mid-80s. SideKick gave you instant access to a slew of interesting little programs, all by pressing the Ctrl-Alt keys at the same time. SideKick would "pop-up" right on top of whatever other program you were running. At the time, this proved immensely handy. Other programmers learned SideKick's secret, and soon dozens of TSRs and pop-up programs appeared. The problem was that Borland cheated to get the pop-up effect, and because of this, none of the TSRs would cooperate with each other. A TSR-laden PC would often crash and the programs would conflict. Today, the pop-up type of TSR program isn't popular any more, thanks to multitasking programs such as Windows and advanced operating systems such as OS/2. TSRs still exist, primarily as programs that enhance DOS's features but without conflicting with other programs. Popular TSRs include the mouse driver, CD-ROM driver, the DOSKEY keyboard enhancer, and certain file undeleting utilities. (See also *memory resident programs.*)

Sentence: "Please, Mr. Cooper, don't get all upset just because the old folks home has adopted *terminate-and-stay-resident* software."

text

Pronunciation: *tek-sta.*

Meaning: Letters, numbers, and other characters or symbols found on your keyboard. Just plain writing, no formatting or other fancy stuff. (See also *ASCII.*)

Sentence: "*Text* is boring."

text box

Pronunciation: *tek-sta bahk-sa.*

Meaning: A box on the screen, outlining an area in which you can type text. This may also be called an input box. Oh, and you can edit text in the text box. What else? Nothing that we can think of right now. It's late, and *Star Trek* is on in three minutes.

Sentence: "Here's a good one: When you're searching for text, type 'my brain' into the *text box.* Then click the OK button. The computer won't find the text, and it will display a message that says 'Error: Can't find my brain.' Ha, ha."

text editor

Pronunciation: *tek-sta ed-i-ter.*

Meaning: A program, actually a crude form of a word processor, that lets you modify ("edit") text files. Text editors are used by programmers to edit program source code files. This is handy because text editors don't use formatting or graphics or anything fancy. All programmers want is something to easily type in their programming instructions without being bothered by the formatting. We mere mortal users can take advantage of text editors as well, even using them as a word processor if we like. They come in handy for working with small files. Indeed, this book was initially created using a text editor so that Dan, Wally, and Chris had a common file format (plain text or ASCII files) in which to work. (Eventually we all moved up to Microsoft Word for Windows because IDG Books told us we were working too fast.) (See also *editor.*)

Sentence: "My award for the worst *text editor* ever goes to DOS's old crummy EDLIN."

text file

Pronunciation: *tek-sta fi-el.*

Meaning: A file that contains only text or ASCII characters. Many word processing, database, and spreadsheet programs give you the option of saving your stuff as "text only," or a text file. This means that you lose all the formatting and special characters not associated with text files, but it also means the information can be easily digested by just about any other program on any other computer. (See also *ASCII*.)

Sentence: "*Text files* are the most common type of file format."

thermal wax printer

Pronunciation: *ther-mel waks print-er.*

Meaning: An old-fashioned type of printing technology that uses a special kind of paper onto which the letters are transferred using heat. For example, Sheryl is lying out at the beach. She's rubbed her bod with this new special wax that gets you tanned quickly. Between Sheryl's back and the sun, Karl, her boyfriend, holds up this piece of cardboard that has his name punched out and, lo, over the course of time, the sun tans this image — KARL — onto Sheryl's back. That's how thermal printing works, but the printer supplies the heat, and the image is burned onto the paper.

Sentence: "My *thermal wax printer* has a reputation for having a smell as bad as a dot-matrix printer's noise."

thesaurus

Pronunciation: *the-saw-rus.*

Meaning: Seriously, this is a collection of words and other words with the same meaning. In computers, it refers to the capability of a word processing program to come up with synonyms to match a word you've chosen. You can highlight a word, ask the thesaurus for some synonyms, and the software generates a list of alternatives or suggestions. There is a Murphy's Law of Thesauruses: the more certain you are that a synonym with exactly the right flavor exists, the more certain your thesaurus is not to even list the word you're referencing, let alone its synonyms.

Sentence: "What would the *thesaurus* offer if you looked up synonyms for 'molecular beam epitaxy'?"

three-dimensional spreadsheet

Pronunciation: *three-dim-en-shun-el spred-sheet.*

Meaning: In spreadsheet technology, the practice of creating a group of spreadsheets and organizing them like pages of a book. Thus, they have depth, besides the usual rows and columns. The depth is the third dimension of the spreadsheet.

Sentence: "I started to learn how to work on a *three-dimensional spreadsheet,* but I got lost because I only had a two-dimensional brain."

tick

Pronunciation: *tik.*

Meaning: (1) Another name for the apostrophe character. (2) In a chart-drawing utility such as found in Excel, a tick mark is a notch on the axis of a chart that denotes an increment. For example, if the Y axis represents Dollars, every tick mark might represent 100 dollars. (3) A beat in your computer's internal clock-ticking, time-keeping thingamabob. PC computers generate 18.5 ticks per second. So if you hear some nerd say, "How many clock ticks was that interrupt?" you know that a clock tick is just about 1⁄18th of a second and can nod your head knowingly.

Sentence: "There was this German POW camp in World War II. And one summer day, the Kommandant assembled all the prisoners out under the hot sun. He said, 'Today we will do special exercises. I want you to tilt your heads left to right, left to right. When you tilt your head to the left, you will say *tick!* When you tilt your head to the right, you will say toc! Everyone!' So all the prisoners started tilting their heads, tick-toc, tick-toc, out under the hot sun — sweat just pouring from their faces. Everyone did this but one prisoner. He just tilted his head to the left over and over, going 'tick, tick, tick.' The Kommandant walked up to the man, looked him over, and said, 'We have ways to make you toc.'"

TIFF

Pronunciation: *Tif.*

Meaning: Acronym for Tagged Image File Format. A bit-mapped graphics file format used frequently for images read in using a scanner. TIFF files are high-resolution dot images.

Sentence: "No, we don't support that graphics standard here. We support PCX, GIF, *TIFF,* and anything painted by Lichtenstein or Klee."

tiling

Pronunciation: *tih-ling.*

Meaning: A technique for arranging various windows in a graphical user interface, such that they're all nicely sized and laid out like a mosaic, without overlapping each other. The key here is "without overlapping." Another arrangement possibility is "cascading." (See also *cascade.*)

Sentence: "*Tiling* is a good choice when it doesn't matter if the images in each window are chopped off and difficult to read."

time sharing

Pronunciation: *tihm shaer-ing.*

Meaning: A strategic use of resources (microprocessor, printer, disk drives) with mainframe or networked computers. The time that is being shared is the computer's processing time. Typically, it's being shared among several users and also may be shared among several programs as well. In a time-sharing situation, the computer is programmed to know how to use its processing resources to attend to a hierarchy of priorities.

Sentence: "Because our computer knows how to manage *time sharing* so well, I think I should have my own time-sharing program so my time will get divided properly among my kids, my spouse, and my job."

time slice

Pronunciation: *tihm slihs.*

Meaning: Amount of processor time allocated to an application, usually measured in milliseconds. For example, if you're running several programs at once in Windows, each program gets a "slice" of the computer's time. The size of the slice can be adjusted, allowing some important programs to use up more time than other not-so-important ones. (See also *multitasking.*)

Sentence: "Roy found this old film from the '40s. It shows Albert Einstein creating *time slices* with a Ginsu knife."

title bar

Pronunciation: *tiht-el bar.*

Meaning: In a GUI like Windows or the Mac system, this is the, well, title, that is prominently displayed in a long bar that stretches across the whole window. It is an especially effective invention because you always know where you are and don't need to call customer service to get you unlost. It typically includes the name of both the application you're using and the document you're working in. Even when you haven't named the new file yet, the program will provisionally call the document something like "Untitled" or "Document," until you come up with your own name for it.

Sentence: "I was hopelessly lost until I looked up at the *title bar,* which said that I was working in Microsoft Word on the T.DOC document."

toaster

Pronunciation: *toh-ster.*

Meaning: A computer device that's so homegrown, so user-friendly, and so intuitive, it's almost like the toaster you use to toast bread. The original Macintosh design was fondly called the "toaster" by its fans. A device called the Video Toaster is used in the Amiga computer to allow you to create studio-quality videos in your own home.

Sentence: "The original Macintosh was fondly called 'the *toaster*' at the height of its popularity. Now it's often called 'the footstool.'"

toggle

Pronunciation: *tog-el.*

Meaning: A type of switch that alternates between two modes, on or off, typically. An example would be the button on your TV that both turns it on and off. When the TV is off, the button turns it on, and vice-versa. In a computer program, a toggle may be a graphical button or some other option that can be either on or off. Selecting the button once turns it on, again turns it off.

Sentence: "I keep *toggling* between slow and slower mode on my PC. I don't think I paid enough money for this thing."

token ring network

Pronunciation: *toh-ken ring net-werk.*

Meaning: A networking format in which PCs are connected in some way. They use this token thing, passed between the computers on the network hose, to decide who's on first. That's the most I can make out of this definition. This is heady, IBM stuff. Most people use Ethernet networks because they are easier to understand. I always think of bus tokens when I see token ring network in print.

Sentence: "Our *token ring network* is crummy."

toner

Pronunciation: *toh-ner.*

Meaning: The black, icky stuff laser printers print with. Technically, toner consists of highly carcinogenic, electronically charged ink particles, just like a photocopier. It's used to form the image on paper.

Actually, the laser printer "welds" the toner to the paper using heat and tiny laser beams manned by elves.

Sentence: "Changing the *toner* can be the chore from hell."

toner cartridge

Pronunciation: *toh-ner kar-trij.*

Meaning: A cartridge, or container, for a laser printer (or other type of machine, like a copier or fax machine) that holds the toner. This technology makes an unbearable job simply horrible. In older machines, you would have to fill the toner container with powdered toner, which had the advantage of allowing you to approximate the effects of six years' worth of cigarette smoking in a mere 10 minutes. Today, toners equate themselves to just about a pack of cigarettes.

Sentence: "You can save money and help save the planet by recycling your *toner cartridges.*"

toolbox

Pronunciation: *tool-bahks.*

Meaning: For software developers, a set of programs that can be used as building blocks for creating applications, so they can avoid the need for re-inventing the wheel every time they write a program. For software users, a collection of tools that serve a common purpose. (See *tools.*)

Sentence: "Using a *toolbox,* anyone can create a cool-looking program with only several weeks of intensive training."

tools

Pronunciation: *toolz.*

Meaning: A set of electronic "tools" that you can use within a given software application which have effects like the real-life tools they're named after. Bear with me on this one. As an example, in a paint program you might have "brushes" of different diameters, a roller, and a spray can. These are tools you can use in the program to get a specific job done.

Sentence: "I'm having such a good time playing with all these *tools* that I don't know when I'll get around to actually painting a picture."

top-down programming

Pronunciation: *tahp-down proh-gram-ing.*

Meaning: Starting a program, and each of its modules, with a statement (in English) about what it's supposed to do and how it's supposed to do it — kind of like a mission statement.

Sentence: "*Top-down programming* doesn't mean you build the program's roof and then the foundation later. It's more along the lines of you write the overall feeling for the program first and then fill in the holes later."

topology

Pronunciation: *tahp-ah-le-jee.*

Meaning: Topology refers to the study of the actor, Topol. In computers, it refers to the configuration of a local area network — how the network is physically laid out. The basic types are centralized and decentralized; the basic formats are the star topology (centralized) and the bus and ring topologies (decentralized). Understand this and you, too, can make massive sums working as a network coordinator.

Sentence: "*Topology* refers to the way your network is laid out."

touch pad

Pronunciation: *tuhch pad.*

Meaning: An input device for which all you need to do is touch a spot and it will register as a signal to the computer. The "spots" are actually cleverly disguised keys or buttons, and the whole front of the touch pad display is a layer of soft plastic.

Sentence: "I was walking down the input aisle in the computer store and came upon the *touch pad* section. They all whispered at me, 'Touch me!' 'No, touch me!' 'Touch me, here!'"

TPI

Pronunciation: *Tee Pee Eye.*

Meaning: Abbreviation for Tracks Per Inch. It measures the amount of information that can be stored on a disk. The more tracks per inch on the disk, the higher the disk's "density" and the more data it can store. It's also a good way to tell some high-density disks from low-density. The lower density disks use 40 or 80 TPI. High-density disks use 135 TPI.

Sentence: "I've been using computers for over 12 years now, and no one I know uses the term *TPI* when she talks about a floppy disk."

track

Pronunciation: *trak.*

Meaning: A "ring" of information on a disk. Most disks record information on disks by storing that information on several concentric rings or "tracks" pre-recorded on the disk's surface. This is complex, disk-formatting stuff. The track contains sectors which each contain 512 bytes of information — the stuff you save on the disk. Knowing about tracks and sectors isn't important in using a disk. The information may only come up when you use special disk utilities (disk repair and diagnosis programs) or when formatting the disk. The term cylinder may also be used to refer to a track of information on a disk.

Sentence: "This disk is no good. I guess my AMTRAK file keeps jumping the *tracks.*"

trackball

Pronunciation: *trak-bahl.*

Meaning: An input device that operates very similarly to a mouse. Where a mouse has a ball you roll on your table top, in the case of the track ball, the ball part is on top and you rotate it using your fingers. Trackballs are very popular with artists, who find the large ball easier to manipulate than the clumsy soap-on-a-rope-like mouse. They're also common on notebook computers because then you don't have to have this device hanging outside the case, nor do you have to roll it around on a flat surface, such as your thigh.

Sentence: "Not only is this *trackball* easier to use than a mouse, it doesn't have a tendency to roll itself off the desk as much."

tractor feed

Pronunciation: *trak-ter feed.*

Meaning: A mechanism for feeding paper through dot-matrix printers. This kind of paper is what is commonly known as "computer paper," the stuff with the holes on either side. This would be a good time to tell you that there is actually a name — chosen in a contest — for the edges of such paper, which form the row of holes that the mechanism grabs to push the paper through. It's called "snaf."

Sentence: "I always have trouble lining up the little holes so that the paper will go through the *tractor feed* without getting overly perfed."

tractor food

Pronunciation: *trak-ter food.*

Meaning: Your most valued documents, caught in the jaws of a tractor feed mechanism.

Sentence: "I watched as my precious annual report became *tractor food* in a matter of seconds."

transparent

Pronunciation: *tranz-par-ent.*

Meaning: A computer function that's pretty close to invisible in its action. Anything that happens without your being directly involved or requiring your input or attention is transparent. For instance, a fax being sent while you continue to work on another document would be a transparent operation.

Sentence: "My communications software sends documents to other users *transparently.* They don't even see the document on the other end."

trash

Pronunciation: *trash.*

Meaning: In the Mac system, a special place to put unwanted documents and files. The trash icon on the Mac desktop looks just like a trash can, and all you have to do to dispose of your unwanted stuff is to click on the item in question with the mouse and drag it to the trash can. A handy feature of the Mac trash can is that its sides bulge out when it has discarded files in it, and it doesn't ultimately dump the stuff until you give it the command to Empty Trash — just like in real life!

Sentence: "The nicest thing about the Mac *trash* can is that the dogs don't knock it over every Thursday night."

tree structure

Pronunciation: *tree struk-cher.*

Meaning: One of the more visual concepts in organizing files on a hard drive. Files are stored in "directories," each of which is connected to other directories like branches in a tree. The main directory on every disk is called the root directory. Other directories branch from the root and still other directories branch from them, making the thing look like an electronic family tree. (See also *path* and *pathname.*)

Sentence: "I almost had a heart attack when Earl walked by with the pruning shears, claiming he was going to fix his hard drive's *tree structure.*"

trigonometry

Pronunciation: *trig-en-ah-me-tree.*

Meaning: A branch of mathematics having to do with relationships of parts of a triangle. If you hear terms like sine, cosine, and tangent, you can nod wisely and say, "Ah, trigonometry!" Trigonometry helps you figure out unknown measurements of a triangle (such as an angle or a side) based on known elements.

Sentence: "You could use *trigonometry* to figure out the height of a distant mountain, if you know how far it is to the mountain and what the angle of view to the peak is, and also if someone whispers its height in your ear."

triple-clicking

Pronunciation: *tri-pel-clik-ing.*

Meaning: Clicking the mouse button three times in rapid succession to access very weird and arcane functions. Triple-clicking is uncommon and is used only in programs whose designers could not figure out more effective means of accessing features.

Sentence: "When I *triple-click* on this icon, I get a message telling me to stop drinking so much coffee."

troglodyte

Pronunciation: *trahg-le-diht.*

Meaning: From the Greek word meaning "cave dweller." A special class of nerd that prefers to dwell in the dark recesses of computer rooms, who have developed nocturnal feeding habits like bats and moles.

Sentence: "The university cafeteria is keeping special hours — not to mention a special diet — for the *troglodytes* on campus."

Trojan horse

Pronunciation: *Troh-jen hors.*

Meaning: A nasty computer program cleverly hidden inside a legitimate program. It comes from a strategy used in the Trojan War, where the Greeks pretended to give a gift of a huge wooden horse as a peace offering to the city of Troy. As Troy slept, the many soldiers hidden inside the horse clambered out and attacked the city, which most historians agree was a sneaky thing to do. Sneaky computer programs that pretend to do one thing but yet disguise a more nefarious deed are called Trojan Horses. You are more likely to find a Trojan horse packaged inside shareware or freeware than in off-the-shelf commercial software.

Sentence: "There is argument behind the notion that Microsoft Windows is a *Trojan horse.*"

true

Pronunciation: *troo.*

Meaning: The opposite of "false." Or it could also mean "yes" or "on." In binary math (also called Boolean math), true means a 1 or positive, and false means a zero or negative.

Sentence: "Believing that a computer would save me time and effort proved too good to be *true.*"

TrueType font

Pronunciation: *Troo-Tihp fawnt.*

Meaning: A category of fonts created jointly by Apple Computer and Microsoft that bypass the need for a page description language (see PDL) or a utility that enables fonts to be displayed on-screen. Instead, the smarts that translate the font to the screen or to the printer are kept inside the font itself. In the olden days, you had to pay dearly for computer programs and printers that understood a multitude of fonts and displayed and printed them well. TrueType fonts take care of the details, making everything look and print swell. TrueType fonts are also called scalable fonts, which means you can select any type size without having to worry about distortions.

Sentence: "Using these widely available and inexpensive *TrueType fonts,* I've been able to design a document that looks just as bad as my handwriting."

TSR

(See *terminate-and-stay-resident program.*)

TTL

Pronunciation: *Tee Tee Ell.*

Meaning: Here's a doozey: Transistor-to-Transistor Logic is what this acronym is all about. What is it? Who knows, who cares, why bother.

You'll often see TTL listed as a type of computer monitor, typically the old style monochrome monitors. Everyone always asked, "What's TTL stand for?" Now you know.

Sentence: "I feel so enriched now that I finally know what *TTL* stands for."

TTY

Pronunciation: *Tee Tee Why.*

Meaning: An abbreviation for teletype. It's also the name of a type of terminal emulation, usually (and this is a secret) meaning "absolutely no emulation whatsoever." TTY rears its ugly head a lot in UNIX and is incorporated into many UNIX commands. Those commands are used to control the various terminals, monitors and keyboards — even modems — connected to the UNIX machine. You need to be a real UNIX dork to understand it all. (See also *terminal emulation.*)

Sentence: "Oh, so you're the jerk who keeps logging in on *TTY*P3 and crashing the system!"

Turing machine

Pronunciation: *Ter-ing ma-sheen.*

Meaning: A simple computer developed by A.M. Turing in the 1930s. It was supposed to be able to diagnose which problems were solvable by machines. It did this by reading a piece of paper tape. Turing's machine could only move the tape forward, put a mark on it, erase the mark, or stop it in its tracks. Turing claimed that the machine could solve any problem that could be expressed as an algorithm (a step-by-step procedure for solving a problem).

Sentence: "I don't think I'd have a use for a *Turing machine.* I just want to solve the problems; I don't care whether they can be solved or not."

turnkey system

Pronunciation: *turn-kee sis-tem.*

Meaning: A computer system all packaged and ready to go for a specific task. The system will be complete with computer, monitor, keyboard, disk drives, software, and other peripherals. The term comes from the automotive industry — where you can put a key into your car, turn it, and operate the vehicle without anything else to buy, install, set up, or learn.

Sentence: "I always thought that *turnkey* had something to do with sardines."

tutorial

Pronunciation: *too-tor-ee-ell.*

Meaning: A training session that guides the student step-by-step through a procedure. Of particular interest are the tutorials that are packaged with many contemporary software programs. Generally, they are interactive, so that you can play along and push keys to get the program to continue.

Sentence: "The *tutorial* for my accounting package comes with instructions for loading a gun."

tweak

Pronunciation: *tweek.*

Meaning: To customize, tailor, adjust, rearrange, cajole, or otherwise mess with. More specifically, it means changing settings on a piece of hardware or software so that your needs are more closely attended to.

Sentence: "I want to *tweak* my word processing program so that it stops beeping when I misspell a word."

Twinkie

Pronunciation: *Twink-ee.*

Meaning: A staple in the diet of computer programmers and other nerds. Fits into most of the four basic food groups. Also, consumption of Twinkies has been used as a defense in the most egregious crimes. Thus, if you need a scapegoat, invoke the Twinkie defense. (See also *M&Ms.*)

Sentence: "Because I had some heavy-duty programming to do, I had some *Twinkies* for a power breakfast."

twisted pair

Pronunciation: *twist-ed paer.*

Meaning: A wire that's secretly a pair of wires wrapped around each other. It is the kind of wire typically used in commercial telephone systems. The wire is "twisted" because you talk into the mouthpiece and it's heard in the ear piece. If the wire weren't twisted, you would talk in the mouthpiece and the sound would come out the mouthpiece. The term is also used in local area networks, especially those that use common phone wiring to connect the computers (common phone wiring is the same thing as "twisted pair"). The good thing about twisted pair is that it's cheap and ubiquitous; the drawback is that it doesn't carry nearly as much information as the thicker coaxial cable (the stuff cable TV comes over).

Sentence: "Here come our network guru and his female companion. Geez. Aren't they a *twisted pair?*"

TXT

Pronunciation: *Tee Ecks Tee.*

Meaning: Abbreviation for Text. A suffix used for text files, generally in DOS-based computing. Examples include LETTER.TXT and GOFISH.TXT.

Sentence: "When I tell my word processor to save my files as 'text only,' it automatically assigns the *.TXT* extension to the filename. Aren't computers smart?"

type-ahead

Pronunciation: *tihp-ah-hed.*

Meaning: A term for a buffer (a part of memory) that allows you to type ahead of what you see on the screen. For example, you can start typing the next DOS command even though DOS is currently copying files to the floppy drive. Of course, DOS's type-ahead buffer is only 15 characters big, so after you type the 15th character, DOS starts beeping at you: Beep! I'm full! Stop typing! Beep! The stuff you type appears as soon as DOS is unbusy.

Sentence: "Because of the *type-ahead* buffer in Windows, I can enter several commands and wait for the computer to catch up. I seem to do that a lot."

typeface

Pronunciation: *tihp-faes.*

Meaning: The design of characters in a font. Typeface refers to the physical characteristics of a family of letters and numbers. Typesetting has grown into a major art form, and the number of available typefaces — even to personal computer users — is almost endless. The main division between the categories of typefaces lies in their use of serifs — the little hooky things at the ends of the letters. Thus, they are called either serif typefaces or sans serif (without serif) typefaces. Other categories include display faces and decorative faces.

Sentence: "One of my favorite *typefaces* is Omar Serif."

UART

Pronunciation: *Yoo-ahrt.*

Meaning: Acronym for Universal Asynchronous Receiver/Transmitter. The UART is the gizmo — actually the integrated circuit — in a computer that changes the parallel data stream inside the computer into the serial data stream. So it takes the bits marching eight abreast inside your computer and lines them up single file for the serial port. This is required for devices that use the serial port, such as a modem. (See also *bit, modem,* and *serial port.*)

Sentence: "There seems to be a traffic jam in my *UART.*"

UMB

Pronunciation: *Yoo Em Bee.*

Meaning: Abbreviation for Upper Memory Block. It's an area of Upper Memory that can be "filled in" with real memory using some sort of memory management magic that only the eggheads can comprehend. A memory device driver, such as DOS's EMM386.EXE, is required to create UMBs. Then, using other memory management magic too mental to mention here, programs can be *loaded high* into those UMBs, which makes more memory available to your programs. It's magic! (See also *conventional memory, low memory, high memory, memory,* and *terminate-and-stay-resident program.*)

Sentence: "Hi. My name is Jim. On my PC I once had a paltry 384K of available memory. Not enough to run WordPerfect. I was devastated. Then I bought a memory manager for my 386 clone. And now, I can stuff all my device drivers and TSRs into *UMBs.* Not only do I have more memory available, but I also learned some really cryptic terms and acronyms that have bolstered my Tech-IQ rating at cocktail parties."

undelete

Pronunciation: *un-duh-leet.*

Meaning: To put something back the way it was before you deleted it. That is, to restore a file after you have deleted it, to resuscitate it, to resurrect it. DOS includes an undelete command that attempts to restore files you may have accidentally blasted to smithereens. Other operating systems have similar commands because it's apparent to those who write computer software that people who use computers (that is, you and me) are apt to accidentally delete things we didn't intend to delete. (See also *Del key* and *unerase.*)

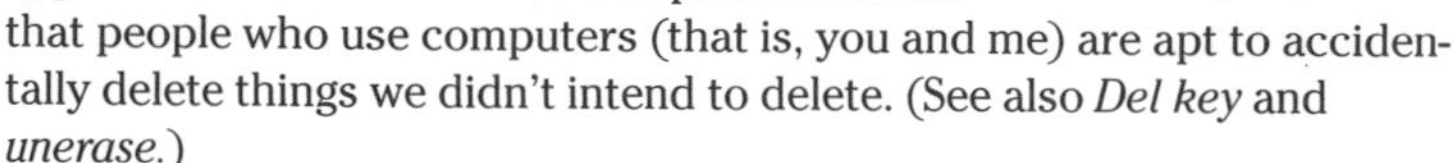

Sentence: "Just because DOS has an *undelete* command doesn't mean you should be careless with the delete command."

underline

Pronunciation: *un-der-lihn.*

Meaning: (1) In word processing or desktop publishing, the attribute applied to text that makes it look underlined. Underlined text was once used in typed manuscripts to indicate that the typesetter should use italics. That's because typewriters could underline but not italicize text. Computers can italicize, so underlining is left as a text attribute for the narrow-minded and bureaucratic out there who are still amazed by underlined text. (2) The underline character on your keyboard, which is a very important character by itself in some programming languages. (See also *underscore.*)

Sentence: "I knew a guy who tried to underline things by typing a word, backspacing (which erased the word), and then typing the *underline* character. While that would work on a typewriter, with a computer you must use a special command that underlines the text for you."

underscore

Pronunciation: *un-der-skor.*

Meaning: Another term for underline, probably introduced by the more musical-minded among computer users. (See also *underline.*)

Sentence: "Now that you're a power user, Michael, you'll need to stop saying underline. It's *underscore.*"

undo

Pronunciation: *un-doo.*

Meaning: To put the situation back to the way it was before you messed it up. It's command in most applications that enables you to cancel the effects of whatever you just did. You can undo typing and formatting commands, but don't get careless about your work because you can't undo everything.

Sentence: "I just hope when I die and get to Heaven, God offers me an *undo* command."

undocumented

Pronunciation: *un-dok-yoo-men-ted.*

Meaning: A feature of your hardware or software that is not explained in the user manual. This happens either because the manufacturer forgot, didn't think it was important, hasn't figured out itself how the feature works, or because the company wants to keep it a secret from you or its competition. Computer book authors love to find undocumented features in software products; it's their life!

Sentence: "I stumbled upon an *undocumented* feature that makes Windows run 100 times faster."

unerase

Pronunciation: *un-ee-raes.*

Meaning: Just like undelete, however, this term was coined by DOS utility guru Peter Norton when he first came upon the idea of undeleting files in the early 1980s. Norton created a program called UnErase — the first of its kind — that recovered deleted files. He made tons of money and founded a complete category of computer software called *utility programs.* (See also *guru, undelete,* and *utility.*)

Sentence: "All praise be to Peter Norton on high! Thank you, O Peter, for thy grace and thine *UnErase*."

UNIX

Pronunciation: *Yoo-niks.*

Meaning: An operating system used especially in multiuser computing contexts, such as with minicomputers and workstations. You also can install UNIX on personal computers and mainframes. UNIX was written in

C and developed in the late 1960s at AT&T's Bell Labs. It first became popular on minicomputers on college campuses and in scientific communities.

The advantages of UNIX lie in its portability from one system to another and in its support of a wealth of applications programs, many programmer's utilities, and programming languages, making it popular among the techno-nerd and geek-whiz faction. Primarily, UNIX is a command-line operating system, very similar to DOS but much more crude and cryptic. Several GUIs are available for UNIX, including X Windows, Open Look, NeXTStep, and others. Incidentally, the name UNIX is a pun of sorts; It's a take-off on an operating system called Multics. Multi, Uni, get it? (See also *C, DOS, K&R, operating system, OS/2, platform,* and *Windows.*)

Sentence: "When a programmer must protect his harem of PCs, he gets some *UNIX.*"

up

Pronunciation: *up.*

Meaning: In the general direction of the sky or ceiling, unless you're in Australia (just checking to see whether you were paying attention). "Up" is used to refer to the direction of the top of the document, even if the top is nowhere on the screen and is in fact just another happy electronic memory to your computer. (See also *down* and *up arrow.*)

Sentence: "To scroll *up,* keep jabbing at the up arrow key."

up arrow

Pronunciation: *up ar-oh.*

Meaning: An arrow pointing upward, as found on one of your cursor keys. Pushing the Up Arrow key moves the cursor up in the document by one line of text. There is also an up arrow at the top of the vertical scroll bar in most graphical applications. Clicking the up arrow in graphical applications with the mouse usually moves the contents of the window down a line or so. Yes, the up arrow moves the contents down, but that's so you can see "up" to the preceding line on the screen. Weird, backward, hard-to-understand — yes, this is how a computer makes life easier for everyone. If only the steering wheel on your car worked that way... (See also *down* and *up.*)

Sentence: "You won't believe this: I pressed the *up arrow* and my computer levitated."

upload

Pronunciation: *up-lohd.*

Meaning: To transmit a file from your computer to another computer. If you're sending a file to another computer, you're uploading. That computer, on the other hand, is downloading the file from you. It doesn't matter who started the file transmission or which computer you're using. If you're sending a file, you're uploading it. (See also *BBS, download,* and *network.*)

Sentence: "I often *upload* my word processing files onto CompuServe to send to publishers in remote parts of the world, such as Indiana."

uppercase

Pronunciation: *up-er kaes.*

Meaning: Capital letters. The terminology comes from the earliest days of typesetting, when the individual metal letters mounted on blocks were stored in trays. The typesetter would pick out the letters that were needed for the job and arrange them on a plate. The capital letters would be stored in the top (or upper) case, and the small letters would be stored in the bottom (or lower) case. (See also *case-sensitive* and *lowercase.*)

Sentence: "Text typed in all *uppercase* letters is hard to read. In fact, it almost seems as if the writer is SHOUTING AT YOU."

upper memory

Pronunciation: *up-er mem-o-ree.*

Meaning: On a PC, this term refers to the portion of memory not used by DOS for running programs. It was originally called Reserved Memory, set aside by IBM in the first PC for "future expansion." DOS was given the rest of memory, a total of 640K, to play with itself and run programs. The rest of the first PC's memory, 384K of memory, was set aside. In memory-management terminology, that area is called Upper Memory. And, in a break with all logic, the memory DOS uses isn't called "lower memory"; it's called conventional memory. (See also *conventional memory, high memory, lower memory, memory,* and *UMB.*)

Sentence: "Every time Phil gets a haircut he loses some *upper memory.*"

UPS

Pronunciation: *Yoo Pee Ess.*

Meaning: Abbreviation for Uninterruptible Power Supply. A fancy term for battery backup — an emergency supply of power in case the power coming out of the wall suddenly stops or when Jim, the dork from Marketing, trips over the PC's cord. Having a UPS often means that you have just enough time to save your stuff and turn off the computer while you're in the dark. You can't really work from the backup battery in the UPS.

Sentence: "This blackout is horrible, but there's Jim, sitting in his office with the only working PC hooked to a *UPS.* Let's unplug him and run something useful instead, like the Nintendo."

uptime

Pronunciation: *up-tyme.*

Meaning: The time that the computer is actually working and you can get stuff done, as opposed to downtime, when the computer isn't feeling well and nothing works. (See also *downtime.*)

Sentence: "The dog is pretty lethargic, Doctor. How can we increase his *uptime?*"

upward compatible

Pronunciation: *up-werd kum-pat-i-bel.*

Meaning: Upward compatible means that something is designed with the future in mind. The item in question, usually a document or file created by some application or piece of hardware, will work with the next version of the product or with components that are not on the market yet. Generally, software is downward compatible only, meaning the newest versions of the application will work with files generated from previous versions, but the previous versions will not work with files created with the new version. (See also *compatibility* and *downward compatible.*)

Sentence: "Wow! This new computer is really designed for *upward compatibility.* There's a plug in the back marked R2-D2 Connection."

USENET

Pronunciation: *Yooz-Net.*

Meaning: Acronym for USEr NETwork. A facility of the Internet that offers a wide variety of newsgroups, bulletin boards, and public forums. It runs on the UUCP (UNIX-to-UNIX copy) network, an international wide area network of all sorts of UNIX computers, all interconnected ala the Tholian Web. (See also *BBS, Internet, network, UNIX,* and *wide area network.*)

Sentence: "From your cozy office chair in Silicon Valley, you can get up-to-the-minute news from, say, Helsinki, Finland, just by accessing *USENET.*"

user

Pronunciation: *yoo-zer.*

Meaning: The person using the computer and software as a tool, as opposed to the programmer or hardware engineers. The term has nothing to do with the skill level of the person at the keyboard. Even nerds of the high programming priesthood are mere users when they sit at a computer. (See also *user-friendly, user group,* and *user-hostile.*)

Sentence: "The computer industry is the only legitimate industry that calls its customers *users.*"

user group

Pronunciation: *yoo-zer groop.*

Meaning: A club or gathering of computer users devoted to the study of a particular piece of software or hardware. There are user groups for the Macintosh, for dBASE, for Adobe Photoshop, and many, many more. User groups often include Special Interest Groups (SIGs) for users that share common interests or products. (See also *CompuServe, GEnie, Internet, network, Prodigy,* and *SIG.*)

Sentence: "*User groups* are a great source of information and a good place to ask questions about your computer or a software package. But if you show up late, stick around and listen to the conversation. You might have accidentally stumbled upon a meeting of the Older Guys with Pen Packs and Pot Bellies Society."

user ID

Pronunciation: *yoo-zer Eye Dee.*

Meaning: Yes, you can get "carded" by your computer. The user ID is a number or code word assigned to you by the system administrator or one you make up yourself. It's used to tell the computer who you are, often in place of your name. For example, Bill Gate's ID on the Microsoft internal mail system is "billg." Don't confuse the user ID with the password. The ID is something that identifies who you are to other people using the computer. In contrast, the password is secret and proves to the computer that the guy who logs in as billg is really Bill Gates and not some joker from the competition who's trying to learn all Microsoft's secrets. (See also *password* and *user.*)

Sentence: Recently overheard in the system administrator's office at a major software vendor: "No, I'm sorry, the *user ID* 'god' is already taken. You'll have to think of something else."

user interface

Pronunciation: *yoo-zer in-ter-fays.*

Meaning: What you see when you turn on the computer. This is the set of prompts, cursors, and software devices with which you interact to get something done in a program. The interface is what you see — in your face — and how you communicate with the computer and (hopefully) get things done. (See also *DOS, GUI, interface,* and *Windows.*)

Sentence: "The best *user interface* is on Star Trek, where they actually tell the computer what to do. Did you ever hear the Enterprise's computer say 'Bad command or file name'?"

user name

(See *user ID.*)

user profile

Pronunciation: *yoo-zer proh-fyle.*

Meaning: In a network or bulletin board situation, a little blurb about a member or user that others on the system can access, so they have a better sense of whom they're talking to. Users write their own blurbs that might include their name, age, geographic location, the kind of computer they're using, and their interests as they relate to that specific bulletin board. (See also *BBS, network,* and *user.*)

Sentence: "Fortunately, my *user profile* didn't include the fact that I have twelve designer pocket protectors."

user-friendly

Pronunciation: *yoo-zer frend-lee.*

Meaning: Supposedly implying that the software or hardware is easy enough for even you or I to understand. Also called intuitive or idiot-proof. It means you can easily figure out what to do without having to look it up in the manual or the on-line help. Yeah, right! (See *user* and *user-hostile.*)

Sentence: "You know, Windows can be a *user-friendly* interface, once you understand what all the gadgets and gizmos are, how to work them, and what they do."

user-hostile

Pronunciation: *yoo-zer hoss-till.*

Meaning: The opposite of user-friendly. This means that no matter how well you treat your computer and the software installed in it, they never lift a finger to make your life any easier. The epitome of user hostility is a cursor blinking on an otherwise totally blank screen — the DOS prompt. (See also *user* and *user-friendly.*)

Sentence: "I worked on a computer that made me enter the code <pi14,69> whenever I wanted to print a plus sign. Now *that* was a *user-hostile* machine."

utility

Pronunciation: *yoo-til-i-tee.*

Meaning: Software intended to help you fix, tweak, or enhance your system. Unlike a true application, a utility doesn't produce any concrete output or documents. Instead, utilities are designed to make working with the computer or your operating system easier. Utilities were once called software tools, and they were intended for use primarily by programmers to help ease programming drudgery. Today, utilities are a legitimate software category. Popular utilities include the Norton Utilities, PC Tools, Stacker, and FastBack. (See also *backup, debugger, file compression, undelete, unerase,* and *virus.*)

Sentence: "At the time of the Michaelangelo virus scare, sales of computer anti-virus *utilities* went way up. It makes you wonder who thought up that Michaelangelo thing."

vaccine

Pronunciation: *vaks-seen.*

Meaning: A disinfectant or anti-virus utility that helps your computer fight computer viruses. It works by looking for the symptoms of virus activity, such as suspicious attempts to infiltrate relatively secluded areas of the hard drive, drowsiness, and high-fever. The vaccine then removes the virus, making your PC infection free. (See also *virus.*)

Sentence: "So let me get this straight, you tried to cure your PC of any possible virus by sticking a moldy orange into your disk drive? Why not just try a *vaccine* next time."

vacuum tube

Pronunciation: *vak-yoom tewb.*

Meaning: An old-fashioned technology used in early computers. It is a device that transmits information by controlling the flow of electrons, as semiconductor diodes and transistors do in modern computers.

Sentence: "A *vacuum tube* is something you can look for in a computer museum, such as the marvelous Boston Computer Museum, which, incidentally, is in Boston."

vaporware

Pronunciation: *vae-per-way-er.*

Meaning: Products, whether hardware or software, that have yet to materialize on the market but are promoted as if they were about to revolutionize the computer industry. In many cases, there is plenty of good reason to believe that the product will never even make it to the market, at least not in the lifetime of its purveyors.

Sentence: "Anything that you've read about or heard about in the computer industry but have yet to see in a store is *vaporware.*"

VAR

Pronunciation: *Vahr.*

Meaning: Acronym for *Value-Added Reseller.* An individual or business that integrates components provided by *Original Equipment Manufacturers* (OEMs) and gets them properly packaged and documented for end users who usually need all the bells and whistles. VARs often package hardware, software, training, documentation, and even custom software services for specialized industries. (See also *OEM, end user,* and *bells and whistles.*)

Sentence: "We purchased a large medical system from a *VAR.* The advantage is that we can complain to one source for all our problems."

variable

Pronunciation: *vaer-ee-a-bowl.*

Meaning: In programming, a symbol that represents a numerical value or string of text used in the program. Using variables gives the programmer the flexibility of changing the value at any point in the program, even if there seems to be no need for that kind of flexibility at the outset. (See also *wildcard.*)

Sentence: "The content of a *variable* can change at any time. This leads me to believe that Bill Clinton's brain contains way too many variables."

VAX

Pronunciation: *Vaks.*

Meaning: A line of computers produced by Digital Equipment Corp. (DEC). In the olden days, the term VAX was often used to mean a large, cumbersome, yet highly capable and powerful computer. The notion of "a VAX on your desktop" used to be thought of in science-fiction terms. In 1988 or thereabouts, it became a reality as the microcomputers of the time reached the processing capabilities of the early VAX computers.

Sentence: "No, it's not true that the first Apple computer was the result of the engineers leaving a Mommy *VAX* and Daddy *VAX* alone overnight."

VDISK

(See *virtual disk.*)

VDT

Pronunciation: *Vee Dee Tee.*

Meaning: Acronym for *Video Display Terminal,* otherwise known as a monitor (with a keyboard). The term VDT, however, is more apt to be used when talking about the negative health effects of these machines, which have been implicated in everything from eye strain to birth defects. They produce a substantial amount of electromagnetic radiation, which may or may not be enough to cause the various maladies that monitors have been accused of causing. For protection, it is possible to get screens that filter out these electromagnetic fields. Screens that polarize the visual output so as to avoid glare are even more widely available. (See also *radiation.*)

Sentence: "I like my *VDT,* but I'm worried about the EMFs it produces. I'm worried that I might get RSI or CTS from all that typing, too. It's that dangerous side of computing that gives me so many of life's thrills."

vector graphics

(See *graphics.*)

verify

Pronunciation: *ver-i-fy.*

Meaning: To confirm the existence of something. In computing, this often refers to the double-checking that takes place after a file is copied. You verify that the duplicate is identical to the original. This makes the copy process take a bit longer because the computer has to double-check, but it ensures that no errors were produced during the duplication process.

Sentence: "Because disk media is much more reliable than in the old days, most DOS users don't bother to *verify* file copies."

version

Pronunciation: *ver-zhun.*

Meaning: An edition of a product. Versions are usually designated with a number, such as "Word 2.0 for Windows," in which 2.0 is the version number, second version, first release. You can't count on the numbers being in numerical order (we don't know why this is so), but typically 1 comes before 2, 2 comes before 3, and so on. The decimal portion of a version number generally represents a small enhancement or bug fix to the initial version release so that version 2.1 is always more reliable than 2.0. Intermediary releases have more digits following the decimal, such as Windows 3.1.1, which is really just Microsoft's way of avoiding the fiasco caused by releasing a whole new version.

Sentence: "*Version* 1.0 of any product — the first one out the shoot — is generally the worst. We recommend waiting until version 1.1 before buying anything."

vertical

Pronunciation: *ver-ti-kel.*

Meaning: Relating to the up-and-down direction. In computers, we can talk about vertical markets, vertical centering, vertical columns, vertical justification, and vertical scrolling. All of which apply in some way to up-and-down-ness.

Sentence: "Yes, I would say that computerized elevators were a *vertical* market."

vertical scroll bar

Pronunciation: *ver-ti-kel skrohl bahr.*

Meaning: The bar on the right side of a window in a graphical application. By clicking the scroll bar with your mouse or using the arrow keys, you can move the contents of the window up or down in various increments. The little marker that travels along the bar is called the *elevator box.* It shows you how far along you are in the document. (See also *horizontal scroll bar.*)

Sentence: "To get to the end of my document, I put these little people in the *vertical scroll bar's* elevator box. Then I say, 'free fall!' and drag the elevator box quickly to the bottom of the scroll bar. It may scare the little people, but I get to the bottom of my document quickly."

VGA

Pronunciation: *Vee Gee Ay.*

Meaning: Acronym for *Video Graphics Array* or *Video Gate Array.* It is a color graphics display standard that was an improvement over its predecessors in terms of color selection, resolution, and accuracy of image. A VGA monitor can display up to 256 colors at one time. The resolution measures image sharpness, and with VGA that's 640 pixels horizontally by 480 lines vertically. Super VGA monitors are even more impressive, with resolutions reaching 1,024 x 768. (See also *monitor, CGA, EGA, graphics, resolution,* and *SVGA.*)

Sentence: "The current standard in PC graphics is *VGA.* If you have anything else, we encourage you to upgrade — especially because we just bought a wad of VGA stock."

video

Pronunciation: *vi-dee-oh.*

Meaning: This word is used loosely to describe all activities in which moving pictures (movies) are involved. More specifically, it can refer to the display function of your computer (that is, video display) or the act of incorporating video devices (VCRs and video recording equipment) with computer technology. Video standards established by the Video Electronics Standards Association help to assure that our computer components work together in such a way that you can actually see something on the screen (which is nice). That's the kind of video that's common to all computers.

Sentence: "I got my father *video* software for his birthday. Now he sits around all day in dark glasses in front of his computer yelling, 'Cut!' into a megaphone."

video adapter

Pronunciation: *vid-ee-oh a-dap-ter.*

Meaning: An expansion card that plugs into one of your PC's expansion slots, allowing your software and your PC's monitor to talk with each other. Standard video adapters include VGA, SVGA, EGA, CGA, and Hercules. Also called a *video card.* (See also *expansion slot, VGA, EGA, CGA,* and *SVGA.*)

Sentence: "The graphics on your PC consist of two elements: the monitor and the *video adapter.* The monitor you see. The video adapter lurks inside your PC's guts."

video card

(See *video adapter.*)

video memory

Pronunciation: *vid-ee-oh mem-er-ee.*

Meaning: A special part of RAM in which the computer stores images displayed on the screen. (See also *memory* and *RAM.)*

Sentence: "The more *video memory* you have, the more colors and sharper resolution you'll get on your PC. But keep in mind that video memory is separate from the memory DOS and your applications use."

video mode

Pronunciation: *vid-ee-oh mohd.*

Meaning: The various resolutions and number of colors available for the different types of graphics adapters used by IBM-compatible computers. Presently, there are 20 video modes, ranging from 0 to 19. Characteristics include whether they display graphics or text only, color or monochrome, the number of colors, the resolution (height and width in pixels), and, in a text-only mode, the number of columns (that means the number of characters you can fit on a line). (See also *mode.*)

Sentence: "I don't care what *video mode* is being used; I just want the screen to match what the printer spits out."

video RAM

Pronunciation: *Vid-ee-oh Ram.*

Meaning: The RAM chips used to make up video memory. These are built into high-end video adapter boards. (See also *RAM* and *video memory.*)

Sentence: "The Megalons used a *video RAM* to break into Captain Video's secret fortress."

videotext

Pronunciation: *vid-ee-oh-text.*

Meaning: Words and numbers that come to your computer (or your TV, for that matter) over the wires. Types of videotext that are commonly transmitted include news, weather information, and stock quotes. In Europe, a videotext system was designed for use with their cable television. Using a special type of computer, you can hook into the system and access information right at home on your TV. Americans must have thought this was too dumb because we never bothered with it.

Sentence: "*Videotext* is an appropriate format for up-to-the-minute news that must be transmitted quickly to be valuable. Stuff such as, 'Hey! Some guy just broke into your house. Go check the bedroom window.'"

virtual disk

Pronunciation: *ver-choo-ul disk.*

Meaning: A make-believe disk that doesn't exist in reality, like most flying saucers. Actually, a virtual disk is a fancy term for a RAM disk, a disk created from the computer's memory. (See also *RAM disk.*)

Sentence: "When the system consultant said he had configured a *virtual disk* on my computer, I told him I'd be sending him a virtual check in the mail."

virtual machine

Pronunciation: *ver-choo-ul ma-sheen.*

Meaning: A software simulation of another computer. A virtual machine is useful for testing software on large computers, such as mainframes. For example, a group of engineers typically create a new computer on a larger mainframe and then run tests to see how the computer performs. All of this is done before the first real machine is created, primarily to work out the bugs. New microprocessors are created in a similar manner. On 386 and later PCs, a virtual machine refers to a special operating mode, the V86 mode, in which the microprocessor can pretend it's actually several 8088 computers all running at the same time. This is how programs such as Windows and DESQview can *multitask* (run more than one program at a time).

Sentence: "Programmers amaze their friends by creating *virtual machines* that contain virtual machines. They can get a job done . . . with virtue."

virtual memory

Pronunciation: *ver-choo-ul mem-er-ee.*

Meaning: Using disk drive storage to simulate RAM. Some operating systems (not DOS) borrow parts of the disk drive and swap out massive chunks of memory to a file on disk — a *swap file.* That way, true memory (RAM) is made available for programs that need it. The memory saved on disk can be put back into real memory when it's needed later. (See also *RAM, memory,* and *hard disk.*)

Sentence: "I use a notepad for my *virtual memory.* I write stuff down on the pad and then forget it. Then I read the pad later and it reminds me of what I need to do. I suppose absent-minded computers need virtual memory as well."

virtual reality

Pronunciation: *ver-choo-ul ree-al-i-tee.*

Meaning: An oxymoron that describes a brave new world of computer technology that creates a simulated multidimensional environment for the user. The user is actually encased in the environment, or can be, with paraphernalia that can include a helmet, goggles, gloves, and a belt, all used as input devices. Getting "inside the space" makes you feel as if you're trapped in a dream world. Within a virtual reality environment,

you can see, hear, and feel your way around a software application. Currently, the main uses of virtual reality are games and design/engineering.

Already, game arcades offer virtual reality setups where you can hunt down and kill your opponent in a place called cyberspace, which is not far from downtown LA. More significantly, virtual reality is used for engineering because it allows the engineer or designer to simulate any view of the product being worked on. For instance, in designing a car, you can actually simulate being inside the engine. (See also *artificial intelligence, knowledge base,* and *expert system.*)

Sentence: "Sometimes I think my whole life is one big *virtual reality* machine — especially when the cat talks to me."

virus

Pronunciation: *vih-ress.*

Meaning: A nasty type of program created by nasty people that is capable of replicating itself and doing severe damage to the contents of other users' systems. To protect your system against viruses, you should: 1) get your software only from reputable places, 2) run an anti-virus utility, and 3) religiously back up your hard drive so that lost data can be quickly and reliably replaced. (See also *vaccine.*)

Sentence: "If you can't cure your computer of a *virus* it's caught, you should at least let it rest and feed it plenty of chicken soup."

visual programming

Pronunciation: *vizh-oo-ul proh-gram-ing.*

Meaning: A way of creating software by making menu choices with the mouse and cutting and pasting items so that actual typing and linear thought are minimized. Examples are Visual BASIC by Microsoft and ObjectVision by Borland. The plus side is that you don't have to know much about programming to be able to work with this technology and produce results. The minus side is that many of your choices are made for you and there is often no way to customize certain options. (See also *programming.*)

Sentence: "*Visual programming* makes it possible for someone such as Uncle Ralph to create custom applications. Remember his spice rack? Doesn't the thought of Ralph programming make you cringe?"

VLSI

Pronunciation: *Vee El Ess Ih.*

Meaning: Acronym for *Very Large Scale Integration,* a technology that refers to semiconductor chips. This means engineering the chip so that it can accommodate a large number of transistors and can do more. (See also *CMOS, MOS,* and *semiconductor.*)

Sentence: "*VLSI* circuits are not larger than other chips; they just contain more information."

voice recognition

Pronunciation: *voys re-kug-ni-shun.*

Meaning: Technology that can recognize and work with the spoken word. It translates sound signals into digital signals that can be processed and analyzed by a computer. The prospect offers a whole new world of opportunity for computers: being able to talk to your computer as you talk to your friends (or, more appropriately, to your children) and being able to repot your plants or remodel your kitchen while you're doing your computer work. Voice recognition technology is in a fairly primitive state at present. (See also *voice synthesis.)*

Sentence: "The first thing I'd do with *voice recognition* technology is tell DOS exactly what it can do with the `Bad command or filename` error message."

voice synthesis

Pronunciation: *voys sin-the-sis.*

Meaning: The opposite of voice recognition. Here, the computer is able to create something that sounds like speech from text that it reads from a hard or floppy disk. Voice synthesis is a lot easier to create than voice recognition, which is why computers talk like computers. (See also *voice recognition.*)

Sentence: "I had always imagined my computer was female. But when I plugged in that *voice synthesis* expansion unit, it sounded like Arnold Schwarzenegger."

volatile memory

(See *RAM.*)

volume

Pronunciation: *vahl-yoom.*

Meaning: Another name for a disk, whether hard or floppy. Comes from the old computer days when instead of having a disk inside your computer, the lab technicians mounted a volume on a high-speed tape machine. The term works for computer storage the same way that a volume is a single book in a larger collection of works. (See also *floppy disk, disk,* and *hard disk.*)

Sentence: "I got an error message that said, `No volume in drive A`, so I turned up my stereo."

volume label

(See *label.*)

von Neumann

Pronunciation: *vahn Noy-man.*

Meaning: The guy who invented an architecture that created a data bottleneck named for him. Basically, it involves a very fast CPU and fast storage, but the processing is slowed down to the rate of the transmission of the data from one place to another. Yes, his name is von Neumann, but you pronounce it von Noyman.

Sentence: "Yes, Dr. *von Neumann* and not two guys named Steve really started this computer revolution."

voodoo

Pronunciation: *voo-doo.*

Meaning: Tried-and-true technology to apply when all else fails. Instead of pressing keys and clicking a mouse, you can chant invocations, do ritual dances, or feed weird concoctions of exotic herbs to your computer in an effort to get it to cooperate. Similar to voodoo economics; see the *Republican Dictionary For Dummies.*

Sentence: "If your PC worked fine yesterday and for some reason it won't today — even though you didn't change a thing — it's *voodoo.*"

wait state

Pronunciation: *wayt stayt.*

Meaning: A short delay that occurs when a microprocessor accesses data from memory. Because the microprocessor is generally faster than the memory chips, it waits for the memory chips to "catch up" by sitting around and having a cup of coffee for the duration of one wait state each time it accesses the memory. A *zero wait state processor* is much faster and takes advantage of faster memory chips. How long is a wait state? It depends on how fast the processor is. In any case, it's a slice of time way too fast for a human to experience. (See also *microprocessor* and *zero wait state.*)

Sentence: "I had to call tech support yesterday about my laptop. They said it had only one *wait state,* but when I took it to the post office it suddenly gained about 40 wait states!"

wallpaper

Pronunciation: *wahl-pay-per.*

Meaning: A graphic image placed on the desktop, or background, of your GUI. If you close all windows in your GUI, you'll see the wallpaper underneath. Wallpaper serves no particular purpose, but it can be interesting and amusing to your friends.

Sentence: "My favorite *wallpaper* is the Nagel painting called 'Sushi.'"

wapro

Pronunciation: *wah-pro.*

Meaning: The Japanese term for word processor. We just thought we'd throw it in here because it's one of those terms you usually don't see in computer dictionaries.

Sentence: "The proper response to the question *'Wapro?'* is 'Wa-kari-mas-en,' or 'I don't understand.'"

warm boot

Pronunciation: *wohrm boot.*

Meaning: The process of restarting your computer by pressing Ctrl-Alt-Delete or an equivalent reset button. A warm boot occurs when you restart the computer without turning it off. Warm booting is much faster than cold booting, which occurs when you turn the computer off and then back on. (See also *cold boot, reboot,* and *Ctrl-Alt-Del.*)

Sentence: "After installing certain software on my hard disk, the programs tell me to restart the computer by pressing Ctrl-Alt-Delete, which *warm boots* the computer. That seems so much cozier than the cold boot approach."

warp coils

Pronunciation: *wohr-pa koy-els.*

Meaning: (1) The massive hoops of metal that allow a starship to glide through space at high speeds without any chronographic dilation. (2) Any sufficiently advanced or mysterious thing inside a computer that you don't understand.

Sentence: "The PC won't boot! Why doesn't someone check the innertubular couplers, quantum phase adjustment wing nuts, or the *warp coils?*"

watch icon

Pronunciation: *wahch eye-kahn.*

Meaning: An icon shaped like a tiny little watch. The watch icon, indigenous to the Macintosh computer, tells you that the computer is thinking and that you'll have to wait. In the early days of the Macintosh, the watch's little hands did not move. Today's watch icons are much more sophisticated. (See also *hourglass icon* and *beachball pointer.*)

Sentence: "Spacelab, this is Houston. You'll have to wait on that emergency meteor collision avoidance program. We're still getting the *watch icon* here."

watt

Pronunciation: *waht.*

Meaning: A unit of measure for power consumption. Watts equal volts times amperes. Hence, a 10 volt, 10 amp power source puts out 100 watts of power. It helps if you think of watts in terms of a light bulb. A 100W light bulb is much brighter than a 60W bulb. TV studios use 1000K bulbs to light their sets, which are terribly bright. The typical PC uses 250W of power, just like a 250W light bulb. (See also *amp* and *troglodyte.*)

Sentence: "I use 50 *watt* light bulbs in my computer room, so I don't get too much glare on the screen. Also, I'm a troglodyte, so it reminds me of my cave-dwelling forefathers."

what if

Pronunciation: *wut ef.*

Meaning: A term used for testing a spreadsheet with various values, generating different results for analysis. Like, "If I made a gazillion dollars, what percentage would my house payment be?" And then you can enter another value, "Now what if I worked at McDonalds? Hey, can this thing deal with negative numbers?" What if testing is commonly used in spreadsheets, in which you can enter different values into cells of the spreadsheet and the formulas recalculate their results based on the different scenarios.

Sentence: "Jimmy used a spreadsheet to calculate various *what ifs* for the money he embezzled. Now he's doing 5–10 but is trying to get the judge to work out a what if for good behavior."

Whetstone

Pronunciation: *Wet-stohn.*

Meaning: The name of a program used for testing the speed of a microprocessor. The Whetstone is used as a standard test for microprocessor speed. (See also *MIPS* and *microprocessor.*)

Sentence: "Hey, my computer can do 1,500 *Whetstones* — and that's with one cable tied behind its back!"

wide area network (WAN)

Pronunciation: *wihd ae-ree-ah net-werk.*

Meaning: A network of computers that spans a large distance, as opposed to a local area network, which involves computers in the same building. (See also *LAN, network, network operating system,* and *node.*)

Sentence: "Realtors can access a *wide area network* that provides multiple listings and other services for your computer. That way they can send messages such as 'Hey! Mr. and Mrs. Turkey looking for duplex — completely real-estate ignorant. Be on the lookout!'"

widow

Pronunciation: *wih-doe.*

Meaning: The first line of a paragraph of text that is separated from the rest of the paragraph. A widow line appears at the bottom of the page, whereas the rest of the paragraph appears at the top of the next page. Many word processors provide widow suppression to avoid this embarrassing problem. (See also *orphan.*)

Sentence: "Sometimes, if your document is full of *widows,* simply writing about a bunch of elderly bachelors makes the widows disappear."

wildcards

Pronunciation: *wihld-kahrds.*

Meaning: Characters or symbols used in place of a number of possible combinations. Wildcards represent one or more characters that "could be anything" in a search or command. For example, if the * symbol is a wildcard, the search text *s*ing* matches any word or item that starts with an *s* and ends in *ing.* (See also **.* ,star-dot-star,* and *?.*)

Sentence: "*Wildcards* come in handy when you search for text and don't know how to spell, when you search for files and don't know their whole names, or when you play Shanghai with the inlaws and have a lousy hand."

WIMP

Pronunciation: *Whimp.*

Meaning: A disparaging acronym for *Windows, Icons, Menus, Pointing device.* It's the wimpy GUI way of using a computer as opposed to using the command line. (See also *window, menu, mouse, icon,* and *command line.*)

Sentence: "Don't show me that *WIMP* interface! I'm a real man! Give me the DOS prompt any day!"

Winchester disk

Pronunciation: *Whin-ches-ter disk.*

Meaning: A type of hard disk. For years, hard drives were called Winchester disks. This had nothing to do with any company named Winchester that made hard drives. Instead, it referred to the first IBM hard drive that stored 30 megabytes of information on each side. Because the drive was a 30-30, people dubbed it a Winchester disk after the famous Winchester rifle. Until the mid-80s, hard drives were often called Winchester disks. This drove everyone nuts because they assumed some person or some company named Winchester made the disks. It just wasn't so. Today they're called hard disks, plain and simple. (See also *hard disk* and *disk.*)

Sentence: "Yes, ma'am, our hard disks come in three sizes: *Winchester,* Colt, and Daisy."

window

Pronunciation: *win-doe.*

Meaning: A window is a *viewport* (outline through which you see stuff) on the screen that displays data, programs, or information. A window can be moved, resized, opened, and closed, allowing you to organize the data on your computer screen. In most GUIs, you can open numerous windows at the same time and juggle information on the screen. You can switch between windows by simply clicking the window you want. However, you can work in only one window — called the *active window* — at a time. (See also *active window.*)

Sentence: "Sometimes I get carried away and open 20 or 30 *windows* at the same time. This usually results in the building inspector coming in with a worried look on his face and muttering something about earthquakes."

Windows

Pronunciation: *Win-dohs.*

Meaning: Short for *Microsoft Windows,* a graphical user interface for DOS computers. Microsoft Windows provides a common way of using programs, making them easier to learn. Plus, Windows manages the way your PC works and takes care of common chores, such as working with the printer and disk drive. For example, when you set up a printer in Windows, that printer is automatically available in all your Windows programs. This lets us poor users concentrate on our work rather than on fussing with the computer and printer drivers or some such. Microsoft Windows provides access also to your computer's *extended memory* (memory above the first megabyte in your computer) and allows multitasking on 386 and higher computers. (See also *GUI* and *Microsoft.*)

Sentence: "Sometimes *Windows* is a fun place in which to work. And then there's now."

wiz

Pronunciation: *wiz.*

Meaning: A computer user who is sharp, fast, and looks good at the computer. A wiz is not quite as adept as a wizard. (See also *wizard, guru,* and *hacker.*)

Sentence: "Thank you for writing and calling me a computer *wiz.* Please note that wiz does not contain an *h.* That means something else entirely."

wizard

Pronunciation: *wiz-erd.*

Meaning: A computer user of high caliber. Not quite a guru, a computer wizard can solve most problems in most cases without assistance of any kind. (See also *guru, wiz,* and *hacker.*)

Sentence: "No, Amy isn't quite a guru. She's a *wizard,* one who knows how to solve a problem but just can't quite explain how."

word

Pronunciation: *werd.*

Meaning: (1) A collection of data bits that are processed as a unit. On the PC and with most microcomputers, a word is 2 bytes of data, 16 bits "wide." Sometimes a word is as little as a byte (8 bits). The size varies, which is why we're being vague here. (2) A word processing program created by Microsoft (Word). (3) A unit of the English language, such as *duh.*

Sentence: "Yes, Microsoft *Word* can write whole documents, which makes us wonder why they didn't call it Microsoft Document."

word processor

Pronunciation: *werd prah-ses-ser.*

Meaning: An application that lets you write and edit documents. Word processors generally include the capability to copy and move text (by individual words, phrases, or paragraphs), search for specific words or phrases, insert and delete text, format the document (including margin settings, fonts, and character styles), and, of course, print the document. Popular word processors include Microsoft Word, WordPerfect, and AmiPro. (See also *application, editor, and text editor.*)

Sentence: "My *word processor* has features that let me create tables and columns. Hey, you'd almost think this was a construction project instead of a memo."

word wrap

Pronunciation: *werd rap.*

Meaning: Word wrap refers to the way a word processor automatically determines whether the word you are typing will fit within the right margin, and if not, places that word on the next line. With word wrap, you don't have to press the Enter key at the end of each line, as you once had to do with a typewriter. You continue typing. Text editors do not have word wrap; you have to press Enter at the end of each line. (See also *hyphenation.*)

Sentence: "*Word wrap* used to be considered a bonus feature for early word processors. Today, a bonus feature is the built-in space shuttle simulator and advanced physics calculation module."

worksheet

Pronunciation: *werk-sheet.*

Meaning: A data file created by a spreadsheet program. Not all spreadsheet programs refer to their data files as worksheets; some call them spreadsheets, others call them pages or sheets, some even call them documents. In any event, a worksheet can be saved as a file on disk. (See also *document* and *spreadsheet.*)

Sentence: "I saved my Budget *worksheet* on disk as BUDGET-A and then saved the Budget I show to the IRS as BUDGET-B."

workstation

Pronunciation: *werk-stay-shun.*

Meaning: A nebulous term used to describe a powerful computer generally used for scientific or engineering applications, such as CAD. A workstation usually has tons of RAM, gobs of disk storage space, a high-resolution graphics adapter and monitor, and a powerful microprocessor. Workstations often use the UNIX operating system, but some high-end Macintosh, DOS, and OS/2 machines qualify as workstations. (See also *network, PC,* and *mainframe.*)

Sentence: "At work I have a 486 computer *workstation,* and at home I have a 386 computer playstation."

WORM

Pronunciation: *Werm* (as in a naked, snake-like, soft-bodied animal).

Meaning: (1) Acronym for *Write Once Read Many.* WORM refers to a disk medium to which you can write data only once but read the data as often as you like. First generation optical disks are WORM media. CD-ROM disks, however, are not WORM media because only the manufacturer can supply the information on the disk. There is no "writing to" a CD-ROM; they are read-only memory (ROM). (2) A type of virus. (See also *RAM, ROM,* and *SCSI.*)

Sentence: "The best two acronyms in all computing are SCSI and *WORM.* It's entirely possible to have a SCSI WORM drive, and if you do, constantly refer to it as that. It's bound to upset someone somewhere."

wristwatch pointer

(See *watch icon.*)

write error

Pronunciation: *rite ehr-er.*

Meaning: An error that occurs when attempting to save data to a disk. Write errors can occur due to glitches on the disk surface, not enough space on the disk, or when trying to save to a write-protected disk. A good user interface "traps" the write error, gives you some clue as to the exact problem that occurred, and maybe, if the computer's in a good mood, tells you how to fix it. Otherwise, the system might crash.

Sentence: "Nothing induces computer panic like having a beautiful document created in memory but not being able to save it to disk, thanks to a *write error.* Try another disk."

write protect

Pronunciation: *rite pro-tekt.*

Meaning: To modify a disk or file so it's unwilling and unable to edit or erase its data. You can write protect a disk by activating the write-protect tab, a doohickey that makes the disk un-writeable. On 3½-inch disks, this is done by flipping the write-protect tab such that it exposes (or opens) the hole in the disk. On 5¼-inch disks, this is done by placing a piece of opaque tape over the write-protect notch on the side of the disk. Write protection is useful when you are copying disks and want to protect the originals.

Sentence: "When I gave my files to a coworker to examine, I *write protected* the disk so that she couldn't change the files. But just in case, I also made a backup copy. And I'm holding her husband and children hostage."

WYSIWYG

Pronunciation: *Whiz-Zee-Wig.*

Meaning: Acronym for *What You See Is What You Get.* WYSIWYG describes the phenomenon of being able to see on the computer screen exactly what you will see on the page when you print your document. There are degrees of WYSIWYG in computerdom, but most people agree that the Macintosh and Windows environments offer true WYSIWYG. In fact, WYSIWYG is so common now that the term is quickly falling out of common usage.

Sentence: "If this page layout program offers a *WYSIWYG* display, why does it need a Print Preview command?"

X ray

Pronunciation: *Eks ray.*

Meaning: An electromagnetic radiation of a short wave length (less than 100 angstroms) that can pass through walls, bodies, and other solid objects. Computers don't produce X rays (but don't quote us on that one). Airport X-ray machines may or may not damage your computer or laptop PC. The best advice is to hand your computer to the guard and not X-ray it.

Sentence: "Superman had *X-ray* vision."

X.25

Pronunciation: *Eks Dot Twentee-Fihv.*

Meaning: A protocol for arranging data in packets that includes identification of the recipient and sender of the data. This is mostly advanced network stuff, not required knowledge unless you plan on someday bringing in the big bucks by being a network guru. (See also *network.*)

Sentence: "Our network no longer functions because someone rewrote all our *X.25* protocols without telling the network manager." (I know, vague sentence, but it makes you sound important when you repeat it.)

Xanadu

Pronunciation: *Zan-uh-doo.*

Meaning: A mythical city in Kubla Khan, known for its incredible beauty and romance. It's also rumored to be an advanced network and information system available to all PCs all over the world. Someday. Soon. (See also *network.*)

Sentence: "I thought I had somehow stumbled into *Xanadu,* but it was only the local computer superstore."

XCMDs

Pronunciation: *Eks-See-Em-Dees.*

Meaning: External commands available for the Macintosh HyperCard programming language. Accessing the XCMDs means a HyperCard programmer has more functions and pizzazz available than when using HyperCard alone. (See also *HyperCard.*)

Sentence: "Josh used a bunch of cool *XCMDs* to spice up his fungi HyperCard database."

XENIX

Pronunciation: *Zee-Niks.*

Meaning: A version of the UNIX operating system that was adapted by Microsoft to run on personal computers. In the old days, you couldn't "buy" a copy of UNIX like you could buy DOS or System 7 or OS/2. So Microsoft packaged its own version of UNIX, which it called XENIX. Now people use SCO XENIX or SCO UNIX from the Santa Cruz Operation, Inc. (See also *UNIX.*)

Sentence: "Dave had the computer science club rolling with his repertoire of archaic *XENIX* puns."

XGA

Pronunciation: *Eks Gee Ay.*

Meaning: Abbreviation for *Extended Graphics Array.* A type of video adapter that provided a higher resolution than previous adapters. (See also *VGA* and *SVGA.*)

Sentence: "No one really needs *XGA* graphics. I'd stick with SuperVGA."

XMODEM

Pronunciation: *Eks-Moh-Dum.*

Meaning: A protocol for transferring files between computers (often across phone lines) and catching errors that occur during transfer. This ensures that the file sent is identical to the file received. XMODEM was actually the name of a program that included the XMODEM file transfer protocol. Today, it refers to the way the file is sent. Other transfer protocols, such as YMODEM and ZMODEM, improve on the XMODEM idea by allowing faster data transmission through larger packets (chunks) of data and the capability to continue transmitting data when the checksum values don't match. (See also *CRC, YMODEM, Kermit, checksum,* and *protocol.*)

Sentence: "Oh, Charles, darling, get with the times! No one uses plain old boring *XMODEM* anymore."

XMS

Pronunciation: *Eks-Em-Ess.*

Meaning: Abbreviation for *Extended Memory Specification.* A memory-management standard for allowing DOS applications to access extended memory. XMS memory-management software provides access to the extended memory through the XMS standard, a set of rules developed by Microsoft and other industry bigwigs. DOS comes with an XMS memory manager called HIMEM.SYS. (See also *expanded memory, extended memory,* and *extended memory specification.*)

Sentence: "I'm going to need a new *XMS* manager on my PC. All my extended memory is threatening to go on strike."

XON/XOFF

Pronunciation: *Eks-Ahn/Eks-Ahf.*

Meaning: Signals for stopping and starting the flow of data during transmission between computers. XON/XOFF lets the receiving computer stop the flow of information so that it may be processed as it comes in. The XON character is actually Control-S, produced by pressing the Ctrl-S key combination. That stops data from being sent and also allows you to catch up and read the screen. For example, if DOS is TYPEing out a file, you can press Ctrl-S and DOS is on hold for a while until you press any other key. The XOFF character is Ctrl-Q. It isn't used by DOS for anything interesting, but on other systems only the Ctrl-Q character gets things moving after being frozen by a Ctrl-S.

Sentence: "We used *XON/XOFF* signals with our walkie-talkies."

XOR

(See *Exclusive OR.*)

XT

Pronunciation: *Eks-Tee.*

Meaning: Abbreviation for *Extended Technology.* XT applied to a model of PC computer that extended the architecture of the original 8080 PC computers by adding extra expansion slots and a larger disk drive. Today, XT computers make good boat anchors. (See also *AT, PC,* and *boat anchor.*)

Sentence: "I asked my son whether he was using the *XT* computer that I gave him for college. He said 'Was that a computer?'"

yacc

Pronunciation: *yack.*

Meaning: Acronym for *Yet Another Compiler Compiler,* a UNIX tool used to create other languages and compilers. (See also *UNIX.*)

Sentence: "The *yacc* tool usually hangs out with *lex,* a UNIX lexical analyzer."

YMODEM

Pronunciation: *Wie Moh-Dum.*

Meaning: A transfer protocol based on the XMODEM standard. YMODEM allows faster data transmission. (See also *XMODEM* and *protocol.*)

Sentence: "My communications package offers XMODEM, *YMODEM,* and ZMODEM protocols. What comes next, AAMODEM?"

Z80

Pronunciation: *Zee Ay-Tee.*

Meaning: The name of an old, 8-bit microprocessor used in the days of CP/M. The Z80 microprocessor was overshadowed by the faster 8080, the brain for the first IBM PC. (See also *CP/M.*)

Sentence: "Nary 10 years ago, the *Z80* was considered the cutting edge of technology. Today, that and $2.25 will buy you a cup of coffee."

zap

Pronunciation: *zap.*

Meaning: To zap a file is to remove it permanently from the disk. Unlike deleting a file, zapping a file removes it without possibly of being undeleted. (See also *undelete.*)

Sentence: "I *zapped* my tax files from the disk, just in case the IRS auditor knows how to undelete files."

Zephram Cochrane

Meaning: The man who invented the *warp drive.* He was lost in deep space and ended up on a remote planet where a feminine energy force was keeping him alive, young, and virile for centuries — like an outer space *Sunset Boulevard.* Of course, Captain Kirk stumbled upon him and rescued him by letting the energy force inhabit the body of Betty from *Father Knows Best.* Zephram and Betty lived happily ever after on that planet.

Sentence: "*Zephram Cochrane* does not really exist."

zero wait state

(See *wait state.*)

ZIP

Pronunciation: *Zip.*

Meaning: A suffix applied to files that have been compressed with the PKZIP utility. A ZIP file may be anywhere from five percent to 95 percent smaller than the original file — or the original group of files, if more than one was compressed at a time. This is useful for transferring files over a modem or for saving disk space.

Sentence: "You need the PKUNZIP program to decompress files stored in a *ZIP* file that was created by using the PKZIP program."

ZMODEM

(See *XMODEM* and *YMODEM.*)

zoom

Pronunciation: *zoom.*

Meaning: The ability to change the way your data appears on the screen. You can zoom in to magnify the data, making it appear quite large on the screen, or you can zoom out to see how the data looks in relation to the page it's on. This is usually accomplished by use of a Zoom command.

Sentence: "I tried using the *Zoom* command to make my computer go faster, but it made my text bigger instead."

zoom box

Pronunciation: *zoom boks.*

Meaning: An area or button on a graphical window that increases the window size to full-screen proportions. (See also *button.*)

Sentence: "I was just poking around the window when all of a sudden, Yikes!, it got as big as a house! I must have stumbled upon the *zoom box.*"

Order Form

Order Center: (800) 762-2974 (8 a.m.-5 p.m. PST, weekdays)

For fastest service, photocopy this order form and fax to: (415) 358-1260

Qty	ISBN	Title	Price	Total

hipping & Handling Charges

ubtotal	U.S.	Canada & International	International Air Mail
p to $20.00	Add $3.00	Add $4.00	Add $10.00
20.01-40.00	$4.00	$5.00	$20.00
40.01-60.00	$5.00	$6.00	$25.00
60.01-80.00	$6.00	$8.00	$35.00
ver $80.00	$7.00	$10.00	$50.00

U.S. and Canada, shipping is UPS ground or equivalent.

or Rush shipping call (800) 762-2974.

Subtotal ______

CA residents add applicable sales tax ______

IN residents add 5% sales tax ______

Canadian residents add 7% GST tax ______

Shipping ______

TOTAL ______

p to:

ne ______

npany ______

lress ______

/State/Zip ______

time Phone ______

ment: ❑ Check to IDG Books (US Funds Only) ❑ Visa ❑ MasterCard ❑ AMEX

d # ______ Exp. ______

nature ______

se send this order form to: IDG Books, 155 Bovet Road, Suite 310, San Mateo, CA 94402.

v up to 3 weeks for delivery. Thank you!

IDG BOOKS WORLDWIDE REGISTRATION CARD

RETURN THIS REGISTRATION CARD FOR FREE CATALOG

Title of this book: Illustrated Computer Dictionary For Dummies

My overall rating of this book: ❑ Very good [1] ❑ Good [2] ❑ Satisfactory [3] ❑ Fair [4] ❑ Poor [5]

How I first heard about this book:

❑ Found in bookstore; name: [6] ❑ Book review: [7]

❑ Advertisement: [8] ❑ Catalog: [9]

❑ Word of mouth; heard about book from friend, co-worker, etc.: [10] ❑ Other: [11]

What I liked most about this book:

What I would change, add, delete, etc., in future editions of this book:

Other comments:

Number of computer books I purchase in a year: ❑ 1 [12] ❑ 2-5 [13] ❑ 6-10 [14] ❑ More than 10 [15]

I would characterize my computer skills as: ❑ Beginner [16] ❑ Intermediate [17] ❑ Advanced [18] ❑ Professional [19]

I use ❑ DOS [20] ❑ Windows [21] ❑ OS/2 [22] ❑ Unix [23] ❑ Macintosh [24] ❑ Other: [25] ________ (please specify)

I would be interested in new books on the following subjects:
(please check all that apply, and use the spaces provided to identify specific software)

❑ Word processing: [26] ❑ Spreadsheets: [27]

❑ Data bases: [28] ❑ Desktop publishing: [29]

❑ File Utilities: [30] ❑ Money management: [31]

❑ Networking: [32] ❑ Programming languages: [33]

❑ Other: [34]

I use a PC at (please check all that apply): ❑ home [35] ❑ work [36] ❑ school [37] ❑ other: [38] ________

The disks I prefer to use are ❑ 5.25 [39] ❑ 3.5 [40] ❑ other: [41] ________

I have a CD ROM: ❑ yes [42] ❑ no [43]

I plan to buy or upgrade computer hardware this year: ❑ yes [44] ❑ no [45]

I plan to buy or upgrade computer software this year: ❑ yes [46] ❑ no [47]

Name: Business title: [48]

Type of Business: [49]

Address (❑ home [50] ❑ work [51]/Company name:)

Street/Suite#

City [52]/State [53]/Zipcode [54]: Country [55]

❑ **I liked this book!**
You may quote me by name in future IDG Books Worldwide promotional materials.

My daytime phone number is ________

IDG BOOKS
THE WORLD OF COMPUTER KNOWLEDGE

YES!

Please keep me informed about IDG's World of Computer Knowledge. Send me the latest IDG Books catalog.

BUSINESS REPLY MAIL

FIRST CLASS MAIL PERMIT NO. 2605 SAN MATEO, CALIFORNIA

IDG Books Worldwide
155 Bovet Rd
San Mateo CA 94402-9833